$\mathcal{I}$nterdisciplinary
RESEARCH

Whether we take a stance on the stem
cell research controversy, interpret a work of art
in a new medium, or assess the reconstruction of Iraq,
a deep understanding of contemporary life requires knowledge
and thinking skills that transcend the traditional disciplines. Such
understanding demands that we draw on multiple sources of expertise to capture
multidimensional phenomena, to produce complex explanations, or to solve intricate problems.

—*Veronica Boix Mansilla (2005),*
"Assessing Student Work at Disciplinary Crossroads"

Interdisciplinary RESEARCH

PROCESS and THEORY

Allen F. Repko

The University of Texas at Arlington

Los Angeles • London • New Delhi • Singapore

For information:

Sage Publications, Inc.
2455 Teller Road
Thousand Oaks,
   California 91320
E-mail: order@sagepub.com

Sage Publications India Pvt. Ltd.
B 1/I 1 Mohan Cooperative
   Industrial Area
Mathura Road, New Delhi 110 044
India

Sage Publications Ltd.
1 Oliver's Yard
55 City Road
London EC1Y 1SP
United Kingdom

Sage Publications Asia-Pacific Pte. Ltd.
33 Pekin Street #02-01
Far East Square
Singapore 048763

Printed in the United States of America

Library of Congress Cataloging-in-Publication Data

Repko, Allen F.
Interdisciplinary research : process and theory/Allen F. Repko.
    p. cm.
Includes bibliographical references and index.
ISBN 978-1-4129-5915-5 (pbk.)
    1. Interdisciplinary research. I. Title.

Q180.55.I48R47 2008
001.4—dc22   2007052937

This book is printed on acid-free paper.

08   09   10   11   12   10   9   8   7   6   5   4   3   2   1

Acquisitions Editor:	Vicki Knight
Editorial Assistant:	Lauren Habib
Associate Editor:	Sean Connelly
Production Editor:	Catherine M. Chilton
Copy Editor:	Diana Breti
Typesetter:	C&M Digitals (P) Ltd.
Proofreader:	Doris Hus
Indexer:	Nara Wood
Cover Designer:	Candice Harman
Marketing Manager:	Stephanie Adams

Contents

Preface   vii

Acknowledgments   xix

Part I: About Interdisciplinary Studies   1

1. Defining Interdisciplinary Studies   3
2. Tracing the Origins of Interdisciplinarity   27

Part II: Theories of Interdisciplinary Studies   49

3. Operationalizing Disciplinary Perspective   51
4. Defining the Elements of Disciplines   83
5. Explaining the Importance of Integration   115

Part III: Drawing on Disciplines   135

6. Beginning the Research Process   137
7. Identifying Relevant Disciplines   160
8. Developing Adequacy in Relevant Disciplines   189
9. Analyzing the Problem and Evaluating Each Insight Into It   217

Part IV: Integrating Insights   245

10. Identifying Conflicts in Insights   247
11. Creating Common Ground   271
12. Integrating Insights and Producing an Interdisciplinary Understanding   295

Conclusion: Interdisciplinarity for the New Century   321

Appendix: Interdisciplinary Resources   327

Glossary of Key Terms   335

References 355

Author Index 371

Subject Index 377

About the Author 395

Preface

A neglected topic in the extensive literature on interdisciplinary studies is how to do interdisciplinary research. This book on the interdisciplinary research process is the first comprehensive treatment of the subject for advanced undergraduate and graduate students. It features an easy to follow step-by-step approach that is grounded in the relevant scholarly debates on interdisciplinarity, research methods (e.g., quantitative versus qualitative), and epistemology (modernism versus postmodernism). Thus, the book integrates theory and practice.

The research process is illustrated by numerous examples, some drawn from professional work, others from undergraduate student projects. Since the research process relies primarily on the disciplines and interdisciplinary fields, the examples are threaded into the text to illustrate interdisciplinary research oriented toward the natural sciences, the social sciences, and the humanities.

In attempting to provide comprehensive coverage, the book defines interdisciplinary studies or interdisciplinarity, traces the origin of the field of interdisciplinary studies, operationalizes the concept of "disciplinary perspective," identifies the defining elements of disciplines, and discusses the importance of integration. The book also explains how to begin the interdisciplinary research process, identify relevant disciplines and their insights, develop adequacy in relevant disciplines, analyze the problem and evaluate each insight into it, identify sources of conflict in insights, create or discover common ground among insights in order to integrate them, and produce an interdisciplinary understanding of the problem. The ideas presented are generic enough to be useful to a variety of interdisciplinary programs and fields.

The Need for This Book

Faculty are concerned that students learn how to do interdisciplinary research and writing. This is one of the important findings reported in the

2003 volume of *Issues in Integrative Studies* titled "Future Directions for Interdisciplinary Effectiveness in Higher Education: A Delphi Study." The study posed this question to its participants, all of whom are leading interdisciplinary practitioners: "What changes in interdisciplinary studies programs need to take place over the next decade in order to better serve the needs of students whose academic goals are not adequately addressed by traditional discipline-based programs?" Under "Curriculum," the participants recommended a textbook that provides an overview of disciplinary perspectives, theories, and methodologies, and especially integrative techniques, along with concrete examples (Welch, 2003, p. 185). Further evidence that the topic is neglected comes from noted interdisciplinary scholar Julie Thompson Klein (2005a), who in *Humanities, Culture, and Interdisciplinarity: The Changing American Academy* criticizes the tendency of scholars to "hover at the level of theory with little or no attention to what is happening on the ground of practice" (p. 7). This book is a response to these concerns. It attempts to apply theory to the "ground of practice" and make the interdisciplinary research process comprehensible and achievable for students.

The major student obstacle in learning the interdisciplinary research process is differentiating it from the research methods of traditional disciplines. An important contribution of the book is that it surveys the dozen or so research methodologies used by the disciplines and explains how these are foundational to, but different from, the interdisciplinary research process. The book also reflects an emerging consensus about the meanings and operations of important interdisciplinary theories and concepts.

The Intended Audience

The book is intended as either a core or a supplemental resource for upper-level and graduate courses that are interdisciplinary. More specifically, the book will be useful in a variety of academic contexts: intermediate-level courses that focus on interdisciplinary research and theory; upper-level topics, problems, or theme-based courses that involve working in two or more disciplines; integrative capstone and senior seminar courses that require an in-depth interdisciplinary research paper/project; keystone courses that integrate general education for upper-level undergraduate programs; graduate courses in interdisciplinary teaching and/or research; teaching assistant (TA) training/certificate courses in interdisciplinary learning, thinking, and research; first semester master's-level research courses; and administrators and faculty who wish to develop interdisciplinary courses and programs at their institutions. The book, particularly its early chapters, can also be used in introductory interdisciplinary studies courses. Multidisciplinary programs calling on students to cross several disciplinary domains will also find this book useful.

The book is aimed primarily at students, though faculty will appreciate the book's glossary of key terms, endnotes, extensive sources, and various teaching aids. Most books on research methods can assume professional consensus about the principles of the field they present. Because the field of interdisciplinary studies has only just reached the point where there is sufficient potential for scholarly consensus on the principles of the field, this book has to point the reader toward a scholarly rationale in the literature for each principle, in addition to explaining the principle itself. In a sense, then, the book is aimed at faculty teaching an interdisciplinary course as much as at students taking that course. Advanced undergraduate and graduate students can learn as much about interdisciplinary studies from the rationale for interdisciplinary principles as from the principles themselves.

The book, because of its extensive discussion of the disciplines and their defining elements, provides students with useful discipline-specific information that is dispersed. This information on disciplinary perspective, phenomena, assumptions, epistemology, theory, and methods is as necessary for multidisciplinary research as it is for interdisciplinary research. Students in disciplinary majors will find this information helpful as they will likely take courses in different disciplines and will want to know how to tie these together.

A Rapidly Growing Field

Interdisciplinary studies (IDS) is not a passing fad; it is here to stay. It is a rapidly growing academic field that offers students undergraduate and graduate degrees. When interdisciplinary undergraduate instructional programs began in the opening decades of the twentieth century, they were truly experimental. By the mid-1990s, they had become established. Today, multi- and interdisciplinary studies degrees are the 13th most popular undergraduate field of 33 listed by the National Center for Educational Statistics (NCES). From 1992 to 2002, the annual average number of students graduating in the United States with a bachelor's degree in multi/interdisciplinary studies was 26,000 per year (NCES, 2003).

Moreover, *Peterson's Four Year Colleges* (2006) shows that students now graduate from 367 programs nationwide and have the possibility of pursuing numerous interdisciplinary master's and doctoral degrees.[1] Additionally, at some institutions, interdisciplinary studies has achieved status as a department or as a separate school within the university (e.g., Arizona State University). IDS programs are growing. Enrollment in the IDS program at the University of Texas, Arlington, for example, has increased from about 325 students in the fall of 2004 to over 600 in January, 2008. Enrollment in ASU's program during the same period has grown from 1,800 students to over 2,300.

The Approach Used and Style of Presentation

The book's sixfold purpose is (1) to describe interdisciplinary studies as an emerging academic field, (2) to explain how the theory that undergirds the field informs the interdisciplinary research process, (3) to demonstrate how this process draws on the disciplines relevant to the problem or focus question, (4) to distinguish this research process from disciplinary methods, (5) to show how to integrate scholarly insights into a complex problem, and (6) to show how to produce an interdisciplinary understanding of a problem and express this new understanding in ways that are meaningful, practical, and purposeful.

This book's approach to interdisciplinary research is distinctive in at least five respects: (1) it describes how one actually conducts interdisciplinary research, whether from a natural science, a social science, or a humanities orientation; (2) it deals comprehensively with interdisciplinary theory, including complexity theory, the theory of common ground, the theory of cognitive interdisciplinarity, and the theory of integration; (3) it presents an easy to follow, but not formulaic, decision-making process. The term *process* is used rather than method because definitionally, process allows for greater flexibility and reflexivity, particularly when working in the humanities. (4) The book highlights the foundational role of the disciplines in interdisciplinary work and the importance of integrating disciplinary insights. (5) The book includes numerous examples of interdisciplinary research from the natural sciences, the social sciences, and the humanities to illustrate how integration is achieved and an interdisciplinary understanding produced and expressed. This book is ideally suited for the newer active learning and problem-based pedagogical approaches as well as for team teaching and other more traditional strategies, though it does not privilege any particular pedagogical approach.

Design Features

The book aids student content comprehension by using current learning strategies that characterize the modern textbook. Conceptual and organizational approaches include chapter outlines, section headings, a glossary of key concepts, boxed definitions and important statements, graphics to illustrate key concepts, italicized and boldfaced key concepts in the narrative, tables, figures, chapter summaries, author index, and subject index. Faculty can profitably use chapter components that correspond to their own approach to interdisciplinary research while omitting others.

Contents

The book is divided into four sections, each organized around a theme that addresses a central issue of the field. Part I defines interdisciplinary studies or interdisciplinarity, and traces its origins. Part II presents the body of theory undergirding interdisciplinarity. Part III shows students how to draw on the disciplines and their insights, and Part IV explains how to create common ground among insights, integrate these, and produce an interdisciplinary understanding of the problem or question.

Part I: About Interdisciplinary Studies

Today, interdisciplinary learning at all academic levels is far more common and there is greater understanding of what it is. Early definitions of interdisciplinary studies were quite general, but the range of meanings has narrowed dramatically over the last decade, though consensus is still lacking. Interdisciplinary learning is more widespread because educators recognize that it is needed and that the disciplines are necessary but insufficient by themselves to address the complex problems that are demanding attention in today's world.

Chapter 1: Defining Interdisciplinary Studies

Chapter 1 answers the question, *What is interdisciplinarity, and how is it different from disciplinarity, multidisciplinarity, and transdisciplinarity?* The popularity of the term *interdisciplinarity* in the Academy, the multiplication of interdisciplinary initiatives and programs, and the persistence of exaggerated claims and outdated suppositions about interdisciplinarity heighten the importance of achieving clarity about its meaning that is grounded in the literature. The chapter traces the etymology of interdisciplinary studies and the term *interdisciplinarity*, examines the differences between disciplinarity and interdisciplinarity, explains how interdisciplinarity is different from multidisciplinarity and transdisciplinarity, identifies the ways the term *interdisciplinarity* is variably used today, and identifies strengths and weaknesses of various metaphors descriptive of interdisciplinary work.

Chapter 2: Tracing the Origins of Interdisciplinarity

Chapter 2 completes the discussion of what interdisciplinary studies is about by asking the question, *How did interdisciplinarity become mainstream by the end of the twentieth century?* At the start of the twentieth century, the modern system of the university and the disciplines had become the engine of knowledge production that far outstripped any other method of learning devised previously. The origin of interdisciplinary studies and the notion of interdisciplinarity can be seen as a response to three developments. The first was the criticism of the disciplines that intensified after World War II. This criticism, influenced by adherents of Nietzsche and French philosopher Michael Foucault, focused on the enormous power that the disciplines had accumulated since the turn of the century. In the 1960s, Foucault argued that the disciplines are not just a way to produce knowledge;

they are, in fact, a sophisticated mechanism for regulating human conduct and social relations. The second development focused on the deepening isolation of the disciplines from each other. Tony Becher and Paul R. Trowler (2001) describe the disciplines in anthropological terms as separate tribes with different cultures and languages (p. 45). The third development is what Klein (2005a) characterizes as "the new generalism," consisting of new forms of interdisciplinarity that were heavily influenced by European philosophy and literary theories. In the 1960s, these forms included structuralism, Lacanian analysis, new kinds of Marxist criticism, and deconstruction. During the 1970s and 1980s, interest grew in feminism and semiotics, and in the 1980s, "poststructural" approaches, including the New Historicism and Cultural Analysis, took root. By the 1990s, these interdisciplinary approaches involving boundary crossing with the social sciences were heightening awareness of difference and were fostering the emergence of a new rhetoric of interdisciplinarity.

Part II: Theories of Interdisciplinary Studies

With definitional issues largely resolved, the field is presently grappling with theoretical issues, and this raises yet another question, *What theory or body of theory underlies interdisciplinary studies?* Part II discusses the theoretical underpinnings of the field, beginning with the role of the disciplines and disciplinary perspective (Chapter 3), the identity of a discipline's defining elements and how these are of interest to interdisciplinarians (Chapter 4), and the theories of integration and complexity (Chapter 5). The theories of common ground and cognitive interdisciplinarity are reserved for Chapter 11.

Chapter 3: Operationalizing Disciplinary Perspective

Interdisciplinary studies is based on the generally held assumption that the disciplines are foundational to interdisciplinarity. If so, then students should know how knowledge is typically structured in the modern Academy and how it is reflected in its organization. They should also know how the disciplines usually associated with each major category—the natural sciences, the social sciences, and the humanities—engage in learning, thinking, and producing new knowledge. There are unresolved questions and significant differences of opinion, however, over precisely what interdisciplinarians should use from the disciplines and how they should use it. The chapter attempts to bridge these differences by clarifying the term "disciplinary perspective" to mean those defining elements of a discipline—the phenomena, assumptions, epistemology, theories, methods, and concepts—that define its character compared to that of other disciplines. This definition differentiates between a discipline's overall view of reality and its scholarly insights into problems that interest it and also enables interdisciplinarians to focus on those particular disciplinary elements that bear on the problem.

Chapter 4: Defining the Elements of Disciplines

Chapter 4 unpacks the meaning of these elements of perspective and explains how they are useful to interdisciplinary students. Though the disciplines are fluid and their boundaries porous, these elements constitute a discipline's intellectual "center of gravity" and constitute much of the raw material that the interdisciplinarian uses in the interdisciplinary research process. The chapter presents two approaches: the traditional or "perspectival" approach, which calls for linking the problem to those disciplines whose perspectives embrace it, and the newer "classification approach," pioneered by Rick Szostak, which calls for linking the problem directly to the appropriate phenomena and bypassing disciplinary perspectives, at least initially. By focusing on phenomena, researchers can broaden their investigation without focusing, at least initially, on particular disciplines. Chapters 6 to 12 draw heavily from the information provided in Chapters 3 and 4.

Chapter 5: Explaining the Importance of Integration

Integration, the focus of Chapter 5, is a distinguishing feature of interdisciplinary work. Lisa Lattuca (2001) finds that the majority of definitions of interdisciplinarity focus on integration, though consensus is lacking concerning what integration should encompass (p. 112). While integration is not easy, it is achievable, even for undergraduate students. The field is moving toward consensus that interdisciplinary studies is uniquely useful for understanding complex problems, such as terrorism, climate change, and illegal immigration, that span multiple knowledge domains.

Part III: Drawing on Disciplines

The general agreement that interdisciplinarity draws primarily upon disciplines, interdisciplines, and schools of thought breaks down when practitioners grapple with the next question, *What is the interdisciplinary research process and how is it achieved?* Parts III and IV argue that the process is not linear but a series of carefully considered decision points called "Steps," leading to integration and ultimately to producing an interdisciplinary understanding of the problem. The process is heuristic, and though step-like, involves a good deal of reflexivity. Chapters 6 to 9 provide information essential to the performance of integration, the subject of Chapters 10 to 12.

Chapter 6: Beginning the Research Process

Chapter 6 presents an integrated and step-based research model of the interdisciplinary research process. This chapter begins the process of identifying decision points and research pathways and provides examples of them from published and student work. It stresses the importance of framing the research or focus question in a way that is appropriate to interdisciplinary inquiry. The chapter also emphasizes the importance of justifying the use of an interdisciplinary approach, as opposed to a multidisciplinary or a disciplinary one. This discussion also addresses the need for greater transparency in interdisciplinary writing that would make these decision points and research pathways explicit. Increasingly, professional interdisciplinary writers, such as Jared Diamond, John L. Jackson, Jr., Mieke Bal, Gary Blesser, and Linda-Ruth Salter, are including in their writing a clear rationale for taking an interdisciplinary approach.

Chapter 7: Identifying Relevant Disciplines

There are two decision points that are the subject of Chapter 7. The first is deciding which disciplines, subdisciplines, interdisciplines, and schools of thought are potentially interested in the problem and then which of these are most relevant to it. A technique that aids in making these decisions is mapping the problem in its complexity so that one can more easily identify variables and relationships that might otherwise escape notice. The second decision point is to conduct a systematic literature search for peer-reviewed insights into the problem. The chapter discusses the purpose of the literature search as it relates to interdisciplinary work, notes the special challenges confronting students, offers practical suggestions about what to do in the very early phase of research, examines the role of the disciplines in the literature search, identifies two challenges facing students in the latter phase of the literature search, and states the importance of providing in-text evidence of disciplinary adequacy. The chapter also addresses library-based computer search techniques, identifies problems that are distinctive to interdisciplinary research, and discusses in general terms nondisciplinary knowledge formations that are available.

Chapter 8: Developing Adequacy in Relevant Disciplines

Chapter 8 introduces another juncture where several decisions must be made concerning how to develop adequacy in relevant disciplines and theories. Since disciplines and the insights they produce are foundational to interdisciplinary work, it is essential that students develop adequacy in those disciplines and their defining elements that pertain to the problem. Developing adequacy involves making decisions about how much knowledge is required from each discipline, subdiscipline, interdiscipline, and school of thought; what kind of knowledge is needed; whether the problem can be adequately illuminated from a handful of disciplinary insights, theories, concepts, assumptions, and methods; and whether the disciplines decided upon earlier remain relevant.

Chapter 9: Analyzing the Problem and Evaluating Each Insight Into It

Once adequacy in the relevant disciplines is achieved, it is then possible to analyze the problem and identify weaknesses of insights into it from the perspective of each discipline and its defining elements. Chapter 9 explains how to analyze the problem from each disciplinary perspective and uses examples of interdisciplinary work from the natural sciences, the social sciences, and the humanities. After addressing how personal and disciplinary bias can complicate and compromise the integrity of the interdisciplinary research process, the chapter explains how to analyze the problem from each disciplinary perspective, primarily in terms of its theories and insights, and evaluate each insight into the problem. Evaluating insights involves identifying the strengths and weaknesses of each writer's theory and understanding of the problem, recognizing that each expert's approach to the problem may be skewed and understanding the implications of this, recognizing that the data or evidence upon which the insight and theory are based may also be skewed, and recognizing that the methods used by disciplinary experts may be skewed as well. A checklist by which to evaluate previous research is also provided.

Part IV: Integrating Insights

Engaging in the interdisciplinary research process raises further questions: *How does one perform the integrative task? What, precisely, is being integrated? What is the interdisciplinary understanding that is produced?* Interdisciplinary integration, as presented here, is a process that involves making a series of step-like decisions that calls for identifying conflicts between insights and the sources of these conflicts (Chapter 10), creating or discovering common ground among the relevant insights by identifying the theory, concept, or assumption that they share (Chapter 11), and then using this commonality (to the extent possible) to integrate these insights and thereby produce an interdisciplinary understanding of the problem. This understanding is tested by its ability to address the problem in a way that is comprehensive, practical, "disciplined," and purposeful (Chapter 12).

Making each of these decisions is essential to achieving integration. Professional and exemplary undergraduate work from the natural sciences, the social sciences, and the humanities are threaded through these chapters to illustrate how others have made these decisions.

Chapter 10: Identifying Conflicts in Insights

Beginning the integrative part of the interdisciplinary research process, the chapter addresses the importance of identifying conflicts between insights and locating the source(s) of these conflicts. The two possible locations of insights are *within* a single discipline or scattered *between* several disciplines that are interested in the problem. The possible sources of conflict between insights are concepts, assumptions, and theories. The chapter explains the importance of identifying theory-based insights produced by the same discipline or by different disciplines and locating the sources of conflict between them. It also offers three different types of interdisciplinary literature to illustrate how to present this information as part of one's analysis of the problem.

Chapter 11: Creating Common Ground

Creating or discovering common ground among conflicting disciplinary insights, theories, concepts, and assumptions is undoubtedly the most challenging, but nevertheless manageable, part of the entire interdisciplinary research process. The chapter discusses the theory of common ground, the theory of cognitive interdisciplinarity, common ground theory in the contexts of narrow versus broad interdisciplinarity, and the findings from the Interdisciplinary Studies Project (Project Zero) at the Harvard Graduate School of Education. The chapter also explains the importance of common ground to the integrative process, identifies the cognitive process required to create common ground, discusses the interdisciplinarian's responsibility in this process, notes the cognitive abilities involved in creating common ground, and explains what common ground is created from. Most important, it identifies the techniques available to create common ground and illustrates their use with interdisciplinary work from the natural sciences, the social sciences, and the humanities.

Chapter 12: Integrating Insights and Producing an Interdisciplinary Understanding

The common ground theory, concept, or assumption having been identified, the two final Steps of the interdisciplinary research process can proceed. The chapter shows how to integrate insights and produce an interdisciplinary understanding of the problem. The cognitive qualities and internal dispositions needed to engage in integration are discussed, including the role of intuition, the necessity of creativity, and how these contribute to the process of integration. The chapter explains how integration is achieved in terms of what is integrated and the importance of paying attention to process. More specifically, the chapter explains the basis of integration, the interdisciplinarian's work in integration, how to recognize when integration occurs, and examples of integrated insights. The chapter concludes by defining the concept of interdisciplinary understanding, identifying its premises, explaining various ways to express the understanding, and suggesting ways to test it. These last Steps are illustrated with the examples of interdisciplinary work threaded throughout Chapters 6 to 11.

The field of interdisciplinary studies is beginning to demonstrate its full potential and generate the volume and scope of new knowledge and understanding that its founders envisioned. The process of knowledge formation can be accelerated and find a wider audience as its practitioners produce more and better interdisciplinary work. To this end, I offer this book with its undoubted limitations to facilitate interdisciplinary learning, thinking, and production of new knowledge.

Professor Allen F. Repko, Ph.D.

Director

Interdisciplinary Studies Program

School of Urban and Public Affairs

University of Texas at Arlington

NOTE

1. See the Association for Integrative Studies online directory of interdisciplinary Ph.D. programs at http://www.units.muohio.edu/aisorg/phd/graddirectoryintro.html.

Acknowledgments _____

Many people have made this book possible. First, my students in the interdisciplinary studies program at the University of Texas at Arlington (UTA) planted the idea that a comprehensive textbook on the interdisciplinary research process was needed. For years they asked me why I did not provide them with one. Having no good answer, I replied (with a mixture of apology and hope), "Someone will eventually write one."

The seed planted by my students was watered in March, 2004 when Stuart Henry and Don Stowe came to our campus to serve as external reviewers of our program. Over lunch, I mentioned that the field of interdisciplinary studies needed a comprehensive textbook. They responded, "Why don't you write it?" After they left, I began transforming class notes into what is now Chapter 1 and, ultimately, this book.

Several have read the entire manuscript and have made many helpful comments, including Deborah DeZure of Michigan State University; Renate Holub of the University of California, Berkeley; Julie Thompson Klein of Wayne State University; Reinhard W. Linder of Western Illinois University; Brian McCormack of Arizona State University; William H. Newell of Miami University of Ohio; and Roslyn Abt Schindler of Wayne State University.

Others have read one or more chapters and offered helpful suggestions, including Richard Castellana of Petrocelli College/Fairleigh Dickenson University; Joan Fiscella of the University of Illinois at Chicago; Don Stowe of the University of South Carolina; and Rick Szostak of the University of Alberta, Canada.

Several of my colleagues at UTA have read portions of the manuscript relating to their expertise and have offered valuable comments, including Beth Wright, Robert Gatchel, Dale Story, Chris Morris, Ben Agger, Barbara Shipman, Larry Standlee, James Welch IV, Diane Lange, Cindy Atha-Weldon, and C. Diane Schepelwich.

I am indebted to my students, who provided valuable feedback as the book developed, and to Christi Romeo and Fleur Wiorkowski for their help in transforming my ideas into graphics.

For his encouragement, his patient reading of several versions of the manuscript, and his many insightful comments, I give special thanks to William H. Newell of Miami University of Ohio.

I also thank Richard Cole, Dean of the School of Urban and Public Affairs; Dana Dunn, former Provost; and Michael Moore, Senior Associate Provost, for their support of the interdisciplinary studies program and me.

Most importantly, I thank Doris, my wife, for her reading and editing of countless versions of each chapter.

I could not have produced this book without the support and encouragement of the people at SAGE Publications. I owe much to Lisa Cuevas, who initially championed this book, to Chris Klein, who continued to support it, and to my editor, Sean Connelly, who guided its production.

Ultimately, I assume responsibility for what is lacking in this book. It is a beginning, and my hope is that it will benefit students, teachers, and administrators and advance the field of interdisciplinary studies.

PART I

About Interdisciplinary Studies

1

Defining Interdisciplinary Studies

Chapter Preview

For over a century, the American educational system at all levels has relied on academic disciplines as platforms from which to impart knowledge and to generate new knowledge. Today, interdisciplinary learning at all levels is far more common as there is growing recognition that it is needed to answer complex questions, solve complex problems, and gain coherent understanding of complex issues that are increasingly beyond the ability of any single discipline to address comprehensively or resolve adequately. As Carole L. Palmer (2001) writes, "The real-world research problems that scientists address rarely arise within orderly disciplinary categories, and neither do their solutions" (p. vii).

This chapter explains the meaning of interdisciplinary studies, defines interdisciplinary studies and the term *interdisciplinarity,* explains the premise of interdisciplinarity and interdisciplinary studies, examines how the terms are variably used today, and identifies metaphors commonly associated with interdisciplinary work.

(★) Source/quote (Palmer)

The Meaning of Interdisciplinary Studies

The meaning of **interdisciplinary studies** or interdisciplinarity continues to be contested by its practitioners and critics. But emerging from this debate are key concepts around which consensus is developing and which inform the integrated definition of interdisciplinary studies that appears in this chapter. The following discussion unpacks the meaning of these terms and, in doing so, introduces students to some of the theory undergirding this developing and diverse academic field.

The "Discipline" Part of Interdisciplinary Studies

Inside the university, the term *discipline* refers to a particular branch of learning or body of knowledge such as physics, psychology, or history

3

(Moran, 2002, p. 2). According to the American Association for Higher Education (AAHE),

> disciplines have contrasting substance and syntax . . .—ways of organizing themselves and of defining rules for making arguments and claims that others will warrant. They have different ways of talking about themselves and about the problems, topics, and issues that constitute their subject matters. (Schulman, 2002, pp. vi–vii)

Mary Taylor Huber and Sherwyn P. Morreale (2002) add that "each discipline has its own intellectual history, agreements, and disputes about subject matter and methods" and its own "community of scholars interested in teaching and learning in that field" (p. 2). Disciplines are also distinguished from one another by several factors. These include the questions disciplines ask about the world, their perspective or worldview, the set of assumptions they employ, and the methods they use to build up a body of knowledge (facts, concepts, theories) around a certain subject matter (Newell & Green, 1982, p. 25).

Disciplines are scholarly communities that define which problems should be studied, advance certain central concepts and organizing theories, embrace certain methods of investigation, provide forums for sharing research and insights, and offer career paths for scholars. A **discipline** is a particular branch of learning or body of knowledge whose defining elements—i.e., phenomena, assumptions, epistemology, concepts, theories, and methods—distinguish it from other knowledge formations. History is an example of a discipline because it meets all of the above criteria. Its **knowledge domain** consists of an enormous body of *facts* (everything that has been recorded in human history). It studies an equally enormous number of *concepts or ideas* (imperialism, slavery, democracy, the American dream). It generates *theories* about why things turned out the way they did (e.g., the great man theory argues that the American Civil War lasted so long and was so bloody because of Lincoln's decision to issue the Emancipation Proclamation in 1862), though many historians strive to be atheoretical. And it uses a *method* that involves critical analysis of primary sources (i.e., letters, diaries, official documents, etc.) and secondary sources (i.e., books and articles about the topic) to present a picture of past events or persons within a particular time and place.

There are four clusters or **categories of traditional disciplines**,[1] the first three of which are examined closely in Chapter 3:

- The *natural sciences* (biology or "life sciences," chemistry, Earth sciences, mathematics, and physics)
- The *social sciences* (anthropology, economics, political science, psychology, and sociology)
- The *humanities* (art and art history, history,[2] literature, music, philosophy, and religious studies)
- The *applied professions* (business and its subfields, communications and its subfields, criminal justice, education, engineering and its various subfields, law, social work, nursing, and medicine)

Disciplines and their defining elements, rather than being rigid and unchanging constructs, are evolving social and intellectual constructs, and as such, are time-dependent. That is, today's discipline may well have been yesterday's subdiscipline or branch of an existing discipline. An example is the evolution of history, which, prior to the mid-nineteenth century, played a minor role in colleges as a branch of literature but grew rapidly as an independent discipline that absorbed those aspects of politics and economics that had a past dimension (Kuklick, 1985, p. 50). Today, history is a well-entrenched professional discipline that is typically included within the humanities but also has allegiances to the social sciences.

The line between the disciplines and interdisciplinarity has begun to blur in recent years with the emergence of interdisciplines. These include a wide variety of interactions ranging from informal groups of scholars to well-established research and teaching communities.

Frequently cited examples are social psychology and biochemistry, though the list also includes environmental engineering, psycholinguistics, ethnomusicology, cultural anthropology, and American Studies (Klein, 1990, p. 43). Interdisciplines differ from disciplines in terms of their origins, character, status, and level of development.[3] For example, molecular biology developed in response to breakthroughs from the discovery of the structure of DNA, new technologies, and complex research problems. Only by bringing together the skills and knowledge of chemists, geneticists, physicists, bacteriologists, zoologists, and botanists could the problems be solved (Sewell, 1989, pp. 95–96).

Klein (1996) speaks of the "concealed reality of interdisciplinarity" where interdisciplinarity is flourishing but is not labeled as such, as in, for instance, medicine, agriculture, and oceanography. The pattern by which the **boundary work** of interdisciplinary studies operates occurs in this way: (1) researchers detach a subject or object from existing disciplinary frameworks; (2) they fill gaps in knowledge from lack of attention to the category; and (3) if the research attains critical mass, researchers "redraw boundaries by constituting new knowledge space and new professional roles" (pp. 36–37).

For the purposes of this book, references to *disciplines* are limited to the traditional disciplines unless otherwise noted. References to specific interdisciplines and schools of thought (e.g., feminism, Marxism) are appropriately identified.

The "Inter" Part of Interdisciplinary Studies

The word *interdisciplinary* consists of two parts: *inter* and *disciplinary*. The prefix *inter* means "between, among, in the midst." **Disciplinary** means "of or relating to a particular field of study" or specialization. So a starting point for the definition of *interdisciplinary* is "between fields of study" (Stember, 1991, p. 4). *Inter* also means "derived from two or more."

Interdisciplinarity is the essence of interdisciplinary studies, which is manifested through research involving two or more knowledge domains.

"Inter" Means Between Fields of Study

This "between" space is **contested space.** Most interdisciplinary study examines **contested terrain**—problems or questions that are the focus of several disciplines. For example, crime in post-9/11 Washington, D.C. is an interdisciplinary problem because it is an economic problem *and* a racial problem *and* a cultural problem. William H. Newell emphasizes that the test of the interdisciplinarity of a problem is not its distance from each contributing discipline but whether the problem is fundamentally multi-faceted or complex (personal communication, June 30, 2004). The important point is that the disciplines are not the focus of the interdisciplinarian's attention; the focus is the problem or issue or intellectual question that each discipline is addressing. The disciplines are simply a means to that end.

Focus on multiple problems.

"Inter" Means Something Derived From Fields of Study

The "something derived from fields of study" is the insights (i.e., scholarly writing on a topic) into a specific problem generated by interested disciplines. The *action taken* on these insights by interdisciplinarians is called integration, the subject of Chapter 5.[4] Integration is the part of the interdisciplinary research process that seeks to reconcile conflicting disciplinary insights. The result of integration—and another aspect of the prefix *inter*— is *something altogether new,* distinctive, apart from, and beyond the limits of any discipline and, thus, *additive* to knowledge. This integrative result is the *interdisciplinary understanding* of the problem, the subject of Chapter 12. This understanding can be used to formulate new policies, frame new questions, produce new products, and foster new avenues of research. Its being additive to knowledge, however, does not preclude interdisciplinarity critiquing the disciplines or interrogating knowledge structures and societal values.

Three important aspects of the prefix *inter* may be summarized as follows:

- The contested space between disciplines
- The action taken on these insights, called integration
- The something altogether new that results from integration and is additive to knowledge

The "Studies" Part of Interdisciplinary Studies

The word *studies* has had a long (since the end of World War II) and respectable history, referring initially to geographical regions (e.g., Soviet

Studies) and historical eras (e.g., Renaissance Studies). Over the past several decades, however, the term has shifted to cultural groups (including women, Hispanics, and African Americans) and also appears in a host of contexts in the natural sciences and social sciences. In fact, "studies" programs are proliferating in the modern university. In some cases, even the traditional disciplines (particularly in the humanities) are renaming themselves as studies, such as English studies and literary studies (Garber, 2001, pp. 77–79).

Why Traditional Disciplines Are Not Referred to as "Studies"

Every established discipline has a universally recognized core of knowledge, and this core is subdivided into specific courses called a **curriculum**. The curriculum of each discipline varies from institution to institution in terms of number of courses offered and the titles of courses. Despite this variety, experts in a discipline recognize these courses as uniquely the "territory" of their discipline. The reason disciplines are not referred to as history "studies" or biology "studies" is that their core of study—their curriculum—is well-established and is recognized as their research and teaching domain.

This traditional arrangement, however, is being upset by the emergence of studies programs such as environmental studies and urban studies and the changing nature and expansion of disciplines. At first, many disciplinary departments simply added "environmental" to their course titles, while others contributed entire courses to a new environmental studies program, such as environmental geology, environmental psychology, and environmental law. A similar situation developed with urban studies. The problem with these and similar "studies" is that they have not resulted in synthesis or integration and, thus, have failed to coalesce into discrete fields (Klein, 1996, pp. 96–100).[5] For example, after three decades, there is still no definition of "urban" that enjoys general agreement, though most definitions include the interrelation between people and space. An exception is ecology, which, despite these difficulties, has managed to develop into a broad field of its own called ecological economics (Rogers, Scaife, & Rizzo, 2005, p. 267).

Studies and other multidisciplinary curricular arrangements arise in the first place because of a "perceived misfit among need, experience, information, and the prevailing structure of knowledge embodied in disciplinary organization" (Caldwell, 1983, pp. 247–249). These new structures represent fundamental challenges to the existing structure of knowledge and formal education. In this sense, these new structures or studies share with interdisciplinary studies (as described in this book) a broad dissatisfaction with traditional knowledge structures and a recognition that the kinds of complex problems facing humanity demand that new ways be found to order knowledge and bridge different approaches to its creation and communication.

Why "Studies" Is an Integral Part of Interdisciplinary Studies

"Studies" is an integral part of interdisciplinary studies because it refers to a wide array of knowledge domains, work, and educational programs that involve crossing disciplinary domains. These studies include (1) interdisciplinary programs that include a core of courses, (2) established interdisciplinary fields such as area studies (e.g., Middle East) and materials science, and (3) newer fields such as environmental studies, urban studies, and cultural studies.

To identify the key differences between the disciplines and interdisciplinary studies and thereby sharpen the contrast between them, a good place to start is to explain why "studies" is an essential component of interdisciplinary studies. The seven main characteristics of the established disciplines are compared and contrasted with those of interdisciplinary studies in Table 1.1.

There are three differences (#1, #2, and #3) and four similarities (#4, #5, #6, and #7). The differences explain why the use of "studies" in interdisciplinary studies is appropriate:

- Interdisciplinary studies does not lay claim to a universally recognized core of knowledge but rather draws on existing disciplinary knowledge (and even nondisciplinary knowledge) while always transcending it via integration (#1).
- Interdisciplinary studies has a research process of its own to generate knowledge but freely borrows methods from the disciplines when appropriate (#2).
- Interdisciplinary studies, like the disciplines, seeks to produce new knowledge, but unlike them, it seeks to accomplish this via the process of integration (#3).

Why "Studies" Is Plural

"Studies" is plural, observes Klein (1996), because of the idea of interaction between disciplines (p. 10). Imagine the world of knowledge wherein each discipline is like a box containing thousands of dots, each dot representing a bit of knowledge discovered by an expert in that discipline. Then imagine similar boxes representing other disciplines, each filled with dots of knowledge. Scholars interested in "studies" are excited by the prospect of examining a broad issue or complex question that requires looking inside as many disciplinary boxes as necessary in order to identify those dots of knowledge that have some bearing on the issue or question under investigation. "Studies" scholars, including those in interdisciplinary studies, are in the business of identifying and connecting dots of knowledge regardless of the disciplinary box in which they reside (Long, 2002, p. 14).

Table 1.1   Comparison of Established Disciplines to Interdisciplinary Studies

Established Disciplines[a]	Interdisciplinary Studies
1. Claim a body of knowledge about certain subjects or objects	1. Claims a burgeoning professional literature of increasing sophistication, depth of analysis, and thus utility. This literature includes subspecialties on interdisciplinary theory, program administration, curriculum design, research process, and assessment. Most important, a growing body of explicitly interdisciplinary research on real-world problems is emerging.
2. Have methods of acquiring knowledge and theories to order that knowledge	2. Makes use of disciplinary methods, but these are subsumed under a research process of its own that involves drawing on relevant disciplinary insights, concepts, theories, and methods to produce new knowledge
3. Seek to generate new knowledge, concepts, and theories, within or related to their domains	3. Produces new knowledge, more comprehensive understandings, new meanings, and cognitive advancements
4. Possess a recognized core of courses	4. Is beginning to form a core of courses
5. Have their own community of experts	5. Is forming its own community of experts
6. Are self-contained and seek to control their respective domains as they relate to each other	6. Is largely dependent on the disciplines for its source material
7. Train future experts in their discipline-specific master's and doctoral programs	7. Is training future experts in older fields such as American studies and in newer fields such as cultural studies through its master's and doctoral programs and undergraduate majors. Interdisciplinary studies still often hires those with disciplinary PhDs.

a. This column is based, in part, on Jill Vickers (1998), p. 34.

Interdisciplinarians are not interested in merely rearranging these ever-changing dots of knowledge but in *integrating* them into a whole that is larger than the sum of its parts.

Studies programs recognize that many research problems cannot easily be addressed from the confines of individual disciplines because they require the participation of many experts, each viewing the problem from their distinctive disciplinary perspective. Critics of studies programs, say Liora Salter and Alison Hearn (1996), charge that they lack disciplinary "substance and good scholarship" (p. 3). "Substance" and "scholarship" are typically code words for **disciplinary depth**—intensive focus on a discipline or subdiscipline. A contrasting view is that a purely disciplinary focus sacrifices breadth, comprehensiveness, and realism for depth. An integrated view recognizes that there is a symbiosis between disciplinary and interdisciplinary research.

Newell speaks for many interdisciplinarians, arguing that interdisciplinary studies is able to achieve as much depth as do the disciplines:

> [T]o the extent that interdisciplinary study harnesses disciplinary depth and rigor, it utilizes similar notions of depth and rigor; but to the extent that it is engaged in a different intellectual enterprise from the disciplines (especially integration), it must have some different notions of depth and rigor in addition. (personal communication, June 30, 2004)

This is not to say that a "studies" program is superior to a disciplinary one. That would be a mistake because the purpose of each is different. Both are needed, particularly in a world characterized by increasing complexity, conflict, and fragmentation.

Other Knowledge Formations

Though the disciplines are widely recognized sources or resources for knowledge and thought, there are other sources of knowledge or knowledge formations of interest to interdisciplinarians. **Knowledge formations** "(alternatives to disciplines) are both bodies of knowledge and processes of coming to know that contain within themselves dynamic patterns from which they have been generated and by which they will be transformed" (Carp, 2001, p. 71). Some of these knowledge formations are

- The knowledge of workers (carpenters, mechanics, Web site designers, farmers)
- The knowledge oppressed peoples have of those who are oppressing them (Carp, 2001, p. 74)[6]
- The knowledge West African immigrants have of "the system" and how it works in New York City (Stoller, 1997, pp. 91–118)
- The knowledge of Songhay sorcerers and other spiritualists
- The knowledge of parents gazing into the eyes of infants
- The knowledge of indigenous peoples about places they traditionally inhabit (Carp, 2001, p. 74)
- The knowledge that Judith Baca (1994) calls "maintaining a relationship with the dust of one's ancestors which requires a generational relationship with the land and a respectful treatment of other life found on the land."
- The knowledge of the varieties of local, vernacular, or cross-cultural knowledge that is sometimes critical for success (Carp, 2001, pp. 74–75)

All sources of potential insight are not equal. These "other sources" of knowledge are useful or even necessary to function well in a particular context or to think about a specific concern. However, they have dramatically different standing from knowledge that has stood the test of expert scrutiny. Under certain circumstances, these other knowledge formations may achieve credibility in the Academy and even find their way into the literatures of the disciplines. In women's studies, for example, testimonial or "lived experience" plays a crucial role. In native studies, "traditional knowledge preserved over centuries through oral tradition and interpreted by elders is central" (Vickers, 1998, p. 23). While knowledge produced by the disciplines, compared to these other sources of knowledge, is generally considered the proper focus of the modern academy, Richard M. Carp (2001) reminds us as scholars, "We do not know what we do not know" (p. 75). Regarding the existence of multiple knowledge formations (i.e., these "other sources" and disciplinary knowledge), interdisciplinarians should be more imaginative, more inquiring, and more open than are disciplinarians about what they do not yet know. Still, we should be skeptical of insights that have not been carefully tested.

A Definition of Interdisciplinary Studies

Three definitions of interdisciplinary studies have gained wide recognition and express an emerging consensus among practitioners on what constitutes interdisciplinary research. The first is the definition advanced by Klein and Newell (1997):

> [Interdisciplinary studies is] a *process* of answering a question, solving a problem, or addressing a topic that is too broad or complex to be dealt with adequately by a single discipline or profession . . . and draws on disciplinary perspectives and integrates their insights through construction of a more comprehensive perspective. (pp. 393–394, italics added)

This definition and its core premises have been incorporated into the definition of interdisciplinary research recently advanced by the National Academy of Sciences, the National Academy of Engineering, and the Institute of Medicine (2005):

> Interdisciplinary research (IDR) is a mode of research by teams or individuals that *integrates* information, data, techniques, tools, perspectives, concepts, and/or theories *from two or more disciplines or bodies of specialized knowledge* to advance fundamental understanding or to solve problems whose solutions are beyond the scope of a single discipline or area of research practice. (p. 39, italics added)

Veronica Boix Mansilla (2005) is particularly concerned with the product of interdisciplinary work or "interdisciplinary understanding." This, she says, is the capacity to integrate knowledge and modes of thinking drawn from two or more disciplines to produce a *cognitive advancement*—for example, explaining a phenomenon, solving a problem, creating a product, or raising a new question—in ways that would have been unlikely through single disciplinary means. (p. 16, italics added)

These definitions agree that interdisciplinarity involves

- A process mode of research
- The disciplines or bodies of specialized knowledge (i.e., disciplinary "perspectives")
- Integration of disciplinary insights
- A cognitive advancement

From these definitions, it is possible to advance an integrated definition of interdisciplinary studies:

Interdisciplinary studies is a process of answering a question, solving a problem, or addressing a topic that is too broad or complex to be dealt with adequately by a single discipline and draws on disciplinary perspectives and integrates their insights to produce a more comprehensive understanding or cognitive advancement.

This definition includes four concepts—process, disciplinary perspectives (the subject of Chapter 3), insights, and an interdisciplinary understanding (the subject of Chapter 12). Research of any kind is a process—a means or a tool, not an end—and to conduct research, it is reasonable to make this process as systematic as possible. Interdisciplinarians typically describe the doing of interdisciplinary research as a "process" rather than "method" because process allows for greater methodological flexibility, particularly when working in the humanities. It also includes the notion of **reflexive scholarship** or self-critique. As Matts Alvesson and Kaj Sköldberg (2000) maintain, "The process of research must include self-reflexivity" (p. 144).

Many disciplinary writers, particularly those in the social sciences and even in the natural sciences, also use the term *process* to describe their approaches to research, even though using specific research methods is part of the "process" (e.g., Neuman, 2006, p. 13).

An **insight** is a scholarly contribution to the clear understanding of a problem. Insights into a problem can be produced either by disciplinary experts or by interdisciplinarians. An **interdisciplinary insight** is produced when the interdisciplinary research process (or some version of it) is used to create an integrated and purposeful understanding of the problem. This process involves drawing on relevant **disciplinary insights** that are expert views on a particular problem. As used in this book, insights refer to scholarship produced by disciplinary experts, unless otherwise stated.

What Interdisciplinary Studies Is Not

Interdisciplinary studies is further clarified by determining what it is not.

Interdisciplinary Studies Is Not Multidisciplinary Studies

Regrettably, the terms "interdisciplinarity" and "multidisciplinarity" have often been seen as synonymous and, consequently, have caused much confusion. **Multidisciplinarity** refers to the placing side by side of insights from two or more disciplines as, for example, one might find in a course that invites instructors from different departments to explain their discipline's perspective on the course topic in serial fashion but makes no attempt to integrate the insights produced by these perspectives into an interdisciplinary understanding of the topic. "Here the relationship between the disciplines is merely one of proximity," explains Joe Moran (2002); "there is no real integration between them" (p. 16). Merely bringing insights from different disciplines together in some way but failing to engage in the hard work of integration is **multidisciplinary studies**, not interdisciplinary studies. The main difference between them lies in the mechanism of the research process and the end product (Rogers et al., 2005, p. 267).

Two metaphors effectively illustrate the essential difference between these two terms: the fruit salad and the smoothie. Multidisciplinary studies can be compared to a fruit salad containing a variety of fruits, each fruit representing a discipline and each fruit being in close proximity to the others. The number of fruits used and the proportions of each in the salad may not be based on anything more than visual appeal. This is not so with interdisciplinary studies, however, which Moti Nissani (1995) compares to a "smoothie." The smoothie is "finely blended so that the distinctive flavor of each [fruit] is no longer recognizable, yielding instead the delectable experience of the smoothie" (p. 125). The metaphor of the smoothie, while limited, illustrates four essential characteristics of interdisciplinary studies:

- The selection of fruits (i.e., the disciplines) was not random but purposeful with the end product clearly in view.
- The process was integrative, meaning that it changed the contribution of each fruit (i.e., disciplinary insight) (Newell, 1998, p. 548).
- The product, compared to the ingredients used, was something new and comprehensive.
- The activity was limited in time and space to creating this new and single product (an integrated result).

Lawrence Wheeler's instructive fable of building a house for an elephant illustrates a typical multidisciplinary approach to solving a complex problem:

Once upon a time a planning group was formed to design a house for an elephant. On the committee were an architect, an interior designer, an engineer, a sociologist, and a psychologist. The elephant was highly educated too . . . but he was not on the committee.

The five professionals met and elected the architect as their chairman. His firm was paying the engineer's salary, and the consulting fees of the other experts, which, of course, made him the natural leader of the group.

At their *fourth* meeting they agreed it was time to get at the essentials of their problem. The architect asked just two things: "How much money can the elephant spend?" and "What does the site look like?"

The engineer said that precast concrete was the ideal material for elephant houses, especially as his firm had a new computer just begging for a stress problem to run.

The psychologist and the sociologist whispered together and then one of them said, "How many elephants are going to live in this house? . . . It turned out that *one* elephant was a psychological problem, but *two* or more were a sociological matter. The group finally agreed that though *one* elephant was buying the house, he might eventually marry and raise a family. Each consultant could, therefore, take a legitimate interest in the problem.

The interior designer asked, "What do elephants do when they're at home?"

"They lean against things," said the engineer. "We'll need strong walls."

"They eat a lot," said the psychologist. "You'll want a big dining room . . . and they like the color green."

"As a sociological matter," said the sociologist, "I can tell you that they mate standing up. You'll need high ceilings."

So they built the elephant a house. It had precast concrete walls, high ceilings, and a large dining area. It was painted green to remind him of the jungle. And it was completed for only 15% over the original estimate.

The elephant moved in. He always ate outdoors, so he used the dining room for a library . . . but it wasn't very cozy.

He never leaned against anything, because he had lived in circus tents for years, and knew that walls fall down when you lean on them.

The girl he married *hated* green, and so did he. They were *very* urban elephants.

And the sociologist was wrong too. . . . they didn't stand up. So the high ceilings merely produced echoes that greatly annoyed the elephants. They moved out in less than six months! (Wheeler & Miller, 1970, n.p.)

This story shows how disciplinary experts usually approach a complex task: They perceive it from the narrow (i.e., monistic) perspective of their specialty and fail to take into account the perspectives of other relevant disciplines, professions, or interested parties (in this case, the elephant), or even of other sources of knowledge.

By contrast, multidisciplinarity and interdisciplinarity seek to overcome disciplinary monism, but in different ways. Multidisciplinarity limits its activity to merely appreciating different disciplinary perspectives. But interdisciplinarity means defying disciplinary limits on what theories, concepts, and methods are appropriate to a problem and being open to alternative methods of inquiry, using different disciplinary tools, and carefully estimating the degree of usefulness of one tool versus another to shed light on the problem (Nikitina, 2005, pp. 413–414).

Interdisciplinary Studies Is Not Transdisciplinary Studies

The contrast between interdisciplinary studies and transdisciplinary studies lies in their differing approaches to the disciplines. Interdisciplinary studies relies primarily on the disciplines for their perspectives, insights, data, concepts, theories, and methods in the process of developing an interdisciplinary understanding of a *particular* problem, not a class of similar problems. **Transdisciplinarity** is "the application of theories, concepts, or methods across disciplines with the intent of developing an overarching synthesis" (Lattuca, 2001, p. 83).

Transdisciplinarity, like interdisciplinarity, is descriptive of collaborative research and problem solving that, unlike interdisciplinarity, crosses both disciplinary boundaries *and sectors of society* by including stakeholders in the public and private domains.

Transdisciplinarity differs from interdisciplinarity in that the theories, concepts, or methods are not borrowed from one discipline and applied to other disciplines interested in the same problem, but rather transcend disciplines and are therefore applicable to many fields. An example of a transdisciplinary approach is sociobiology, which applies the principles of natural selection and evolutionary biology to the study of animal social behavior (Lattuca, 2001, p. 83). In **transdisciplinary study**, a problem or theme such as "the city" or "sustainability" becomes the focus of interest. Such mega and complex problems require collaboration among a hybrid mix of actors from different disciplines, professions, and sectors of society (Klein, 2003, pp. 12, 19).[7] In the 1990s, transdisciplinarity began appearing more often in the humanities as a label for critical evaluation of knowledge formations. For example, in women's and gender studies, Dölling and Hark (2000) associated transdisciplinarity with critical evaluation of terms, concepts, and methods that cross disciplinary boundaries (pp. 1196–1197).

The Premise of Interdisciplinary Studies

A major **premise of interdisciplinary studies** is that the disciplines (including interdisciplines) themselves are the necessary preconditions for and foundations of interdisciplinarity.[8] This premise is implicit both in the definition of interdisciplinary studies and, as already noted, in the very concept of interdisciplinarity itself. "Precondition" means prerequisite; it also means preparation. The disciplines, despite their limitations, are appropriate starting points for doing interdisciplinary research. They have, after all, produced "the historical and cultural artifacts embodying, participating in, and regenerating a complex of factors tied to psychological, economic, structural, and intercultural developments in Western Europe and the United States over the past two-and-a-half centuries" (Carp, 2001, pp. 78–79).

Furthermore, to ignore the disciplines and the wealth of knowledge that they have generated would severely constrain the interdisciplinarian's ability to research almost any conceivable topic. "Foundation" means the basis upon which something stands, like a house standing on a foundation. The disciplines are foundational to interdisciplinary research because they provide the perspectives, epistemologies, assumptions, concepts, theories, and methods that inform our ability as humans to understand our world. The "house" or integrated understanding that the interdisciplinarian ultimately constructs on this disciplinary foundation may well include other sources of knowledge, as previously noted. Saying that the disciplines are the necessary "preconditions for" and "foundations of" interdisciplinarity does not mean that the other sources of knowledge that Carp and others insist on using in their interdisciplinary work should be excluded or even marginalized in every instance. However, when these other sources of knowledge—these other knowledge formations—are used, the interdisciplinary researcher must integrate them with disciplinary knowledge at some point in order to achieve the goal or result of the interdisciplinary research process—an interdisciplinary understanding. This understanding provides new meaning to the object of inquiry. The term **meaning** is important in the humanities, where it is often equated with the intent of the author or artist (Bal, 2002, p. 27).[9]

Competing Impulses Behind the Term *Interdisciplinarity*

Interdisciplinarians have differing views on the role of the disciplines. There are, writes Moran (2002), two "competing impulses" behind the term *interdisciplinarity* (p. 15). On the one hand, there is the search for a wide-ranging, total knowledge; on the other hand, there is a more radical questioning of the nature of knowledge and our attempts to organize and communicate it. In this sense, says Moran, interdisciplinarity "interlocks with concerns of epistemology—the study of knowledge—and tends to be centered around problems and questions that cannot be addressed or solved within the existing disciplines" (p. 15).

These two differing impulses have implications for the meaning of interdisciplinarity. As Geoffrey Bennington (1999) points out, *inter* is an ambiguous prefix that can mean forming a communication between or joining together. Indeed, the term *interdisciplinarity* is slippery: "It can suggest forging connections across the disciplines; but it can also mean establishing a kind of undisciplined space in the interstices between disciplines, or even attempting to transcend disciplinary boundaries altogether" (p. 104). This ambiguity of interdisciplinarity, says Moran (2002), is a major reason why some critics have come up with other terms, such as "post-disciplinary," "anti-disciplinary," and "transdisciplinary." These terms that are often loosely defined and used interchangeably suggest that being interdisciplinary is not quite enough and that there is another intellectual level where disciplinary divisions can be subverted or even erased (p. 15).

The integrated definition of interdisciplinary studies noted earlier assumes "the existence and relative resilience of disciplines as modes of thought and institutional practices" (Moran, 2002, p. 17). This book agrees with Moran and other practitioners who view interdisciplinarity as complementary to the disciplines. The disciplines and the knowledge they produce in terms of insights, theories, and methods make interdisciplinary studies possible. This book explores how students can profitably use the disciplines, interdisciplines, and schools of thought to produce new understandings.

How the Term *Interdisciplinarity* Is Variably Used Today

The term *interdisciplinarity* has undergone a metamorphosis since it was coined by the Organization for Economic Cooperation and Development (OECD) in France in 1972. The OECD distinguished multi-, pluri-, inter-, and transdisciplinary forms of knowledge formation from disciplinarity (pp. 25–26). According to this typology, the most basic distinction is between "multidisciplinarity" and "interdisciplinarity." As noted earlier, multidisciplinarity juxtaposes disciplinary perspectives. The disciplines speak with separate voices on a problem of mutual interest. However, the disciplinary status quo is not interrogated, and the distinctive elements of each discipline retain their original identity. In contrast, interdisciplinarity consciously integrates separate disciplinary data, concepts, theories, and methods to produce an interdisciplinary understanding of a complex problem or intellectual question (Klein & Newell, 1997, p. 393).

Forms of Interdisciplinarity

Klein (2005a) cautions, however, that not all interdisciplinarities are the same. "Disagreements about definition," she says, "reflect differing views of the purpose of research and education, the role of disciplines, and the role of critique" (p. 55). There are three major forms of interdisciplinarity: instrumental interdisciplinarity, conceptual interdisciplinarity, and critical interdisciplinarity. **Instrumental interdisciplinarity** is a pragmatic approach that focuses on research, methodological borrowing, and practical problem solving in response to the external demands of society. However, borrowing alone is not sufficient for instrumental interdisciplinarity but requires integration. The key distinction between instrumental interdisciplinarity and critical interdisciplinarity (discussed later in this chapter) is the objective: Instrumental interdisciplinarity seeks to solve real-world problems or to illuminate and critique the assumptions of the perspectives (disciplinary, ideological, etc.) on which interdisciplinarity draws. This book reflects an instrumental approach. Interdisciplinarity is seen to result from "disciplinary slippage" or the space between disciplines that leads to the establishment of new interdisciplines (Klein, 1990, p. 42). Cellular biology is an example of an interdiscipline that developed out of physics, chemistry, and biology.[10]

Conceptual interdisciplinarity, also pragmatic, emphasizes the integration of knowledge and the importance of posing questions that have no single disciplinary basis (Salter & Hearn, 1996, p. 9). This notion of interdisciplinarity often implies a critique of disciplinary understandings of the problem, as in the case of cultural studies, feminist, and postmodern approaches. An example of conceptual interdisciplinarity, where the integrative concept is identity, is a study of the role of reggae music in affirming the cultural and political identity of postcolonial black Jamaicans (Lattuca, 2001, pp. 83–84).

The third form of interdisciplinarity is **critical interdisciplinarity**, which aims to interrogate existing structures of knowledge and education, raising questions of value and purpose. Critical interdisciplinarians fault the pragmatists for merely combining existing disciplinary approaches without advocating transformation. Rather than building bridges across academic units for practical problem-solving purposes, critical interdisciplinarians seek to transform and dismantle the boundary between the literary and the political, treat cultural objects relationally, and advocate inclusion of low culture (Klein, 2005a, pp. 57–58).

Yet, these distinctions between pragmatic and critical interdisciplinarity are not absolute. Research on systemic and complex problems such as the environment and healthcare often reflects a combination of critique and problem-solving approaches. The integrated definition of interdisciplinary studies noted earlier reflects an emerging consensus approach to the field: It is pragmatic, yet leaves room for critique and interrogation of the disciplines as well as economic, political, and social structures.

Interdisciplinarity, then, "has developed from an idea into a complex set of claims, activities, and structures" (Klein, 1996, p. 209). Identification of some of the more important of these follows.

Interdisciplinarity Is Used to Describe Work

There are four aspects of the work of interdisciplinary studies.

The Work of Integrating Knowledge

According to Boix Mansilla and Howard Gardner (2003), the principal work of interdisciplinary studies is the integration of knowledge and of modes of thinking from two or more disciplines. "Integration," they say, is the "blend[ing] into a functioning or unified whole" (p. 1). The **integration of knowledge**, then, means identifying and blending knowledge from relevant disciplines to produce an interdisciplinary understanding of a particular problem or intellectual question that is limited in time and to a particular context that would not be possible by relying solely on a single disciplinary approach. For example, a single disciplinary perspective cannot possibly explain the complex phenomenon of terrorism, much less craft a comprehensive solution to it. Understanding terrorism in an interdisciplinary sense calls for drawing on insights from history, political science, cultural anthropology, sociology, law, economics, religious studies, and psychology and integrating these to produce a more comprehensive understanding of it. By drawing on multiple disciplines, says Boix Mansilla (2002), interdisciplinary study "advances our understanding [by explaining complex phenomena, crafting comprehensive solutions, and raising new questions] in ways that would have not been possible through single disciplinary means" (p. 7). The work of integrating knowledge is also about practical problem solving (Boix Mansilla & Gardner, 2003, p. 2).[11] Interdisciplinary work often leads to the formation of new fields. Examples of the growing variety of such fields include ecology; environmental sciences; resource management; landscape development; industrial ecology; medical ecology; human ecology; social ecology; public health; cancer research; biotechnology; sociology of knowledge; discourse studies; science, technology, and society studies; future studies; conflict studies; cultural studies; media studies; communication studies; information sciences; cybernetics; computer sciences; systems sciences; and knowledge management (Klein, 2003, p. 16).

The Work of Integrating Disciplinary Modes of Thinking

Mode of thinking means the way of thinking and perceiving reality that characterizes a discipline—i.e., its perspective. Identifying and blending information from various disciplines about a problem or question is difficult enough; harder still is learning how each discipline thinks, approaches problem solving, conducts research, and creates new knowledge. This discipline-specific information that interdisciplinarians use in their research to produce an interdisciplinary understanding is characteristic of the symbiosis noted earlier between disciplinary and interdisciplinary research. Chapters 3 and 4 examine this discipline-specific information. The disciplines, though difficult to master and constantly changing in character, remain invaluable ways to perceive and understand the world (Boix Mansilla & Gardner, 2003, p. 8).

The Work of Recognizing and Confronting Differences

Recognizing and confronting differences stands in contrast to the initial transdisciplinary ideal that believed in a world in which differences were to be overcome, thus making the unity of knowledge possible. "The reality," Klein (1996) argues,

> is that differences matter. Even if negotiated and mediated, differences do not go away—they continue to create "noise." Misunderstandings, animosities, and competitions cannot be mitigated or glossed over. They must be taken seriously as attempts are made to spell out differences and their possible consequences. Interdisciplinarity . . . does not trust that everything will work out if everyone will just sit down and talk to each other. (p. 221)

The differences that Klein and others say that interdisciplinary studies must recognize and confront include differences over values such as political agendas, cultural traditions, and religious animosities. Klein's straightforward statement is a realistic assessment of the human condition as it is, not as it ought to be. Interdisciplinarity embraces reality. But, despite claims to the contrary, life is not inherently interdisciplinary. An example of a topic reflecting political and cultural differences is a study of education for democratic citizenship in which the student uses political liberalism and civic republicanism to critique each one's assumption and expose each one's over-reliance on rights and duties.

Interdisciplinary study seeks to integrate knowledge (as it pertains to a particular problem) rather than to unify knowledge. **Unifying knowledge** implies blending differences out of existence in subservience to an "overarching idea" such as feminism or Marxism. Integration, however, confronts differences, looks for common ground despite those differences, and, ultimately, produces an interdisciplinary understanding that takes those differences into account.

Each interdisciplinary studies research project requires drawing on a different combination of disciplines and insights because knowledge and problems are contextual and contingent. One practitioner expresses it this way: For interdisciplinarians, the "definition of intellectuality shifts from absolute answers and solutions to tentativeness and reflexivity" (Klein, 1996, p. 214). Chapters 2 and 5 discuss the kind of thinking that students should ideally exhibit.

Interdisciplinarity Is Used to Describe a Research Process

The interdisciplinary research process is the subject of Chapters 6–12. As noted in the integrated definition of interdisciplinary studies, the purpose or product of the research process is a cognitive advancement or interdisciplinary understanding of a particular problem. Integration is a means to that end, not an end in itself. The integrative part of the interdisciplinary research process involves identifying relevant disciplinary insights into the problem; evaluating ways in which these may conflict; creating or discovering the common ground concept, theory, or assumption by which the insights can be reconciled; and thereby producing an interdisciplinary understanding of the problem. This research process is described in Figure 1.1.

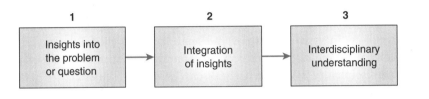

Figure 1.1   The Interdisciplinary Research Process

Interdisciplinarity Is Used to Describe the Kind of Knowledge Produced

Veronica Boix Mansilla, William C. Miller, and Howard Gardner (2000) are concerned about the kind of knowledge that interdisciplinary studies produces. "Individuals demonstrate **disciplinary understanding** [boldface added] when they use knowledge and modes of thinking in disciplines such as history, science, or the arts, to create products, solve problems, and offer explanations that echo the work of disciplinary experts." By contrast, "individuals demonstrate **interdisciplinary understanding** when they integrate knowledge and modes of thinking from two or more disciplines in order to create products, solve problems, and offer explanations, in ways that would not have been possible through single disciplinary means" (pp. 17–18).

Interdisciplinarity Is Used to Describe a Change in Knowledge Production

Knowledge production refers to scholarly research published in the form of peer-reviewed articles and books. The discussion about interdisciplinarity is a dialogue about innovation—that is, *change*—in the means of knowledge production. Disciplinary researchers traditionally are trained to produce knowledge differently than are interdisciplinarians. Interdisciplinarians borrow from the disciplines and integrate this information to produce new insights and meanings.[12] This activity, which goes against the grain of what many disciplinary researchers have been taught to do and to protect, is needed because knowledge is increasingly interdisciplinary and boundary crossing is commonplace.

Metaphors Commonly Used to Describe Interdisciplinary Work

A **metaphor** is a figure of speech in which a word or phrase, a story, or a picture is likened to the idea that one is attempting to communicate, as shown in the metaphors of the smoothie and the elephant house. Metaphors are extremely useful in helping us visualize an unfamiliar concept (Lakoff & Johnson, 1980, p. ix). Metaphors are important to interdisciplinary work and thinking in two ways: They communicate to disciplinarians the nature of interdisciplinary work in an overall sense, and they model the integrative result of a specific research project. Commonly used metaphors descriptive of interdisciplinary work in a general sense warrant discussion.

The Metaphor of "Boundary Crossing"

Boundary crossing is the process of moving across knowledge formations for the purpose of achieving an enlarged understanding. Boundaries between knowledge units—academic disciplines—are in a continuous, though imperceptibly slow, process of breaking down and reformulating. Indeed, boundary crossing with respect to knowledge production has become the defining characteristic of our age (Klein, 1996, p. 1).

Boundaries exist in many forms, including political, social, economic, religious, and ethnic. Surrounded by boundaries, we are mostly unaware of their existence until we find one blocking our progress. Boundary-related topics include the boundaries between science, religion, and humanist ethics concerning embryonic stem cell research and human cloning; the boundaries between religion, politics, and education concerning private school vouchers and the Bush administration's faith-based initiative; and the boundaries between politics, business (management), and sociology (race) concerning governmental (at all levels) responses to disasters such as Hurricane Katrina.

One boundary that is less known but no less important is the boundary between academic disciplines, or, as Klein (1996) calls it, a "specialist domain." "Boundary," she says, "has become a new keyword in discussions of knowledge" (p. 1). Words related to "boundary" include "turf," "territory," and "domain."

The metaphor of "boundary crossing" is useful to interdisciplinarians because it calls attention to the ways that disciplines have historically staked out their differences, claims, and activities and have built institutional structures to define and protect their knowledge practices (Klein, 1996, p. 1). "Boundary" can also be descriptive of something that is artificial and needlessly obstructive. This is the sense that Steve Fuller (1993) ascribes to the metaphor when he calls disciplinary boundaries "artificial barriers to the transaction of knowledge claims. Such boundaries are necessary evils that become more evil the more they are perceived as necessary" (p. 36).

There are at least two problems, though, with the boundary metaphor. First, it conveys the incorrect notion of a static line or space that fails to allow adequately for changes within a discipline or overlapping aims and activities among disciplines. Also, territorial metaphors fail to describe adequately the role of language between disciplines (Lyon, 1992, p. 682). Few boundaries or languages remain fixed—at least not for very long. This is certainly true in the Academy.

Reasons for crossing boundaries are several and will be discussed in later chapters. For interdisciplinarians, the primary reason for crossing boundaries is to develop a more comprehensive understanding of the problem that would not otherwise be possible by examining it from the perspective of a single discipline.

The Metaphor of Bridge Building

The metaphor of **bridge building** connotes the borrowing of tools and methods from disciplines (Squires, 1975, pp. 42–47). There are two attractions to this metaphor. The first is the idea of showing how interdisciplinary activity, like the spun cables suspended from the piers of the Golden Gate Bridge and firmly anchored in the bedrock on either shore, is something that takes place between two disciplines. The second attraction is the idea that interdisciplinary study has an applied orientation that students find attractive. Possible bridge building topics include explorations of how environmentalists can work with business and government to sustain the environment while meeting the economic development needs of the indigenous society, and how better communication and understanding can be developed between hostile racial, religious, and other groups.

There is, however, a problem with using "bridge building" to describe interdisciplinary studies, the interdisciplinary process, and integration: "Bridge builders do not tend to engage in critical reflection on problem choice, the epistemology of the disciplines being used, or the logic of disciplinary structure" (Klein, 1996, pp. 10–11). In other words, this metaphor suggests that interdisciplinary study is less concerned with the knowledge, perspectives, theories, and methods of those disciplines relevant to the problem or question under investigation than with the construction of a theory (i.e., cable) that would connect the disciplines.

The Metaphor of "Mapping"

Mapping or mapmaking is a metaphor based on the idea that the carving up of knowledge space is like the practice of cartography or mapmaking. Mapping involves using a "combinational" or integrative method to map or display information that is gathered from a variety of sources (Szostak, 2004, p. 143). European cartographers produced a system of mapping geographical and political space by lines of longitude and latitude forming territorial quadrangles that symbolically represented the world. These divisions were further subdivided into smaller units and, in turn, into still smaller units. In the absence of global positioning systems, inaccuracies abounded and disputes inevitably arose over who owned what sliver of territory (Stoddard, 1991, p. 6).

The classic illustration of this errant approach to mapping was the 1884 partitioning of Africa. Someone has calculated that of the colonial borders that dissected the continent and its peoples, fully 30% were arbitrary (Stoddard, 1991, p. 6). The remapping of the Earth's surface in our own day is occurring at the same time we are remapping knowledge.

Mapping a problem—breaking it down into its component parts and seeing how these parts behave and relate to one another—is an important strategy used by disciplinarians and interdisciplinarians to analyze complex problems. Mapping a problem such as spousal battery, for example, is likely to require the researcher to seek insights from several disciplines to explain its causes. Chapter 7 introduces various ways to map the problem.

The usefulness of the metaphor of mapping or remapping is that it reveals new interdisciplinary fields and the extent of border crossing between disciplines (Klein, 1996, p. 3). The weakness of this metaphor, however, is that it compares knowledge (which is fluid) to land (which is more stable). Another weakness is that maps tend to emphasize some aspects over others, constrain thought, and even mislead at times. Szostak (2004) notes that "maps may represent the concerns and interests of the powerful, as when black population centers were ignored on maps of South Africa" (pp. 143–144).

The Metaphor of "Bilingualism"

Bilingualism is a popular, but inappropriate, metaphor for interdisciplinary work that implies mastery of two complete languages. Its attraction is that it compares disciplines to foreign languages. For many, developing proficiency in a foreign language is as difficult and time-consuming as developing knowledge of a new discipline. The problem with this metaphor is that mastery of two complete languages rarely, if ever, occurs. Klein (1996) says that pidgin and Creole are the typifying forms of interdisciplinary communication (p. 220). **Pidgin** is a simplified speech used for communication between people with different languages for a limited purpose; **Creole** is a new first language among a hybrid community of knowers (Fuller, 1993, p. 45; Stoddard, 1991). The minimal condition for the possibility of interdisciplinary work involving teams of experts from different disciplines, cautions Klein (1996), must be "communicative competence" (p. 220).

Lest students feel that they must find just the right metaphor to express visually what they are attempting to do, Klein's (1996) point that "interdisciplinary activities cannot be depicted in a single image" (p. 19; Klein, 2000, p. 9) is well taken.[13] Interdisciplinarians are able to communicate the concept of interdisciplinarity to disciplinarians more effectively when they are mindful of the aspect of interdisciplinarity that each of these metaphors illuminates while being aware of its limitations.

CHAPTER SUMMARY

Interdisciplinary studies and interdisciplinarity are evolving dynamic concepts that are now mainstream in the Academy. Still, many disciplinarians use the terms multidisciplinarity and interdisciplinarity interchangeably and are unaware of the role of integration and of the goal of the interdisciplinary enterprise. This chapter has defined these terms, explained the differences between the disciplines and interdisciplinary studies, examined how interdisciplinarity is different from multidisciplinarity and transdisciplinarity, and identified the ways that interdisciplinarity is variably used today. Lastly, this chapter has identified strengths and weaknesses of various metaphors descriptive of interdisciplinary studies.

Chapter 2 presents the etymology of interdisciplinarity, examines the interdisciplinary critique of the disciplines, traces the origins of interdisciplinarity, and describes the interdisciplinary approach to learning, thinking, and research.

NOTES

1. For the limited purposes of this book, I am using traditional lists of major disciplines rather than the much fuller contemporary taxonomies.

2. History can be studied in two broad ways—the social science version that is theory-driven and often quantitative in its scientific testing of hypotheses, and the humanities version that is qualitative, narrative, and nonscientific, painting mental pictures with words rather than testing formal hypotheses, or with a conceptual and methodological pluralism that draws on both approaches.

3. See Klein, 1996, pp. 78–84, for a detailed discussion of these differences.

4. Not all interdisciplinarians agree that integration is the hallmark of interdisciplinarity. Lisa Lattuca (2001) prefers to distinguish between types of interdisciplinarity by focusing on the kinds of questions asked rather than on integration (p. 80). Joe Moran (2002) understands interdisciplinarity loosely to mean "any form of dialog or interaction between two or more disciplines" (p. 16). For Moran and others, the terms *interdisciplinarity* and *integration* are synonymous with *teamwork*, as in team teaching and cross-disciplinary communication on research projects (Klein, 2005b, p. 23; Lattuca, 2001, p. 12; J. R. Davis, 1995, p. 44).

5. However, some argue that some fields of studies have achieved this state.

6. This is an example of what Salter and Hearn (1996) call "critical interdisciplinarity," which poses a challenge to the disciplines. See the discussion of this form of interdisciplinarity in Lattuca (2001), pp. 117–118.

7. For a thorough discussion of the strengths and limitations of transdisciplinarity, see Somerville & Rapport (Eds.) (2000), *Transdisciplinarity: Recreating Integrated Knowledge*, particularly the chapters by Klein and Newell.

8. However, as Klein (2005a) notes, interdisciplinarity can no longer be regarded as a single kind of activity framed against a stable disciplinary system (p. 69).

9. In the humanities, students are required to choose a definition of meaning: artist intent, audience reaction, and so on. However, Rick Szostak (2004) argues that the interdisciplinary conception of "meaning" should urge students to embrace all possible definitions and the causal links they imply. Students "could still choose

to specialize with respect to one of these (or not) without needing to assume the others away" (p. 44).

10. This form, also known as "strategic" or "opportunistic," gained increased visibility during the 1980s in science-based areas of intense international economic competition, especially computers, biotechnology, manufacturing, and high technology. "Pragmatic" interdisciplinarity serves the political economy of the market and national needs. It seeks to build bridges within academia and between academia and society at large (Klein, 2005a, p. 57).

11. They talk about a variety of forms of interdisciplinary work. In their work in total, though, they emphasize epistemic goals that are contingent upon "practical" contexts.

12. Klein (1990) states, "There are no standards for excellence in borrowing" (p. 94).

13. More recently, Klein (2000) concludes that "territorial metaphors may be obsolete" and suggests that organic metaphors, such as boundary crossing, that highlight connection may be more useful because "knowledge production is no longer strictly within disciplinary boundaries" (pp. 8–9).

Review Questions

1. What are the characteristics or defining elements of a discipline?

2. Why is history a discipline and not "studies," and interdisciplinary is "studies" and not a discipline?

3. What are the three important aspects of the prefix *inter?*

4. Which of the seven main characteristics of the established disciplines are shared by interdisciplinary studies, and which ones are not?

5. What four concepts are embedded in the integrated definition of interdisciplinary studies used in this book?

6. What are some other sources of knowledge that interdisciplinarians such as Carp argue should be used in interdisciplinary work?

7. Why is Nissani's "smoothie" analogy of interdisciplinarity more useful than the fruit salad analogy?

8. In what ways is Lawrence Wheeler's fable of building the elephant house illustrative of a typical multidisciplinary approach to solving a complex problem?

9. How would an interdisciplinary approach to building an elephant house differ from a multidisciplinary approach?

10. What is the premise of interdisciplinary studies?

11. How is the term *interdisciplinarity* variably used today?

12. Of the metaphors descriptive of interdisciplinary work identified at the end of the chapter, which seems to be most appropriate and useful?

2

Tracing the Origins of Interdisciplinarity

Chapter Preview

The origins of interdisciplinarity converge around four insights. The first is that interdisciplinarity has a philosophical grounding in ideas extending from the Greco-Roman classics. The second is that when faced with new challenges of the modern world, particularly the proliferation of specialization, higher education looks to interdisciplinarity as an alternative. Third, the idea of disciplinarity is not much older than the idea of interdisciplinarity when one factors in the beginnings of general education, American studies, and comparative literature. Finally, interdisciplinarity has traditionally found itself at the forefront of change in higher education and thus involved in controversy. The old ideal of liberal humanism and integration of knowledge survives and thrives in a growing number of interdisciplinary programs across the nation.

This chapter discusses the etymology and research model of interdisciplinarity, explains the interdisciplinary critique of the disciplines, and traces the formation of the disciplines and interdisciplinarity and the field of interdisciplinary studies. The chapter then examines the assumptions underlying interdisciplinary studies and identifies the traits and skills of interdisciplinarians.

Interdisciplinarity: Etymology and Research Model

The etymology or origin of the noun *interdisciplinarity* is uncertain, though the term began to appear in the early twentieth century. One writer attributes its first use to the Social Science Research Council that used the term in the 1920s as shorthand for research that crossed the Council's disciplinary divisions (R. Frank, 1988, p. 91). Some scholars date the beginning of interdisciplinarity to the general education, core curriculum, and comparative literature movements that arose in the early part of the century, while others point to the rise of area studies and American studies in the 1930s and 1940s. Still others highlight problem-focused work in science and technology, beginning with agricultural and defense research in the 1940s, or cite educational experiments in the 1960s and 1970s (Klein, 2005a, pp. 2–3).

Today, interdisciplinary research and education are "inspired by the drive to solve complex questions and problems . . . and lead researchers in different disciplines to meet at the interfaces of those disciplines" (National Academy of Sciences et al., 2005, p. 16). Although various disciplines have differing approaches to research, especially in the types of phenomena they investigate, *all* research—including interdisciplinary research—involves identifying problems, discovering source material, generating data, organizing and analyzing that information, and drawing conclusions substantiated by it. Research in the sciences, and even more so in the social sciences, is increasingly interdisciplinary because the complexity of phenomena under investigation often defies a single disciplinary approach and requires crossing disciplinary domains. Interdisciplinary study involving the humanities is likewise increasingly interdisciplinary, reflecting what anthropologist Clifford Geertz (1980) describes as the **"blurring of the genres"** (i.e., disciplinary knowledge domains). Responding to the **four "posts"** that have transformed modern thought—postpositivism, poststructuralism, postmodernism, and postcolonialism—the **new humanities** is reflected in the development of interdisciplinary identity fields and new specialties such as urban studies, social history, film studies, women's and feminist studies, gender theory, and black studies as well as Hispanic American, Asian American, and Native American studies (Arthurs, 1993, pp. 265–267).

The Interdisciplinary Critique of the Disciplines

The interdisciplinary critique of the disciplines touches on at least six problematic characteristics of the disciplines and of **disciplinary specialization,** which is the focus on a particular portion of reality that is of interest to the discipline to the exclusion of other portions of reality.

Specialization Can Blind the Student to the Broader Context

A bit of dialogue found in *The Little Prince* by Antoine de Saint-Exupéry (2000) reveals the narrow focus of specialization:

"Your planet is very beautiful," [said the little prince]. "Has it any oceans?"
"I couldn't tell you," said the geographer . . . .
"But you are a geographer!"

"Exactly," the geographer said. "But I am not an explorer. I haven't a single explorer on my planet. It is not the geographer who goes out to count the towns, the rivers, the mountains, the seas, the oceans, the deserts. The geographer is much too important to go loafing about. He does not leave his desk." (pp. 45–46)

This humorous exchange shows that disciplinary specialization can blind the student to the broader context and leave unanswered the larger, more important, and practical issues of life. The fable of building a house for an elephant makes the same point. Interdisciplinarians believe that specialization *alone* will not enable us to master the pressing problems facing humanity today. The more specialized the disciplines become, the more *necessary* interdisciplinarity becomes.

Specialization Tends to Produce Tunnel Vision

Interdisciplinarians argue that the many complex practical problems confronting society can be understood only by examining them from various disciplinary perspectives and then integrating their insights to produce a more comprehensive understanding of them. They point out that disciplinary experts are prone to tunnel vision when it comes to examining important issues. For example, the experts who advocated the damming of the Columbia and Snake Rivers system were certain that this complex of hydroelectric dams would not harm the many salmon species that spawned in the rivers' tributaries. But the experts were wrong. Today, despite the extensive building of fish ladders and other costly efforts to mitigate the effects of these dams, several species are on the verge of extinction, and an industry that employed tens of thousands of workers is in ruins. In this world of specialists, even highly educated persons can be unaware of the social, ethical, and biological dimensions of a policy or action. Indeed, one may know a great deal about a particular subject but know little about its consequence (Dietrich, 1995).

Disciplinarians Sometimes Fail to Appreciate Other Disciplinary Perspectives

Before 9/11, few policy experts on the Middle East paid much attention to the central role that religion plays in the region, in particular its role as a motivating force behind much of the organized violence against Western interests there. But since 9/11, scholars are taking a fresh look at how religion, in interdisciplinary combination with other perspectives, informs our understanding of terrorist organizations such as Al-Qaeda. The need is to develop a more comprehensive understanding of such terrorist organizations in hopes of learning how to neutralize their appeal.

Some Worthwhile Topics Fall
in the Gaps Between Disciplines

In their critique of the disciplines, interdisciplinarians argue that some problems are neglected because they fall between disciplinary boundaries. An example of a new **integrative field** is strategic organization, which is an effort to bridge the disciplinary divide between strategic management, usually housed in sociology departments, and organization theory, usually housed in management departments (Baum, 2002, p. 21). According to Giles Gunn (1992), important dimensions of human experience and understanding lie unexplored in the spaces between disciplinary boundaries or the places where they cross, overlap, divide, or dissolve (p. 239). These gaps between the disciplines are being filled by new knowledge domains, such as sociobiology and biochemistry, that are allowing researchers to address new questions and pursue new topics (Klein, 2000, p. 16).

Creative Breakthroughs Often
Require Interdisciplinary Knowledge

The interdisciplinary critique of the disciplines extends to the need for creative breakthroughs when addressing complex problems. **Creative breakthroughs** often occur when different disciplinary perspectives and previously unrelated ideas are brought together (Sill, 1996, pp. 136–149). C. P. Snow (1964) states, "The clashing points of two subjects, two disciplines, two cultures—of two galaxies, so far as that goes—ought to produce creative changes. In the history of mental activity that has been where some of the breakthroughs came" (p. 16). Those who wish to speed up the production of knowledge and the solution to pressing problems should promote, or at least tolerate, an interdisciplinary approach.

The Disciplines Are Unable to
Address Comprehensively Complex Problems

A further problem with the disciplines is their inability to address comprehensively, much less solve, complex problems such as global warming. One might examine global warming from a biological perspective and hypothesize the effects of warmer ocean temperatures on coral reefs. One might examine it from an economic standpoint and conclude that the immediate financial costs of global warming are simply too great to warrant the United States signing the Kyoto Protocol. Or, one might examine the issue from the perspective of domestic politics and conclude that partisan political considerations are to blame for inaction on the problem. All these disciplinary contributions may be valuable, but they fail to provide the truly comprehensive perspective on the problem that policymakers and the public really need. On too many issues of public importance, the disciplines tend to talk past each other.

Most interdisciplinarians do not seek the end of the disciplines, for reasons already discussed in Chapter 1. They believe, however, that although the disciplines are useful for producing, organizing, and applying knowledge, too much specialization narrows and distorts one's view of the world.

Daniele C. Struppa (2002) argues that the need for interdisciplinary studies "is now stronger than ever" because modern objects of investigation require an interdisciplinary approach (p. 97). Steve Fuller (1993) agrees: Certain kinds of problems, increasingly those of general public interest, are not being adequately addressed by individual disciplines. Analyzing and solving these problems, says Fuller, requires an interdisciplinary approach (p. 33).

These concerns about specialization and fragmentation and the desire for integration of knowledge are not new but have a long history extending from ancient Greco-Roman times. The following brief history of the origins of interdisciplinarity and of interdisciplinary studies shows that they arose in response to a series of cultural and educational challenges that required alternatives.

The Formation of the Disciplines and the Origins of Interdisciplinarity and Interdisciplinary Studies

By the time of the ancient Greeks, knowledge had accumulated to such an extent that Plato's Academy, founded in 387 BC, offered instruction in gymnastics, music, poetry, literature, mathematics, and philosophy. The purpose of this experience was to promote the physical, moral, and social development of the "whole person," a concept foundational to integrative values in modern humanities, liberal education, general education, and many interdisciplinary studies programs (Hirst, 1974, pp. 30–31; Nussbaum, 1985, pp. 6–7).

Aristotle, the great philosopher, began the practice of dividing knowledge into disciplines. He established a clear hierarchy between the different academic subjects with the theoretical subjects of theology, mathematics, and physics on top; the practical subjects of ethics and politics in the middle; and the productive subjects of the fine arts, poetics, and engineering at the bottom. Aristotle found this structuring of knowledge necessary but regrettable because it violated the fundamental notion of the unity of all knowledge. To integrate these subjects, he placed philosophy as the universal field of inquiry at the top of his hierarchy, as a way to bring together all the different branches of learning (Moran, 2002, p. 4). Significantly, this **classical division of knowledge** remained intact until the nineteenth century, when a new scheme of disciplinarity arose.

The Origins of the University and the Disciplines

The twelfth century (1100–1200 AD) saw the development of a new institution that was to play a major role in the ascendancy of European civilization and the development of the disciplines: the **university**. The modern university is an institution of higher learning that provides teaching and research and is authorized to grant academic degrees. It evolved from the medieval cathedral schools and "rested on the conviction that there was an essential and universal unity of knowledge and through Christianity, that faith was the highest order of knowledge" (Briggs & Micard, 1972, p. 186). The first recorded appearance of the word "university" is in a letter of Pope Innocent III in 1208 or 1209 (Bishop, 1970, p. 266). The first universities appeared in Salerno, Bologna, Paris, Oxford, and Cambridge, where groups of students and teachers (or masters) would meet, often in rented halls or rooms. Interestingly, the original meaning of the word "university" does not refer to either "universe" or "universal" but rather to the totality of a group, as in a group of students (Haskins, 1940, p. 14; Rashdall, 1936, pp. 4–5).

By the thirteenth century, the universities were teaching a serial curriculum that included both letters and the sciences in the customary divisions of the trivium and the quadrivium. "Until at least the end of the eighteenth century," writes Moran (2002), "university students tended to study a core curriculum of the liberal arts, divided into the trivium (logic, grammar, rhetoric) and the quadrivium (arithmetic, geometry, astronomy and music)" (p. 5). This curriculum served as the basis of and preparation for the professions. Students went on to specialize in theology, medicine, or law much as students today choose to "major" in a subject. These studies corresponded to modern courses in the arts and sciences (Bishop, 1970, p. 267).

The term "discipline," introduced as "disciplina" by the Romans, was applied to these professions because of the perceived need to relate education to specific economic, political, and ecclesiastical ends (Klein, 1990, p. 20). Interestingly, Medieval scholars largely excluded contemporary cultural developments as well as the mechanical arts, including agriculture, navigation, war, weaving, and the theater arts (Saffle, 2005, p. 14). Not until the twentieth century would these fields be absorbed into the academic curriculum of the Western university. The university and the disciplines became an engine of knowledge production that far outstripped any other method of learning devised by any previous civilization.

The Impact of the Enlightenment and Scientific Revolution on the Disciplines

The production of knowledge and disciplinary specialization accelerated during the late seventeenth and eighteenth centuries. Two movements hastened this process. The first was the **Enlightenment**, a Europe-wide intellectual movement that emphasized the progress of human knowledge through the powers of reason and provided justification for the movement known as modernism. The second was the **scientific revolution** that occurred at about the same time and that emphasized greater specialization (i.e., reductionism) and heightened research activity (i.e., empiricism), initially in the sciences and then in all the disciplines. The significance of the Enlightenment and the rise of modern science is that they challenged the idea of the unity of knowledge. The early division of the empirical sciences dates from this period.

Not everyone, however, saw greater disciplinary specialization as a positive development. In the early 1700s, the Italian thinker Giambattista Vico called for a new approach to learning. He claimed that the ascendancy of science and mathematics in the curriculum had led to a neglect of broad education in favor of specialized knowledge. He argued that the "human sciences" such as history, philosophy, and law can achieve knowledge and understanding "from within" and, in fact, were superior to the natural sciences, which can only describe the external phenomena in nature (Moran, 2002, p. 7). Nevertheless, Vico's call for less specialization and a more comprehensive approach to learning largely fell on deaf ears.

The Consolidation of the Disciplines in the Late Eighteenth and Early Nineteenth Centuries

Between 1750 and 1800, the disciplines consolidated their hold on the teaching and production of knowledge by embracing three new revolutionizing techniques: writing, grading, and examination. These practices were introduced in three new teaching settings: the seminar (beginning in the German universities around 1760), the laboratory (beginning in the French *Grandes Ecoles* before the Revolution), and the classroom (beginning in Scotland around 1760).

Disciplines also began publishing disciplinary journals and hiring their own PhDs, making it difficult for scholars to cross disciplinary lines. Combined, these practices and settings enabled the disciplines to strengthen their position and accelerate the production of new knowledge (Hoskin, 1993, pp. 275–277). These practices and settings have been so successful that today they are used the world over.

The Professionalization of Knowledge in the Late Nineteenth and Early Twentieth Centuries and the Rise of the Modern Disciplines

The academic disciplines of today and the modern concept of disciplinarity are largely the product of development in the late nineteenth and early twentieth centuries (Klein, 1990, pp. 21–22; Lattuca, 2001, p. 23). This period saw the formation of disciplines in the physical and natural sciences such as biology, chemistry, and physics, though the division process was underway between the mid-seventeenth century and late eighteenth century. By the middle of the nineteenth century, the social sciences were fragmenting into anthropology and economics, followed by psychology, sociology, history, and political science. Though the humanities include the oldest subjects, the humanities were the last to assume modern disciplinary form (Easton, 1991, p. 11).

Along with the rise of scientific specialties came increased competition for university resources, so universities began to organize themselves around the disciplines. These new disciplines were accompanied by new professional societies: history in 1884, economics in 1885, political science in 1903, and sociology in 1905 (Hershberg, 1981, p. 23). Disciplinary journals allowed isolated specialists to keep abreast of the latest research and also gave them a forum for presenting their own research. Specialists did not need to consider perspectives other than those of their own specialty (Swoboda, 1979, p. 62).

As the modern university took shape, disciplinarity was reinforced in two major ways, according to Klein (1990). First, industries demanded and received specialists from the universities. Second, the disciplines recruited students to their ranks (pp. 21–22). The trend toward specialization, especially in the sciences, was further propelled by increasingly more expensive instrumentation, elaborately equipped laboratories, and highly trained personnel. "Although the 'Renaissance Man' may have remained an ideal for the well-educated baccalaureate, it was not the model for the new professional, specialized research scholar" (Hershberg, 1981, p. 23). Clearly, the impression that is often conveyed to students that the disciplines have always existed is incorrect.

The proliferation of academic disciplines raised concerns about overspecialization, in particular how these new disciplines were connected to issues of power and self-interest. Late nineteenth-century German philosopher Friedrich Nietzsche and early twentieth-century Spanish philosopher José Ortega y Gasset saw the new disciplines as symptoms of a more general phenomenon: the growing interdependence of government, business, and education. Driving this interdependence was an economic system that increasingly depended on the availability of specialists and professionals. Under this system, the disciplines and the universities served two vital functions: They trained persons for careers in government and business, and they gave these new professions legitimacy and status by providing them with academic credentials (Moran, 2002, pp. 11, 13).

The Emergence of Interdisciplinary Studies

The notion of interdisciplinarity and the emergence of interdisciplinary studies can be seen as a response to two broad developments in the twentieth century. The first is the general education movement that dates from the early decades of the century. The second concerns the cultural revolution of the 1960s and the resulting reforms in higher education.

The General Education Movement

The **general education movement** that arose after World War I was a response to several problems besetting American culture and education at the time, including the lack of national unity and the eroding cohesiveness of general education (Boyer, 1981, pp. 4–5). The philosophy animating the general education movement was the belief that these problems could be solved by reemphasizing the arts and the values associated with classical humanism that emphasized wholeness of knowledge and of human nature. These arts and values are "general" in four ways: (1) they apply to all subject areas; (2) they embrace all basic skills; (3) they affect the formation of the whole person; and (4) they provide guidance for all humans (McKeon, 1964, pp. 159, 171–172).

At the heart of the general education movement and of liberal humanism was the implicit notion of interdisciplinarity. There were two differing conceptions of interdisciplinarity at work: the **traditional interdisciplinarity** and the **pragmatic interdisciplinarity**. The former focused on the classical and secular ideals of liberal culture and education. The latter focused on the study of historically situated problems of society (Hutcheson, 1997, pp. 109–110). What both conceptions held in common, though, was the notion of general education as "the place where all the parts would add up to a cohesive whole" (Klein, 2005a, p. 31). The magnet holding these diverse pieces together was thought to be a common core of great books and ideas based on two millennia of Western cultural development. Requiring students to study this common core, advocates believed, would stem the rising tide of "materialism, vocationalism, empiricism, relativism, specialism, and departmentalization" (Graff, 1987, p. 162). Thus, one of the first motivations for interdisciplinary studies in the United States, states Charles Anderson (2001), was to demonstrate unity of knowledge (pp. 456–457). By contrast, Columbia University began to move away from the traditional unity of knowledge model, toward one of shared interdisciplinary knowledge. Its well-known course, Contemporary Civilization, promoted shared interdisciplinary knowledge with emphasis on the process of knowing and examination of contemporary problems (Hutcheson, 1997, p. 110).

The Cold War Era and Interdisciplinarity

After World War II, a second general education reform movement emerged, triggered by the 1945 Harvard report, *General Education in a Free Society*. The report called for a new general education curriculum based on the sciences and writings of the European humanist tradition. Against the backdrop of fascism and communism, proponents intended the curriculum to provide a common core of knowledge, beliefs, and values centered on the ideals of freedom and democracy—in short, a national ideology opposed to communism in the Cold War era (Bender, 1997, pp. 20–21).

At the same time, criticism of the disciplines intensified and focused on two themes. The first was the enormous power that the disciplines had accumulated since the turn of the century. Influenced by Friedrich Nietzsche, French philosopher Michael Foucault argued in the 1960s that the disciplines are not just a way to produce knowledge; they are a sophisticated mechanism for regulating human conduct and social relations. He found the examination to be the "quintessential practice that epitomizes both the modern power of knowledge and the modern practice of meticulous disciplinary control" (Hoskin, 1993, p. 277).

The second criticism focused on the deepening isolation of the disciplines from each other. Tony Becher (1989) uses the anthropological metaphor of **tribes** to describe the disciplines, each having its own culture and language:

> Men of the sociology tribe rarely visit the land of the physicists and have little idea what they do over there. If the sociologists were to step into the building occupied by the English department, they would encounter the cold stares if not the slingshots of the hostile natives. . . . The disciplines exist as separate estates, with distinctive subcultures. (p. 23)

Echoing Foucault, Moran (2002) complains that the disciplines exercise their considerable power by "permitting certain ways of thinking and operating while excluding others" (p. 14).

University Reforms in the 1960s and Interdisciplinary Studies

This critique of the disciplines was strengthened by the confluence of three major developments in the 1960s: the Vietnam War, the student revolution, and dramatic changes in social mores. Combined, these served as a catalyst from which emerged new thinking about how the Academy should relate to society (Mayville, 1978, p. 3). This new thinking called for radical university reforms, one central element of which was the elimination of the traditional academic disciplines in favor of holistic notions of training that were closer to the practical problems of life (Weingart, 2000, p. xii). The disciplines and the scholarship that they produced had failed to explain, or even ignored, the great social movements and struggles that characterized the period. These included the civil rights, anti-imperialist, anti-racist, and women's rights movements. To that generation of students and young faculty, "The disciplines seemed increasingly irrelevant or even obstructionist to their quest to understand, address, and solve the great issues of the day" (Katz, 2001, p. 520). By contrast, interdisciplinarity became a programmatic, value-laden term that stood for reform, innovation, progress, and opening up the university to all kinds of hitherto marginalized publics (Weingart, 2000, p. xii). The radicalism of the 1960s produced new fields such as African American studies, women's studies, and ethnic studies, and new definitions of culture and politics.

But by the late 1970s, when the social struggles had subsided and mundane academic routine had returned to the universities, the call for interdisciplinarity became much less urgent. "What had seemed progressive only a few years earlier appeared outdated, if not quaint" (Weingart, 2000, p. xii). Yet, under the surface calm, young interdisciplinarians such as William H. Newell and Julie Thompson Klein were persistently questioning what constituted legitimate subjects of inquiry, and by their work, they began slowly to reconfigure the contours of knowledge and the methods through which such knowledge was produced (Katz, 2001, p. 520).

Interdisciplinary Studies Emerges as an Academic Field

In 1979, a group of 50 interdisciplinarians led by Newell decided that they needed to have their own professional organization and journal and formed the **Association for Integrative Studies (AIS)**. Its purpose was to study interdisciplinary methodology, theory, curricula, and administration. In 1982, AIS launched a peer-reviewed journal, *Issues in Integrative Studies.* Within a decade, AIS, under Newell's leadership, became a national voice for interdisciplinary studies and a professional home for several hundred interdisciplinarians where they could work together to develop the potential of the field.

The founding of AIS converged with a broader development that reflected a fundamental change in the way knowledge is produced in the United States. There is, observes Peter Weingart (2000), "a growing pluralism both in the locations of knowledge production and in the patterns of initiation, production, and use of knowledge as well as its disciplinary combinations" (pp. xi–xii). This development is uneven and does not affect all the disciplines in the same way. Where production of knowledge is fast, as in the natural sciences, the disciplinary boundaries seem to be more fluid than in the social sciences where the rate of production is far slower. Inside the university, where the disciplines command great respect, the goal of knowledge production is to *understand*. However, outside the university, where the goal is to generate practical knowledge in order to *solve problems,* the disciplines command less respect and "are even frowned upon as obstacles to innovation or as providing a skewed perspective" (p. xii).

Finally, as disciplinary boundaries are becoming more permeable and as the number of new fields and specialties grows by the day, interdisciplinarity is becoming a fairly common experience. This development, however, does *not* signal the beginning of the end of the disciplines and their replacement by interdisciplinarity. Rather, it shows the limits of the disciplines and the need for and the expansion of the concept of interdisciplinarity. The interdisciplinary research process offers a way to apply basic research from relevant disciplines to complex, real-world problems that transcend individual disciplines. Both the disciplines and interdisciplinarity are needed and should be viewed as complementary rather than contradictory ways to produce knowledge and solve problems, as shown in Figure 2.1.

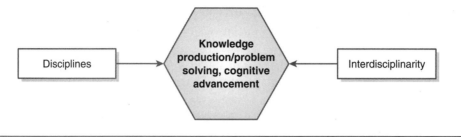

Figure 2.1   Complementary Ways to Produce Knowledge and Solve Problems

The Interdisciplinary Approach to Learning, Thinking, and Producing Knowledge

The interdisciplinary approach to learning, thinking, and producing knowledge distinguishes this academic field from the disciplines. Although the field still lacks a cohesive and agreed-upon theory, there is a set of assumptions that are well established.

Interdisciplinary Assumptions

At least five assumptions undergird the field, though consensus on each of them varies.

The Reality Beyond Academia Requires an Interdisciplinary Approach

Interdisciplinarity reflects the reality that is beyond academic boundaries. It is, according to a recent study by the Carnegie Foundation for the Advancement of Teaching, uniquely able to "address real-world problems, unscripted and sufficiently broad to require multiple areas of knowledge and multiple modes of inquiry, offering multiple solutions and benefiting from multiple perspectives" (Huber & Hutchings, 2004, p. 13). It is an oversimplification, however, to say that life is interdisciplinary. It is more appropriate to say that gaps in human knowledge and fragmentation of human organization abound and, consequently, that integrated approaches to problems are required (Klein, 1996, pp. 12–13).

The Disciplines Are Foundational to Interdisciplinary Studies

Speaking for many interdisciplinarians, Deborah DeZure (1999) says, "Interdisciplinarity is not a rejection of the disciplines. It is firmly rooted in them but offers a corrective to the dominance of disciplinary ways of knowing and specialization" (p. 3). Newell (1992) argues that we need the depth and focus of disciplinary ways of knowing, but we also need interdisciplinarity to broaden the context and establish links to other ways of constructing knowledge. Indeed, interdisciplinary study, grounded by definition in the disciplines, is both complementary and critical of them at the same time (pp. 212, 220).

Some interdisciplinarians, though, share an **antidisciplinary** view, preferring a more "open" understanding of "knowledge" and "evidence" that would include "lived experience," testimonials, oral traditions, and interpretation of those traditions by elders (Vickers, 1998, pp. 23–26). There is a problem, however, with this approach. Without some grounding in the disciplines relevant to the problem, borrowing risks becoming indiscriminate and the result rendered suspect. Moreover, those who reject the knowledge claims of the disciplines altogether may be uncertain how to make knowledge claims other than on grounds of life experience. In academic work, says Klein (2005a), it is still necessary to develop **disciplinary adequacy** or minimum understanding of the cognitive map of each of the disciplines, interdisciplines, and schools of thought relevant to a particular problem (p. 71). How to achieve adequacy in the disciplines relevant to the problem is the focus of Chapter 8.

The Disciplines by Themselves Are Inadequate to Address Complex Problems

Disciplinary inadequacy is the view that the disciplines by themselves are inadequate to address complex problems. Disciplinary inadequacy stems from several factors, beginning with the pressing need for an integrated approach to increasingly complex social, economic, and technological problems. This was one of the findings of the first authoritative national report on interdisciplinary studies that was published in 1990 by the Association of American Colleges. The report of the Interdisciplinary Studies Task Force confirmed a widely held belief that knowledge has become increasingly interdisciplinary. The reasons included new developments in research and scholarship, the formation of new hybrid fields, the expanding influence of interdisciplinary methods and concepts, and the pressing need for integrated approaches to complex social, economic, and technological problems (Klein & Newell, 1997, pp. 395–396). Wolfram W. Swoboda (1979) uses even stronger language: "Individual specialties on their own, it is now clear, simply do not have the breadth of perspective nor probably the willingness to assume responsibility for offering extensive and intensive solutions to social problems" (p. 83).

Disciplinary inadequacy stems from a second factor, namely, its claim that the disciplines provide all that is needed to make sense of the modern world. This is so, states Ananta Kuma Giri (2002), observing that there comes a point when disciplinary certainty has to be abandoned in order "to discover the unexpected truths of reality in the borderland." The disciplinary approach fails, she argues, because "whatever categories and concepts we use to make sense of reality, they are not adequate to provide us a total picture" (p. 110). Stanley Fish (1991) notes, "As soon as disciplines are fully established they come quickly to believe in the priority of their own concerns." He complains that the disciplinary boundaries that characterize the university "are not natural but historical" (pp. 101–102, 105). "The problem with disciplinary thinking," says Giri, "is that it fails to realize that its claim to universality needs to be relativized by recognizing the significance of other disciplines in gaining multiple perspectives about the world to which both one's as well as another's discipline contribute" (p. 106).

A third factor explaining disciplinary inadequacy is that the world is undergoing a **paradigm shift.** This refers to a profound and transformative change in the philosophical and theoretical framework that dominates a discipline or approach to knowledge formation. Accelerating globalization of cultural, technological, economic, and demographic flows is rapidly and profoundly transforming the institutions that produce and disseminate knowledge (Friedman, 2001, p. 504). Interdisciplinarity can aid in this process. Underlying the calls for an interdisciplinary component to liberal education is the recognition that interdisciplinary study encourages "breadth of vision and the development of the skills of integration and synthesis so frequently demanded by the problems of a culture in the midst of a profound transition" (Newell & Green, 1982, p. 23).

As society and its problems become more complex, the traditional academic disciplines will not always be able to prepare students for the complex issues they will face in the professions (McCall, 1990, p. 1319). A value inherent in the concept of complexity is that interdisciplinarity prepares future professionals to confront the complex behaviors and problems they will certainly face in a profession.

Disciplinary Perspectives Reveal Only a Portion of Reality

Academic disciplines provide their own unique perspective on a given problem, as illustrated in the fable of the blind men and the elephant (see Chapter 3). For example, although "power" is a concept relevant to virtually all the social sciences, each discipline has its own definition of power, and each definition is undergirded by certain assumptions, methods, and so forth that are unique to each discipline. To gain a more balanced and comprehensive understanding of "power" as it relates to a problem, interdisciplinarians must develop adequacy concerning the perspective of each relevant discipline (Hursh, Haas, & Moore, 1983, pp. 44–45).

The ability to do this is called **cognitive decentering,** which is the intellectual capacity to consider a variety of other perspectives and thus perceive reality more accurately, process information more systematically, and solve problems more efficiently. The term *decentering* denotes the ability to shift deliberately among alternative perspectives and to bring each to bear upon a complex problem. This type of thinking allows the student to make connections between disciplines and theories, between practical problems and accumulated knowledge, and between a society's assumptions and those of other cultures, as shown in Figure 2.2.

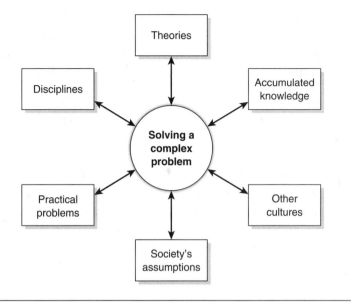

Figure 2.2   Cognitive Decentering

Above all, cognitive decentering enables interdisciplinarians to evaluate the usefulness of various disciplines to understanding complex problems. The importance of this thinking process is evident in everyday decision making, as well as in scientific pursuits. For example, the cognitive process described above is essential in the search for solutions to such problems as energy depletion, environmental pollution, health care delivery, and urban decay, or in considering aesthetic qualities of line, color, form, and texture from the standpoint of music, art, dance, or theater (Hursh et al., 1983, pp. 44–45).

Integration of Insights Will Produce a Cognitive Advancement That Would Not Be Possible by Relying on Single Disciplinary Means

Integration, the focus of Chapter 5, is a core feature of interdisciplinary studies and of the interdisciplinary research process. Narrowly speaking, integration requires understanding the disciplinary perspectives on the problem and paying careful attention to evaluating and rectifying the elements of these perspectives (identified in Chapters 3 and 4) that conflict.

Traits and Skills of Interdisciplinarians

Interdisciplinary studies is not just a way to obtain a degree; it is a systematic method of training one's mind and developing one's character. "The effect, if not the purpose, of interdisciplinarity is often nothing less than to alter the way we think about thinking" (Geertz, 1980, pp. 165–166; Gunn,

1992, p. 240). From the extensive literature on interdisciplinary studies, it is possible to identify no fewer than 15 traits and skills common to inter-disciplinarians. **Traits** are distinguishing qualities of a person, whereas **skills** are cognitive abilities to use one's knowledge effectively and readily in performing a task.

Traits

Enterprise. The interdisciplinarian is like an entrepreneur in the sense that both are willing to assume risk in order to achieve the objective. The inter-disciplinarian, like the entrepreneur, sees connections and the possibility of obtaining new information, novel insights, and an interdisciplinary under-standing of complex problems. Cognitive psychologist Rainer Bromme (2000) compares crossing a disciplinary boundary to "moving about in for-eign territory" (p. 116). Interdisciplinarians enjoy venturing into unfamiliar places and entertaining new ideas.

Love of Learning. Students drawn to interdisciplinary studies are intensely interested in the world they live in, and they welcome opportunities to view the world and its problems from differing perspectives (Trow, 1984, p. 15). Since interdisciplinarians often find themselves in new situations, they must also know how to learn and adapt. They need to know what information to ask for and how to acquire a working knowledge of the language, concepts, and analytical skills pertinent to understanding a given problem (Klein, 1990, p. 183).

Reflection. Learning is a process of cognitive and emotional transformation. Students in interdisciplinary studies are interested in understanding the know-ing process. **Reflection** occurs when students evaluate sources of information, demonstrate lines of reasoning from conflicting perspectives, evaluate com-plex problems or objects, discuss controversial issues, or justify an important decision. Reflection also occurs when students examine, perhaps in a reflec-tive paper, their responses to an emotionally charged question (Myers & Haynes, 2002, pp. 191–192). Consequently, students engaged in interdiscipli-nary learning develop a strong self-concept (Bromme, 2000, pp. 116–118).

Tolerance for Ambiguity and Paradox in the Midst of Complexity. Interdisciplinarians accept that sometimes there are irreconcilable differences in the ways different disciplines view the same problem or issue. They must be able to see all sides of an issue, reconcile conflicting perspectives by cre-ating common ground among them, and live with ambiguity where reconcil-iation proves impossible (Bromme, 2000, pp. 116–118; Hursh et al., 1983, pp. 44–45). Ambiguity can be unsettling, especially for those who demand quick and clear-cut solutions to problems. But ambiguity is a fact of life and of complexity, too. Real-world problems are often so complicated that it is impossible to know everything that one needs to know to understand them, let alone solve them. Interdisciplinarians know that interdisciplinary understanding is a constant process that never quite achieves total understanding. Accepting that there is always something more to know keeps interdisciplinarians from becoming too settled in their knowledge about a problem. They remain open to new information and perspectives.

Receptivity to Other Disciplines and to the Perspectives of Those Disciplines. **Receptivity to other disciplines** means being open to information or insights from any and all relevant disciplinary perspectives. This, in turn, means being willing, even eager, to learn about other fields of knowledge, gaining both an intuitive and intellectual grasp of them (Newell, 1992, p. 215). Receptivity to other disciplines and to their perspectives is essential to developing an interdisciplinary understanding of any problem. Understanding a discipline's perspective involves not simply knowing what knowledge the discipline offers, but a willingness to deal with its perspective on its own terms, appreciating its assumptions, epistemology, concepts, theories, and methods (Armstrong, 1980, p. 54; Gunn, 1992, p. 239). In other words, the interdisciplinarian needs to be ready, willing, and able to walk in the shoes of the disciplinarian in a selective fashion pertinent to specific problems and questions. Chapters 3 and 4 emphasize the primary importance that interdisciplinarians attach to knowing the commonly used elements of the major disciplines in the sciences, the social sciences, and the humanities. But this chapter emphasizes that knowing must be preceded by receptivity.

Willingness to Achieve "Adequacy" in Multiple Disciplines. Being receptive to multiple perspectives is one thing; successfully understanding them is another. The disciplines have each developed a daunting array of skills and knowledge, and at first glance it seems impossible to comprehend fully, let alone master, any one or two of them in a single lifetime. However, there is a difference between achieving mastery and adequacy in a discipline. According to Klein (1996), the difference between disciplinary mastery and disciplinary adequacy lies in the difference between learning a discipline thoroughly in order to practice it (i.e., mastery) and merely comprehending how that discipline characteristically looks at the world in terms of its perspective, assumptions, epistemology, concepts, theories, and methods (i.e., adequacy) (p. 212). The interdisciplinarian needs only to achieve adequacy, meaning knowing the discipline's defining elements relevant to the problem. This knowledge allows the student to have a basic "feel" of the discipline and an understanding of how it approaches the problem. **Interdisciplinary learning** develops the ability to know the limitations and biases of a discipline, to discover the benefits and perspectives of a discipline, and to understand how a discipline works simply by forcing us to see one discipline in light of another (Carlisle, 1995, p. 10). Interdisciplinary learning also develops the ability to integrate disciplinary insights relevant to a problem or question and produce a new and more comprehensive understanding of it than would be possible using single disciplinary means.

Appreciation of Diversity. Appreciating diversity means, simply, having respect for people holding different views, devoted to different faith traditions and different cultures, and coming from different ethnic or racial backgrounds. Interdisciplinarians, acutely aware of their own biases, acknowledge that different points of view are necessary for an interdisciplinary understanding (Newell, 1990, p. 71).

Willingness to Work With Others. Interdisciplinarity is often a collaborative process. No one person, no matter how thoroughly trained, will ever have a complete understanding of any given problem or issue. This includes the interdisciplinarian investigating it. The interdisciplinarian often has to draw upon the insights of disciplinary experts. An **expert interdisciplinarian** is one who is able to integrate the input of others to address an issue, which may include coordinating team members. This trait applies especially to interdisciplinarians engaged in technical and scientific studies that most commonly involve teamwork. Effective participation in interdisciplinary team activities is not so much a matter of individual traits as it is of learned behavior. People develop intellectual skills, such as dialectical and metaphorical thinking, and patterns of group communication skills that permit them to learn from and be taught by other members of the team (Newell, 1998, p. 551).

Humility. Humility is the one learned behavior that all scholars, including interdisciplinarians, surely need when faced with a complex problem that exposes the limits of one's training and expertise (Newell, 2001, p. 22). While disciplinarians can take comfort in knowing all there is to know about some sliver of reality that is their specialty, interdisciplinarians cannot hope to achieve this level of mastery of every facet of a complex problem. Instead of experiencing pride of mastery, the interdisciplinarian is humbled by knowing how much the relevant domains of knowledge do not know about the complex problem.[1] Practitioners of interdisciplinary studies bring to their craft a humility that comes from knowing what they do not know. Students and teachers involved in interdisciplinary investigations quickly discover that they do not know and cannot know everything about a topic. But by using the interdisciplinary process, they are at least moving toward knowing more about the topic than they would otherwise be able to learn using a purely disciplinary approach. "Through this process students discover the need for further learning, and they develop respect for different views" (Wentworth & Davis, 2002, p. 17).

Interdisciplinarity, according to the Organization for Economic Cooperation and Development (OECD), "is first and foremost a state of mind" (1970, p. 192).

Skills

Ability to Communicative Competently. Interdisciplinarity is a highly interactive field, requiring **communicative competence**, the ability to comprehend and translate terminology that is discipline-specific. Each discipline has not only its own set of skills and knowledge but also its own language that it uses to describe its assumptions, concepts, and theories. Though discipline-specific language is an effective "shorthand" for experts to use to communicate with each other, it is often incomprehensible to those outside the discipline. This places an additional burden on the interdisciplinarian, who must grasp this terminology and make it accessible to others, regardless of their field of expertise (Klein, 1996, p. 217).

The variety of disciplinary perspectives involved in interdisciplinary practice often necessitates the building and coordination of teams of individuals with different training and expertise. An interdisciplinarian must possess keen interpersonal relations skills and be able to engage in productive communication with people who hold a variety of interests, beliefs, and mind-sets, even if some of these sharply conflict.

Interdisciplinarity facilitates communication across disciplinary boundaries. This communication is possible because, despite the differences in jargon, there is overlap among the assumptions, concepts, theories, and methods used by the disciplines as well as underlying recurring patterns in both natural phenomena and human behavior that generally hold true in all of them. In many cases, each of the disciplines is saying something similar about the nature of the world, only in a different language.

Ability to Think Abstractly. **Abstract thinking** is a higher-order cognitive ability that enables one to understand and express an interdisciplinary understanding or meaning of a problem symbolically in terms of a metaphor, or to compare a hard-to-understand and complex phenomenon to a symbol that is simple, familiar, and easy to understand. Abstract thinking is an essential skill for many professions and is particularly desirable for the interdisciplinarian, especially when working in the humanities. To achieve the objective of an interdisciplinary understanding, the interdisciplinarian must integrate differing disciplinary insights into the problem and, ideally, should be able to express this understanding or meaning symbolically in terms of a metaphor. Abstract thinking and metaphors are important tools in the interdisciplinarian's toolbox. However, "abstract thinking represents '*an* end, not *the* end' of the thinking process" (Seabury, 2002, p. 47).

Ability to Think Dialectically. In many ways, dialectical thinking is the opposite of disciplinary thinking, but it is an important skill of the interdisciplinarian and is a method that underlies interdisciplinary work. **Dialectical thinking** means any systematic reasoning or argument that places side-by-side opposing ideas for the purpose of seeking to resolve their conflict. It is a method of determining the truth of any assertion by testing it against arguments that might negate it. Composition expert Anne Berthoff (1981) believes that there is a natural dialectic of the mind, "a dialectic of sorting and gathering, of particularizing and generalizing" (p. 105). Indeed, one writer goes so far as to state that dialectical thinking "is *the* underlying method of interdisciplinary work" (W. Davis, 1978). Rather than viewing differences, tension, and conflict as barriers that must be overcome, the interdisciplinarian views these as part of the integrative process.

Ability to Engage in Nonlinear Thinking. **Nonlinear thinking** is the ability to approach a problem creatively, thinking about it "outside the box" without being influenced by solutions attempted in the past, and viewing it from different perspectives. As noted in Chapter 1, interdisciplinary studies is similar to the disciplines in that it has a "method" or way of conducting research and producing new knowledge. However, the progression of the interdisciplinary research process—from identifying the disciplines and their perspectives relevant to the problem, to identifying conflicts between them, to integrating insights, and ultimately to producing an interdisciplinary understanding of the problem—is not linear (Nikitina, 2002, p. 41). Rather, it more resembles a **feedback loop** that requires the researcher to periodically revisit earlier activity.

Ability to Think Creatively. Interdisciplinarity requires creativity. The creative idea is a "combination of previously unrelated ideas, or looking at it another way, a new relationship among ideas" (G. A. Davis, 1992, p. 44). As applied to interdisciplinary work, **creativity** is a process that involves rethinking underlying premises, assumptions, or values, not just tracing out the implications of agreed-upon premises, assumptions, or values. Creativity involves iterative (i.e., repetitive) and heuristic (i.e., experimental) activity (Spooner, 2004, p. 93). Creating common ground among conflicting insights, for example, may well involve iterative and heuristic activity. The techniques and methods useful in creating or discovering common ground, engaging in integration, and producing an interdisciplinary outcome are identified in later chapters.

Ability to Think Holistically. **Holistic thinking** involves thinking about the problem as part of a complete system. According to Irene Dabrowski (1995), "A holistic perception of reality—*seeing things whole*—requires interdisciplinary focus" (p. 3, italics added). Aspects of holistic thinking include inclusiveness that accepts similarities as well as differences, comprehensiveness that balances disciplinary breadth and disciplinary depth (disciplinary specialties privilege depth over breadth), ability to associate ideas and information from several disciplines and connect these to the problem, creativity that is dissatisfied with the partial insights available through individual disciplinary specialties and that produces an interdisciplinary understanding, and metaphorical thinking that visually expresses the resultant integration.

Some of these skills and traits, such as holistic thinking, typically receive greater emphasis in interdisciplinary contexts than in disciplinary contexts. These skills and traits are arguably desirable for anyone who wishes to lead a meaningful and productive life in any field of endeavor.

CHAPTER SUMMARY

An examination of the origins of interdisciplinarity and interdisciplinary studies shows that the historical curriculum of European and American universities was a common core of undergraduate studies deeply rooted in the humanities and the ideals of the generalist model. By the late nineteenth century, however, the generalist model was challenged by a combination of cultural and educational factors that led ultimately to the modern system of disciplinarity. The negative impacts of knowledge fragmentation, in turn, led to calls for reform of the general education curriculum at the end of both world wars and the rediscovery of interdisciplinarity. The social and political upheavals of the 1960s led to a concerted effort to inject interdisciplinarity into academic culture beyond the confines of general education through the establishment of interdisciplinary courses and programs. This effort continued, though with less intensity, into the 1980s and 1990s. By the turn of the new century, the increasing importance of interdisciplinarity was established, and there is now far more agreement on what interdisciplinarity is and what it assumes. Students are benefiting from the traits and skills that interdisciplinarity fosters.

The commonality undergirding these developments is the growing recognition of the importance of integration to interdisciplinary studies and its ability to produce new knowledge. The integrative process draws on the disciplines and their insights to address problems and questions that require an interdisciplinary approach. The disciplines and their defining characteristics are the subjects of Chapters 3 and 4.

NOTE

1. Paul Stoller (1997) in *Sensuous Scholarship* speaks of the importance of humility in academic life (pp. 135–137).

REVIEW QUESTIONS

1. What is the difference between "instrumental" and "conceptual" interdisciplinarity?

2. What are the six problematic characteristics of the disciplines and of disciplinary specialization? Give examples.

3. What was the impact of the Enlightenment on the development of the disciplines?

4. How did the academic disciplines that exist today and the modern concept of disciplinarity arise? What role did economic and technological development play in this process?

5. What is the difference between the professionalization of knowledge model that developed in the late 1880s and the traditional liberal humanist and generalist model of education?

6. What role did the first general education movement and the Cold War play in the development of interdisciplinarity?

7. How did the university reforms in the 1960s contribute to the origins of interdisciplinary studies?

8. What factors contributed to the emergence of interdisciplinary studies in the twentieth century?

9. What are the assumptions underlying interdisciplinarity and interdisciplinary studies?

10. What role does "cognitive decentering" play in interdisciplinary learning and research?

11. What are the traits and skills of interdisciplinarians?

PART II

Theories of
Interdisciplinary Studies

3 Operationalizing Disciplinary Perspective

Chapter Preview

This chapter and the next introduce the traditional disciplines and the concept of disciplinary perspective that is a key component of the theory of interdisciplinarity and foundational to the interdisciplinary research process. This chapter describes the structure of knowledge and how it is typically reflected in the organization of the Academy and explains why the traditional disciplines are of interest to interdisciplinarians. The chapter also defines "disciplinary perspective," clarifies its meaning, and explains its significance for interdisciplinary work. Most important, the chapter explains how the disciplines are of practical interest to interdisciplinary students and discusses the distinctive ways each category of disciplines (the natural sciences, the social sciences, and the humanities) approaches understanding.

The Structure of Knowledge and Its Reflection in the Organization of the Academy

Scholars developed fields of knowledge that exist today as academic disciplines. Most academic departments represent a particular discipline, and clusters of related disciplines form larger units within a university called **colleges,** such as the college of liberal arts or the college of social sciences. In most university settings, academic departments are foundational to the institution's structure.

Disciplinarity

The widely used term **disciplinarity** refers to the system of knowledge specialties called disciplines, which is little more than a century old.

Discipline is used throughout this book as an umbrella term that also includes subdisciplines and interdisciplines, defined as follows:

- A **subdiscipline** is a subdivision of a traditional discipline. The discipline of anthropology, for example, has developed several subdisciplines, including cultural anthropology, physical anthropology, anthropology of religion, urban anthropology, and economic anthropology. The formation of subdisciplines is a logical outcome of a cognitive division of labor and is a process driven by research (Bruun & Toppinen, 2004, p. 5).
- An **interdiscipline** literally means "between disciplines"—i.e., between the bodies of knowledge defined by the theories and methods of the established disciplines (Karlqvist, 1999, p. 379). An interdiscipline often begins as an interdisciplinary field, but over time becomes like a discipline, developing its own perspectives, journals, and professional associations. The interdisciplines of biochemistry and neuroscience, for example, both emerged as interdisciplinary fields that eventually grew to become their own mainstream disciplines. The transition from interdisciplinary field to interdiscipline is still underway for women's studies (Grace, 1996, pp. 59–86).

Categories of Disciplines

Disciplinary knowledge is produced in the form of books, journals, databases, and conferences—all of which are vetted by the disciplines. Departments and programs structure and organize the passing on of that knowledge to the next generation, create new knowledge, and guide the careers of faculty members who do the teaching and conduct the research. Within departments, disciplines have considerable impact on what is taught and what is researched (and how it is researched) and influence how teaching is done. They are organized into broad **disciplinary categories** that typically include the sciences, the social sciences, the humanities, and the applied fields and professions such as communications, engineering, law, nursing, education, and business. Though useful, these categories do add to the "borders-and-territories" map of modern intellectual life.[1]

Table 3.1 is a conventional classification of the disciplines that includes only traditional disciplines, excluding the applied fields and professions.[2] A discipline may be considered part of one category at one university but belong to a different category at another. History, for example, is considered a discipline within the social sciences in some institutions but part of the humanities at others. Though history has elements of both social science and humanities, this book follows the traditional taxonomy of including history in the humanities.

Disciplinary Perspectives in Interdisciplinary Work _____

Interdisciplinary research requires an understanding of the disciplines. This is consistent with the definition of interdisciplinary studies noted in Chapter 1.

Table 3.1 Categories of Disciplines

Category	Discipline
The Natural Sciences	Biology
	Chemistry
	Earth Science
	Mathematics
	Physics
The Social Sciences	Anthropology
	Economics
	Political Science
	Psychology
	Sociology
The Humanities	Art and Art History
	History
	Literature (English)
	Music and Music Education
	Philosophy
	Religious Studies

According to this definition, interdisciplinarity has a high degree of dependence upon and interaction with the disciplines. Therefore, understanding the role of the disciplines and their perspectives in interdisciplinary work is important to a full understanding of interdisciplinarity and in distinguishing interdisciplinary studies (as defined in this book) from alternative conceptions of interdisciplinarity.

Disciplinary Perspective

Disciplinary perspective, in a general sense, is each discipline's characteristic view of that portion of reality that it is interested in. The first to assert that disciplines have distinct perspectives or worldviews that are pertinent to interdisciplinary understanding, Raymond C. Miller (1982) states that perspective should be "the primary means of distinguishing one discipline from another" (p. 7). A discipline's worldview or "perspective" is a lens through which to view reality. Each discipline acts like a lens when it filters out certain phenomena so that it can focus exclusively on phenomena that interest it. Disciplines such as history and biology are not collections of certified facts; rather, they are *lenses* through which we look at the world and interpret it (Boix Mansilla et al., 2000, p. 18). In the sciences, disciplines are most easily distinguished by the phenomena they study. A conventional physicist, for example, would not be interested in studying the declining salmon populations in the Columbia and Snake Rivers, but a biologist would. A conventional sociologist would not be interested in theological representation in a fifteenth-century oil painting, but an art historian would. Similarly, a conventional historian would likely not be interested in the regulatory hurdles involved in the building of a new oil refinery, but a political scientist would.

Misconceptions About the Term *Perspective*

There are several misconceptions about disciplinary perspective that have developed over the years. One misconception is taking a narrow focus, seeing perspective as referring only to a discipline's overall view of reality. Understood in this limited way, perspective is but one of several elements of a discipline, including its phenomena, assumptions, epistemology, concepts, theories, and methods.[3] Other scholars take a much broader view of perspective, arguing that it is the *source* of all other disciplinary elements.[4] Rick Szostak (2004), for example, explains how disciplinary perspective both reflects and influences a discipline's choice of phenomena, theory, and method. The problem with the narrow conception of perspective is that it is of little use in interdisciplinary work other than to help students identify disciplines that are relevant to the problem, but only in a general way.

The second misconception about disciplinary perspective is that other terms, such as "purview," for example, can easily be substituted for it. However, "purview," which means limit or scope of authority, is far from the meaning of "perspective," which is the capacity to view things in their true relationship and relative importance to other things. Intended or not, substituting "purview" for "perspective" emphasizes limitation instead of viewpoint. In the end, attempts to substitute other terms for "perspective" only serve to muddy the definitional waters and make more problematic the operational utility of the term for interdisciplinary work.

Another misconception about the term "perspective" is that it is similar to, if not identical with, *insight*. Interdisciplinary studies, as defined in Chapter 1, is a process of drawing on disciplinary perspectives and integrating their insights. It is, therefore, important to clarify the relationship between a discipline's "perspective" and its "insights" and briefly explain how these relate to the objective of the interdisciplinary research process, which is to produce a more comprehensive understanding of the problem. A discipline's experts produce insights into a problem or class of problems. These insights typically reflect the discipline's perspective. Students draw on relevant disciplinary insights, identify the sources of conflict between them, create common ground among them, integrate them, and produce an interdisciplinary understanding of the problem.

A fourth misconception about the term "perspective" is that the research process involves integrating perspectives from disciplines relevant to the problem. The interdisciplinary process involves integrating disciplinary *insights*—not perspectives (i.e., a discipline's overall view of reality)—into a particular problem or question. These three examples illustrate the point:

- Earth science views planet Earth as a large-scale and highly complex process involving the four subsystems of geosphere, hydrosphere, atmosphere, and biosphere. When this *perspective* is applied to a particular problem, say damming a river system such as the Columbia, the *insight* that earth science may generate (in the form of a scholarly monograph, journal article, or report to a public agency) is that building the system of dams is feasible given the geological characteristics of the Columbia Basin.
- Sociology views the world as a social reality that includes the range and scope of relationships that exist between people in any given society. When this *perspective* is applied to a particular problem, say repeated spousal battery, the *insight* into the problem that sociologists may generate is that it is caused by male unemployment or the desire for patriarchal control.
- Art history views art in all its forms as representing a culture at a given point in time and therefore providing a window into that culture. When this *perspective* is applied to a specific work of art, say a post-Civil War Currier & Ives lithograph, the *insight* that art historians may generate concerning the meaning of the work is that it expresses the optimism of a culture that has embraced the concept of progress by conquering Nature.

It is important to remember that before students can identify disciplinary insights into a particular problem, they must first identify the relevant disciplines (and their perspectives).

Merely examining the same object or phenomenon from different disciplinary perspectives does not *by itself* constitute interdisciplinary work. Without integration, these different perspectives would lead to mere multidisciplinary work (Hacking, 2004, p. 5). The reason is illustrated in a poem by American poet John Godfrey Saxe (1816–1887) based on an Indian fable about six blind men and an elephant. Each of them thoroughly investigated a particular part of the massive beast, and each emphatically concluded that what he had "observed" was very much like a wall (its sides), a spear (its tusk), a snake (its swinging trunk), a tree (its leg), a fan (its ear), and a rope (its tail). The poem ends,

> And so these men of Indostan
>
> Disputed loud and long,
>
> Each in his own opinion
>
> Exceeding stiff and strong,
>
> Though each was partly in the right,
>
> And all were in the wrong! (Saxe, 1963)

The lesson is that simply having six different experts from six different disciplines examine an object will likely yield at least six different insights into the object. This is the nature of multidisciplinarity. What is lacking, of course, is any attempt to integrate these conflicting insights, insofar as this is possible, into one composite description or explanation of the object so as to provide a more comprehensive understanding of it. All of the disciplines involved contribute to that integrated understanding, but it is not "owned" by any of them. This analogy can be extended to include a seventh blind person representing the interdisciplinarian who queries the other six about the object. The person then integrates the information provided by the six disciplinarians in an attempt to construct an interdisciplinary understanding or coherent "theory" of the elephant.[5]

Other Problems With the Concept of Disciplinary Perspective

In addition to these misconceptions about the meaning of "perspective," there are problems with the term as it relates to the character of the disciplines themselves. For one thing, the disciplines are heterogeneous families, not monolithic structures (Lenoir, 1997, p. 61). The overall nature and content of the disciplines are constantly changing, as are their external boundaries and their degree of unity. Over time, the changing nature of disciplinary knowledge domains impacts the identities and cultural characteristics of disciplines and, thus, of their perspectives (Becher & Trowler, 2001, pp. 38, 43).

This point about the changing character of the disciplines themselves is underscored by the **cognitive discord** that today characterizes so many disciplines (Dogan & Pahre, 1989). This discord consists of disagreement by the discipline's practitioners over the defining elements of the discipline. Henrik Bruun and Aino Toppinen (2004) state, "Disciplines are actually quite heterogeneous, from a cognitive and epistemological perspective, and . . . research seldom follows any strict disciplinary boundaries" (p. 5). The American Sociological Association (ASA), for example, states on its Web site, "Sociology provides many distinctive perspectives on the world" (ASA, 2008). These "distinctive perspectives" within sociology, openly acknowledged by the ASA, are reflective of sociologists having aligned themselves with various theories and schools of thought that currently inform the discipline. It is the case today, writes David M. Newman (2004), that most social research and the insights it is generating into social problems "is guided by a particular theory" (p. 72). Any clarification of disciplinary perspective, then, must include theory as one of its elements.

Cognitive discord also characterizes art history, a discipline experiencing divisive theoretical conflicts. Consequently, art historian Donald Preziosi (1989) says that there is no such thing as an Olympian perspective in the discipline, despite what might be inferred from numerous textbooks (p. xi). Indeed, some scholars go so far as to claim that a dominant perspective, as defined in interdisciplinary literature, is lacking in almost every discipline in the social sciences and humanities (Dogan & Pahre, 1989).

This raises the question of whether some disciplines in their fragmented state, such as art history and sociology, even have a general perspective on reality. The answer is "yes" because the very idea of a discipline as something entirely coherent, in terms of strict adherence to its defining elements (theories, concepts, assumptions, methods, etc.), is an idealization. The reality of disciplinarity, past and present, is ferment and fragmentation.[6] Counterbalancing these centripetal forces to a large degree is an **intellectual "center of gravity"** that enables each discipline to maintain its identity and have a distinctive (but not undisputed) disciplinary perspective.

Compounding this cognitive discord are the well-documented phenomena of boundary crossing and borrowing from other disciplines (Gaff, Ratcliff, & Associates, 1997; Klein 1999). Studies show two interrelated trends. The first is a "historical reversal" of the long-term trend of growing specialization and proliferation of undergraduate programs and courses (Gaff et al., 1997, p. xiv).

The second is an increase in the crossing of disciplinary boundaries. Disciplines borrowing concepts, theories, and methods from one another, says Klein (1999), skews the picture of knowledge depicted in conventional maps of the Academy. She observes, for example, how textuality, narrative, and interpretation were once thought to belong within the domain of literary studies. Now, she says, they appear across the humanities and the social sciences, including science studies, and the professions of law and psychiatry. Similarly, research on the body and on disease occurs in disciplines as varied as art history, gerontology, and biomedicine. The movement of methods and analytical approaches across disciplinary boundaries, she contends, has become an important feature of knowledge production today (p. 3). However, these new developments do not mean the end of "discipline" in a conventional sense.

Along with the **cognitive fluidity** of the disciplines and increasing boundary crossing between them, there is a third characteristic of contemporary disciplines that has bearing on the concept of perspective. Disciplinarians in the social sciences and the humanities are more apt to use the term *perspective* when referencing grand theories or schools of thought that are informing their disciplines, such as modernism and postmodernism, rather than associating the term with the disciplines themselves (Agger, 1998, pp. 2–3; Wallace & Wolf, 2006, pp. xi, xii, 5, 7–8). To avoid these problems altogether, interdisciplinarians, such as Moran (2002), who use the term in the broadest possible sense are resorting to defining interdisciplinarity without referring to either perspective or insights (p. 16). This raises the question, addressed in Chapter 5, of what knowledge interdisciplinarians are supposed to integrate.

Disciplinary Perspective Clarified

Clearly, then, the problems with using the term *perspective* are formidable. Narrow conceptions of the term and errant substitutions of other terms for it, combined with the fluid character of the disciplines themselves, have meant that there has been little discussion of the specific elements of this important term and sparse analyses of how they might profitably be used by students. The solution is to clarify the term *perspective* in a way that highlights these elements.

The **defining elements of a discipline's perspective** include the phenomena it studies, the kind of data it collects, the assumptions it makes about the natural and human world, its epistemology or rules about what constitutes evidence or "proof," its theories about the causes and behaviors of certain phenomena, and its methods (the way it gathers, applies, and produces new knowledge). Members of each discipline, interdiscipline, or school of thought agree on what constitutes an interesting and appropriate question to study, what constitutes legitimate evidence, and what a satisfactory answer to the question should look like. These shared emphases also comprise perspective. From perspective, the discipline frames the "big" questions or "perennial issues and problems" that give the discipline its definition and signature (Becher & Trowler, 2001, pp. 26, 31).

A clarified definition of **disciplinary perspective** that takes all of these considerations into account is this:

> Disciplinary perspective refers to the ensemble of a discipline's defining elements that include phenomena, assumptions, epistemology, concepts, theory, and methods.

The interdisciplinary emphasis on perspective-taking is supported by research from cognitive psychology and the emerging cognitive science of interdisciplinary collaboration. This research shows that confrontation of different perspectives is a condition for any kind of cognitive development "both in interdisciplinary dialog and in individual thought" (Bromme, 2000, pp. 115–116). Accordingly, interdisciplinarity aids discovery of new knowledge by juxtaposing different disciplinary perspectives along with their defining elements and attempting to create common ground among them (pp. 116, 119–131).[7] Howard Gardner (1999) contends that a multiple perspective approach can enhance understanding in at least three ways: (1) by providing powerful points of entry to the topic, (2) by offering apt analogies of the problem, and (3) by conveying key ideas (pp.186–187).

The clarified definition of disciplinary perspective is consistent with the definition of interdisciplinary studies noted in Chapter 1 that emphasizes drawing on disciplinary perspectives and integrating their insights to produce an interdisciplinary understanding. This clarified definition of perspective also captures the messy reality of what occurs in actual interdisciplinary work—drawing not just on disciplinary perspectives in a general sense, but more especially on those defining elements of disciplines that relate directly to the problem.

Drawing on Disciplinary Perspectives in a General Sense

Students should draw on disciplinary perspectives in two ways: in a general sense as they begin their research and in a more particular sense as they examine specific elements of those perspectives that bear on the problem. Drawing on perspectives in a general sense typically occurs early in the research process when the focus is on identifying disciplines that might be interested in the problem. Identifying which disciplinary literatures should be consulted at the outset is made easier if the student knows the perspectives of disciplines and which of these may pertain to the problem. Drawing on the defining elements of particular disciplines typically occurs later in the research process as the student develops adequacy in each relevant discipline (discussed in Chapter 8).

The perspectives in Tables 3.2 are separated into three clusters and are stated in the most general terms. These are not comprehensive generalizations about each discipline, but central tendencies that are a matter of consensus. The purpose in presenting the following information is to help students decide at the outset of the research process which disciplines might be interested in the problem and which disciplines should be mined for further information. Disciplines are defined primarily in terms of phenomena in order to provide insight into their general or overall perspective.

The defining elements of each discipline and its perspective are examined in Chapter 4.

Caveats Concerning the Clarification of Disciplinary Perspective

Though the disciplines are foundational to interdisciplinary studies and to the interdisciplinary research process, "foundational" does not mean exclusive. Students should be aware of two caveats or explanations to avoid misinterpretation. The first caveat is that knowledge relevant to all interdisciplinary inquiry should not be limited to the disciplines.

The work of Richard Carp and other practitioners shows that knowledge outside the disciplines can and does play a legitimate and sometimes defining role in interdisciplinary understanding. Even so, the disciplines provide the regimen of investigation and analysis with which to examine many phenomena and combine these to provide the depth of insight or requisite knowledge and information for what Klein and Newell (1997) call the "working balance among breadth, depth, and synthesis that characterizes 'interdisciplinarity'" (p. 406).

Table 3.2   Overall Perspectives of Science and Humanities Disciplines Stated in General Terms

Discipline	Overall Perspective
Natural Sciences	
Biology	While the other natural sciences focus on the principles that govern the nonliving physical world, biology studies the behavior of the living physical world. When biologists venture into the world of humans, they look for physical, deterministic explanations of behavior (such as genes and evolution) rather than the mental ones (such as the decisions of individuals or groups based on free will or norms) on which the social sciences focus.
Chemistry	Chemistry focuses on the distinctive properties of the elements, individually and in compounds, and their interactions. Chemistry sees larger-scale objects, organic as well as inorganic, in terms of their constituent elements and compounds.
Earth Science	Earth science focuses on the large-scale physical processes of planet Earth and is concerned with both the details and functions of the four subsystems and their interactions.
Mathematics	Mathematics is interested in abstract quantitative worlds mathematicians create with postulates, assumptions, axioms, and premises and then explore by proving theorems.
Physics	Physics focuses on basic physical laws connecting objects (atoms and subatomic particles, quanta) and forces (gravity, electromagnetic, strong, weak) that often cannot be directly observed but that establish the underlying structure of observable reality.
Social Sciences	
Anthropology	Cultural anthropology sees individual cultures as organic integrated wholes with their own internal logic and culture as the set of symbols, rituals, and beliefs through which a society gives meaning to daily life. Physical anthropology seeks to understand former cultures through the artifacts it uncovers.
Economics	Economics emphasizes the study of market interactions, with the individual functioning as a separate, autonomous, rational entity, supreme within them. It perceives groups (even societies) as nothing more than the sum of the individuals in them.
Political Science	Political science views the world as a political arena in which individuals and groups make decisions based on the search for or exercise of power. Politics at all levels and in all cultures is viewed as a perpetual struggle over whose values, not just whose interests, will prevail in setting priorities and making collective choices.
Psychology	Psychology sees human behavior as reflecting the cognitive constructs individuals develop to organize their mental activity. Psychologists also study inherent mental mechanisms, both genetic predisposition and individual differences.

Discipline	Overall Perspective
Sociology	Sociology views the world as a social reality that includes the range and scope of the relationships that exist between people in any given society. Sociology is particularly interested in voices of various subcultures, analysis of institutions, and how bureaucracies and vested interests shape life.
Humanities	
Art and Art History	Art history views art in all of its forms as reflecting the culture in which it was formed and therefore providing a window into a culture. Art, and thus art history, has a place for universal aesthetic tastes.
History	Historians believe that any historical period cannot be adequately appreciated without understanding the trends and developments leading up to it, that historical events are the result of both societal forces and individual decisions, and that a picture or narrative of the past can be no better than the richness of its details.
Literature (English)	Literature believes that cultures, past and present, cannot be adequately understood without understanding the literature produced by the culture.
Music and Music Education	Music educators believe that a critical component of culture past and present cannot be adequately understood without understanding the music produced by the culture.
Philosophy	Philosophy recognizes a variety of limits to human perceptual and cognitive capabilities. Philosophy views reality as situational and perspectival. Reality is not a collection of imperfect representations that reflect an "absolute reality" that transcends all particular situations. Rather, these representations are the reality that is the world.
Religious Studies	Religious studies views faith and faith traditions as human attempts to understand the significance of reality and cope with its vicissitudes through beliefs in a sacred realm beyond everyday life.

A second caveat is the omission of "concepts" from the list of defining elements, though the term is used throughout this book. A **concept** is a symbol expressed in language that represents a phenomenon or an abstract idea generalized from particular instances (Wallace & Wolf, 2006, pp. 4–5; Novak, 1998, p. 21). For example, chairs come in various shapes and sizes, but once a child acquires the concept *chair*, that child will always refer to anything that has legs and a seat as a chair (p. 21).

Mieke Bal (2002) agrees that concepts "need to be explicit, clear, and defined" because they are "the key to intersubjective understanding" (i.e., involving or occurring between separate conscious minds). She notes, however, that in interdisciplinary humanities, concepts "are neither fixed nor unambiguous." Though concepts look like words, they are not ordinary words, nor are they labels. As a cultural analyst, Bal argues that "interdisciplinarity in the humanities must seek its heuristic [i.e., aid to learning] and methodological basis in *concepts* rather than *methods*" (pp. 5, 22–23, italics added). An example of Bal's work is threaded into later chapters.

One reason for omitting examples of concepts for each discipline is that the term lacks clarity as it relates to other terms such as phenomena, causal link, theory, and method. Rick Szostak (2004) finds that many concepts can be defined in terms of phenomena, causal links, theory, or method. Some concepts, such as culture, are clearly phenomena. Others, such as oppression, are results of phenomena—in this instance, political decision making. Still others, such as revolution, globalization, and immigration, describe processes of change within or between phenomena (p. 41). But most of these, he observes, can best be understood as illustrating features of causal links—in this example, the link between art and human appreciation (pp. 42–43). In addition to the difficulty of differentiating concepts from phenomena and causal links is the more formidable problem of dealing with the huge number of concepts that each discipline has generated. Perhaps this is why so few scholars have attempted exhaustive surveys of scholarly concepts in particular disciplines, let alone across entire disciplinary categories. The student who will certainly encounter what are purported to be concepts is well advised to consult Szostak's classification of phenomena presented in Chapter 4 to see whether the concept is, in fact, a concept.

This **taxonomy** or orderly classification of selected disciplines and their perspectives raises the question of how students can find perspectives of disciplines, subdisciplines, interdisciplines, and theories not included in this book. A good place to obtain leads is Chapter 4, which has tables that define elements of disciplines (their epistemologies, theories, methods, etc.) and cite standard disciplinary sources. Students may also consult content librarians who specialize in certain disciplines. Another strategy is to ask disciplinary experts to recommend sources. This combined approach should produce aids that are authoritative and useful. The issue of finding scholarly research aids is addressed more fully in Chapter 7.

How the Disciplines and Their Perspectives Are of Interest to Interdisciplinarians

Table 3.1 places the disciplines in the context of the structure of knowledge that is common to many universities. The following discussion explains how each of these categories, and the disciplines typically associated with them, is of interest to students working in these disciplinary categories. This discussion also provides some sense of what the disciplines within each category hold in common and how they differ, and how the various elements of disciplines are mutually supportive and thus constitute a unique perspective.

The Natural Sciences

The **natural sciences**, says philosopher of science Robert Klee (1999), tells us "what the world is made of, how what it is made of is structured into a complex network of interdependent systems, and why what happened in a given localized system happened." Successful **science**, he says, claims to give us empirical information that, combined with rational thought, leads to *knowledge* of what *exists* in the universe, and also claims to *explain* why it behaves the way it does (p. 2).[8]

The natural sciences are of interest to interdisciplinary students because of their subject matters, their common use of the scientific method, and the empirical facts they uncover. According to the National Academy of Sciences, the National Academy of Engineering, and the Institute of Medicine (2005), "Some of the most interesting scientific questions are found at the interfaces between disciplines." These questions lead researchers beyond their own disciplines to invite participation of researchers in adjacent disciplines and even "stimulate the development of a new interdisciplinary field" (p. 33). Examples include biochemistry, cognitive science, genomics, proteomics, epidemiology, microbiology, structural biology, ecology, and ecologic economics.

Biology is concerned with organisms at many levels, from one-celled organisms to those with many organs and systems to entire ecosystems of organisms, individually as they interact today and as they have evolved over generations. Biology incorporates some of the reductionism of chemistry and physics into more holistic thinking at a variety of levels in the lifetime of a species and over the deep time of Earth science (Donald, 2002, p. 127). The revolution in biology has led to its morphing into "life sciences." Biology is increasingly intersecting with other disciplines such as cultural anthropology and mathematics. The interdisciplinary field of biological anthropology studies human biological variation and the relationship of human groups with climatic, geographic, and other physical conditions and with social and cultural influences (Lasker & Mascie-Taylor, 1993).

Students working on environmental problems such as global warming, sustainable development, and other environment-related issues are naturally interested in biology and several of its subdisciplines such as environmental biology and ecology, which embrace holism (while often taking a reductionist approach to studying it). Students examining public health issues should be interested in the subdisciplines of epidemiology and toxicology, while those considering the ethical implications of human cloning, stem cell research, and when life should end (as debated in the Terry Schiavo case) should be interested in bio-ethics, which many classify as an interdisciplinary field.

Chemistry focuses on the distinctive properties of chemical elements and their compounds and reduces large-scale phenomena to the interactions among their constituent chemical elements and compounds. Knowledge of basic chemistry is important for understanding just about any area of biology, such as making sense of the structure of cells and organisms (Coppola & Jacobs, 2006). Students researching environmental problems, for instance, are interested in the subdisciplines of analytical chemistry, environmental chemistry, and organic chemistry. Analytical chemistry seeks to develop new ways of measuring the properties of matter that enable detection of trace amounts of harmful substances in the environment and to better understand the universe. Environmental chemistry and organic chemistry explain the chemical mechanisms by which pollution alters and spreads in the atmosphere, water, and soil. Another example of interdisciplinary activity and the branching of knowledge is the formation of molecular biology that developed to decipher the DNA code. This effort involved physicists, biologists, geneticists, and biochemists (Bechtel, 1986, p. 33).

Earth science is the study of planet Earth, the materials of which it is made, the physical and chemical processes that act upon these materials, and the history of the planet and its inhabitants. Earth science no longer focuses on just "rocks and minerals" but takes a systems view of the planet Earth. It studies the details of and the interactions between four subsystems—the geosphere, the hydrosphere, the atmosphere, and the biosphere—and how these affect life on this planet. In contrast to biologists, who also study the biosphere consisting of all the myriad forms of life on Earth, geologists study the origins and changes of these systems and organisms during their geological history through their interactions with the other three subsystems over geologic time. Geologists are concerned with a large variety of scientific tasks and therefore must use knowledge from diverse fields. Plate tectonics, a comprehensive theory that explains mountain building, earthquakes, and vulcanism, has brought together geologists, oceanographers, geophysicists, paleomagneticists, and seismologists in an interdisciplinary research effort to understand the Earth's crust (Levin, 2003, pp. 1–3). Complex problems such as global climate change and the efficient and economic utilization of Earth resources, particularly fossil fuels, play increasingly major roles in human society and are, therefore, of interest to students.

Mathematics is the science of numbers, including their operations, interrelations, and abstractions. The discipline plays a significant role in all of the natural and social sciences by focusing on the properties of various abstract systems that can be expressed quantitatively. Some of those systems can be applied to aspects of reality, but mathematicians themselves work in hypothetical realities of their own creation. Applied mathematics is foundational to the sciences and has greatly impacted, directly or indirectly, almost all of the other disciplines. For example, one undergraduate student has integrated history, geometry, and art to explain the development of perspective in painting (*Book of Fours*). Another example is knot theory, a branch of mathematics that has been used to explain the twisting and knotting of DNA, in particular the problems with DNA that occur in cancer cells. Mathematics provides other disciplines with tools for understanding, such as mathematical modeling. Statistics, an important sister discipline, provides tools for empirical tests of that understanding (Taper & Lele,

2004). For example, ecology operates under a mixture of philosophies and statistical approaches, each of which provides unique functions in the discovery of ecological knowledge (Maurer, 2004, pp. 17–31).

Physics occupies an exceptional space among the sciences because in this discipline, two characteristics are united that are only found separately in the other sciences. Whereas mathematics is interested in quantitative modes of representation themselves, physics applies them to the physical phenomena in which it is interested. Unlike the laws of the other sciences that are approximations, the laws of physics are generally mathematically precise; yet, unlike mathematics, its subject matter is empirical. It accomplishes this feat by expressing its laws in terms of idealized concepts that are presumed to underlie observed empirical reality, such as mass and energy, while abstracting from messy characteristics, such as friction. The goal of physics is to "understand the universe and the physical laws that govern it" (National Research Council, 2002, p. 1).

Interdisciplinary students are interested in physics when they seek to understand border-crossing problems such as U.S. energy policy and global warming. Concerning energy policy, physics can help us understand the theoretical limitations of the efficiency of power plants, electrical power transmission, photovoltaic cells, and hydroelectric dams. Physics is essential in understanding the greenhouse effect that underlies global warming, the physical basis of meteorological phenomena such as El Niño and the jet stream (for distributing pollution worldwide), and the intrinsic problems associated with nuclear power.

The Way the Natural Sciences Approach Problem Solving

Finally, interdisciplinarians are interested in how the natural sciences typically engage in problem solving. This involves making decisions and taking steps consisting of the following:

- *Describing the problem:* identify its context, state its conditions, specify the facts, state assumptions, and state the goal of the research
- *Selecting the relevant information*: identify critical elements and critical relations
- *Representing the problem:* identify the organizing principles, laws, and methods that arrange the problem in a systematic way; arrange the parts and connections between things into a systematic whole; illustrate elements and their relations
- *Inferring:* discover connections among parts, hypothesize by supposing or forming a "what-if" statement
- *Synthesizing:* combine parts to form a whole, elaborate in great detail, generate missing links, and develop a course of action
- *Verifying:* see whether the final result makes sense (Donald, 2002, pp. 26–27)

Though some aspects of this problem-solving strategy correspond to the interdisciplinary research process, there is much that is different between the two approaches. These similarities and differences, stated in general terms, are identified as follows:

- *Describing the problem:* The nature of the problem is typically different. The natural sciences try to focus on a problem as narrowly as possible, reducing it until it does not require input from outside the sciences. For interdisciplinary students, the problem should be complex and/or broad enough to require input from two or more disciplines (as likely drawn from the social sciences and the humanities as from the natural sciences).

- *Selecting relevant information:* The source of relevant information is typically different. The natural sciences define "relevant information" narrowly in terms of that which can be scientifically apprehended and reduced to quantification through experimentation. Interdisciplinarians define "relevant information" much more broadly to include information from any discipline, even including, under certain circumstances, extradisciplinary information.

- *Representing the problem:* The way in which the problem is represented is typically different. The natural sciences use the language of mathematics to represent the problem. Though interdisciplinarians may also do this, they are more likely to map or diagram the problem to reveal its component and subcomponent parts and combine this with carefully worded descriptive statements.

- *Inferring:* Both the natural sciences and the interdisciplinary process are concerned with discovering connections between the parts of the problem and with making inferences about the significance of these connections. The connections identified by interdisciplinarians are between concepts or variables typically studied by different disciplines.

- *Synthesizing:* The meaning of synthesis and the process by which it is achieved are similar for the natural sciences and interdisciplinary studies. For both, synthesis or integration means combining parts that *may* be in conflict to form a whole and is a trial and error process of putting elements together into a structure or pattern not there before.[9] This is especially true for interdisciplinarians because the parts come from different disciplines or different theories, whereas the parts combined by scientists typically do not conflict. For the interdisciplinary student, the step of combining insights—i.e., integration—must be preceded by the step of discovering or creating the common ground theory, concept, or assumption among parts that conflict so that integration can proceed.[10]

- *Verifying:* This final step in the scientific process is similar to the final step in the interdisciplinary process, with this caveat: The complex problems generally studied by interdisciplinarians make it difficult (but not impossible) to evaluate the understanding produced by the research process. The problems studied by scientists, however, because they are so narrowly focused, make it easier to judge the effectiveness of a solution. Complex problems are messy, such that small changes in one part produce large changes in another part. This is especially true concerning problems involving the humanities, where novelty and creativity are valued.

The Social Sciences

The **social sciences** seek to explain the human world and figure out how to predict and improve it. In their approach to problem solving, the social sciences can be either quantitative or qualitative, either scientific or humanistic. The social sciences, from their inception, "have been torn between the ideals of scientific objectivity and those of humanistic reform-mindedness" (Hendershott & Wright, 1997, p. 301). The social sciences are of interest to interdisciplinary students because they focus on human behavior and advance insights about the human condition. Social scientists, though, are more than mere observers: "They are also participants in the behavior they explore" (Frankfort-Nachmias & Nachmias, 2008, p. 10). As Hans Zetterberg (1967) writes,

> Symbols are the stuff out of which cultures and societies are made. . . . For example, a sequence of conception, birth, nursing, and weaning represents the biological reality of parenthood. But in analyzing human parenthood we find, in addition to the biological reality, a complex of symbols [e.g., values, norms] dealing with the license to have children, responsibilities for their care and schooling, rights to make some decisions on their behalf, obligations to launch them by certain social rituals. . . . Our language contains codifications of what parents are and what they shall do and what shall be done to them, and all these sentences in our language represents the social reality of parenthood. Social reality, then, in this as in other cases, consists of symbols. (pp. 1–2)

Anthropology studies two domains: the biological (physical) and the cultural.[11] Biological anthropology is the scientific study of the genesis, evolution, and variation of humans in prehistory. Cultural anthropology is divided into three major subfields—archeology, linguistics, and ethnology (the study of recent cultures). Cross-cutting these subfields is applied or practicing anthropology (Ember & Ember, 2004, p. 3). Cultural anthropology is the scientific study of the development of human cultures based on ethnologic, ethnographic, linguistic, social, and psychological data and methods of analysis. Cultural anthropology makes some use of the subject matter of these disciplines but has its own distinctive perspectives, theories, concepts, assumptions, and methods. An added use of anthropology (as a whole) is to provide models of the "human-nature interface," meaning that anthropology understands cultures within their environmental contexts. For example, this discipline can provide useful insights into a complex problem such as the Israeli-Palestinian conflict by viewing it as a conflict between two distinct cultures in a physical context that exacerbates competition and division. Cultural anthropologists are increasingly interested in big subjects such as nationalism and ethnicity and are starting to look at the idea of "development" as a product of a particular culture and history (Barnard & Spencer, 1996, p. x–xi).

Economics studies the nature and functioning of economic systems (both macro and micro) and develops criteria for assessing efficiency in the provision of goods and services. "Micro" refers to the study of individual markets or behaviors; "macro" refers to the study of the aggregate economy—economic growth, business cycles, inflation, and unemployment. Economists study the production, distribution, and valuation of products and services, rational decision making, market mechanics, government regulation, taxation and expenditure, labor markets, management, productivity, monetary policy, environment and transportation issues, and international trade. Decision making under scarcity is the general focus of economics, though the discipline is equally concerned with the institutions within which and the mechanisms through which that decision making takes place. Though economics has been more resistant to interdisciplinarity than other disciplines have been, a promising development is "a tentative dialog with sociology and other social sciences, such as psychology and history" (Smelser & Swedberg, 2005, p. 19).

Recently, debates surrounding modernism and postmodernism have emerged within the discipline. Almost invisible to most economists, postmodernists are challenging modernist notions such as economic "progress" and "knowledge" and the reduction of most human motives to a single purpose: individual gain (Cullenberg, Amariglio, & Ruccio, 2001, pp. 3–7). Students are interested in these discussions because they bear directly on a wide range of public policy issues.

Psychology seeks internal (inside the skin) explanations for behavior, whereas the other social sciences seek explanations that are external to the individual, such as income and wealth (economics), social status (sociology), or power (political science). Economics, for instance, assumes rationality and thus avoids careful analysis of how humans actually make decisions, though this is beginning to change. It views consumer behavior as grounded in the balance of internal tastes and external prices and income but takes all of the variables it measures from *outside* the individual. In contrast, psychology develops models comprised largely or even exclusively of constructs or schemata *internal* to the individual. Psychology asks how humans perceive, learn, interact casually or informally with others, and evolve throughout the life cycle. The goals of this rapidly developing discipline are to describe, explain, predict, and change behavior (Huffman, Vernoy, & Vernoy, 2000, p. 5). As a natural science, psychology seeks the laws of nature in examining the biological basis for the relationship between the brain and behavior. As a social science, psychology examines behavior reflecting the emotions and thoughts of the individual singly, in dyads, or in groups.

Psychologists are interested in observed behavior (both human and animal), mental processes, and the relationships between them. The basic fields include developmental (cognitive and social), learning behavior (traditional animal and human learning and sexual behavior), neuroscience (biophysiology, health psychology, behavioral genetics), cognitive processes (senses and perception, memory, language, decision making, creativity, consciousness), and social psychology (individual perceptions and self-awareness that is social in origin), all of which are interdisciplinary. Psychology is split between clinical and experimental psychologists. Both focus on individual human behavior, the mental life of individuals, and the constructs through which individuals organize their mental life. The discipline incorporates the practice of psychology as well as the study of psychology, whereas economics excludes businessmen, political science excludes politicians, and even an applied field in sociology such as criminology trains police officers but excludes them from the Academy (unless they have appropriate academic credentials).

Interdisciplinary students are typically interested in psychology and its subdisciplines because of the diversity and range of theories extending from the natural sciences to the behavioral sciences. Developmental theories and neuroscience, for example, often converge with biology for nature versus nurture discussions. Learning and motivational theories combine with cognitive theories of intelligence, memory, and language and may be connected to current strategies in education. Personality theories, gender roles, and the fundamentals of group behavior overlap with decision-making models that are easily merged with various fields involving communication and management. Interdisciplinary students seeking to understand issues as diverse as discrimination, spousal abuse, and suicide terrorism should be interested in using these theories.

Sociology is the systematic study of social structures (i.e., frameworks that exist above the level of individuals), collective human action, social relationships, culture, and even the impact of social context on individual behavior. Sociologists examine social behaviors from a group, rather than an individual, perspective and study patterns of behavior shared by members of a group or by the larger society. This rapidly changing discipline includes three major theoretical perspectives: **functionalism** (or its most recent reincarnation in systems theory), which focuses on the functional contributions of each part of society and tends to be associated with a focus on order in society and lesser attention to conflict in society; **symbolic interactionism**, a major theoretical perspective of sociology that focuses on the use of signs and symbols in interaction among people; and **critical social theory**, which looks at conflict, competition, change, and constraint within a society.[12] The American Sociological Association lists some 40 subfields such as stratification/inequality, health, family, gender, race/ethnicity, education, law, crime and social control, demography, aging, social psychology, social movements, organizations and bureaucracy, and theory. Each has ties to the others and, most importantly, to other disciplines and is interdisciplinary (Calhoun, 2002, pp. 455–457). Judith Blau (2001) reports that the discipline is increasingly receptive to theories and methodologies from other fields. Another change is the more rapid pace of the development of subspecialties in sociology (p. x).[13] For example, the field of economic sociology represents one of the "leading edges of sociology" and "one of its most important interdisciplinary adventures" (Smelser & Swedberg, 2005, p. ix).[14] These new developments, while posing serious challenges to sociology, do not necessarily portend its disintegration.

Interdisciplinary students are interested in sociology because sociologists tend to believe that answers to questions of meaning may be found in "contextual processes—in social, historical, cultural, economic, political, psychological, and biological properties—that are extrinsic to an event but imbue it with meaning and significance" (Klein, 2005a, p. 141). Of interest also is sociology's emphasis on developing theoretical perspectives on social relationships and group behavior and on its application of theory, both grand and narrow range. Additionally, students are interested in the discipline's explanation of the impact of social structure on one's life and on the lives of others, its focus on how traditions and existing social structures mold people's belief systems, and its analysis of far-reaching concepts such as class, conflict, engagement, family, gender, modernity, race, and social context.

Political science is the study of power (raw and constrained) and its influence in government, political processes, institutions, ideologies, and relationships involving rule and authority. Political science draws on history, sociology (especially political sociology), economics (especially public choice theory), and psychology (especially social psychology) for its theories. Political science is at least as influenced by sociology (which believes decisions are based on norms, mores, and morals more than rationality and on group interests more than self-interest) as it is by economics (which believes decisions are based on rational self-interest). Whereas sociology focuses primarily on status and economics focuses on income and wealth, political science focuses on power as motivation for human behavior.

Interdisciplinary students are interested in political science because it provides insights into decision-making processes, political ideologies, the workings of institutional structures, the ways power is acquired, used, and lost. Indeed, students who are knowledgeable about postmodernist theory know that power infuses many (if not all) human interactions and that the power dimension of topics falls well outside the domain of government and, hence, of political science.

The Way the Social Sciences Approach Problem Solving

Students are also interested in the social sciences because of the way they approach problem solving. All disciplines and subdisciplines within the social sciences—anthropology, economics, history,[15] political science, psychology, and sociology—are problem-solving disciplines. A leading textbook on methods argues that the work of social science is usually divided into three interdependent tasks: concept formation, proposition formation, and research design (Gerring, 2001, p. 20). Concepts answer the *what* question, that is, what to call the phenomena under investigation. This is the problem of concept formation which lies at the heart of much social science work. Progress in the social sciences occurs, says John Gerring, through changing terms and definitions called concepts. Social science requires a specialized vocabulary. Consequently, social scientists cannot accept words simply as they present themselves in ordinary speech because ordinary usage is unsettled. Concept formation in the social sciences is an attempt to bridge the world of language and the world of things (pp. 54, 58). For example, economists have clear, distinct definitions of "demand/supply" and "quantity demanded/supplied." Interdisciplinarians must be aware of how different disciplines define and use a particular concept when addressing the same problem.

Interdisciplinary studies students are interested in social science concepts because defining key concepts that bear on the problem allows them to set the boundaries of the problem and communicate about the problem across disciplinary boundaries. The problems caused by the multiple meanings of a term in ordinary language and the resulting confusion of talking past one another lead to the need for concept formation in the social (and natural) sciences. Interdisciplinarians have developed techniques to integrate concepts that appear similar but have different meanings in different disciplines. These integrative techniques and illustrations of their use are found in Chapter 11.

Proposition formation involves generating statements about the world or some aspect of it. The statement can be a simple declaration, "The United States is a religious nation," or a question, "Should the Arctic Wildlife Refuge be opened to oil drilling?" **Research design** involves establishing criteria for evaluating evidence, selecting appropriate methods of analysis, and choosing verification strategies. Both proposition formation and research design are important components of the interdisciplinary research process introduced in Chapter 6.

The Humanities

The humanities[16] are sometimes conflated with the "liberal arts" and "liberal education," but these latter terms include the sciences and the social sciences along with the humanities. Some taxonomies also separate the fine and performing arts from the humanities. The **humanities** express human aspirations, interpret and assess human achievements and experience, and seek layers of meaning and richness of detail in written texts, artifacts, and cultural practices.

The humanities also concern themselves with process: how to read, look at, understand, and enjoy these human expressions (Minor, 2001, p. 4). The humanities imagine, create, and interrogate. The humanities permit us to look at the relationship of individuals to groups and groups to each other over time. The humanities enable us to respond emotionally, imaginatively, and aesthetically to writers' expressions of inner conflict, fears, hopes, and joys along with the details of their particular experiences and contexts. The humanities also permit reflection on human relationships to the natural world and human beliefs about a supreme being or supernatural order in various eras and cultures. They provide tools for logical analysis and modes of discussing and debating moral and ethical questions (White, 1997, p. 264).

The humanities and the social sciences are engaged in a lively trade of concepts, theories, methods, and even subject matter. Former keywords in the social sciences such as "cause," "variable," "force," or "function" are being replaced by a new vocabulary from the humanities such as "rules," "representation," "attitude," and "intention" (Geertz, 1983, pp. 23–24).

The humanities are split between the older traditional humanities and the newer critical humanities. The **traditional humanities** focus on human culture in terms of its meaning, its values, and the significance of its art, literature, music, philosophy, religion, and performing arts. The newer interdisciplinary "**critical humanities**—feminism, critical theory, postcolonial studies, culture studies, gender studies, queer theory, postmodernism, poststructuralism, deconstructionism, etc.—on the other hand, focuses not so much on human culture itself as on *our knowledge of it, and on disciplinary knowledge in general*" (Davidson & Goldberg, 2004, pp. 42–62, italics added). An example of this change of focus is the shift in "culture" from a discipline-bound to an interdisciplinary concept. Newell (2007) points out that while these fields have much in common with interdisciplinarity— that is, they value multiple perspectives and see knowledge as constructed— they also have the potential to provide a critique of interdisciplinarity because they offer a fundamental critique of disciplinary knowledge in which interdisciplinary studies is grounded (p. 251).

The disciplines encompassed by the humanities—art and art history, history, literary studies, music and music education, philosophy, and religious studies—are of interest to interdisciplinary students because they offer strategies for addressing dilemmas and acknowledging ambiguity and paradox. Theories generated by the humanities can help us face the tension between the concerns of individuals and those of groups. They help us confront the large questions of human existence—the meaning of life, truth, beauty, and justice. They also give voice to feeling and artistic shape to experience, balancing passion and rationality and exploring issues of morality and value. The study of the humanities provides a venue in which the expression of differing interpretations and experiences can be recognized and areas of common interest explored (White, 1997, p. 263). Even more, the humanities offer narratives that bring home the human impact of behavior studied more dispassionately by the social sciences and descriptions that show in rich detail how patterns of behavior explained by the social sciences uniquely impact individual lives.

Art responds to universal aesthetic tastes, though these vary because of cultural and personal differences. Art is split between the practice and history of art and between the study of the object itself and its context. Traditionally, the study of Western art has focused on the object and its intrinsic worth. By the 1980s, however, there was growing interest in non-Western cultures and a corresponding emphasis on placing the art of all cultures within a broad cultural context. Art differs from the sciences in at least one critical respect: The arts are multicultural but not universal in the way that physical laws are universal (Harris, 1997, p. 328).[17] Although art and art history may seem unrelated to external "practical" problems interdisciplinarians often seek to resolve, art is a useful window into a culture. For students, art objects can embody the essence of a cultural belief or value. Visually sophisticated interdisciplinary students can use photographs, in particular, as a window into a culture.

History studies all aspects of human experience over time and seeks to understand important events, personalities, developments, and civilizations. However, what historians find "important" changes from one generation to the next as current societal issues change and as the discipline evolves. Peter Burke (1991) reports that over a century ago, historians tended to focus more narrowly on diplomatic, military, and political topics involving mainstream society and famous men. Today, historians focus more diversely on economic, social, political, and cultural history of everyday women and men from a variety of cultural, racial, and sexual backgrounds. Individual historians tend to rely on a particular theoretical lens—feminist, Marxist, neoconservative, New Left—to interpret the topic at hand. The new scholarship draws on a greater variety of evidence such as statistics, oral accounts, and material culture (pp. 1–23). Recreating contexts and generating insights into a historical period often require the historian to "borrow" information from other disciplines, such as sociological models and psychological theories, without utilizing their perspectives and thus fail to provide a fully interdisciplinary understanding of an event or personality.

In the case of American studies, says Klein (2005a), "the field at large may be interdisciplinary, but practitioners may not be or one discipline may dominate over another" (p. 171). Like history students, interdisciplinary students are concerned to place the problem in a historical context or to identify the developments that caused the problem as part of the interdisciplinary process. History is "one of the busiest areas of cross-disciplinary combinations"

(Dogan & Pahre, 1990, p. 87) because historians borrow from the methodologies and research materials of many disciplines to create new areas of interest such as psychohistory and social history (Vess & Linkon, 2002, p. 98).

Even though literature is really many disciplines, one for each language (e.g., English, German, French) and comparative literature that seeks to connect them, the disciplines are lumped together under literature or "literary studies" because they have so much in common. The discipline studies the literature of a culture or period. However, the discipline is divided on many issues, among them how to deal with race, class, gender, and countries that are former colonizers or former colonies. Like history, literature touches on every aspect of human existence. But unlike history, which limits itself to facts expressed in nonfiction, much of literature takes the form of fiction that addresses what might or should be as well as what has been. The "what should be" is the subject of the emerging interdisciplinary field of ethical criticism that is based on two ideas: "literature possesses moral dimensions" and "philosophical conceptions of morality can be illustrated by literary forms" (Gunn, 1992, p. 241).

Rejecting the arbitrariness of disciplinary boundaries, interdisciplinarians are increasingly associating literature with a wide range of disciplines including philosophy, anthropology, psychology, politics, religion, linguistics, and history. Examples of interdisciplinary subjects that have emerged are the materialism of the body, the psychoanalysis of the reader, the sociology of conventions, the ideology of gender, race, and class (Klein, 2005a, p. 93). Interdisciplinary students are interested in literature when they seek to gain a deeper or richer understanding of a culture, human relations, or one's self. Since writers are often concerned with problems facing society (even sometimes before they are recognized as problems), students draw upon these literary insights to gauge the relative importance of or human impact on a problem. For example, novels such as *The Jungle, Crime and Punishment,* or *Uncle Tom's Cabin* profoundly impacted public perceptions of the effects of the factory on the family, the meaning of justice, and the evil of slavery.

In the twentieth century, music divided into separate disciplines of musicology, ethnomusicology, theory, and composition, each having its own professional societies. Consequently, it is hard to talk about music in the singular anymore because different kinds of music are proliferating and multiplying along with their meanings (Bohlman, 1996, p. 197). Anahid Kassabian (1997) describes the discipline as a "web of critiques" that illuminate each other. Their effect is not to correct or alter the existing canon or practices but to transform the discipline into a "heterogeneous intersection" of its traditional branches of theory, musicology, and ethnomusicology. The lines of these subdisciplines are increasingly being blurred by their interfacing with cultural studies, ethnic studies, postcolonial studies, Marxism, and feminist anthropology (pp. 8–9; Pasler, 1997, p. 21).

Music as a major expression of human culture is of interest to interdisciplinary students studying, for example, a cultural period. For one thing, music, especially through its lyrics, often serves as the voice of an otherwise silenced subculture. One can achieve a more comprehensive understanding of youth gang culture, for example, by studying its music and lyrics. The emergent field of jazz studies addresses its subject within a broad framework, integrating ethnicity and aesthetics with economics, politics, and culture (Klein, 2005a, p. 148). Though extended reflections on interdisciplinary process are rare in music, one example offers an in-depth demonstration of what applying the process can achieve. Linda and Michael Hutcheon's (2001) study of opera, literature, and medicine shows the connections among sex, venereal disease, and race in Richard Wagner's opera *Parsifal* in the death of the character Amfortas.

Philosophy is divided into five major branches of inquiry: aesthetics, ethics, metaphysics, epistemology, and logic. Aesthetics studies the nature of beauty. Ethics or moral philosophy studies human behavior in light of moral values and rules. Metaphysics is the "study of ultimates, of first and last things" that "give us some judgment about the nature of reality" (Reese, 1980, p. 353). Epistemology is the study or theory of the origin, nature, methods, and limits of knowledge. And logic is the branch of philosophy that studies inference. Philosophy is an abstract way of thinking about the world in general. Prior to the 1960s, philosophy saw its role not as a participant in a common intellectual enterprise with other disciplines but as an overseer of the standards, terminology, and practices of other disciplines. Philosophers focused on analyzing the meaning of disciplinary terms using extremely technical language that was mostly unintelligible to outsiders (Nehamas, 1997, pp. 232–233).

Developments in the 1960s and 1970s, however, began to change the discipline. One of these was the emergence of artificial intelligence that offered the possibility of modeling the human brain. Philosophers became interested in the mind and the new field of cognitive science, one of the most active interdisciplinary specialties within philosophy. Another, and perhaps more important, development of interest to philosophers and to interdisciplinarians was the reentry of philosophy into the public values arena with the publication of John Rawls' *A Theory of Justice* (1970). Rawls examines the conditions that a just society must satisfy and mounts a philosophical defense of political liberalism. The book's significance is its justification for philosophy taking an active role in the discussion and resolution of public problems and its laying the groundwork for the field of "applied philosophy." Of interest to interdisciplinary students is the field's fruitful interaction with business and medicine, for example, on issues of ethics, reproductive technologies, as well as with social scientists who are interested in rational choice theory. The branch of philosophy that has been most successful in entering public discourse, and of interest to interdisciplinarians, has been feminism (Nehamas, 1997, pp. 233–236). **Feminism** is both a social movement and a grand theoretical perspective on society. As a social and sociological perspective, it examines the roles that "sex and gender play in structuring society, as well as the reciprocal role that society plays in structuring sex and gender" (Calhoun, 2002, p. 162).[18] Also because it works with fine gradations of meaning, philosophy can be a powerful tool for interdisciplinarians, placing multifaceted investigations into a cohesive framework and teaching how to assess knowledge for truth and to delineate relationships between different aspects of reality by examining their underlying concepts.

Religion or religious studies, a relatively new subject-field, concerns specific religions or faith traditions in which people believe.[19] Religious studies makes the subject of religion intelligible by using "prescribed modes and techniques of inquiry" (Capps, 1995, p. xiv). The discipline has its own schools of thought, movements, and seminal theorists. Religious studies includes theology, which understands a religion from an insider's (i.e., believer's) perspective, but also draws on history, philosophy, anthropology, and literature to understand the religion from an outsider's perspective. Like anthropology in the social sciences, religious studies as a discipline tries to understand where sacred beliefs come from without passing judgment on them. Since religion is a universal phenomenon and one that is growing in importance, interdisciplinary students should not overlook its impact. Indeed, a wide variety of phenomena, such as the debates over abortion and euthanasia, human cloning, stem cell research, terrorism, the Israel-Palestinian conflict, and the uses of religion in political debate, clearly have a religious component.

The Way the Humanities Approach Understanding

The humanities typically leave explanation and problem solving to the scientists and social scientists, focusing instead on understanding, interpreting, and meaning-making. The humanities have been characterized by a (nonexclusive but extensive) stress on the use of textual analysis as method. However, this is changing. The humanities, especially interdisciplinary fields such as transatlantic studies, increasingly draw on methods and subjects of other disciplines. In fact, the distinction between those aspects of the social sciences that have humanistic methods and those that do not is increasingly difficult to make. As Lyn Maxwell White (1997) notes,

> The humanities and the social sciences now share a wider range of methods, and the humanities are increasingly likely to be engaged in reflection on contemporary life and social and political concerns that were considered the province of the social sciences twenty-five years ago. (p. 266)

Scholarship in English literature, for example, now incorporates approaches from fields such as history, philosophy, and anthropology, while scholars in historical studies may borrow narrative and interpretive theories from literature and quantitative methods from sociology.

Whereas the natural sciences tend to use experimental methods based on empirical (often quantitative) data and take "replicability as a touchstone of validity" (White, 1987, p. 265), the humanities generally do not. Significantly, humanistic and scientific methods may both be used to examine subject matter in interdisciplinary core curricula and in new fields such as environmental studies.

The clearest remaining distinction between the humanities and the natural and social sciences is their respective epistemological practices. The social sciences embrace rationalism, empiricism, and quantification of evidence, though some social scientists contend that quantitative and qualitative analysis can be mixed. The objective of using multiple research methods increasingly favored by social scientists is to reduce or eliminate many of the shortcomings associated with each individual method (Dorsten & Hotchkiss, 2005, pp. 26–27, 39). The presumption of **rationalism** is that reason aided by observation can discover basic truth regarding the world. **Empiricism** holds that all knowledge is derived from our perceptions (transmitted by the five senses of touch, smell, taste, hearing, and sight), experience, and observations.

Science assumes that a communication tie between man and the external universe is maintained through his own sense perceptions. Knowledge is held to be a product of one's experience, as facets of the physical, biological, and social world play upon the senses (Sjoberg & Nett, 1968, p. 26).

However, knowledge is not acquired only from our perceptions. Many phenomena, such as quarks, cannot be experienced or observed directly. Observation is required to back up what we have perceived. As a mental activity, observation "is neither self-evident nor entirely detached from the scientific terms, concepts, and theories employed by scientists" (Frankfort-Nachmias & Nachmias, 2008, p. 6). **Quantification of evidence** means discovering or expressing the numerical quantity of something, as, for example, in quantitative chemical analysis where one needs to determine the exact amount of each element in a substance. Each science adapts these epistemologies differently to its respective domains—that is, both empirical evidence and quantification take somewhat different forms in the physical and biological sciences, and all three are used to varying degrees alongside postmodern epistemologies in the social sciences (other than economics). Finally, in contrast to the epistemological preferences and practices of the natural sciences and the social sciences, the humanities are organized around the production of consensual and **qualitative knowledge** arrived at through contention rather than the empirical testing of theories.[20]

What Each Category Has in Common

Though the discussion above emphasizes differences among categories and among disciplines within categories, it is also true that each category has in common its learning and thinking processes and its overall view of humanity. These are identified in Table 3.3 in alphabetical order and are stated in the most general terms.

Table 3.3   Categories of Disciplines Reflecting Their Learning and Thinking Processes and
              Their View of Humanity

Category	Disciplines	Learning and Thinking Process	View of Humanity
The Natural Sciences	• Biology • Chemistry • Earth Science • Mathematics • Physics	Inductive, knowledge-intensive, analytic[a]	Humanity is subject to the forces and laws of nature.
The Social Sciences	• Anthropology • Economics • Political Science • Psychology • Sociology	Theory construction, measurement, and textual analysis[b]	Human behavior is patterned, lawful, and principled.
The Humanities	• Art and Art History • History • Literature (English) • Music and Music Education • Philosophy • Religious Studies	Contemplative perception and expression of particular significant texts, objects, and behaviors[c]	Human behavior is idiosyncratic, unique, and the result of free will, not determined.

SOURCE: Based on Repko (2005), p. 49.

a. "Learning in the sciences is inductive, knowledge intensive, and analytic, going from specific phenomena to explanation that requires developing an extensive vocabulary to describe elements and relations between them" (Donald, 2002, pp. 127–129).
b. "Learning in the social sciences involves developing an abstract vocabulary, theoretical frameworks, analytic reasoning, and research methods that emphasize theory construction, measurement, and textual analysis" (Donald, 2002, p. 132).
c. "Learning is concerned with understanding human culture—with aesthetics, where meaning is found in the contemplative perception of particular significant things, and synoptics, where meaning is comprehensive and integrative" (Donald, 2002, p. 232).

CHAPTER SUMMARY

The disciplines are clearly foundational to interdisciplinary inquiry. The role of the disciplines in the interdisciplinary research process has generally depended upon the researcher connecting the problem or topic to disciplines whose general or characteristic view of reality—their perspective—addresses the problem or topic. However, relying on an understanding of perspective in this way is clearly problematic, given the increasing cognitive fluidity of the disciplines, their porous borders, and the extent to which grand theories such as interpretivism, postmodernism, feminism, and others are informing the human sciences. A clarified definition of disciplinary perspective serves two practical purposes. It differentiates between a discipline's overall view of reality and the specific insights it generates into a particular problem. It also enables the student to focus on each discipline's defining elements—phenomena and data, assumptions, epistemology, concepts, theories, and methods—as these pertain to the problem. In this latter sense, perspective is integrative, holistic, and more useful to students. Chapter 4 unpacks the meaning of these several defining elements of perspective.

NOTES

1. The term "borders-and-territories" is from Clifford Geertz and is cited in Julie Thompson Klein (2005a), p. 40.

2. Among the applied fields and professions, Geertz (1983) includes education, communications, criminal justice, management, law, and engineering (p. 7). Elsewhere, Geertz (2000) characterizes these broad categories as "rather baggy" because of their indeterminacy (p. 156). Mary Taylor Huber and Sherwyn P. Morreale (2002) use the term "disciplinary domains," referring to the humanities, the social sciences, and the sciences (p. 8). I do not use the term "core disciplines" because the notion implies a hierarchy of knowledge that many would contest (Salter & Hearn, 1996, p. 6).

3. Early on, interdisciplinarians such as Newell and Green (1982) opted for a narrow definition: "Disciplines are . . . distinguished from one another by the questions they ask about the world, by their *perspectives or world view,* by the set of assumptions they employ, and by the methods which they use to build up a body of knowledge (facts, concepts, theories) around a certain subject matter" (p. 24, italics added). According to this definition, "perspective" is but one of four primary disciplinary elements and is co-equal with the questions that the disciplines ask about the world, the set of assumptions they employ, and the methods they use to build up a body of knowledge (facts, concepts, theories).

4. Newell (1992) now argues that "perspective" should be defined in broader terms, even suggesting that it is the *source* of all other disciplinary elements. He refers to "perspective" as that "*from which* those concepts, theories, methods, and facts emerge" (p. 213, italics added). He adds, "the interdisciplinary researcher must understand how the relevant concepts, theories, and methods underlying each discipline's perspective are *operationalized*" (1998, p. 545, italics added). Janet Donald (2002) apparently agrees, emphasizing that "to understand a field of study [i.e., a discipline], students must learn its perspectives and processes of inquiry" (p. xii–xiii). By "perspective" she means a discipline's epistemology, vocabulary, theory, and methods or processes of inquiry (pp. 2, 8). Jill Vickers (1998) states that interdisciplinarians "must accept that the different disciplines . . . have different cognitive maps" (p. 17). For Hugh Petrie (1976), reliable borrowing from the disciplines requires that the interdisciplinarian know quite a lot about the "cognitive and perceptual apparatus utilized" (p. 35).

5. I am indebted to Richard Castellana for this insight.

6. Rogers et al. (2005) explain that much of this discord within disciplines "may owe more to internal political agendas than we would like [to admit]" (p. 268). The reason why scholarly disciplines do not become inert and settled, explains Marjorie Garber (2001), is "the *disciplinary libido,*" meaning the ways in

which disciplines seek to differentiate themselves from each other while at the same time desiring to become "its nearest neighbor, whether at the edges of the Academy (the professional wants to become an amateur and vice versa), among the disciplines (each covets its neighbor's insights), or within the disciplines (each one attempts to create a new language specific to its objects, but longs for a universal language understood by all)" (p. ix).

7. Three recent studies support Bromme's claim. Svetlana Nikitina (2002) finds that the key elements essential for success in integrative work are "students' and faculties' disposition for boundary-crossing [and] their intellectual breadth and ability to cope with unanswered questions in science" (p. 27). In "Pathways of Interdisciplinary Cognition" (2005), she writes, "interdisciplinary thinking is fundamentally similar to dialogical exchanges occurring in language and in collaborative activities in which epistemological positions are bartered" and argues that "Bakhtin's (1981) theory of dialogic understanding and subsequent linguistic theories of conceptual metaphor and blending serve as a constructive theoretical framework for the understanding of interdisciplinary cognition" (p. 389). The study by Sharon J. Derry, Christian D. Schunn, and Morton Ann Gernsbacher (Eds.), *Interdisciplinary Collaboration: An Emerging Cognitive Science* (2005), reflects on the current state of scientific knowledge regarding interdisciplinary collaboration and encourages research that studies interdisciplinary cognition in relation to the ecological contexts in which it occurs.

8. Klee italicizes these words to indicate the specifically philosophical aspects of science.

9. Donald (2002) cites the example of Maxwell's equations that represent "a tremendous synthesis of physical behavior, extending from X-rays through light and through electric and magnetic fields and phenomena that appear totally dissimilar" (p. 50).

10. Scientists do not normally need to create common ground because it already exists, since the parts typically do not conflict.

11. According to the *Encyclopedia of Social and Cultural Anthropology*, the biggest and most influential area of anthropology is generally known as cultural anthropology in North America and social anthropology in Europe (Barnard & Spencer, 1996, p. x).

12. When functionalism came under attack in the last quarter of the twentieth century, Marx's work shaped such new orientations as world-systems theory. "Microeconomics informed the development of rational-choice theory, which applied economic models of maximizing behavior to social phenomena and introduced more sociological analysis into economic reasoning" (Calhoun, 2002, pp. 456–457).

13. Blau notes two additional changes: (1) the diminishing influence of the classic analytical distinctions, such as macro verses micro and interpretive versus explanatory, because these do not apply to such current concepts as social construction, social capital, engagement, and contextualism; and (2) the increasing tendency of scholars to ignore the quantitative-qualitative division because of "an interest in advancing descriptive understanding and in achieving more synthetic accounts" (p. x).

14. Economic sociology is "the sociological perspective applied to economic phenomenon" (Smelser & Swedberg, 2005, p. 3).

15. John Gerring (2001), for example, finds the question of whether or not to classify history, cultural anthropology, and the theory subfields of political science and sociology as social sciences "the most troublesome." "They are clearly social," he writes, "but are they science? About all one can say without risk of offense is that many writers in these fields see their own approaches as systematic, rigorous, evidence-based, generalizing, non-subjective, and cumulative—as scientific, in the loose sense in which we have employed it here. . . . These divisions will always be blurred around the edges" (pp. xv–xvi). Though this book includes history with the humanities, it is mentioned here because historians, like social scientists, engage in problem solving by asking questions such as, "Why did the Truman administration drop atomic bombs on Japan?"

16. On how to define the humanities, see the views of James Mehl, Walter Gulick, and Charles Cree (1987).

17. The claim that the arts are multicultural but not universal is controversial. The formal elements of art (e.g., line, color, form) may have universal applications, according to Semir Zeki (2000) in *Inner Vision*. Zeki takes an important first step toward providing a scientific theory of aesthetics.

18. For an evenhanded and extended definition of feminism, see Calhoun (2002), pp. 162–163.

19. Walter H. Capps (1995) says that the intellectual discipline of religion "is most frequently referred to as religious studies" (p. xiii).

20. Szostak (2004) argues extensively that distinctions between "explanation" and "interpretation" and also "quantitative" and "qualitative" are overdrawn. "Both understanding and interpretation involve causal arguments, and many social scientists and biologists make qualitative arguments. . . . Participant observation can be done in a quantitative fashion and experiments in a qualitative fashion" (personal communication, May 7, 2007).

REVIEW QUESTIONS

1. What are the characteristics of academic disciplines?

2. What are some misconceptions about the term "disciplinary perspective" as it has developed over the years?

3. How is the fable of the blind men and the elephant by Saxe descriptive of the nature of multidisciplinarity? What is lacking for the fable to be descriptive of interdisciplinarity?

4. How is "cognitive discord" manifesting itself in many of the traditional disciplines, such as art history?

5. How does the clarified definition of disciplinary perspective differ from the traditional understanding of the term?

6. How is the clarified definition of disciplinary perspective consistent with the widely accepted definition of interdisciplinary studies?

7. What are some caveats concerning the clarification of disciplinary perspective?

8. Why are the natural sciences of interest to interdisciplinarians?

9. What are the similarities and differences, stated in general terms, between the problem-solving strategy used by the sciences and the interdisciplinary approach?

10. How do the social sciences approach problem solving compared to interdisciplinary studies?

11. How do the humanities approach understanding and meaning?

12. How does the humanities' view of humanity differ from that of the natural sciences and of the social sciences?

4 Defining the Elements of Disciplines

Chapter Preview

Chapter 3 examined the role of the disciplines in the interdisciplinary research process. It also clarified the definition of disciplinary perspective as meaning a discipline's overall view of reality *and* a discipline's defining elements. These include phenomena, assumptions, epistemology, concepts, theories, and methods. Chapter 4 unpacks the meaning of each of these elements and explains how they are useful to students. This information can profitably be used to develop adequacy in disciplines relevant to the problem.

The Defining Elements of a Discipline

As clarified, disciplinary perspective means not just a discipline's general view of reality but its constituent parts as well. Consistent with this clarified definition, perspective is not among the defining elements identified here because it subsumes them. The term **elements** is used when referring to the constituent parts of a discipline that provide its essential and formative character.

Phenomena

Phenomena are enduring aspects of human existence that are of interest to scholars and are susceptible to scholarly description and explanation (Szostak, 2004, pp. 30–31). As Szostak explains, economic and political institutions evolve and assume different forms in every society, but the classification of possible types of institutions need not change to capture this diversity. Similarly, individuals may differ in terms of personality, but a set of personality characteristics is always with us (p. 30).

The sorting out of distinctions between disciplines in this chapter does not imply that disciplines are static. Indeed, their character is ever changing and their borders are elastic and porous. This reality and the absence of a logical classification of phenomena to guide the disciplines have produced two unfortunate effects. The first is that several disciplines may share a phenomenon, often unmindful of the efforts of other disciplines to comprehend it. For example, psychology and religious studies share an interest in the phenomenon of suicide terrorism, but one rarely finds in their work references to the theories and research of the other discipline. The second effect is that the disciplines may ignore a particular phenomenon.

Interdisciplinary students, like disciplinary students, must identify the phenomena relevant to the research question. They can attempt this in one of two ways: approach the disciplines serially in hopes of locating a particular phenomenon in one or more of them, or focus on the phenomenon itself. Table 4.1 presents the traditional approach of first identifying relevant disciplines and searching their literatures in hopes of finding insights into a particular phenomenon. The success and speed of this search naturally depends on the researcher's familiarity with each discipline. Table 4.1 links the disciplines to illustrative phenomena of interest to them. It is based on the classification of phenomena developed by Rick Szostak (2004). These phenomena are linked to particular disciplines for the purpose of helping students identify which disciplines are relevant to the problem in order to decide which disciplines to mine for insights.[1]

The boundaries of disciplines are evolving, fluid, and overlapping in places while leaving some unexplored territory between themselves and other disciplines. The increasingly common practice of disciplinary scholars borrowing concepts, theories, and methods from other disciplines has implications for interdisciplinary work. The cognitive fluidity that today characterizes the disciplines means that students should not approach disciplines as self-contained repositories of information but be aware that today the disciplines are open to a wider range of concepts, theories, and methods that transcend disciplinary boundaries. That is, students should not only examine the characteristic elements of relevant disciplines for insights into the problem but also search for information from sources that transcend disciplines, such as grand theory (e.g., feminism) and the categories of phenomena appearing in Table 4.1. The classifications provided in this table and elsewhere in this book should help students see how each discipline's perspective contributes to an overall understanding of a multifaceted problem.

Phenomena Classified

Until recently, only the **perspectival approach** (i.e., relying on each discipline's unique perspective on reality) was available to interdisciplinarians because no system of classifying all human phenomena existed. Szostak (2004) meets this need in his pioneering work that classifies phenomena about the human world. His **classification approach**, shown as Table 4.2, moves left to right from the most general to the most specific. A practical benefit of Szostak's approach is that all phenomena can be linked rather easily to particular disciplines, provided that one knows the discipline's general perspective and the phenomena it typically studies.

Table 4.1   Disciplines and Their Illustrative Phenomena

Category	Discipline	Phenomena
The Natural Sciences	Biology	Biological taxonomies of species; the nature, interrelationships, and evolution of living organisms; health; nutrition; disease; fertility
	Chemistry	The periodic table of chemical elements that are the building blocks of matter—their composition, properties, and reactions
	Earth Science	Planet Earth's geologic history, processes, and structures, soil types, topography and land forms, climate patterns, resource availability, water availability, natural disasters
	Mathematics	The logic of numbers, statistics, mathematical modeling, computer simulations, theoretical counterpoint to sensitivity analysis
	Physics	Subatomic particles, the nature of matter and energy and their interactions
The Social Sciences	Anthropology	The origins of humanity, the dynamics of cultures worldwide
	Economics	The economy: total output (price level, unemployment, individual goods and services), income distribution, economic ideology, economic institutions (ownership, production, exchange, trade, finance, labor relations, organizations), the impact of economic policies on individuals
	Political Science	The nature and practice of systems of government and of individuals and groups pursuing power within those systems
	Psychology	The nature of human behavior as well as the internal (psychosociological) and external (environmental) factors that affect this behavior
	Sociology	The social nature of societies and of human interactions within them
The Humanities	Art and Art History	Nonreproducible art—painting, sculpture, architecture, prose, poetry—and reproducible art—theater, film, photography, music, dance
	History	The people, events, and movements of human civilizations past and present
	Literature	Development and examination (i.e., both traditional literary analysis and theory as well as more contemporary culture-based contextualism and critique) of creative works of the written word
	Music and Music Education	Development, performance, and examination (i.e., both traditional musicological analysis and theory as well as more contemporary culture-based contextualism and critique) of creative works of sound
	Philosophy	The search for wisdom through contemplation and reason using abstract thought
	Religious Studies	The phenomena of humans as religious beings and the manifestations of religious belief such as symbols, institutions, doctrines, and practices

SOURCE: Szostak (2004), pp. 26–29, 45–50.

Table 4.2   Szostak's Categories of Phenomena About the Human World[a]

First Level	Second Level	Third Level
Genetic Predisposition	Abilities	Consciousness, subconsciousness, vocalization, perception (five senses), decision making, tool making, learning, other physical attributes (movement, eating, etc.)
	Motivations	Food, clothing, shelter, safety, sex, betterment, aggression, altruism, fairness, identification with group
	Emotions	Love, anger, fear, jealousy, guilt, empathy, anxiety, fatigue, humor, joy, grief, disgust, aesthetic sense, emotional display
	Time Preference	
Individual Differences	Abilities:	
	• Physical Abilities	• Speed, strength, endurance
	• Physical Appearance	• Height, weight, symmetry
	• Energy Level	• Physical, mental
	• Intelligences	• Musical, spatial, mathematical, verbal, kinesthetic, interpersonal
	Personality:	
	• Emotionality (Stable/Moody)	• Contentment, composure vs. anxiety, self-pity
	• Conscientiousness	• Thoroughness, precision, foresight, organization, perseverance vs. carelessness, disorderly, frivolous
	• Affection (Selfish/ Agreeable)	• Sympathetic, appreciative, kind, generous vs. cruel, quarrelsome, faultfinding
	• Intellectual Orientation	• Openness, imagination, curiosity, sensitivity vs. closed-mindedness
	• Other Dimensions?	• Dominant/submissive, strong/weak, in/dependent, humor, aggression future/present oriented, happiness
	• Disorders?	• Schizophrenia, psychoticism . . . ?
	• Sexual Orientation	
	• Schemas	• View of self, others, causal relationships
	• Interpersonal Relationships	• Parent/child, sibling, employee/r, romance, friendship, casual acquaintance
Economy	Total Output	Price level, unemployment, individual goods and services
	Income Distribution	
	Economic Ideology	
	Economic Institutions	Ownership, production, exchange, trade, finance, labor relations, organizations
Art	Nonreproducible	Painting, sculpture, architecture, prose, poetry
	Reproducible	Theater, film, photography, music, dance
Politics	Political Institutions	Decision-making systems, rules, organizations
	Political Ideology	
	Nationalism	

First Level	Second Level	Third Level
	Public Opinion	Issues (various)[b]
	Crime	Versus persons/property
Culture	Languages	By descent?
	Religions	Providence, revelation, salvation, miracles, doctrine
	Stories	Myths, fairy tales, legends, family sagas, fables, jokes and riddles
	Expressions of Culture	Rituals, dance, song, cuisine, attire, ornamentation of buildings, games
	Values	
	• Goals	• Ambition, optimism, attitudes to wealth, power, prestige, beauty, honor, recognition, love, friendship, sex, marriage, time preference, physical and psychological well-being
	• Means	• Honesty, ethics, righteousness, fate, work, violence, vengeance, curiosity, innovation, nature, healing
	• Community	• Identity, family vs. community, openness to outsiders, trust, egalitarianism, attitude to young and old, responsibility, authoritarianism, respect for individuals
	• Everyday Norms	• Courtesy, manners, proxemics, tidiness, cleanliness, punctuality, conversational rules, locomotion rules, tipping
Social Structure	Gender	
	Family Types/Kinship	Nuclear, extended, single parent
	Classes (various)	Occupations (various)
	Ethnic/Racial Divisions	
	Social Ideology	
Technology and Science	Fields (various)	Innovations (various)
	Recognizing the Problem	
	Setting the Stage	
	Act of Insight	
	Critical Revision	
	Diffusion/ Transmission	Communication, adoption
Health	Nutrition	Diverse nutritional needs
	Disease	Viral, bacterial, environmental

(Continued)

Table 4.2 (Continued)

First Level	Second Level	Third Level
Population	Fertility	Fecundity, deviation from, maximum
	Mortality	Causes of death (various)
	Migration	Distance, international, temporary
	Age Distribution	
Non-Human Environment	Soil	Soil types (various)
	Topography	Land forms (various)
	Climate	Climate patterns (various)
	Flora	Species (various)
	Fauna	Species (various)
	Resource Availability	Various resources
	Water Availability	
	Natural Disasters	Flood, tornado, hurricane, earthquake, volcano
	Day and Night	
	Transport Infrastructure	Mode (various)
	Built Environments	Offices, houses, fences, etc.
	Population Density	

SOURCE: Szostak (2004), pp. 27–29.

a. The table undoubtedly appears daunting at first. Closer examination of it, though, shows that there are only 11 categories of phenomena and relatively small sets of second-level phenomena. The third-level phenomena in the table can be further unpacked into subsidiary phenomena. Szostak says that the table was developed using a mix of deduction and induction, and thus can be extended if/when new phenomena are discovered (personal communication, May 7, 2007).

b. "Various" here and elsewhere in this table covers a lot of phenomena that are not equal. Distinguishing between these will require the student to consult more specialized disciplinary literatures.

Using Table 4.2, the student should be able to link most topics readily to one or more of the particular phenomena in the table. For example, the phenomenon of fresh water scarcity in Texas concerns the nonhuman environment. Moving from left to right, one can see multiple links to a wide array of subphenomena that may pertain to the problem. These subphenomena, in turn, provide links to other phenomena identified in the right-hand column that may be of further interest. Reading the literature pertaining to the several subphenomena may lead the researcher to broaden the investigation to include the categories of economics and politics and their respective subphenomena. In short, the student using Szostak's classification approach should be able to identify connections to neighboring phenomena that may touch on the research question. Making these connections aids the research process and integrative work, as will be demonstrated in later chapters.

Assumptions

An **assumption** is something taken for granted, a supposition. Assumptions are the principles that underlie the discipline as a whole and its overall perspective on reality. As the term implies, these principles are accepted as the truths upon which the discipline's theories, concepts, methods, and curriculum are based. Stated another way, a discipline's theories, concepts, and insights are simply the practical outworking of the assumptions of its members about *what* ought to take place and *how* it should take place.

Grasping the underlying assumptions of a discipline as a whole provides important clues to the assumptions underlying its particular insights. Assumptions underlying specific insights are important to the integrative part of the interdisciplinary process that calls for identifying possible sources of conflict between them. Once these conflicts are identified, the student can then work to create common ground among them. This, in turn, makes possible integrating insights, and ultimately producing an interdisciplinary understanding of the problem.

The basic assumptions of science are six: that nature is orderly, that we can know nature, that all natural phenomena have natural causes, that nothing is self-evident, that knowledge is based on experience, and that knowledge is superior to ignorance (Frankfort-Nachmias & Nachmias, 2008, pp. 5–6). The particular *combination* of assumptions is unique to each discipline, but disciplines can share assumptions. The assumptions in Tables 4.3, 4.4, and 4.5 are not comprehensive generalizations but central tendencies and, thus, can be challenged by disciplinarians who might prefer different representational selections. The purpose in presenting these tables is to help students decide which disciplines are relevant to the problem so that their literatures can be mined for insights.

The hallmark assumptions that most scientists make are two. The first is that scientists can transcend their cultural experience and make definitive measurements of phenomena. The second is that "there are no supernatural or other a priori properties of nature that cannot potentially be measured" (Maurer, 2004, pp. 19–20).[2] This assumption is reflected to varying degrees in the characterizations of disciplinary assumptions underlying the natural sciences and mathematics noted in Table 4.3. The sources cited in this and in following tables are good starting points for further reading.

The social sciences are grounded in essentially the same set of basic assumptions that characterize the sciences (Frankfort-Nachmias & Nachmias, 2008, p. 5). Assumptions in the social sciences are closely related to the research methods, theories, and schools of thought embraced by members of each discipline's community of scholars. For example, a popular textbook on behavioral research methods (i.e., psychology, communication, human development, education, marketing, social work, and the like) states the assumption underlying the scientific approach and systematic empiricism as these methods are applied to the behavioral sciences: "Data obtained through systematic empiricism allow researchers to draw more

Table 4.3   Assumptions of Disciplines in the Natural Sciences

Discipline	Assumptions
Biology	Biologists assume that the hypothetico-deductive approach (i.e., deductive reasoning used to derive explanations or predictions from laws or theories) based on the principle of falsification (i.e., the doctrine whereby theories or hypotheses derived from them are disproved because proof is logically impossible) is superior to description of pattern and inductive reasoning (Quinn & Keogh, 2002, p. 2).
Chemistry	The function of the whole is reducible to the properties of its constituent elements and compounds and their interactions. "All living organisms share certain chemical, molecular, and structural features, interact according to well-defined principles, and follow the same rules with regard to inheritance and evolution" (Donald, 2002, p. 111).
Earth Science	The principle of uniformitarianism leads geologists to assume that the present is the key to understanding the past. Earth processes have not significantly changed during the several billion years that Earth has been a dynamic planet similar in many ways to the other planets constituting the solar system. In the past decade, Earth system scientists have assumed that natural and social systems are strongly coupled and act in nonlinear ways (Steffen et al., 2004, p. 287).
Mathematics	Assumptions (or axioms) in mathematics form the starting point for logical proofs of its theorems. They constitute the "if" part of a statement: "If A, then B." The consequences of the assumptions are found through logical reasoning, which leads the mathematician to discover the conclusion, "then B" (Shipman, personal communication, April, 2005).
Physics	Logical empiricism assumes the existence of a finite set of laws that governs the behavior of the universe and that there is an objective method for discovering these truths. Natural realism, by contrast, assumes (1) that the universe works in a law-like manner, though the nature of the universe may be extremely complex and much of it may even be unfathomable; and (2) "scientists can build models that approximate nature sufficiently to allow further progress in understanding particular phenomena" (Maurer, 2004, p. 21). This atomistic approach to knowledge further assumes that separate parts together constitute physical reality, that these separate parts are lawfully and precisely related, and that physics events can be predicted.

confident conclusions than they can draw from casual observation alone" (Leary, 2004, p. 9). Modernists share a "grizzled confidence" in such ideas as "progress" and "knowledge" grounded in empirical and replicable data (Cullenberg et al., 2001, p. 3). This modernist assumption is present, to varying degrees, in many of the social science disciplines but is being challenged by postmodern notions. Both sets of assumptions—modern and postmodern—are noted in Table 4.4.

Assumptions in the humanities, more so than in the social sciences, are pluralistic and even conflicted, as is shown in Table 4.5.

Table 4.4 Assumptions of Disciplines in the Social Sciences

Discipline	Assumptions
Anthropology	Cultural relativism (the notion that people's ideas about what is good and beautiful are shaped by their culture[a]) assumes that systems of knowledge possessed by different cultures are "incommensurable" (i.e., not comparable and not transferable) (Whitaker, 1996, p. 480). Cultural relativism has been the driving ethic of anthropology for generations, but it is being challenged by feminists, postcolonialists, and advocates for other marginalized groups on the grounds that relativism supports the repressive status quo in other cultures (Bernard, 2002, p. 73).
Economics	Modernist approaches predominate. Modernist economists assume that the same dominant human motivation (rational self-interest) transcends national and cultural boundaries, in the past as in the present. Also, they assume that both usefulness and value are implicit in rational choices (on which they prefer to focus) under conditions of scarcity. Postmodernists assume that all things, including economic motivation and behavior, are intimately bound up with the situatedness (i.e., the cultural, political, and technological context) of those engaged in these activities and thus are not generalizable (Cullenberg et al., 2001, p. 19).
Political Science	Political science has been influenced primarily by history, but more recently it is being influenced by theories from sociology, economics, and psychology. Consequently, its assumptions reflect whichever discipline and theory it is drawing from at the moment. Modernists assume rationality: "Human beings, while they are undeniably subject to certain causal forces, are . . . in part intentional actors, capable of cognition and acting on the basis of it" (Goodin & Klingerman, 1996, pp. 9–10). Behavioralists (who are also modernists) assume that political science can become a science capable of prediction and explanation (Somit & Tanenhaus, 1967, pp. 177–178). Proponents of the scientific method of research assume that empirical and quantitative, rather than normative and qualitative, analysis is the most effective way of knowing political reality (Manheim, Rich, Willnat, & Brians, 2006, pp. 2–3).
Psychology	Psychologists assume that "data obtained through systematic empiricism allow researchers to draw more confident conclusions than they can draw from casual observation alone" (Leary, 2004, p. 9). Generalizations about larger populations may be inferred from representative sample populations. Psychologists also assume that group behavior can be reduced to individuals and their interactions, and that humans organize their mental life through psychological constructs.
Sociology	Assumptions vary widely in this discipline. Empiricists assume an independent social reality exists that can be perceived and measured through gathering of data. Critics of modernism assume that our perceptions of social reality are filtered through a web of assumptions, cultural influences, and value-laden vocabularies, that individual human behavior is socially constructed, with rationality and autonomy playing modest roles at best; groups, institutions, and especially society have an existence independent of the individuals in them. People, they assume, are motivated primarily by the desire for social status (Alvesson, 2002, pp. 2–3).

a. Cultural relativism does not equate to ethical relativism (that all ethical systems are equally good since they are all cultural products), as Merrilee Salmon (1997) makes clear. Szostak notes that there are two distinct issues associated with relativism. The first is incommensurability (which, if true, would challenge the very idea of interdisciplinarity). "The second is that there are no universal standards for evaluating cultural elements. Both flow from the idea that cultural elements are tightly bound into a monolithic structure that is best analyzed as a whole (but then it is hard to understand both cultural evolution and subcultures) (personal communication, July 7, 2007).

Table 4.5   Assumptions of Disciplines in the Humanities

Discipline	Assumptions
Art and Art History	Modernists assume that the intrinsic value of the object is primary. Radical art historians—i.e., Marxist, feminist, psychoanalytical, and poststructuralist—"share a broad historical materialism" of outlook: that all social institutions such as education, politics, and the media, are exploitative and that "exploitation extends to social relations, based, for instance, on factors of gender, race, and sexual preference" (Harris, 2001, p. 264). In general, these critics assume that intrinsic values remain primary, but understanding the social context completes one's grasp of the work (Harris, 2001, p. 264).[a]
History	Modernist (positivist and historicist) historical scholarship rests on the idea that objectivity in historical research is possible and preferred (Iggers, 1997, p. 9). In general, social history (e.g., Marxian socioeconomic history, the Braudelian method, women's history, African American history, and ethnic history) assumes that those whom traditional history writing had ignored (the poor, the working class, women, homosexuals, minorities, the sick) played an important but unappreciated role in historical change (Howell & Prevenier, 2001, p. 113).
Literature	Literature (broadly defined) or "texts" are assumed to be a lens for understanding life in a culture and an instrument that can be used to understand human experience in all of its complexity. Texts "encompass the continuous substance of all human signifying activities" (Marshall, 1992, p. 162). Another assumption is that these texts are "alien" to the reader, meaning that "something in the text or in our distance from it in time and place makes it obscure." The interpreter's task is to make the text "speak" by "reading" the text using extremely complex skills so as to give the text "meaning." *Meaning* is "an intricate and historically situated social process" that occurs between the interpreter and audience (i.e., reader) that neither fully controls (pp. 159, 165–166).
Music and Music Education	Modernists assume that empirical investigation produces verifiable and objective "knowledge" (i.e., in the sense of infallible theories, laws, or general statements) and "truth" that is context free. Postpositivists (interpretivists, critical theory advocates, gender studies scholars, and postmodernists) deny the possibility of objectivity because human values are always present in human minds (Elliott, 2002, p. 99).
Philosophy	There are two schools of thought about how to get knowledge. Rationalists assume that the chief route to knowledge is the exercise of systematic reasoning and "looking at the scaffolding of our thought and doing conceptual engineering" (Blackburn, 1999, p. 4). The model for rationalists is mathematics and logic. Empiricists assume that the chief route to knowledge is perception (i.e., using the five senses of sight, smell, hearing, taste, and touch and the extension of these using technologies such as the microscope and telescope). The model for empiricists is any of the natural sciences where observation and experiment are the principle means of inquiry (Sturgeon, Martin, & Grayling, 1995, p. 9).

Discipline	Assumptions
Religious Studies	Religious studies often queries faith, and the history of religions focuses on understanding the phenomenon of man as a religious being. One key assumption of the discipline is that there is something inherently unique about religion and those who study it must do so without reducing its essence to something other than itself, as sociologists and psychologists tend to do. A related assumption is that even though religion is freighted with human emotion, objectivity is possible (Stone, 1998, p. 5).

a. Marxists assume that class struggle is the primary engine of historical development in capitalist society and that other forms of exploitation are either a product of the basic antagonism of class or peripheral to it. Feminists assume connections and causal links between patriarchal dominance within the society as a whole and its art. Psychoanalytic art historians assume that a full understanding of "the subject" requires inquiry into the complex nature of the embodied human psyche and its conscious and unconscious outworkings (Harris, 2001, pp. 262, 264, 195).

Assumptions often play an important role in the process of creating common ground among conflicting insights. For example, in examining insights into the problem of the causes of suicide terrorism, students found that an important assumption underlying scholarly insights from psychology and political science is that the behavior of the terrorists is rational (as defined by both disciplines), not irrational as many in the class had initially supposed.

Epistemology

Epistemology is the branch of philosophy that studies how one knows what is true and how one validates truth (Sturgeon et al., 1995, p. 9). It has to do with the nature, validity, and limits of inquiry (Rosenau, 1992, p. 109). An epistemological position reflects one's views of what can be known about the world and how it can be known. Literally, an epistemology is a theory of knowledge (Marsh & Furlong, 2002, pp. 18–19). Each discipline's epistemology is its way of knowing that part of reality that it considers within its research domain (Elliott, 2002, p. 85).

A researcher's epistemological position is reflected in what is studied and how it is studied. For example, **positivists** are concerned with establishing causal relationships between social phenomena through direct observation, attempting to develop explanatory, and even predictive, models. Positivist researchers believe that (a) the world exists independently of our knowledge of it, (b) social phenomena exist independently of our interpretation of them, and (c) objective analysis is possible. The polar opposite of this position is the interpretivist position. **Interpretivists** believe that (a) the world is socially constructed, (b) social phenomena do not exist independently of our interpretation of them, and (c) objective analysis is impossible (Marsh & Furlong, 2002, p. 20, 26).

The **epistemic norms of a discipline** are agreements about how researchers should select their evidence or data, evaluate their experiments, and judge their theories. Science philosopher Jane Maienschein (2000) states, "It is epistemic convictions that dictate what will count as acceptable practice and how theory and practice should work together to yield legitimate scientific knowledge" (p. 123). The experimental approach is based on the epistemological assumption that stresses the value of experimental control and replicability, whereas the field approach is based on the value of studying the "messy, muddled life-in-its-context" (p. 134).

The statements on epistemologies in Tables 4.6, 4.7, and 4.8 are not definitive but central tendencies. Any way of classifying the epistemological positions of the disciplines can be contested.[3] These tables draw heavily from disciplinary experts, with the recognition that no two scholars may give precisely the same description of their disciplines. The approach chosen here was done so in awareness of the possible criticisms of it.

Table 4.6 Epistemologies of the Natural Sciences

Discipline	Epistemology
Biology	Biology stresses the value of classification and experimental control. The latter is the means of identifying true causes, and which therefore privileges experimental methods (because they are replicable) over all other methods of obtaining information (Magnus, 2000, p. 115).
Chemistry	Chemists use both empirics and theory (especially thermodynamics). Even more than physics, chemistry relies on lab experiments, data collection in the field, and computer simulations. Chemistry involves less field work than Earth science and biology do.
Earth Science	In much of Earth science, the theory of uniformitarianism is used. Since geologists are concerned about the history of the Earth but can't directly observe it, they accept that natural laws and processes have not changed over time (L. Standlee, personal communication, April, 2005). Geologists stress the value of field work.
Mathematics	Mathematical truths are numerical abstractions that are discovered through logic and reasoning. These truths exist independently of our ability or lack of ability to find them, and they do not change. These truths or forms of "invariance" enable us to categorize, organize, and give structure to the world. These mathematical structures—"geometric images and spaces, or the linguistic/algebraic expressions"— are "grounded on key regularities of the world or what we 'see' in the world" (Longo, 2002, p. 434).
Physics	Like all the physical sciences, physics is empirical, rational, and experimental. It seeks to discover truths or laws about two related and observable concepts— matter and energy—by acquiring objective and measurable information about them (Taffel, 1992, pp. 1, 5).

These characterizations are empiricist. Empiricism, as Alex Rosenberg (2000) notes, is the "ruling 'ideology' of science."[4] Empiricism assures us that observation and experimentation make scientific explanations credible and the predictive power of its theories ever-increasing (p. 146). However, the epistemologies of the sciences make scientific approaches inadequate for addressing value issues (Kelly, 1996, p. 95).

The disciplines in the social sciences, more so than in the natural sciences, tend to embrace more than one epistemology, as shown in Table 4.7. For example, reflecting the growing postmodernist criticism of positivism's empiricism and value neutrality, most social scientists now agree that knowledge in their disciplines is generated by the "continual interplay of personal experience, values, theories, hypotheses, and logical models, as well as empirical evidence generated by a variety of methodological approaches" (Calhoun, 2002, p. 373).

Given the **epistemological pluralism** in the human sciences, it is problematic to associate a particular epistemology with a particular discipline. This is because of the deep divide between the modernist and newer critical approaches to knowledge formation within the humanities, as shown in Table 4.8.

Interdisciplinary students are interested in epistemology for at least three reasons. First, a writer's epistemological position is reflected in what is studied, how it is studied, and the status the writer gives to the findings. For example, a positivist looking for causal relationships will tend to prefer quantitative analyses that are "objective" and "generalizable." By contrast, a writer in the interpretivist camp is concerned with *understanding* and will, consequently, use qualitative methods to discover the *meaning* that behavior has for agents (Marsh & Furlong, 2002, p. 21).

Second, good interdisciplinary work requires a strong degree of **epistemological self-reflexivity** (Klein, 1996, p. 214). Students should be aware of the advantages and disadvantages of different epistemological approaches. Also, students should be aware that their epistemological choices tend to influence their selection of research methods that, in turn, influence research outcomes (Bell, 1998, p. 101). Accordingly, students should be concerned that their embrace of certain assumptions, epistemologies, theories, methods, and political views do not bias the interdisciplinary research process and thus skew the resulting interdisciplinary understanding.

Third, the major epistemological approaches discussed inform much of the literature in the natural sciences, social sciences, and humanities. Faced with growing epistemological pluralism across the disciplines, but especially in the social sciences and even more so in the humanities, students need to know the nature and limits of the truth claims made by these major epistemological approaches. Disciplinary students are more likely to base their epistemological commitments on their affinity for either modernist (including positivist) or postmodernist approaches, rather than on their attachment to some disciplinary grouping (Lattuca, 2001, p. 104). In her study of

Table 4.7   Epistemologies of the Social Sciences

Discipline	Epistemology
Anthropology	Epistemological pluralism characterizes anthropology. Empiricists hold that people learn their values and that their values are therefore relative to their culture. The rationalist notion is that there are universal truths about right and wrong. Both physical and cultural anthropologists embrace constructivism, which holds that human knowledge is shaped by the social and cultural context in which it is formed and is not merely a reflection of reality (Bernard, 2002, pp. 3–4).
Economics	The epistemological dominance of modernism is being challenged by postmodernism that generates a pluralistic understanding of reality. Postmodernists see reality, and the self, as fragmented. Therefore, human understanding of reality is also fragmented. Nevertheless, the beliefs of economists are still largely determined by empirical evidence in direct relation to the mathematical theories and models they hold. It stresses fixed definitions of words, employs a deductive method, and examines a small set of variables (Dow, 2001, p. 63).
Political Science	Political science embraces a rationalist epistemology. However, logical positivists in the discipline are trying to cast the "science" of politics in terms of finding some set of "covering laws" so strong that even a single counterexample would suffice to falsify them. But human beings, according to others in the discipline, while they are undeniably subject to certain external forces, are also in part intentional actors, capable of cognition and of acting on the basis of it. Consequently, these scholars study "belief," "purpose," "intention," and "meaning" as potentially crucial elements in explaining the political actions of humans (Goodin & Klingerman, 1996, pp. 9–10).[a]
Psychology	The epistemology of psychology is that psychological constructs and their interrelationships can be inferred through discussion and observation and applied to treatment (clinical) or a series of experiments with slight variations (experimental). A critical ingredient of a good experiment is experimental control that seeks to eliminate extraneous factors that might affect the outcome of the study (Leary, 2004, p. 208).
Sociology	Modernist (i.e., positivist) sociology shares a rationalist epistemology with the other social sciences, but this epistemology is opposed by critical social theory, a theory cluster that includes Marxism, critical theory, feminist theory, postmodernism, multiculturalism, and cultural studies. What unites these approaches in the most general sense is their assumption that knowledge is socially constructed and that knowledge exists in history that can change the course of history if properly applied (Agger, 1998, pp. 1–13).

a. Marsh and Furlong (2002) see the discipline divided among three epistemological positions: positivism, interpretivism, and realism (pp. 22–32).

Table 4.8   Epistemologies of the Humanities

Discipline	Epistemology
Art and Art History	Modernists determine the value of works of art by comparing them with standards of aesthetics and expertise. But practitioners of the new art history who emerged in the 1960s determine the value of works of art in relation to contestation between values of competing groups; that is, it understands them in social and cultural contexts (Harris, 2001, pp. 65, 96–97, 130–131, 162–165, 194–196, 228–232, 262–288). Postmodern critics (active from about 1970 to the present) "argue that the supposedly dispassionate old-style art historians are, consciously or not, committed to the false elitist ideas that universal aesthetic criteria exist and that only certain superior things qualify as 'art'" (Barnet, 2008, p. 260).
History	Modernists focus on the authenticity and appropriateness of how an event, person, or period is interpreted by evaluating the work in terms of its faithfulness to appropriate primary and secondary sources. "Truth," they believe, "is one, not perspectival" (Novick, 1998, p. 2). Believing that "structure" is fundamental to understanding the past, social historians focus on structure and infrastructure—on material structure, on the economy, on social and political systems—but do not eliminate the individual. More recently, some social historians have begun to employ "micro-history" or the new cultural history (a blend of social history and intellectual history) as a way of studying ideological structures, mental structures (such as notions of family and community), isolated events, individuals, or actions, borrowing from anthropology the ethnographic method of "thick description," which emphasizes close observation of small details, carefully listening to every voice and every nuance of phrase (Howell & Prevenier, 2001, p. 115).
Literature	In general, modernists focus on the text and employ text-based research techniques. Newer approaches see meaning-making as a relational process. The close reading of texts is being informed by background research into the context of the text, such as the circumstances surrounding its production, content, and consumption. Other newer approaches abound. For example, notions of auto/biographic writing have shifted from an idea of presenting "the truth" about someone to presenting "a truth." Oral history is viewed as a means of understanding the workings of "literary and cultural phenomena in and on people's imagination." Critical discourse analysis examines patterns in language use in order to uncover the workings of an ideology to see how it exerted control or how it was resisted. Quantitative researchers are using computers to calculate the frequency with which certain words appear in a text so that they can better interpret its meaning (Griffin, 2005, pp. 5–14).
Music and Music Education	For modernists, knowledge is often primarily technical knowledge. Modernists determine the value of musical works by comparison with standards of aesthetics and expertise and examine their meaning and structure through various methods of interpretation. Postmodernists embrace a much more pluralistic view of knowledge than modernists do and view it as elusive, fragile, temporary, and conjectural. Postmodernists argue that there are an infinite number of potentially "true" statements that can be developed about any phenomenon, and that no single form of research can possibly account for the complete "truth" or reality of anything. "The goal of research, then, is continuously to seek relevant descriptions and explanations of a phenomenon based on the best and most complete knowledge we can garner about that phenomenon" (Elliott, 2002, p. 91).

(Continued)

Table 4.8 (Continued)

Discipline	Epistemology
Philosophy	Recently, philosophical questions about perception have become more important. For both empiricist and rationalist positions, one of the major concerns is to ascertain whether the means of getting knowledge are trustworthy. The chief concerns of epistemology in this regard are memory, judgment, introspection, reasoning, and "a priori-a posteriori" distinction, and the scientific method (Sturgeon et al., 1995, pp. 9–10).
Religious Studies	Religious studies is concerned about the "assumptions and preconceptions that influence the analysis and interpretation of data, that is, the theoretical and analytical framework, even personal feelings, one brings to the task of organizing and analyzing facts" (Stone, 1998, p. 6). Though all humanities disciplines are concerned about the problem of subjectivity, few are as self-critical as religious studies (p. 7).

interdisciplinarity at colleges and universities, Lisa Lattuca finds that professors committed to traditional **modernist approaches** (belief in objective, empirically based, rationally analyzed truth that is knowable) chose theories and methods from different disciplines that were epistemologically consistent with their own way of thinking (p. 105). James A. Bell (1998) agrees, finding that most disciplinary writers tend to fall into one of two epistemological camps. At the one extreme, he says, are the followers of **epistemological positivism** or "law and order" approach, who point to any flexibility in matters epistemological as a guise for relativism or at least a mask for being weak or lacking conviction in expressing one's views. At the other extreme are **epistemological postmodernists** who view epistemology as "totally arbitrary, being nothing more than a political power game to legitimize one's favored views" (p. 103). This latter conception, says Bell, is at the heart of **postmodernist approaches** that typically operate under the assumption that there is no such thing as objective truth. Instead, knowledge is explained discursively because the social and political context is a discursive construction, usually as a weapon in the hands of some individuals or groups to dominate and intimidate others (p. 103). Students are wise to recognize that both extreme positions are harmful because they limit one's own thinking and denigrate the thinking of others.

In searching for disciplinary insights into the problem, students will inevitably encounter writings that reflect adherence to one of the major epistemological approaches. While writers may not explicitly reveal their epistemological preferences, their writings will often provide clues detectable to the informed interdisciplinarian. Students should know these approaches—their strengths and limitations—so as to be able to select the one most appropriate to the problem. The left-hand column of Table 4.9 shows theories about how the world works that purport to explain a wide range of phenomena and causal links: modernism, interpretivism, postmodernism, and feminism.

Postmodernism is of particular interest to students, especially those working in the humanities and the social sciences. This critical approach offers a way to understand society by questioning modernism's notion of objectivity. The postmodern challenge radiates across the disciplines but is concentrated most heavily in the social sciences and the humanities.[5] In political science, for example, it calls into question the authority of hierarchical, bureaucratic decision-making structures, while in psychology it questions the conscious, logical, and coherent subject (Rosenau, 1992). The battle between modernists and postmodernists has been largely settled, but the postmodernist critique of modernism has left a lasting impact.

Each of these broad theoretical approaches to explaining reality has its own epistemological position, as shown in Table 4.9. (The middle column of the table shows the various schools of thought within modernism.) The epistemological position of each theory and school of thought is stated in the right-hand column in general terms.

Table 4.9   Epistemology

Theory About How the World Works	School of Thought	Epistemological Position
Modernism		A real world exists independent of our knowledge of it.
	Positivism	External reality is discoverable through empirical observations.
	Realism	Direct observation should not be privileged because deep structures, which cannot be directly observed, have crucial effects on outcomes.
	Behavioralism	General laws about the way things work are discoverable by studying observable behavior.
	Rational Choice	Theoretical models can be constructed that permit us to predict outcomes.
	Marxism	Reality is discoverable by examining the political dimensions of class relations and economic structures.
Interpretivism		The world can be interpreted on an individual basis, but it can never really be known.
Postmodernism		The world is discursively constructed (see **"discourse"** in Glossary)
Feminism		Some adherents to feminist theory embrace a modernist (i.e., realist) epistemology while others embrace a postmodern approach.[a]

SOURCE: Based on Gerring (2001), pp. 11–12; Stoker & Marsh (2002), p. 11; Elliott (2002), pp. 88–89.

a. Critics of feminist epistemology such as Cassandra Pinnock (1994) point out that feminist epistemology "should not be taken seriously" because it "is unable to resolve the tension between (a) its thesis that every epistemology is a sociopolitical artifact, and (b) its stated aim to articulate an epistemology that can be *justified* as better than its rivals" (p. 646).

Students should be aware of the common criticisms of their favored epistemological approach. The limitations of modernism and postmodernism, for example, are shown in Table 4.10 and are stated in general terms.

The implication for truth claims of the modernist/positivist and postmodernist/interpretivist approaches is this: Modernist empirical research under the label of positivism assumes an independent reality out there that can be perceived and measured. Based upon the careful design of procedures, the data collected and processed enables empirical research to validate or invalidate a hypothesis about that part of reality under investigation. For positivists, this great faith in data and empirical inquiry is the cornerstone of knowledge production and reliability (Alvesson, 2002, pp. 2–3).

In recent years, **interpretivist approaches** such as postmodernism, feminism, and critical theory are challenging this bedrock assumption, claiming that the perceptions and interpretations of what we perceive are filtered through a web of values, expectations, and vocabularies that influence understanding (Frankfort-Nachmias & Nachmias, 2008, p. 11). Feminists, for example, point to how "male domination has produced a masculine social science built around ideals such as objectivity, neutrality, distance,

Table 4.10   Limitations of Each Epistemology

Theory	Weaknesses
Modernism	1. All forms of human observation are judgmental, conceptual, or theory-laden.
	2. Even a very large number of empirical statements do not add up to "knowledge" in the sense of infallible theories, laws, or general statements (Elliott, 2002, p. 89).
	3. Often there are possible alternative explanations for whatever data scientists gather.
	4. Modernists insist on the empirical-observational definition of research that requires that all other fields involving qualitative judgments to be excluded, including education (p. 89).
Postmodernism	1. It embraces extreme relativism, arguing that no single interpretation is more defensible than another.
	2. Deconstruction, a postmodern approach to understanding texts, is destructive, not constructive, because it reduces all texts in the same way to the same conclusions.
	3. Postmodernists insist that their way of investigating an issue has more merit than any other and that the social and political agendas they support are superior to others (Rosenau, 1992, p. 124).
	4. Society is fractured into disjunct groups of people who cannot meaningfully associate with the others outside their group (Elliott, 2002, p. 113).
	5. There are no "right" procedures of investigation because there is no verifiable and universal meta-system of knowledge (p. 96).

control, rationality and abstraction" and that these have "marginalized alternative ideas such as commitment, empathy, closeness, cooperation, intuition, and specificity." Critical theorists charge that knowledge production is grounded in politics and interests (Alvesson, 2002, p. 3). These other critical approaches are calling into question even the possibility of objectivity and the reliability of knowledge.

Theory

The root meaning of the word "theory" is looking at or viewing, contemplating or speculating. As generally used, **theory** refers to a generalized scholarly explanation about some aspect of the natural or human world, how it works, and why specific facts are related, that is supported by data and research (Bailis, 2001, p. 39; Calhoun, 2002, p. 482; Novak, 1998, p. 84).

Two Kinds of Theory

There are two kinds of theory. **Grand theories** or grand narratives or schools of thought cross disciplines and "attempt to tell a particular Big Story—such as the rise of capitalism, patriarchy, or the colonial subject" (Klein, 2005a, p. 58). Grand theories or narratives such as Marxism, feminism, and rational choice inform more than one discipline.[6] Grand theories or schools of thought are general analyses that attempt to explore and explain interrelationships between phenomena that extend beyond the borders of two or more disciplines. Each school of thought is like a discipline only in that it has its own perspective, assumptions, epistemology, concepts, and methods.

Unlike grand theories that transcend disciplinary boundaries and are used by two or more disciplines, **narrow-range theories** are often specific to the discipline and, thus, have limited applicability. In the social sciences, narrow-range theories are designed to account for a relatively small number of phenomena and produce insights into a specific problem of interest to a segment of the discipline's community of scholars. Each narrow-range theory has its own epistemology, concepts, and methods.

Theories, both grand and narrow range, about the causes or consequences (real or possible) of a problem are important components of the interdisciplinary research process because they generate so many of the insights into the problem. Integrating these insights to the extent possible is a critical step toward producing an interdisciplinary understanding of the problem.

Theories, states Stanley Bailis (2001), that explain and predict behavior are considered adequate. Theories that lead to many successful applications in the world of human experience are considered powerful. The practice of a discipline's community of scholars, he says, "is largely a matter of trying to determine whether its theories are adequate and powerful." Indeed, theories are the basic source of the questions scholars ask, of the evidence and methods they use to find answers, and, ultimately, of the meaning and significance of what is learned. This, says Bailis, "is why theories are both necessary and dangerous—necessary because they organize work, dangerous because they do so by deliberately limiting attention, perception, and inquiry" (p. 39).

Concepts and How They Relate to Theory

How do concepts relate to theory? Concepts are the most elementary "building blocks" of any theory.[7] Some concepts are found in only a single theory, but most are found in a wide range of theories. For example, the concepts of "class," "socioeconomic status," and "social stratification" are found in several sociological theories.

Each discipline has created a large number of concepts that constitute its technical jargon or language. Introductory disciplinary textbooks are excellent sources of concepts and their definitions. Though each discipline has its own specialized vocabulary, it is common to find that a concept in one discipline is also found in the vocabulary of another discipline but has a different meaning. For example, the concept of "rational" in sociology may refer to values and behavior that is normative for the group or for society at large, whereas for religion the concept may be conditioned by one's belief in and behavior governed by the sacred writings of a faith tradition. Students are interested in concepts because they often serve as the basis for creating common ground among conflicting insights (the focus of Chapter 11).

In interdisciplinary work, concepts can facilitate making general connections across disciplinary boundaries. Each concept typically exhibits the characteristics of its disciplinary location (Klein, 1996, p. 50). To create common ground among differing insights, the student may use one of the several integrative techniques discussed in Chapter 11, such as redefining a concept so that it can be extended to other disciplines and their insights into the problem. Once achieved, integration of differing insights can proceed and the interdisciplinary understanding can be produced.

The Importance of Grand Theory or Schools of Thought to Interdisciplinary Work

The clarified definition of disciplinary perspective, repeated here, highlights the importance of theory: Disciplinary perspective refers to the ensemble of a discipline's defining elements that include phenomena, assumptions, epistemology, concepts, theory, and methods. Students need a basic understanding of theory, both grand and narrow range, for three practical reasons. First, as Donald (2002) emphasizes, for students to work in a discipline, they "must have the vocabulary and the theory of the field" because "each discipline requires a different mindset" (p. 2).

Second, more than ever before, theory dominates the scholarly discourse within the disciplines and determines the questions asked, the phenomena investigated, and the insights produced. Klein (1999) notes the increasingly common practice of disciplines borrowing theories and methods from other disciplines and, in some cases, making the borrowed theory or method its own (p. 3). Szostak (2005) observes that many scholars "are influenced by various modern or postmodern theories" (p. 1). Ben Agger (1998) notes "the ongoing theory explosion across the humanities and social sciences" (p. 10). Lattuca (2001) comments on the "qualitative-quantitative cross currents in the social sciences and the increased use of poststructuralist theories in the humanities and social sciences" as examples of ferment in and among disciplines (p. 3).

Third, since these theories explain particular or local phenomena, they provide many of the disciplinary "insights" into a particular problem, and it is these insights that students need to integrate in order to produce an interdisciplinary understanding of the problem.

Grand narratives, particularly postmodernism and its offshoots (e.g., New Historicism and Cultural Analysis), are heavily influencing the social sciences and the humanities (Rosenau, 1992, p. 3). Increasingly, these anti-modernist theories are reflected in the growing volume of scholarship produced by social science and humanities scholars, and this scholarship is adding new insights into a wide range of issues. For example, New Historicist scholars such as Catherine Gallagher and Stephen Greenblatt (2000) are delving deeply into particular historical cultures to understand how certain products of these cultures (e.g., paintings and other art objects) are important signs and embodiments of the freedom of the human imagination (p. 11). Cultural analysis scholars such as Mieke Bal (1999) are keenly aware of the critic's (or viewer's) situatedness in the present and seek to understand the past as part of the present, as what is around us (p. 1). Consequently, in order to profitably read and use these literatures, one must have, at a minimum, some basic understanding of the theories that they so vehemently oppose and that they so fervently embrace.

Finally, students need to develop a basic understanding of theory because of the interrelationship between theory and disciplinary research methods. In his discussion of how to do interdisciplinarity, Szostak (2002) emphasizes the importance of ascertaining "what theories and methods are particularly relevant to the question at hand. In the conduct of interdisciplinary work," he says, "there are complementarities such that borrowing a theory from one discipline will encourage use of its methods, study of its phenomena, and engagement with its worldview" (p. 106). As with phenomena, he cautions students not to ignore theories and methods that may shed some lesser light on the question.[8]

Understanding each theory, if only in general terms, will enable students to approach many topics with greater sophistication and depth of insight than is possible by ignoring them. Explanation of precisely how theory may actually be used in interdisciplinary work is reserved for later chapters.

To sum up, theory is important to interdisciplinary work for three reasons:

- Theory is a major component of what any discipline is. It is virtually impossible to conduct research in any discipline on any topic and not have to deal at some level with theory.
- Because theory is so fundamental to disciplinary scholarship, knowing the basics of these grand theories or schools of thought (including newer theories such as cultural analysis and new historicism) will at least enable the student to detect them when reading the disciplinary literature relevant to the topic.
- Insights are embodied in theories. Theories produce insights into a specific problem.

Method

Method is the final defining element of a discipline and its perspective. **Method** concerns how one conducts research, analyzes data or evidence, tests theories, and creates new knowledge (Rosenau, 1992, p. 116).[9] Methods are ways to obtain evidence of how some aspect of the natural or human world functions (Szostak, 2004, pp. 99–100). Each discipline tends to devote considerable attention to discussing the method(s) it uses, and it does this by requiring students majoring in the discipline to take a research methods course. The reason is simple: The methods a discipline favors correspond to the theories it embraces. Students should be aware of this linkage between disciplinary methods and theories. Though a discipline favors one method to investigate a theory, there may be other methods that would shed less favorable light on it.

Tables 4.11, 4.12, and 4.13 associate particular disciplines with particular methods. The methods associated with each discipline are not definitive and are stated in the most general terms. Any statement of disciplinary practices can be contested on the ground that it disguises the pluralistic and even conflicted view of disciplinary practice. The following descriptions are written in awareness of the possible criticisms of them. The purpose of these tables is to help students decide which research method(s) are appropriate to the problem, or topic.

There is an underlying logic to how disciplinarians proceed in producing new knowledge, and there's another overlapping but distinct logic to how interdisciplinarians proceed. All the natural sciences use the **scientific method**.[10] The method, idealized, has four steps: (1) observation and description of phenomena; (2) formulation of a hypothesis to explain the phenomena; (3) use of the hypothesis to predict the existence of other phenomena, or to predict quantitatively the result of new observations; (4) execution of properly performed experiments to test those hypotheses or predictions. The scientific method is based on beliefs in empiricism

Table 4.11   Research Methods Associated With the Natural Sciences

Discipline	Methods
Biology	The epistemological debate between the naturalist or field position versus the experimental or laboratory position is also about which methods (i.e., lab or field) produce "good science" (Maienschein, 2000, p. 134). Laboratory (i.e., experimental design and data analysis) methods extract life from its natural ecological setting and examine specimens under controlled conditions using electron microscopy and positron emission tomography (PET) to produce visual images of the structure of systems (Bechtel, 2000, p. 139). Systems ecologists and developmental biologists insist on studying life in its living, functioning, active form using "philosophical, sociological, anthropological, and cognitive explanatory schemata" (Holmes, 2000, p. 169). For biology, the scientific method must take into consideration ethical limits to experimentation.
Chemistry	One way in which the approach of chemistry differs from that of the other sciences is that it attempts to develop new materials using the foundational principles discovered and developed by chemistry, and chemistry seeks to understand the observed macroscopic properties in terms of atomic and molecular behavior (J. Rogers, personal communication, April, 2005). "Understanding the properties of a substance and the changes it undergoes leads to the central theme in chemistry: macroscopic properties and behavior, those we can see, are the results of submicroscopic properties and behavior that we cannot see" (Silberberg, 2006, p. 5).
Earth Science	Like physics and chemistry, Earth science relies on a variety of quantitative methods of displaying and analyzing data, including statistics, geographic information systems (GIS), computer modeling such as finite elements and discrete elements, X-ray diffraction and florescence, mass spectronomy, emission and absorption spectronomy, gravity and magnetic resonance, acoustic (seismic) wave propagation (reflection and refraction), remote sensing using the electromagnetic spectrum, and well logging techniques that include sonic, electrical resistivity, and neutron absorption. Increasingly, however, geologists are relying more on field work because processes taking place in Deep Time cannot be replicated (J. Wickham, personal communication, August, 2006).
Mathematics	Mathematics is totally abstracted from the empirical world, though other disciplines that are empirical apply mathematics. The worlds mathematicians create are rational simply because rationality is a requirement mathematicians impose on themselves. Mathematics uses proven theorems about the properties (e.g., consistency, transitivity, completeness) of the abstract realities they create.
Physics	Like chemistry, physics takes objects apart to study their constituent parts (atoms and subatomic particles, quanta) to see how they are related; but unlike chemistry, it also studies overall characteristics such as mass, velocity, conductivity, and heat of evaporation. The methods of physics are split into theoretical and experimental. "Theoretical" physicists solve problems using mathematical modeling rather than experimentation. Experimental physicists use experiments and computers to measure and quantify objects and phenomena and to test and verify or falsify the theories produced by the theoretical physicists (Donald, 2002, pp. 32–33). In physics, the hypothesis often takes the form of a causal mechanism or a mathematical relation.

(whether the observation is direct or indirect), quantifiability (including precision in measurement),[11] replicability/reproducibility, and free exchange of information (so that others can test or attempt to replicate/reproduce). The term "scientific method" has celebrated quite different methods at different points in time. There is no one "scientific method" but a dozen legitimate scientific methods that emphasize carefully stating and testing hypotheses. But it has predominantly followed (with some notable and relatively recent exceptions such as ecology) the strategy of **reductionism**. This is an approach to understand the whole of something by examining its parts.

The scientific method assumes that there is a single explanation of how phenomena that appear to be separate entities are intrinsically unified (Donald, 2002, p. 32). Similarly, the assumption underlying interdisciplinarity is that conflicting disciplinary insights into a complex problem are intrinsically unified by an underlying common ground theory, concept, or assumption that can be created or discovered by the student. This assumption is unlike the assumption underlying the scientific method, however, in that the resulting general "law" is applicable to all similar phenomena, whereas the resulting interdisciplinary understanding is "local" and limited to the problem at hand.

Not all the sciences use the scientific method in the same way. The physical sciences, such as physics and chemistry, use experimental forms of the method involving experiments to gather numerical data from which relationships are identified and conclusions are drawn. The more descriptive social sciences, such as anthropology, may use a form of the method that involves gathering information by making visual observations or interviewing. Among the differences between the sciences that are addressed in Table 4.11 are what each discipline considers data and how each gathers and processes data. For example, chemistry's approach to research is quite similar to that of the other physical sciences, such as physics and Earth science, in that it seeks to measure and describe observed phenomena. But unlike Earth science, it relies first and foremost on lab experiments.

The social sciences use modernist scientific techniques, such as mathematical models and statistical analysis of empirical data, in conducting much of their research. But this approach to methodology has lost force largely because of developments in the philosophy of science that have long since moved beyond methodological monism. It is in methodology that postmodernism is having it greatest impact on the social sciences and the humanities by "deflating the confidence previously held in the capacity to identify best practice" (Dow, 2001, p. 66). Today, says H. Russell Bernard (2002), "the differences *within* anthropology and sociology with regard to methods are more important than the differences *between* those disciplines" (p. 3). Consequently, the description of methods in Tables 4.12 and 4.13 reflects both modernist and postmodernist approaches.

Table 4.12   Research Methods Associated With the Social Sciences

Discipline	Methods
Anthropology	Anthropology uses a wide variety of scientific and interpretive techniques to reconstruct the past including experiments, sampling, cultural immersion, field work, interviewing (unstructured and semistructured), structured interviewing (questionnaires and cultural domain analysis), scales and scaling, participant observation, field notes, direct and indirect observation, thick description, analysis of human interaction, language, archaeology, and biology (Bernard, 2002).
Economics	Modernist methods include data analysis involving regression analysis, Monte Carlo simulations, plugging the data into systems of large numbers of simultaneous equations, etc. What is distinctive about most economic data sets is that they are generated for other purposes (e.g., governmental policy) and often do not directly measure the variables of interest to economists, so economists end up working with inferential indicators more than direct measurements. Mainstream economics, however, is experiencing some degree of methodological fragmentation by postmodernists who oppose the reduction of human behavior and motives to a single purpose: individual gain. Concluding that "an overarching methodology is rendered impossible by the fragmented nature of discourse-based knowledge," postmodernism denies the role of methodology altogether. Recently, a corrective "synthetic" approach has adopted a pluralistic approach to methodology, holding that the methodology of each economic school of thought should be analyzed critically on its own terms (Dow, 2001, pp. 66–67).
Political Science	Political science does not have a single big methodological device all its own, the way that many disciplines do. Rather, "political science as a discipline is defined by its substantive concerns, by its fixation on 'politics' in all its myriad forms" (Goodin & Klingerman, 1996, p. 7). More specifically, practitioners describe legal governments, examine ideas, normative doctrines, and proposals for social action (Hyneman, 1959, p. 28). Political scientists rely heavily on mathematical modeling and statistical testing. A method distinctive to political science is polling data on voter behavior. Like other social sciences, political science believes that "research should be theory oriented and theory directed," and that "findings [should be] based upon quantifiable data (Somit & Tanenhaus, 1967, p. 178).
Psychology	Psychology and its many subfields use the scientific method. Within this method there are many approaches to gaining knowledge, and some of these are more demanding than others. The continuum of demands on the adequacy of information is called "levels of constraint" that focus on precision, structure, and control of the various phases of the research project. These levels of constraint include (from least to most demanding) naturalistic observation, case study research, correlational research, differential research, and experimental research (Graziano & Raulin, 2004, pp. 48–51). There are two primary types of research: basic research to understand psychological processes and the primary goal of which is to increase knowledge, and applied research to find solutions for certain problems such as employee morale. Other applied researchers conduct evaluation research to assess the effects of social or institutional programs on behavior (Leary, 2004, p. 4).

(Continued)

Table 4.12 (Continued)

Discipline	Methods
Sociology	The intellectual labor of sociology, not unlike other disciplines, is divided among theorists, methodologists, and researchers. The effect of this cognitive separation in sociology is "that theorists do not deal with the relationship of theory to evidence" and, thus, to method (Alford, 1998, pp. 11–12). Methodologists are usually divided into quantitative and qualitative specialties. "Quants" are further divided between applied and theoretical statisticians. "Quals" are divided into ethnomethodologists, symbolic interactionists, grounded theorists, historical methodologists, and ethnographers, each having its own specialized terminology and research techniques. Researchers analyze the substantive problems defined as part of the discipline's subfields of social stratification, political sociology, the family, education, and the sociology of organizations (pp. 1, 11). Though sociology has been long dominated by modernist approaches to research, this is being seriously challenged by methodologies inspired by the humanities that are qualitative (i.e., meaning-based), constructionist, interpretative, narrative, and contextualized (situated in power, race, and gender). Qualitative research methods do not rely heavily on mathematical and statistical analysis but "study people in their natural setting and attempt to make sense of phenomena in terms of the meanings that people bring to them" (Dorsten & Hotchkiss, 2005, p. 147).

Students draw on fields of scholarship in which different beliefs hold. Table 4.13 shows that the humanities rarely insist on quantifying observations. Part of the challenge of interdisciplinary integration is reducing conflict in insights drawn from disciplines and theories so that common ground can be created or discovered. Common ground makes integration of conflicting insights possible, and once achieved, enables the development of an interdisciplinary understanding. Science leaves the integration of knowledge out of the scientific method altogether, while interdisciplinary studies focuses on it. The scholarly enterprise needs both specialized and integrative research.

The correlation between theory and method noted earlier is shown in Table 4.14 to contrast the methods used by the widely divergent theories of positivism, interpretivism, and postmodernism. Interpretivists assume that there are significant differences among individuals in how they perceive the same phenomenon. Postmodernists, by contrast, argue that using any methodology is rendered impossible by the fragmented nature of discourse-based knowledge (Dow, 2001, p. 66). The methods associated with each theory are not definitive and are stated in the most general terms. The purpose of this table is to aid students in linking methods to these theories.

Interdisciplinary studies students should be interested in research methods because they have to decide when and whether to use quantitative or qualitative methods, or both. Though the furor over this difference is dying down, disciplinary researchers remain deeply divided about which approach is

Table 4.13   Research Methods Associated With the Humanities

Discipline	Methods
Art and Art History	Modernist art historians examine art objects in terms of the artists' mastery of appropriate technique, their structure and meaning within particular historical, political, psychological, or cultural contexts. Formalist analysis of a work of art, for example, considers primarily the aesthetic effects created by the component parts of the design, while iconography studies focuses on content rather than form. Two methodological reactions against formalism are Marxism, which studies the economic and social context of art, and feminism, which is predicated on the idea that gender is an essential component to understanding art. Biographical and autobiographical methods rely on texts (if they exist) and approach works of art in relation to the artist's life and personality. Semiotics, a recent methodological approach derived from linguistics, philosophy of language, and literary criticism, assumes that cultures and cultural expressions such as language, art, music, and film are composed of "signs" and that each sign has a meaning beyond, and only beyond, its literal self (Bal & Bryson, 1991, p. 174). Other approaches include deconstruction, which assigns meaning according to contexts which themselves are continually in flux, and the complex psychoanalytic method that deals primarily with unconscious significance of works of art (Adams, 1996). Postmodern critics, who see the artist as deeply implicated in society, "reject formal analysis and tend to discuss artworks not as beautiful objects produced by unique sensibilities but as works that exemplify society's culture, especially its politics" (Barnet, 2008, p. 260).
History	Historians engage in research that involves identification of primary source material from the past in the form of documents, records, letters, interviews, oral history, archaeology, etc., or secondary sources. They also practice critical analysis involving interpretation of historical documents and forming these into a picture of past events or the quality of human life within a particular time and place. To write good history, historians need a combination of well-reasoned arguments based on solid evidence combined with objectivity and interpretive scrutiny. In the twentieth century, the narrative, event-oriented history characteristic of nineteenth-century professional historiography gave way to "various kinds of social science-oriented history spanning the methodological and ideological spectrum from quantitative sociological and economic approaches and the structuralism of the Annales School to Marxist class analysis" (Iggers, 1997, p. 3). As applied to history, postmodernists question whether there are objects of historical research accessible to clearly defined methods of inquiry, asserting that every historical work is a literary work because historical narratives are verbal fictions, the contents of which are more invented than found (pp. 8–10).
Literature (English)	Research methods emphasize the centrality of texts and include auto/biographical, oral history, critical discourse analysis (i.e., analyzing patterns in language) for exploring visual signs (e.g., illuminations of manuscripts, graphic novels, photographs), computer-aided discourse analysis, ethnography (concerns cultural and social practices), quantitative analysis (i.e., how numbers are used as interpretive tools and as a means of calculating

(Continued)

Table 4.13 (Continued)

Discipline	Methods
	the frequency with which certain words occur and the contexts in which they are set), textual analysis that sees meaning-making as a relational process (which relies on other research methods such as feminist and deconstructionist ones), interviewing living authors, and creative writing (which must be accompanied by a theoretical piece of writing) (Griffin, 2005, pp. 1–14). Literary theories are also approaches to literature and include New Criticism (that insists on the preeminence of the text itself and its literary properties), psychoanalytic criticism, reader-response criticism, structuralism, deconstructionist criticism, Marxist criticism, feminist criticism, Bakhtinian criticism, Foucaultian criticism, and multicultural criticism that attends to cultural perspectives such as African American or postcolonial (Bressler, 2003).
Music and Music Education	Music education research is multimethod. Positivist scholars use expertise (i.e., mastery of techniques involved in the production of works of art) and criticism (i.e., interpretation of compositions in terms of their aesthetic qualities, techniques employed, and their meaning within specific historical, political, psychological, or cultural contexts). However, the basic trend in music education research methods is on interpretivist forms of inquiry (i.e., phenomenology, action research, ethnography, narrative inquiry that focuses on human actions, beliefs, values, motivations, and attitudes), critical theory (that stresses that teaching and learning are deeply related to social practices and injustices), feminist or gender studies (that argues that gender issues are implicit in all research methods and interpretations, though most in the field reject the idea of a distinctly feminist research methodology), and postmodernism (that rejects the idea of "methods" altogether and holds that there are no rules of procedure that must be followed and no "right" procedures of investigation, though it does embrace introspection, individualized interpretation, and deconstruction) (Elliott, 2002, pp. 85–96).
Philosophy	The method of philosophy is the making and the questioning of distinctions (a distinction is a difference displayed). Philosophy explains by distinguishing between concepts, as, for example, how responsible action is to be distinguished from the nonresponsible (Sokolowski, 1998, p. 1). Philosophers use a variety of techniques to examine a written composition including dialectic, syllogism and logic, contemplation, linguistic/symbolic analysis, argument and debate, and also thought experiments.
Religious Studies	Today, there is no real distinction between the methods of science (natural and social) and those of the academic study of religion. Scholars of religion employ a variety of research and analytical methods that cut across disciplinary lines when examining religious phenomena, religious actions, religious groups, and religious ideas. The methods used by researchers are largely dictated by the questions they ask and the issues they seek to explore. The common ground among scholars of religion is their efforts to describe and explain religious phenomena as an aspect of human culture and experience and do this by engaging in self-reflection, self-criticism, self-censorship, and self-control (Stone, 1998, pp. 6–8).

Table 4.14   Positivism, Interpretivism, and Postmodernism: Their Methods Contrasted

Theory	Methods
Positivism	1. Scholars should study only that which is observable, such as actions, and not attitudes. 2. People should be studied independent of their natural environment. 3. Quantification of evidence is essential.
Interpretivism	1. Since humans are intentional and self-reflective, scholars should study attitudes over actions. 2. Scholars should study people in their natural environment, seeking to understand rather than to explain. 3. Qualitative analysis is emphasized over quantitative analysis.
Postmodernism	1. It denies both the prescriptive and descriptive role of methodology because methodology requires some regularity in techniques for acquiring knowledge (Dow, 2001, p. 66).

SOURCE: Based on Szostak (2004), pp. 62–65, 105.

preferable. Students should be open to both approaches. The **quantitative approach,** such as the number of molecules and the size of the ozone layer, emphasizes that evidence can be expressed numerically over a specified time frame. The **qualitative approach** focuses on evidence that cannot easily be quantified, such as cultural mannerisms and personal impressions of a musical composition. In reality, the quantitative/qualitative distinction is becoming increasingly blurred. For example, theories in natural science that focus on nonintentional agents—such as the germ theory of disease or cell theory—are inherently qualitative. Interpretivists often quantify by using words such as "most" rather than percentages (Szostak, 2004, p. 111).

Students should be interested in methods for the additional reason that they must make decisions about particular ones to use. Just as students must have at least a general knowledge of the theories informing the disciplines relevant to the problem, so, too, must students have a working knowledge of the methods used by these same disciplines. Interdisciplinary programs whose courses cross only a few disciplinary boundaries emphasize, naturally, only a few methods. Interdisciplinary programs or courses that take interdisciplinarity itself as a focus tend toward a much broader coverage of methods, though this coverage is far from exhaustive. The latter kind of program clearly demands that one read widely in the disciplinary literature to develop at least a general understanding of all the standard methods. Fortunately, the number of these is relatively small. Table 4.15 links commonly used quantitative and qualitative methods with the positivist, interpretivist, and postmodern approaches.

The description and strengths and weaknesses of each method is reserved for Chapter 8.

Table 4.15   Method Types Linked to Grand Theories and Their Approaches

Grand Theory	Approach	Method Typologies
Positivism	Quantitative	Experiments
		Surveys
		Statistical Analysis
		Mathematical Modeling
		Classification
Interpretivism	Qualitative	Participant Observation
		Interviews
		Case Studies
		Hermeneutics
		Intuition/Experience
Postmodernism		Discourse Analysis

CHAPTER SUMMARY

This chapter and Chapter 3 provide information that is foundational to inter-disciplinary theory and practice in two ways. First, they explain the role of the disciplines and clarify the definition of disciplinary perspective to mean a disci-pline's characteristic view of reality *and* its defining elements: phenomena, assumptions, epistemology, theory, and method. This broadening of the term's meaning is consistent with the widely accepted definition of interdisciplinary studies. Second, these chapters provide the student with two ways of beginning interdisciplinary inquiry. The one is the traditional perspectival approach that involves linking the problem to those disciplines whose perspectives embrace it. The other is Szostak's classification approach that involves linking the topic to the appropriate phenomena. The virtue of this latter approach is that it enables researchers to identify more readily neighboring phenomena that may other-wise be overlooked but may well be relevant to the problem. Students, then, can broaden their investigation without focusing, at least initially, on particular dis-ciplines. Students can profitably use both approaches to delve deeply into the scholarship on the problem, thus countering the occasional criticism that inter-disciplinary studies is shallow and lacks rigor. Using both approaches shows that interdisciplinary analysis can be systematic and cumulative.

NOTES

1. Members of various disciplines will likely find the descriptions of their respec-tive disciplines not comprehensive enough. But experience using these descriptions in interdisciplinary classrooms validates their intended purpose: to point the student to

those disciplines that are *potentially* relevant to the problem. Once these are identified, the student should then consult each discipline's research aids, many of which are cited in tables in this chapter. These include handbooks, companions, journals, and bibliographies to validate the relevance of each discipline to the problem.

2. R. N. Giere (1999) calls this philosophical approach "naturalistic realism" and states that it is closest to the actual mind-set that most scientists take.

3. For example, Alan Bryman (2004) states, "There is no agreement on the epistemological basis of the natural sciences" (p. 439). Competing epistemological values in biology, for example, are fueling the debate over how much can be learned in the laboratory versus how much can be learned in the field—in other words, what constitutes "good science"? Admittedly, there is overlap between assumptions, epistemology, and preferred method in Tables 4.6, 4.7, and 4.8.

4. Empiricism has come under fire from postmodernists, particularly from feminist philosophers of science who identify a role for value judgments in science and advocate tolerance and willingness to encourage a variety of approaches and multiple judgments of significance to the same scientific problem (Rosenberg, 2000, p. 183).

5. For a more complete discussion of postmodernism, see Chris Baldick (2004), pp. 201–202.

6. Transdisciplinarity operates like a grand theory in that it seeks unity of knowledge through a single overarching epistemology. According to Newell (2000), "transdisciplinarity has not advanced beyond theoretical appeal, while interdisciplinarity has gained widespread usage" because it "is largely pragmatic" (pp. 42–43).

7. Mieke Bal (2002) argues that concepts constitute interdisciplinary method in the humanities and that their use is inclusive of social science methodology (p. 5).

8. Polkinghorne (1996) says that philosophers of science, if not practicing scientists, now accept that scientific methods can neither prove nor disprove any theory (nor even any narrow hypothesis). Nevertheless, the application of scientific methods to theories provides scientists with invaluable, if imperfect, evidence with which they can judge whether a theory is in accord with reality (pp. 18–19).

9. Szostak (2004), in *Classifying Science: Phenomena, Data, Theory, Method, Practice,* is careful to distinguish between methods "from techniques or tools, such as experimental design or instrumentation, or particular statistical packages" (p. 100). Tools and techniques and so on are a subset of methods. His chapter on "Classifying Methods" is indispensable reading for students.

10. Alexander Taffel (1992) states, "The combination of activities in which scientists engage to achieve the understanding they seek is sometimes called the *scientific method.* There is however no single method of science, but rather a variety of activities in which scientists use different combinations of these to solve difficult problems. Scientific activities include recognizing and defining problems, observing, measuring, experimenting, making hypotheses and theories, and communicating with other scientists" (p. 5).

11. Modern science relies heavily on statistical methods in the testing of hypotheses (Rosenberg, 2000, p. 112). Taper and Lele (2004) discuss the two schools of statistical thought, frequentist and Bayesian, and how these approaches impact quantitative statements. "There cannot be such a thing as quantification of support for a single hypothesis," they argue. Scientific evidence "is necessarily comparative," meaning that "one needs to specify two hypotheses to compare, and data may support one hypothesis more than the other" (p. 527).

REVIEW QUESTIONS

1. What are the characteristics of academic disciplines?

2. How may Szostak's "Classification of Phenomena" table help the student to determine which disciplines are relevant to the following problems: the problem of greenhouse gas emissions from coal-fired generators, the problem of how to pay for national health insurance, and the question of when life should end?

3. How may Szostak's "Categories of Phenomena About the Human World" help students identify subphenomena that may pertain to the problem of fresh water scarcity in Texas?

4. How can assumptions play an important role in the process of creating common ground among conflicting insights?

5. What are three reasons that interdisciplinary students should be interested in the epistemologies of disciplines?

6. What are some limitations of modern and postmodern epistemologies?

7. How is a narrow range (i.e., disciplinary) theory different from a grand theory or grand narrative or school of thought?

8. How are concepts related to theory (whether it is a disciplinary theory or a school of thought)?

9. What is the importance of schools of thought to interdisciplinary work?

10. How is the assumption underlying the scientific method similar to and unlike the assumption underlying the interdisciplinary approach?

11. How do the research methods associated with the humanities differ from those used in the social sciences and the natural sciences?

12. How do the methods used by positivism, interpretivism, and postmodernism contrast with each other?

13. Explain why interdisciplinary students should be interested in disciplinary research methods.

5 Explaining the Importance of Integration

In 2000, an interdisciplinary team of cognitive psychologists, curriculum specialists, teacher educators, and researchers updated Bloom's classic taxonomy of levels of intellectual behavior that are important in learning. They identified six levels within the cognitive domain, from the simple recognition or recall of facts at the lowest level through increasingly more complex and abstract mental levels, leading ultimately to the highest order ability, creating, shown in Figure 5.1.

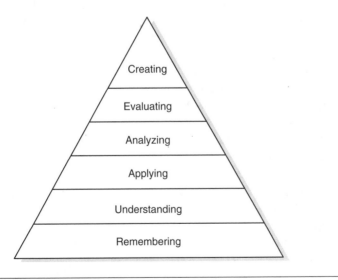

Figure 5.1   The Updated Bloom's Taxonomy

SOURCE: Anderson et al. (2000).

NOTE: One of the features of the Anderson et al. (2000) taxonomy that differentiates it from Bloom's 1956 taxonomy is that it reverses the order of evaluation and synthesis or integration, placing "creating," which involves integration, at the highest level of cognitive activity. For a comparison of Bloom's taxonomy with Anderson et al.'s revision of it, see the useful discussion by Leslie Owen at www.uwsp.edu/education/lwilson/curric/newtaxonomy.htm.

The significance of this taxonomy for interdisciplinary research is that it elevates the cognitive abilities of creating and integrating to the highest level of knowledge. Creating involves putting elements together—integrating them—to produce something that is new, coherent, and a functional whole. The focus of this chapter is on integration: what it is, its importance to interdisciplinary inquiry, the prerequisites for integration, and the product of integration. Integration is central to understanding the nature of interdisciplinary studies and is its distinguishing feature. Integration is also at the heart of the interdisciplinary research process.

What Integration Is

Interdisciplinarians substantially agree on the centrality of integration to interdisciplinarity and the interdisciplinary research process, and they are moving toward consensus about what integration should encompass.[1] Though achieving integration is not easy, it is possible, even for those new to the field.

Toward a Definition of Integration *or* Synthesis and Its Critical Elements

The verb *integrate* means "to unite or blend into a functioning whole." **Interdisciplinary integration**, then, is the activity of critically evaluating and creatively combining ideas and knowledge to form a new whole or cognitive advancement. A synonym of integration is the noun **synthesis**. Klein (1996) states, "synthesis connotes creation of an interdisciplinary outcome through a series of *integrative actions*" (p. 212, italics added). What these "integrative actions" or steps involve is the subject of Chapters 10–12.

Several traits attend the terms *integration* and *synthesis*:

- They are synonyms.
- They convey the meaning of activity leading toward a certain result.
- Central to the integrative process is critically evaluating and analyzing.
- The nature of the activity or process is combining or uniting.
- What is combined or united are ideas, data, and knowledge. (Since the ideas and knowledge take the form of insights into a specific problem, the combining, uniting, and integrating of these insights is valid only for that context. This topic is explored in later chapters.)
- The object of this activity is the creative formation of something new and greater than the sum of its individual parts—a new whole.
- The distinctive characteristics of the new whole are that it is more comprehensive and is a cognitive advancement. (The complexity of the object of interdisciplinary scrutiny implies that the "whole" achieved via integration only partially coheres and has only quasi-stability and quasi-predictability.)

Because the terms *integration* and *synthesis* are so close in meaning, many practitioners use them interchangeably. This book uses the term *integration* because it appears in the prominent definitions of interdisciplinary studies noted in Chapter 1. To be complete, the definition of integration must reference three critical elements: the nature of the "new whole," the cognitive activity involved in integration, and the contribution of the disciplines to its formation.

The Nature of the "New Whole"

The **new whole** that the activity of integration produces is greater than the sum of its constituent parts. The "constituent" or essential "parts" are those individual disciplinary insights into a particular problem or object. Though separate, they relate directly to the problem or question.

Interdisciplinarians have not always been clear about integration. Newell (1990), for example, relates how he used to think of integration as analogous to completing a jigsaw puzzle (p. 74). For a time, this analogy was commonly used. However, comparing the product of integration to a completed jigsaw puzzle is problematic in several critical respects. For one thing, the pieces of a jigsaw puzzle are finely milled to fit together as tightly as possible. This is not so with disciplinary insights. Disciplinary insights pertaining to a particular problem or object fit to varying degrees. The problem of fit is minimized in the natural sciences where fit is achieved merely by reconciling alternative conceptualizations of the same phenomenon. For example, when addressing the energy crisis, physics may focus on how a power plant works (i.e., the alternative formulations of thermodynamics) and chemistry on how energy is released from chemical bonds in coal. The insights may be fully complementary but require using the integrative technique of redefinition (see Chapter 11), perhaps to address differences in scale (Newell & Green, 1982, pp. 25–26). When an issue connects the natural sciences to the humanities or social sciences, however, as in the embryonic stem cell research controversy, insights become less complementary, so the problem of fit becomes more challenging (Kelly, 1996, p. 95).

The reason why fit is so challenging when investigating a problem such as human cloning that spans the natural sciences, the social sciences, and the humanities is that there are deep epistemological fissures between these disciplinary categories. Although the sciences are "geared up to tell us what the facts are," says James S. Kelly (1996), science does not ascribe value or morality to these facts. "The only recognized epistemological powers operative in the scientific realm are those of the five senses. And we do not (literally) see, hear, smell, touch, or taste wrongness or rightness." Kelly calls this understanding of interdisciplinarity "narrow" (not to be confused with the earlier definition **narrow interdisciplinarity**) because it focuses on factual situations and structures in need of modification, not on the rightness or wrongness of the activity, which is the realm of the humanities. This conception of interdisciplinarity would, therefore, focus on cloning techniques, not on the rightness or wrongness of cloning. Instead, Kelly argues for practicing a **"wide interdisciplinarity,"** which enables interdisciplinary practitioners from the sciences and the humanities to work together to identify, solve, or resolve normative problems, both practical and theoretical, having to do with the satisfaction of human needs (p. 96). This book embraces Kelly's wide interdisciplinary approach.

Second, the jigsaw puzzle and its pieces are designed according to a predetermined pattern or picture that appears on the cover of the puzzle box. With disciplinary insights, however, there is no predetermined pattern that the student can consult to see if the "new whole" or new understanding or new meaning or cognitive advancement is consistent with it and if one is "getting it right." In fact, working with disciplinary insights is comparable to working with puzzle pieces from different puzzles mixed together with no picture for guidance. The absence of pattern is particularly challenging when working in the social sciences and the humanities where insights from different disciplines tend to conflict more sharply. For example, in examining the meaning of the Temple Mount in Jerusalem to Judaism, Christianity, and Islam, religious studies scholars may focus on the sanctity of the Mount based on the sacred writings of these faith traditions, whereas political scientists may focus on the political benefits and symbolism of physical control of the site. Because the disciplinary insights conflict, they make the task of discovering the common ground theory, concept, or assumption difficult, though not impossible. Once common ground is created or discovered and the new understanding achieved, the student can see whether the new understanding is consistent with or can accommodate the conflicting disciplinary insights.

Third, the jigsaw puzzle pieces, when assembled, form a picture that is not new because it existed before the pieces were assembled. However, when disciplinary insights are integrated, they generally form something that is truly new—a new understanding, a new meaning, or a new solution. When a disciplinary expert produces an insight into a problem and the insight appears as a book aimed at a disciplinary audience or as an article published in a peer-reviewed journal, the insight is considered new, complete, and authoritative in the view of the discipline. It is not perceived as missing some piece from another discipline.

From an interdisciplinary standpoint, however, the same insight is only partial and only one of many possible explanations of the problem or interpretation of the object, especially if other disciplines have produced insights into the problem. In fact, students should view the integrated result, though new, as only partial. In her study of interdisciplinary cognition, Svetlana Nikitina (2005) argues for the notion of "provisional integration" and for researchers to critically question the interdisciplinary understanding (p. 390). This is sound scholarly advice.

This understanding—i.e., interdisciplinary insight or **integrated insight**—is "new" because it is the result of the integrative process and encompasses the conflicting disciplinary insights. It is truly new because it did not exist prior to the integration of the separate disciplinary insights. It is new also because it is not merely a reassemblage of the separate disciplinary insights or a juxtaposition of them in a multidisciplinary fashion.

Janet Delph's (2005) student essay, "An Integrative Approach to the Elimination of the 'Perfect Crime,'" provides one example of how an interdisciplinary understanding is new compared to any of its contributing disciplinary insights. Delph mined insights from criminal justice, forensics, and psychology. Insights from criminal justice emphasize the necessity of protecting, searching, and documenting a crime scene so as not to compromise the investigation and infringe on suspects' constitutional rights. Insights from forensic science or "criminalistics" emphasize how scientific findings (DNA, drugs, etc.) are interpreted by law, whereas insights from forensic psychology focus on gathering information on the behavior, personality, and physical attributes of the offender. Her new understanding is that criminal profiling would greatly benefit from combining the investigatory and profiling methods of all three approaches in order to increase understanding by law enforcement officials about what each branch needs to solve the crime.

Fourth, the puzzle picture before it was cut up encompassed a predetermined area expressed in square inches or centimeters. When the pieces are fitted together, the completed puzzle is not larger (or smaller) than the sum of its pieces. By contrast, the new whole created by the activity of integration is larger than its constituent parts (i.e., insights), not in spatial terms but in cognitive terms. Delph's (2005) interdisciplinary understanding or integrated insight is larger than its constituent parts because it involves a new approach to criminal investigation that is inclusive of all three major disciplinary approaches.

This example shows that the interdisciplinary understanding is more comprehensive than what could be achieved by merely gathering up individual specialty insights and using them to view the problem from a series of disciplinary perspectives the way multidisciplinarity does. The new whole is larger than its constituent parts because it cannot be reduced to the separate disciplinary insights from which it emerged (Newell, 1990, p. 74). The interdisciplinary understanding is likewise new in that nothing relevant has been excluded. Disciplinarity tends to exclude, whereas interdisciplinarity strives for inclusion. The new humanities field of cultural analysis, for example, uses integrative interdisciplinary analysis of objects from everyday culture, the very "rejects" of the conventional disciplines (Bal, 1996, p. 11).

The defining characteristics of the new whole created by the integrative interdisciplinary process, then, are these:

- It is formed from disciplinary and specialty insights that do not fit together naturally or easily, though they may be somewhat complementary.
- It is created without benefit of a preexisting integrative pattern (though a recognized approach is used).

- It has never existed before and has characteristics that differ from any of those of the specialty insights.
- It is inclusive of relevant information, and in this sense it is integrative (since complexity reduction is inevitably part of the process).

The Cognitive Activity Involved in Integration

At least two cognitive activities are involved in integrative activity: perspective taking and holistic thinking.

Perspective Taking

Perspective taking involves viewing some problem, object, or phenomenon from a particular dimension or viewpoint other than one's own. As applied to interdisciplinary work, perspective taking involves examining a problem from the standpoint of interested disciplines (in serial fashion) and identifying the differences between them. Hursh et al. (1983) illustrate this type of perspective taking through a simple analogy where items of fruit are compared to disciplines:

> If four pieces of fruit—an apple, an orange, a pear, and a peach—are placed on a table, specialists in each of those varieties may readily describe their differences. Their very existence as separate entities invites discrimination, given the predilections of Western thought toward specialization and analysis. (p. 47)

If, however, these four pieces of fruit are placed tightly together in a basket, the specialists must shift their perspectives to recognize that a new entity is created: a fruit basket. This is a higher order construction, fitting into one construct the common attributes of the four entities. The sheer existence of the basket creates order—or unity—out of four disparate yet related items (Hursh et al., 1983, p. 47). Hursh et al.'s attempt to represent interdisciplinary integration of insights with the fruit basket analogy, however, fails to depict what integration produces because the fruit, though situated compactly in the basket, retain their separate identities. Nissani's (1995) metaphor of the smoothie, noted in Chapter 1, comes closest to depicting the disciplinary insights once integrated because the parts (i.e., individual fruit) are indistinguishable from the whole (i.e., the smoothie). The actual process by which integration takes place is explained as Step 9 in Chapter 12.

Another type of perspective taking is **role taking**, which is used by interdisciplinary research teams. This is the act of adopting a set of perspectives associated with a person, a culture, or even an animal.[2] The literature from social psychology and its research on role taking offers insights that are applicable to interdisciplinarity. The first is that people's judgments are biased in the direction of their own knowledge. This was one of the important findings of a series of studies conducted by Susan G. Fussell of Carnegie Mellon University's Human-Computer Interaction Institute and Robert Kraus of Columbia University. Their studies found that judges are prone to "false consensus bias," meaning that they assume that others are more similar to themselves than they actually are (Fussell & Kraus, 1991, 1992). The implication of Fussell and Kraus's research for students involved in interdisciplinary teamwork and solo research is that they need to be aware of their own biases, including disciplinary biases, so that these do not color (consciously or unconsciously) the integrative outcome.

Other insights on perspective taking come from research on leader-member exchange (LMX) theory, an approach to understanding leader-member relationships in the workplace (Martin, Thomas, Charles, Epitropaki, & McNamara, 2005, p. 141). Central to this theory are the three role-taking aspects of perspective taking. Each of these aspects is pertinent to interdisciplinary integration. The first role-taking aspect is that role-takers must accurately perceive how others see and understand the world. This finding of the Society for Industrial and Organization Psychology (1998) echoes the research by Fussell and Kraus on "false consensus bias." Students, whether as solo researchers or members of a research team, need to see themselves as role-takers. To integrate differing insights, students must consciously assume in turn the role, if only briefly, of a disciplinarian researching in each of the disciplines relevant to the problem.

LMX theory also calls for role-takers to have "large role-taking ranges." This simply means that role-takers should be able to view a situation from many perspectives (Martin et al., 2005, p. 141). The implications for integrative work are obvious: Students must not limit their inquiries to only those disciplines with which they are familiar or to those insights with which they agree.

A third role-taking aspect is that role-takers "should be able to perceive the other's perspective in depth and have a full understanding of the other's perspective" (Martin et al., 1995, p. 141). In interdisciplinary work, achieving depth of understanding sufficient for full understanding of another's (i.e., discipline's) perspective is called developing adequacy in the discipline, the focus of Chapter 8.

The key points of perspective taking as it pertains to interdisciplinary integration are as follows:

- Students must reflect on their biases, disciplinary as well as personal.
- Students must assume the role of disciplinarian, though briefly, as they mine each discipline for insights into the problem.
- Students must not limit their inquiries to only those disciplines with which they are familiar or to those insights and theories with which they agree.

Holistic Thinking

The second cognitive ability required for integrative work is holistic thinking, a skill characteristic of interdisciplinarians noted in Chapter 2 and discussed more fully here. This is the ability to understand how ideas and information from relevant disciplines relate to each other and to the problem (Bailis, 2002, pp. 4–5). Holistic thinking differs from perspective taking in this important respect: Whereas perspective taking (the subject of Chapter 3) is the ability to understand how each discipline would typically view the problem, holistic thinking is the ability to see the problem in terms of its constituent disciplinary parts (i.e., its defining elements identified in Chapter 4). In holistic thinking, the focus is on the relationships of parts to the whole and on the differences and similarities between these parts. The object of holistic thinking is not unified knowledge and a unitary concept of the world; that is the goal of transdisciplinarity. The object of holistic thinking is to view the problem in the broadest possible context rather than under controlled or restrictive conditions favored by disciplinary specialties. Holistic thinking sees characteristics of a problem that are not apparent when studying the problem in disciplinary isolation (p. 7). For example, a study of community art, usually seen as separate from urban economic development, may show how the community benefits socially, culturally, and economically (i.e., holistically) from various kinds of art. The goal or product of holistic thinking is a more comprehensive understanding of the problem.

The Role That the Disciplines and Interdisciplinary Fields Play

Achieving this new integrated whole involves, primarily, the disciplines but also includes interdisciplinary fields as well as schools of thought. The premise of interdisciplinary studies is that the disciplines themselves are the necessary preconditions for and foundation of interdisciplinarity. The student's task is to identify the perspective of each discipline and interdiscipline and their defining elements relevant to the problem, the subjects of Chapters 3 and 4. The process involved in achieving integration involves identifying, evaluating, and rectifying differences between disciplinary insights (Klein, 1996, p. 221).

A Definition of Interdisciplinary Integration

From the discussion of what integration is, two important ideas about integration emerge and should appear in its definition:

- The "new whole" is something larger and more complex than the sum of its constituent parts. (This statement is designed to emphasize the distinctiveness of the new whole from its constituent parts, that is, from the disciplines themselves.)

- Achieving this new whole involves combining insights and knowledge from disciplines, interdisciplines, and schools of thought.

Additionally, practitioners repeatedly refer to interdisciplinary integration as a *process* as opposed to an *activity*. This is deliberate. *Process* conveys the notion of making gradual changes that lead toward a particular (but often nonlinear) result, whereas *activity* has the more limited meaning of vigorous or energetic action not necessarily related to achieving a goal. Consequently, the earlier partial definition of interdisciplinary integration is amended as follows:

Interdisciplinary integration is the process of creatively combining ideas and knowledge from disciplinary and other sources to produce a more comprehensive understanding or cognitive advancement.

The Importance of Integration to Interdisciplinarity and the Interdisciplinary Research Process

Since interdisciplinary studies became an academic field, leading interdisciplinarians have insisted that it should be defined in terms of integration. The concept appears in one of the first attempts to define interdisciplinary studies by Newell and William J. Green in 1982 and in the more prominent definition offered by Klein and Newell in 1997 (noted in Chapter 1). Jay Wentworth and James R. Davis (2002), writing on interdisciplinary learning, stress the importance of teachers moving students "patiently toward *integration* or new conceptualization" (italics added). And as students develop the habit of interdisciplinarity, "the search for *integration* can be intensified" (pp. 17–18, italics added). Michael Seipel (2002) concurs, writing "interdisciplinary analysis requires *integration* of knowledge from the disciplines that is brought to bear on the issue, question or problem at hand" (p. 3, italics added). Boix Mansilla (2002) states, "Individuals demonstrate interdisciplinary understanding when they *integrate* knowledge and modes of thinking" (p. 9, italics added).

Increasingly, practitioners are recognizing that integration is what ultimately distinguishes genuine interdisciplinarity from multidisciplinarity. According to Donald G. Richards (1996), multidisciplinarity merely seeks to "arrange in serial fashion the separate contributions of selected disciplines to a problem or issue, without any attempt at synthesis" (p. 124). Klein (1990) is even more explicit in identifying the deficiencies of multidisciplinarity, stating that it "signifies the juxtaposition of disciplines [and] is essentially additive, *not integrative*" (p. 56, italics added). The critical failure of the multidisciplinary approach to learning, explains Richards, is that "it leaves the task of providing *integration* largely or entirely to the student without explicit guidance from the course or instructor(s). Under these circumstances the interdisciplinary relations will be lost if they are ever identified in the first place" (p. 116, italics added).

The critical importance of integration to interdisciplinary studies and the interdisciplinary research process is summarized in this important statement by Newell (1998):

> The pragmatic and epistemological value of interdisciplinary study is ultimately determined by the success of interdisciplinarians in carrying out . . . *integration*, because all save the antidisciplinarians identify that as its distinguishing feature. Theoretical clarity and agreement concerning the nature of interdisciplinarity, its outcomes, the role of the disciplines, and the nature of . . . integration would be of no avail if interdisciplinarians were unable to accomplish *integration*. The respect of disciplinarians in the academy, the demand for interdisciplinarians to assist in solving complex societal problems, the success of radical critiques, and the long-term prospects for interdisciplinary education are all dependent on the proven success of *integration*. (p. 550, italics added)

While integration is not the goal of interdisciplinary work, it is the means to attain it. The goal is to produce an interdisciplinary understanding of the problem and apply this understanding to solving the problem that prompted the inquiry.

The Prerequisites for Integration

Interdisciplinary studies requires the triangulation of depth, breadth, and integration. **Triangulation,** in an interdisciplinary sense, means achieving balance between disciplinary depth, disciplinary breadth, and interdisciplinary integration, as shown in Figure 5.2.

Interdisciplinarity requires all three, not just depth and breadth. The **depth** required for successfully engaging in the first half of the interdisciplinary research process (i.e., drawing on disciplines and their insights) is developing adequacy or sufficiency in each discipline relevant to the problem (the subject of Chapter 8). The depth required for engaging in the second half of the research process (i.e., integrating insights) involves identifying conflicts between insights and locating their sources, creating common ground, integrating insights and producing an interdisciplinary understanding of the problem, and testing the understanding.

Adequacy (the subject of Chapter 8) means that the student borrower does not claim expertise or professional command of all the disciplines used but rather acquires a *sufficient* understanding of each discipline's cognitive map and is thus able to identify the insights, concepts, theories, and methods necessary to understand a particular problem, process, or phenomenon (Klein, 2005a, p. 68). How much adequacy is required depends on what each project requires. The notions of "depth" and "rigor," says Klein (1996),

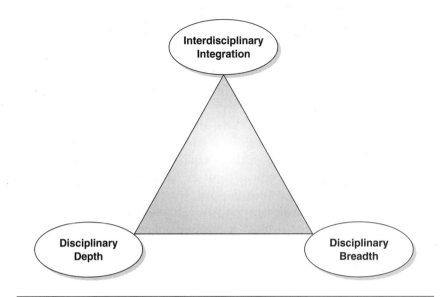

Figure 5.2   Triangulation of Disciplinary Depth and Breadth and
                   Interdisciplinary Integration

NOTE: In her discussion of the metaphor of the triangulation of "depth," "breadth," and
"synthesis," Klein (1996) uses the term "synthesis" because, as she explains, it "connotes
creation of an interdisciplinary outcome through *a series of integrative actions*" (p. 212, italics
added). Her preference for synthesis over integration in this context is understandable.
However, in my graphic that attempts to depict this metaphor, I substitute the term *integration*
because it is the term used in the definition of interdisciplinary studies that this book embraces.
See the Association of American Colleges (1991, p. 74) for an early reference to the notion of
interdisciplinary triangulation.

are usually associated with disciplinarity. However, in interdisciplinary
work, they are redefined: "Depth in interdisciplinary work derives from
competence in pertinent knowledges and approaches, [and] rigor derives
from attention to integrative process" (p. 212). Interdisciplinary **rigor**, then,
derives from attention to integrative process, the product of integration,
and the testing of that product.

Interdisciplinary **breadth** refers to interdisciplinary work that draws on
disciplines that are epistemologically distant (e.g., a natural science discipline and a humanities discipline) in contrast to narrow interdisciplinarity
that draws on disciplines that are epistemologically close (e.g., physics and
chemistry). Clearly, the burden on the interdisciplinary student is far greater
than it is for the disciplinary student.

Integration, explains Klein (1996), does not result from "simply master-
ing a body of knowledge, applying a formula, or moving in linear fashion
from point A to point B. . . . It requires active triangulation of depth,
breadth, and synthesis [i.e., integration]" (p. 212). Integration requires using
(1) disciplinary knowledge (i.e., depth and breadth), (2) integrative skills,
(3) integrative knowledge, and (4) an integrative mind-set.

Disciplinary Knowledge

Disciplinary knowledge includes (1) an understanding of the overall perspective of each relevant discipline and (2) adequacy in each discipline's defining elements that pertain to the problem. These elements and the discipline's overall perspective are generally reflected in its literature, from which insights into particular problems are drawn. The movement here is from the most general knowledge of a discipline—its overall perspective—to more specific knowledge about the discipline's defining elements, to still more specific knowledge of how each of its elements informs its insights into the problem. The movement, in short, is from understanding a discipline's overall perspective on reality, to more focused reading on the defining elements, to intensive "digging" into the discipline's scholarly literature.

Integrative Skills

The second prerequisite for conducting integration is having **integrative skills**. These include (1) familiarity with models of integration, (2) familiarity with techniques of integration, (3) self-conscious awareness of the interdisciplinary research process, and (4) critically evaluating disciplinary insights.

1. Familiarity With Models of Integration. Students should be aware of the **models of integration** because they characterize much of the interdisciplinary work occurring inside and outside the Academy today. These models are approaches to interdisciplinary work and are described in terms of their vision, theory, practice, and primary strength or weakness.[3]

Model #1: Integration as an Overarching Conceptual Framework

- *Vision:* Proponents of this transdisciplinary approach share a lofty vision that is succinctly described by Joseph J. Kockelmans (1979) as "the discovery of overarching conceptual frameworks" (p. 142). By **overarching conceptual framework** or **conceptual bridging** is meant a single concept, principle, or law that accounts for phenomena typically studied by a broad range of disciplines (Boix Mansilla, 2002, p. 18). These "overarching conceptual frameworks," Kockelmans (1979) believes, "will facilitate the unification of the sciences and eventually the solution of important problems with which the existing disciplines acting in isolation are incapable of dealing effectively" (p. 142). Creating them, however, is admittedly a formidable task even for expert researchers.[4]

- *Theory:* Regarding the theory that undergirds this transdisciplinary vision, Kockelmans further explains that those who work exclusively in the realm of the natural sciences usually have no great difficulty in discovering a common framework. "In most cases," he says, "it will consist of the basic principles and methods of physics, chemistry, or biology. On the other hand, [interdisciplinary] research projects in the social sciences, and particularly those involving both the natural and the social sciences, confront us with great theoretical and methodological problems" (1979, p. 142).

- *Practice:* In practice, this approach to interdisciplinary work is conducted most effectively by groups of scientists trained in various scientific disciplines. Cooperation among them requires that they "try to discover common ground . . . [that] could serve as a basis to deal meaningfully with all large-scale problems" (Kockelmans, 1979, p. 145).

- *Strength or weakness:* Students should be mindful of two problems with the overarching conceptual framework approach. For one thing, so much effort is consumed in theory construction that little educational or practical benefit has yet come forth. Another problem is that it seeks to eliminate tension among the disciplines and their perspectives, the very thing that drives interdisciplinary studies. An overarching theory that unifies everything (if this were possible) would remove that tension. Since reality is so complex, the very nature of complexity militates against the unity of reality, and thus knowledge of that reality.

Model #2: Integration as Comprehensive Perspective

- *Vision:* Advocates of this model have two goals in mind. The first goal is educational and seeks to balance increasing disciplinary specialization with interdisciplinarity. Barbara Hursh, a social/educational psychologist, Paul Haas, an economist, and Michael Moore, a humanist, propose developing an integrative interdisciplinary approach that stresses multiple perspectives on specific issues in order to teach skills of comparison, contrast, analysis, and, above all, synthesis (1983, p. 43). The second goal is more practical and calls for interdisciplinary studies to be pragmatic and to focus on real world problems. It is the practicality of interdisciplinary studies that is attracting growing interest in the field.

- *Theory:* This comprehensive perspective model is grounded in the theories of learning associated with John Dewey, Jean Piaget, and William Perry and emphasizes **generic skills**. These skills "include such cognitive functions as recognizing and defining problems; analyzing the structure of an argument; assessing the relationship of facts, assumptions, and conclusions; and performing **hypothetico-deductive processes**" (Hursh et al., 1983, pp. 43–44). These involve proposing hypotheses and testing their acceptability or falsity by determining whether their logical consequences are consistent with observed data.

- *Practice:* Hursh, Haas, and Moore (1983) illustrate this model by using the metaphor cited earlier of a fruit basket that creates a new entity out of four distinct entities—an apple, an orange, a peach, and a pear—and thus unity, order, and synthesis. The utility of this model is its focus on generic skills and multiple perspectives, which, they argue, are "essential in the search for solutions to such [complex] problems as energy depletion, environmental pollution, health care delivery, and urban decay, or in considering aesthetic qualities of line, color, form, and texture from the standpoint of music, art, dance, or theater" (p. 45). Their model calls for identifying interdisciplinary salient concepts such as "power," "energy," "modernization," "globalization," or "progress," which require students to examine the concept from the perspectives, assumptions, and modes of reasoning of different disciplines.

- *Strength or weakness:* The virtue of this model for many practitioners is that it calls for "a more comprehensive perspective," that is, "a larger, more holistic understanding of the question, problem, or issue at hand" (Newell, 1998, p. 547). While this is, in itself, no easy task, it is far more manageable for a single researcher in the social sciences, the humanities, or the applied fields to deal with integrating disciplinary insights than it is to construct an overarching theory that encompasses the disciplines as described in the first model. Integration as comprehensive perspective is the model that this book embraces, but with modification. For one thing, Hursh, Haas, and Moore's (1983) model is too general because it fails to address *how* integration actually occurs. Also, their model fails to identify *what* is integrated. This book stresses that the product of integration (the subject of Chapter 12)—the interdisciplinary understanding or cognitive advancement—should correspond more closely to Nissani's metaphor of the smoothie than to a basket of different fruit.

Model #3: Integration as Interpenetration

- *Vision:* **Interpenetration** is a term Steve Fuller (1993) uses to describe his model of interdisciplinary research. It calls into question the differences between the disciplines involved and calls for the "renegotiation of disciplinary boundaries" (p. 33). Supporters of this third model critique the way disciplines divide rather than connect knowledge and call for nothing less than the redefinition of disciplines in the same ways that feminism and cultural studies have already done. Jeffrey M. Peck (1989), who takes a postmodern deconstructionist view of boundaries, argues that disciplinary boundaries should not be dissolved but continually crossed, enabling alternative knowledge structures and new inquiries to emerge (as cited in Klein, 1996, p. 7). What Peck (1989) and others have in mind is that these multiple border crossings between disciplines, or interpenetrations, will reveal "new emerging places where our [interdisciplinary] profession can be practiced" (pp. 179–180).

- *Theory:* This interpenetration model of interdisciplinarity is based, in part, on the ideas of cultural archeologist Michael Foucault, whose pioneering work in cultural history cut across disciplinary boundaries and revealed patterns of cultural domination and oppression. Under his influence, for example, the concept of "culture" has undergone a radical redefinition in which literary texts are products of historical, social, political, and economic environments once deemed "outside" of the text but which are now seen as shaping it (Klein, 1996, p. 152).

- *Practice:* Peck (1989) applies this model of interdisciplinary analysis to German cultural studies that, in the past, had been characterized by "a particularly German form of intellectual domination" (p. 179). Peck sees German studies as the kind of *in between space* where one can study the clash of multiple disciplinary perspectives and the variety of discourses about Germany—the literary, political, and sociological (p. 184). Peck believes the interpenetration model of cultural analysis is applicable to the study of other cultures, whether advanced or so-called primitive, and allows scholars to "uncover and 'make visible'—in Foucault's archeological sense—patterns of domination and oppression" (p. 179).

- *Strength or weakness:* The weakness of this postmodernist model is its heavy emphasis on conflict and on exposing competing and culturally imposed disciplinary vocabularies struggling for power. Identifying disciplinary insights, critically evaluating them, and identifying the sources of conflicts is certainly part of the integrative process. As important as these steps are, they are but preparatory to further steps that include creating or discovering common ground, integrating insights, and producing a more comprehensive understanding or new meaning.

What These Models Agree on

Though marked by sharp differences, all three of these models of interdisciplinary integration agree on three important points:

- The integrative activity should be limited to the specific problem or question at hand. This means, in practical terms, that the integration produced cannot necessarily be used as a template to solve other similar problems. The ideas and knowledge take the form of insights into the specific problem, and their integration is valid only for that specific context.
- The problems selected for investigation should be clearly beyond the ability of any one discipline to address comprehensively or resolve.
- The disciplines, interdisciplines, and professional fields are essential for the conduct of interdisciplinary work.

Two Fundamental Questions Raised by These Models Concerning the Nature of Interdisciplinary Integration

- *Question #1: What does integration change?* Does integration change only the contribution of each discipline, or are the disciplines themselves somehow changed? The answer is that depending on which model is used, integration can change both and is, in fact, doing so. The model that is most "user friendly," typical to students new to interdisciplinary studies, and favored in this book is the second: integration as comprehensive perspective. Most interdisciplinary scholars agree that disciplinary contributions—i.e., insights, theories, and concepts—must change for interdisciplinary integration to proceed. Precisely how this occurs will be demonstrated in Chapters 10–12, which focus on the integrative process.

- *Question #2: Must integration result in a clear-cut solution to a problem for a study to be "successful" and truly interdisciplinary?* As Newell (1998) has observed, "Most authors talk about solving complex problems as though they have clear-cut solutions," which, of course, many do not (p. 548). To conclude that the integrative effort has "failed" because of the absence of a feasible solution, even though the effort revealed a new understanding or new areas to be investigated, would be a mistake. Any integrative work that contributes *something* "new" to the understanding of a complex problem, even an increased appreciation of its complexity, should be viewed as successful.

2. Familiarity With Techniques of Integration. Familiarity with techniques of integration (Chapter 11) is another critical integrative skill. Integration involves comparing and contrasting disciplinary insights, creating or discovering common ground among them, integrating insights, and producing a new understanding or new meaning. The identity of specific proven integrative techniques commonly used in creating common ground is reserved for Chapter 11.

3. Self-conscious Awareness of the Interdisciplinary Research Process. Students must understand the interdisciplinary research process because it is the way in which interdisciplinary knowledge is created. This process consists of two parts that arise out of the integrated definition of interdisciplinary studies stated in Chapter 1: (1) It draws critically on disciplinary insights, and (2) it integrates these to produce an interdisciplinary understanding. This process is introduced in Chapter 6.

Integrative Knowledge

The third prerequisite for conducting integration is having **integrative knowledge**. This means being able to identify the disciplinary elements relevant to the problem; identify conflicts between disciplinary insights and evaluate their sources; apply the appropriate integrative technique(s) to create or discover common ground; integrate these conflicting insights by applying the common ground theory, concept, or assumption to them; and produce the new understanding or cognitive advancement.

An Integrative Mind-set

The fourth and final prerequisite for conducting integration is developing an **integrative mind-set**. This means cultivating these five qualities of mind:

- Seeking what is useful even if it is problematic
- Thinking inclusively and integratively, not exclusively
- Being responsive to each perspective but beholden to none (i.e., not allowing one's strength in a particular discipline to influence one's treatment of other relevant disciplines with which one is less familiar)
- Striving for balance among disciplinary perspectives
- Maintaining intellectual flexibility

These five integrative qualities correspond to several of the traits and skills of interdisciplinarians identified in Chapter 2.

The Goal of Integration

Not a Position But a Motion

The integration that results from the integrative process is valued not as an end in itself but for the interdisciplinary understanding or cognitive advancement it makes possible. Marsha Bundy Seabury (2002), an expert in interdisciplinary pedagogy, writes of her hope that interdisciplinary studies students will *move toward integration*, and thus reach a more comprehensive understanding. The metaphor of "moving toward integration" does *not* mean "a graph-like progression whereby students gradually move from lower forms of thinking on up to more holistic, abstract thinking, ending in the upper-right quadrant of the page." Sometimes the "'goal' may be *not a position but a motion*, meaning that students should be able to move among levels of abstraction and generalization," which is part of the integrative process (p. 47, italics added).

It May Be Messy

Michael Seipel (2002) cautions students and teachers alike that the focus on integration should not imply that the outcome of interdisciplinary analysis will always be a neat, tidy solution in which all contradictions between the alternative disciplinary insights are resolved. "Interdisciplinary study," he writes, "may indeed be 'messy,'" meaning that sometimes the attempt at integration will succeed only partially or not at all. Differing insights into a problem and accompanying tensions between disciplines may not only provide further understanding, he says, but should be seen as a "healthy symptom" of interdisciplinarity. The richest interdisciplinary work is that resulting from a research process that works through these tensions and contradictions between disciplinary systems of knowledge with the goal of integration, the creation of new knowledge (p. 3). One such example of integrative work is William Dietrich's (1995) *Northwest Passage: The Great Columbia River*, which will be referenced in later chapters to illustrate certain steps of the integrative process.

The Integrated Result

Consequently, the integrated result, which is the interdisciplinary understanding or cognitive advancement, must have the following characteristics:

- It must explain a specific phenomenon comprehensively.
- It must be greater than the sum of its separate disciplinary parts.

Methods for Assessing Integration

Lisa Lattuca (2001) identifies three methods for assessing the level of integration of an interdisciplinary teaching or research project:

1. *Examine the process by which interdisciplinary research is accomplished.* For example, one could count how often researchers meet to coordinate their work (p. 113). [One weakness of this approach, however, is that meetings may vary considerably in their productivity and movement toward integration of disciplinary terminology. However, this approach could profitably serve as a key indicator of integration if the process is sufficiently detailed, explicit, and proven.]

2. *Judge the final product of an interdisciplinary research project.* Typically, the participants or the researchers themselves do this (p. 113). [A weakness of this approach is that different groups of researchers may devise widely varying standards by which to judge the same or similar work. However, this weakness can be overcome if the standard is part of a widely accepted model of the research process; Wentworth & Davis, 2002, p. 33]. Jay Wentworth and James R. Davis argue, "The central purpose of evaluation ought to be to assess this integrative process in the work of students. Becoming explicit about evaluation is simply another way of gaining clarity about the integrative process" (p. 33).

3. *Look at the point of origin (i.e., the research question) to understand interdisciplinarity.* Lattuca (2001) argues for this third approach (p. 113). [A weakness of this approach is that it places the emphasis entirely on the question, even though initiating questions are frequently modified during the course of research. Also, the approach fails to explain and provide examples of why question posing is superior to approaches #1 and #2. Moreover, the approach does not recognize that the interdisciplinary research process is *a whole* and that its constituent parts contribute to achieving an integrated result.]

The issue is not which approach should prevail but how all three approaches—the research question, the research process, and the integrated result—should be used in performing integration and assessing its outcome.

CHAPTER SUMMARY

Integration is a defining characteristic of interdisciplinary studies and of the interdisciplinary research process. It is what differentiates interdisciplinarity from multidisciplinarity and transdisciplinarity. This chapter examines the nature of the "new whole" resulting from integration, the cognitive activity involved in integration, and the contribution of the disciplines to its formation.

At least two cognitive activities are involved in integration: perspective taking and holistic thinking. The integration required for disciplinary depth and breadth in interdisciplinary work includes disciplinary knowledge, integrative skills, integrative knowledge, and an integrative mind-set. The chapter critiques various models of integration and discusses integration as the means to an end—a new and more comprehensive understanding of the problem. "Integration as comprehensive perspective" is a model that is widely accepted and the one this book embraces. Chapter 6 focuses on following this model and identifies the initial steps one would take in beginning an interdisciplinary research project.

NOTES

1. Lattuca (2001), however, speaks for those interdisciplinarians who prefer to focus on the type of question justifying interdisciplinary research rather than on developing models of the interdisciplinary research process. She identifies three types of questions: "*synthetic interdisciplinary questions* that bridge disciplines and are questions that cannot be answered completely by a single discipline; *transdisciplinary questions* that are applicable across disciplines and therefore transcend a single disciplinary identity; and *conceptual interdisciplinary questions* that have no compelling disciplinary basis" (p. 112). Integration, she argues, "seems too narrow a term for the other forms of interdisciplinary scholarship" because "only synthetic interdisciplinary questions are *implicitly* integrated in the sense that they bridge disciplines and require contributions from more than one discipline" (p. 115, italics added). The problem with limiting the notion of interdisciplinarity to the initiating questions is that questions often change during the research process. This book agrees with Lattuca on the importance of framing questions in a way that justifies using an interdisciplinary approach (see Chapter 6), but differs with her in emphasizing the importance of developing a model of the interdisciplinary research process that applies to all interdisciplinary work. What defines interdisciplinarity is not only the research question, but also the research process and the product resulting from it.

2. Cindy Atha-Weldon provided this insight (personal communication, March, 2006).

3. I have excluded grounding in particular theories because these typically fall outside interdisciplinary curricula.

4. It is most unlikely that undergraduate interdisciplinary studies students would be involved in such a daunting enterprise.

REVIEW QUESTIONS

1. What are six statements that characterize interdisciplinary integration?

2. What is the difference between narrow interdisciplinarity and wide interdisciplinarity, as conceived by Kelly?

3. How is the analogy of the jigsaw puzzle deficient in describing the "new whole" resulting from interdisciplinary integration?

4. What two cognitive activities are involved in the integrative process, and what are the differences between them?

5. What role do the disciplines play in the integrative process?

6. What are three important ideas of what integration is?

7. What is a definition of interdisciplinary integration?

8. What is the importance of integration to interdisciplinarity and the interdisciplinary research process?

9. What are the prerequisites for integration?

10. Which of the three models of integration does this book embrace and why? What do these models agree on?

11. What two fundamental questions do these models raise concerning the nature of interdisciplinary integration?

12. What is the goal of interdisciplinary integration?

PART III

Drawing on Disciplines

6

Beginning the Research Process

Chapter Preview

Chapters 1 and 2 define interdisciplinarity and interdisciplinary studies and trace the origins of these concepts. Chapters 3 through 5 introduce theoretical aspects of interdisciplinarity, including the role of the disciplines in interdisciplinary work, the concept of disciplinary perspective, the defining elements of disciplines useful to interdisciplinarians, and the concept of integration. These chapters provide the definitional and theoretical grounding for the practice of interdisciplinary work described in Chapters 6 through 12.

Chapters 6 through 9 explain how to draw on the disciplines and mine their insights. Chapters 10 through 12 show how to integrate insights and produce an interdisciplinary understanding of the problem. Chapters 6 through 12 operationalize interdisciplinarity, which is manifested through research. The research process described in these chapters, and especially its integrative aspect, is the way interdisciplinarians produce new knowledge, defined as interdisciplinary understanding, cognitive advancement, or new meaning. This chapter focuses on the beginning of the research process that calls for making two important decisions: defining the problem or stating the focus question (Step 1) and justifying the use of an interdisciplinary approach (Step 2).

What the Interdisciplinary Research Process Is

Interdisciplinary research is a decision-making process that is heuristic, iterative, and reflexive. Each of these terms—decision making, process, heuristic, iterative, and reflexive—requires explanation.

A *Decision-Making* Process

Decision making, a uniquely human activity, is the cognitive ability to choose after considering alternatives. Decision making is necessitated by the prevalence of complex problems in our personal lives, in business, in society as a whole, and in the international realm. Interdisciplinarity focuses primarily on complex problems, questions, and objects. A characteristic of these is that there are many variables involved, each of which may be studied by a different discipline, subdiscipline, interdiscipline, or school of thought. The interdisciplinary research process is a practical and proven way to make decisions about how to approach these problems, deciding which ones are appropriate for interdisciplinary inquiry, and constructing more comprehensive understandings, new meanings, and possible solutions (Newell, 2007, p. 247).

A Decision-Making *Process*

Doing interdisciplinary research, whether individual or collaborative, is characterized by Newell (2007) as a decision-making process (p. 246). The term *process* means following a procedure or strategy, especially one that involves synthesis or special modification. Process also entails moment-to-moment interactions as well as interactions over the course of the project (Seabury, 2004, p. 63). The interdisciplinary research process is indeed special compared to the research methods employed by the disciplines because integration is at the very core of interdisciplinary activity, whereas it is not at the core of disciplinary activity. The interdisciplinary research process, then, entails making a series of decisions to produce the end product: an interdisciplinary understanding.

A Decision-Making Process That Is *Heuristic*

A **heuristic** is an aid to understanding or discovery or learning. The heuristic method places the student in the role of the discoverer of knowledge. The student finds how to solve the problem individually or in groups rather than being told about the solution to the problem (Lyman, 1997, p. 304). The instructor intervenes only to suggest a certain methodology for approaching the problem. Hursh et al. (1983) state, "The process of searching, more than the process of finding, is exceedingly important in stimulating cognitive development" (p. 54).

The interdisciplinary research process is heuristic in that it provides a way to understand a problem that otherwise would be impossible to achieve using a disciplinary or multidisciplinary approach (Newell, 2007, p. 248). The process aids discovery by introducing multiple decision points or steps.[1] These provide occasions for students to learn using experimentation or trial and error. The process by which integration is achieved, say Hursh et al. (1983), necessitates a two-level approach. The first level focuses on the disciplines and how they approach the topic from their particular perspectives. The second level focuses on integrating the different disciplinary insights (pp. 52–53).

In a research process that features decision making and step taking, the process is by no means linear, wherein the research proceeds mechanically along a straight upward sloping line to the goal. That is, the process is not a simple matter of moving from point "A" to point "B" to point "C" and on to the end. Rather, when the interdisciplinarian gets to point "B," point "A" may need to be revisited and revised. In fact, revising work performed under earlier Steps is likely to happen at any given point in the process. The process, for example, of selecting the most relevant disciplines (Step 3) may lead to reformulating the problem identified in Step 1. The literature search (Step 4) actually occurs over several Steps, beginning with Step 1. As Klein (1990) notes, there is no formula for doing interdisciplinary work (p. 73). Throughout the research process, the student should expect to revisit earlier work

A Decision-Making Process That Is *Iterative*

The interdisciplinary research process is **iterative** or procedurally repetitive. Its Steps or procedures involve repetition of a sequence of operations yielding results successively closer to the desired outcome. For example, one of these procedures, Step 5, concerns developing adequacy in each of the relevant disciplines. Typically, the procedure used to develop adequacy in one relevant discipline will apply to the other relevant disciplines.

A Decision-Making Process That Is *Reflexive*

The interdisciplinary research process is also **reflexive**. This means being self-conscious or self-aware of disciplinary or personal bias that may influence one's work and possibly skew the evaluation of insights and thus the product of integration. As students make decisions about which insights to use and which to discard, they should avoid the temptation of eliminating a perspective or theoretical approach that is unfamiliar to them or that challenges their beliefs. Throughout the research process, say Hursh et al. (1983), the process of challenging one's work must occur. A systematic reexamination process provides the "warning device" that some important information or idea was omitted during the early phases of the project (p. 55).

Two Additional Characteristics of the Interdisciplinary Research Process

Two additional characteristics of the interdisciplinary research process warrant comment. For one thing, it requires an act of "creative imagination" (Newell, 1990, p. 74). While the student must have some grasp of the defining elements of relevant disciplines, one must also exercise imagination and creativity to perform several of the Steps in the process. The term *Steps* is used to clarify the point of decision or operation that one would normally take in almost any research project and to differentiate a particular decision or operation from others. Students working in the "softer" social sciences and in the humanities will no doubt wish to stress the elements of creativity, intuition, and art in the interdisciplinary process, more than Steps. Nevertheless, the interdisciplinary process, and especially the integrative part of that process, involves intuition *and* method, creativity *and* process, art *and* strategic decision making.

Second, the interdisciplinary research process "is a tall order for even the best of learners" (Haynes, 2002, p. xiii). The main reason the interdisciplinary process, and particularly the integrative Steps in that process, is such a "tall order" is that most school learning is **rote learning** (that occurs when the learner memorizes new information without relating it to prior knowledge) involving no effort to integrate new knowledge with existing concepts, experience, or objects (Novak, 1998, pp. 19–20). Our method of education is so focused on analysis, reductionism, and duality that we lack guides to integration and holism. Consequently, few are able to integrate knowledge that requires developing disciplinary depth and breadth (Klein, 1996, p. 212).

In the end, each interdisciplinary research project presents its own unique combination of challenges and difficulties. The many examples of professional work and exemplary student projects threaded throughout these chapters clearly show that there is no one way to do interdisciplinary work. This is not to say that the process is haphazard. Interdisciplinary research has in common with all disciplinary research an overall plan or approach. Reduced to its simplest terms, all research has these three steps in common: (1) the problem is recognized as needing research, (2) the problem is approached using a research strategy, and (3) the problem is solved or at least a tentative solution is devised. Each discipline has developed its own methods and preferred research strategy, as noted in Chapter 4. Likewise, interdisciplinary studies has developed a research process that differs in important respects from disciplinary methods and subsumes them, as shown in Figure 6.1. These differences between interdisciplinary and disciplinary approaches to research are noted along the way.

The interdisciplinary research process is an overarching approach (noted by the arching line) that draws on disciplinary methods (see Tables 4.11, 4.12, and 4.13) that are appropriate to investigating the problem.

An Integrated Model of the Interdisciplinary Research Process

Interdisciplinarians generally agree on the need to specify, at least to some extent, how to draw on disciplinary perspectives and, especially, how to integrate their insights. Those who oppose any greater specificity do so

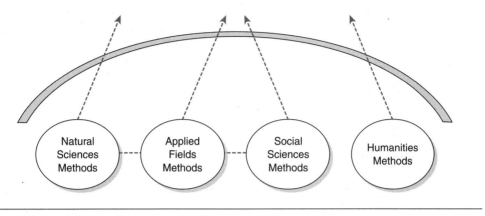

Figure 6.1   Interdisciplinary Research Process

NOTE: The dotted lines connecting the Applied Fields to the Natural Sciences and the Social Sciences show that the Applied Fields (such as education, criminal justice, communication, law, and business) use research methods drawn from these other disciplinary categories.

reasoning that it might constrain freedom of activity, stifle creativity, or suggest objectivist modernism (Newell, 2007, p. 245). What these critics overlook is that all research, whether disciplinary or interdisciplinary, uses some method of approaching the problem and collecting data. After ordering this data to help identify patterns, the researcher then applies theory to discern the meaning of those patterns, and it is from that meaning that one derives insights into the problem. The interdisciplinary research process in its most simplified form is shown in Figure 6.2.

Though helpful, Figure 6.2 lacks the detail necessary to proceed from the problem to the understanding. The integrated model of the interdisciplinary research process presented in Table 6.1 describes a proven approach to conducting interdisciplinary research, finding new meaning, and creating new knowledge.

The Benefit to Students of Clear Guidelines

Neither freedom nor creativity is compromised by providing some structure to the research process. In fact, as a practical matter, students, especially

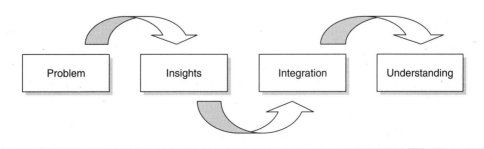

Figure 6.2   From Problem to Understanding

Table 6.1   An Integrated Model of the Interdisciplinary Research Process

A. Drawing on disciplinary insights[a]

    1. Define the problem or state the focus question

    2. Justify using an interdisciplinary approach

    3. Identify relevant disciplines

    4. Conduct a literature search

    5. Develop adequacy in each relevant discipline

    6. Analyze the problem and evaluate each insight into it

B. Integrating insights and producing an interdisciplinary understanding

    7. Identify conflicts between insights and their sources

    8. Create or discover common ground

    9. Integrate insights

    10. Produce an interdisciplinary understanding of the problem and test it

SOURCE: Repko (2006, p. 123).

a. The term "disciplinary insights" includes insights from disciplines, subdisciplines, interdisciplines, and schools of thought.

those who are new to interdisciplinary studies, benefit from having clear guidelines to help them engage in the process and achieve some measure of integration. To this end, Table 6.1 offers a procedural model that integrates the prominent models of the interdisciplinary research process.[2]

While the various research models on which the integrated model is based differ in the number, description, and order of some Steps, they agree on the need to perform certain essential tasks to prepare for integration and then to perform it. The explanation of each Step provides examples of how the model is being applied to actual research inside and outside the classroom.

Cautions Concerning These Steps

Before describing these Steps in detail, several cautionary words are in order. First, dividing what is essentially a fluid process into discrete Steps gives the misleading but unavoidable impression that these Steps do not overlap. They often do. For example, some researchers begin conducting the literature search (shown as Step 4) as early as Step 1, while others continue reading the literature during the later Steps of the research process. It is good to consider Step 4 as a fluid process within the overall research process, especially in its early phases.

Second, numbering the Steps implies a unidirectional sequence, but this is not the true nature of the interdisciplinary research process. The research process depicted in Figure 6.2 is much more like a feedback loop than a ladder.

Feedback is corrective information about a decision, operation, event, or problem that compels the researcher to revisit an earlier phase of the project. This corrective information typically comes from previously overlooked scholarship or other knowledge formations (discussed in Chapter 7). Researchers must be careful to recognize the existence of feedback as they perform these various Steps. Yet, there is movement from the simple (the statement of the problem) to the complex (the interdisciplinary understanding).

Throughout the integrated model, the process of challenging and reexamining must occur (Hursh et al., 1983, p. 55). Significantly, all the models, including the integrated model, emphasize the **nonlinearity** of the interdisciplinary process, meaning that along the way the researcher should reflect on, and may need to revisit, or even revise, earlier work. The researcher should periodically ask questions such as the following:

- Have I defined the problem or question too broadly or too narrowly?
- Have I correctly identified the parts of the problem?
- Have I identified the disciplines *most* relevant to the problem?
- Have I gathered the most important insights concerning the problem?
- Am I privileging one discipline's literature or terminology over another simply because I am more comfortable working in the discipline?
- Have I allowed my personal bias to shape the direction of the study?

Third, there is the temptation to avoid difficult Steps and leap ahead to later Steps. By keeping in mind the Steps in the interdisciplinary process, students are more likely to realize that they have skipped over an important Step and need to return to complete it. Since each Step typically requires the completion of previous Steps, it is important to regularly reexamine the work done in earlier Steps. For example, one might be tempted not to spend much time developing adequacy in the disciplines relevant to the problem (Step 5) and proceed with analyzing the problem and evaluating expert insights into it (Step 6). This impatience to "get on with the project" can prove costly, however. Unless the student knows what specific information to look for when developing adequacy—the discipline's concepts, theories, and methods—the time and effort invested may fail to yield the quality information that is needed to perform later Steps. Ultimately, the student will have to develop adequacy in each relevant discipline before reading and comprehending the disciplines' insights profitably. Avoiding difficult Steps and decisions will make the task of integration problematic.

Fourth, describing the process in terms of Steps may give the impression that each relevant discipline is "mined separately for nuggets of insights before any integration takes place, and that when integration occurs, it happens all at once." Nothing could be further from actual practice. Students should partially integrate as they go, meaning that they should incorporate disciplinary insights into a broader understanding of the problem as they proceed (Newell, 2007, p. 249).

> **Step 1: Define the problem or state the focus question**

Defining the research problem or stating the focus question is the first and most basic activity that the student should undertake in conducting research or engaging in problem solving of any kind. This initial Step involves paying careful attention to (1) selecting a problem that is researchable in an interdisciplinary sense, (2) defining the scope of the problem or focus question, (3) avoiding three tendencies that run counter to the interdisciplinary process, and (4) following three guidelines for stating the problem.

Selecting a Problem or Focus Question That Is Researchable in an Interdisciplinary Sense

A problem is **researchable** in an interdisciplinary sense (1) when it is the focus of two or more disciplines and (2) when there is a gap in attention to a problem beyond one domain. In the second instance, a problem may be complex but for some reason has failed to generate scholarly interest outside a particular discipline. Such was the case with the problem, "The Effects of Physician Shortages on Society." The problem is complex and is certainly important to society. But for whatever reason, it has failed to attract much scholarly attention outside the field of medicine (though it is a subject of discussion in multiple arenas that draw on economic, sociological, political, and demographic perspectives). The discovery of such gaps in research opens the door to potentially fruitful interdisciplinary inquiry.

Defining the *Scope* of the Problem or Question

Defining the scope of the problem is the first decision that must be made. The **scope** refers to the parameters of what is included and excluded from consideration. In other words, how much of this problem will be investigated? What are the limits of the investigation? (Szostak, 2002, p. 105; Wolfe & Haynes, 2003, p. 140). For example, if the problem being addressed is repeat spousal battery, how will this be approached? Will the focus be on the *causes* of repeat spousal battery or the *prevention* of spousal battery? Will it focus on the *treatment* of the perpetrator and/or the victim of spousal battery? Or will it focus on the *effects* of repeat spousal battery on the children? Though all these options are clearly related to the overall problem of repeat spousal battery, narrowing the scope of the problem at the outset, to the extent possible, will facilitate the literature search and subsequent Steps in the research process. The extremes to be avoided are conceiving the problem too broadly, so that it is unmanageable, or too narrowly, so that it is not interdisciplinary and not researchable.

Christopher Myers and Carolyn Haynes (2002) offer three criteria for developing a good **interdisciplinary question** for students at any level: (1) it should be open-ended and too complex to be addressed by one discipline alone, (2) it should be researchable, and (3) it should be verified using appropriate research methods (p. 186). Subsequent Steps in the research process may require students to revisit the statement of the problem or focus question and modify it in some way.

Three Tendencies That Run Counter to the Interdisciplinary Research Process

In defining the problem or stating the focus question, one should avoid three tendencies that may be acceptable in discipline-based research projects, but which run counter to the interdisciplinary research process: disciplinary bias, disciplinary jargon, and personal bias.

Disciplinary Bias

The statement of the problem should be free of **disciplinary bias**. This means that students should not use words and phrases that connect the problem to a particular discipline. For example, the problem statement "The Responsibility of Public Education for Sex Education" is biased in favor of education. Stating the problem in *discipline-neutral* terms makes it easier to justify using an interdisciplinary approach. To remove the disciplinary bias in the above example, the problem could be worded like this: "Sex Education in Public Education: An Interdisciplinary Analysis." The exception to this "rule" is when the disciplines involved are so closely related that there is no need for a neutral vocabulary (Wolfe & Haynes, 2003, p. 155).

Disciplinary Jargon

The statement of the problem should be free of **disciplinary jargon**. This means avoiding the use of terms and concepts that are not generally understood outside the discipline. If a term or concept must be used in the statement introducing the problem, then the student must define the term or concept in the next sentence or two so that the reader has a clear understanding of what is being investigated. A rule of thumb is to assume that the reader is unfamiliar with a term or concept. Here is an example of a statement that introduces a problem that is appropriate to interdisciplinary inquiry but contains disciplinary jargon: "The recidivism of domestic batterers is a significant problem in the United States because of the short-term and long-term psychological effects on the victim." This statement of the problem contains three terms that require definition: recidivism, domestic batterers, and psychological effects. (If the student wants to limit the investigation to "psychological effects on the victim," then a simple disciplinary approach will do. Otherwise, the statement should omit the term "psychological," to expand the search to other disciplines. Students must learn what terms mean and factor them into the interdisciplinary frameworks they construct.[3]) Even disciplinary experts working on interdisciplinary research teams must first develop a common vocabulary before the work of research can begin.

The following are student-written examples of discipline-neutral statements introducing a problem relying on multiple disciplines:

- "Euthanasia is the intentional killing by act or omission of a dependent human being for his or her alleged benefit, be it voluntary or involuntary. The controversy over euthanasia was rekindled recently in the case of *Sue Rodriguez vs. the Province of British Columbia*, which involved a woman in her forties who was suffering from Lou Gehrig's disease and who wanted to choose the time and manner of her inevitable death." From this wording, the reader can readily discern that the three disciplines deemed by the student as most relevant to the problem of euthanasia are ethics, medicine, and law.
- "Recent ACT scores show that a growing number of students are failing to grasp basic scientific knowledge. Science and technology play an integral role in modern society. Without scientifically and technically trained students, there will be a shortage of trained professionals in critical fields such as medicine, biology, engineering, and information technology. Even fields that are not normally thought of as scientific, including business, agriculture, journalism, and sociology, now rely heavily on science and technology." The disciplines that the student found to be most relevant to this topic are biology, psychology, and education.

An interdisciplinary problem should not privilege any one discipline because using disciplinary jargon or terminology unique to the discipline tacitly favors (perhaps unconsciously) one perspective at the expense of another.

Personal Bias

A second tendency is for students to inject their **personal bias,** or their point of view, when introducing the problem. While stating a personal opinion and arguing a personal point of view is appropriate in many academic contexts, it is not appropriate in most interdisciplinary contexts where the purpose is quite different: to produce a more comprehensive understanding of the problem that is as inclusive of as many conflicting viewpoints as possible. Certainly, the student should take a position at the outset (i.e., in the introduction) that the problem requires an interdisciplinary approach and argue against narrow disciplinary positions. The trap that some students fall into is to marshal evidence from various disciplines to support their personal bias before they identify and evaluate the important perspectives on the problem. Unwittingly, they are simply adding their personal bias to the biased insights of the disciplines. We note the bias in this student's introduction of the problem: "Taxpayer dollars should not be used to finance sports complexes for professional teams." The student obviously believes this and would prefer to write a paper advancing this point of view. However, the interdisciplinarian is not to play the role of prosecuting attorney or defense counsel for the accused. *The role of the interdisciplinarian is to produce an understanding of the problem that is more comprehensive and more inclusive than the narrow understandings that the disciplines have produced.* This calls for approaching the problem with a frame of mind that is decidedly different from that of the disciplinarian. This frame of mind is one of neutrality (or at least suspended judgment) and objectivity until all the evidence is in. This means openness to different disciplinary perspectives as well as to their insights into the problem, even if these insights challenge one's deeply held beliefs. A defining characteristic of interdisciplinary work should be to mitigate conflict by finding common ground among conflicting perspectives, including one's own.

Three Guidelines for Stating the Interdisciplinary Problem or Question

If a problem appears suitable for interdisciplinary inquiry, the student should phrase it keeping in mind these important guidelines:

• *The problem should be stated clearly and concisely.* This statement demonstrates lack of clarity: "The majority of complaints registered by the Childcare Licensing Agency (CLA) concern unsafe childcare facilities." It is unclear what is the focus of the investigation: the complaints (whether or not they are valid), lack of enforcement of safety regulations by the CLA, lack of funding of the CLA by the federal government, or the lack of legislation that establishes strict enforcement procedures.

• *The problem or focus question should be sufficiently narrow to be manageable within the specified limits of the essay.* The problem of "Securing the Southern Border of the U.S." was too broad for an essay requiring only three disciplinary perspectives. Upon discovering that the literature on border security was vast, the student narrowed the problem to the more manageable one of "Perspectives on Securing the Southern Border of the U.S. Against Human Smuggling: An Interdisciplinary Study."

• *The problem should appear in a context (preferably in the first paragraph of the introduction) that explains why it is important—that is, why we should care.* The following introduction places the problem of wife battery in a context that not only engages the reader but, more important, indicates why the problem warrants our interest:

> Wife battery is a widespread and growing problem in the United States. It is urgent that a solution be found because of its devastating effects on the victim, including debilitating depression and redirected violence against her children. The wife's extended family and associates also feel the effects of her physical and emotional pain. Most tragically, studies show that children who grow up in abusive homes tend to be abusive to their own children, thus perpetuating a vicious cycle of violence.

Note that one way to identify the essay as an interdisciplinary work is to include "An Interdisciplinary Analysis" or "An Interdisciplinary Study" in the title.

Examples of Statements of an Interdisciplinary Problem or Question

The following are examples from published work and student projects of well-written statements introducing the problem that illustrate the above criteria. The student projects are identified by an asterisk.

From the Natural Sciences: Dietrich (1995), Northwest Passage: The Great Columbia River

William Dietrich introduces the problem of how dams on the Columbia River system in the Northwest are impacting the salmon populations and the people who depend on them for their livelihood:

> To a Pacific Northwest journalist such as myself, the river was inescapable as a subject. Its energy powered the region and its history dictated the region's history. . . . Many of the people I encountered, however, looked at the river from the narrow perspective of their own experience. One colleague said it was as if everyone looked at the Columbia River through a pipe. . . . Each interest group looked at the Columbia and saw a different river.
>
> That experience dictated the approach of this book.
>
> One of the mistakes of the past . . . has been our tendency to focus narrowly on development of some part of a river without considering the consequences for the whole. "When we [whites] are confronted by a complex problem, we want to take a part of the complexity and deal with that," remarked Steve Parker, a fish biologist hired by the Yakima Indian tribe. The Henry Ford assembly line is an example of this kind of specialization, Parker said. Its economic success is why narrow focus and admiration of specialists became ingrained in American culture. (pp. 23–24)

From the Natural Sciences: Smolinski (2005),* Fresh Water Scarcity in Texas

Joe Smolinski introduces the problem of fresh water scarcity in Texas in this clearly written introductory paragraph:

There is little doubt among experts that fresh water is one of the most valuable natural resources in the state of Texas. Experts, in a variety of disciplines, have not yet been able to reach agreement as to the cause and effect of the widespread fresh water shortages currently experienced across the state. With population predictions calling for a dramatic increase in the number of residents over the next fifty years, the competition between these uses will only become more intense. How we address the use and allocation of water will have a dramatic impact on the environment and the quality of life for all Texans. (p. 1)

From the Social Sciences: Fischer (1988), *"On the Need for Integrating Occupational Sex Discrimination Theory on the Basis of Causal Variables"*

Charles C. Fischer introduces the problem of occupational sex discrimination (OSD) in the workplace as follows:

The majority of complaints filed with the Equal Employment Opportunity Commission under Title VII of the Civil Rights Act involve sex discrimination. Complaints of sex discrimination pertain mainly to pay discrimination, promotion (and transfer) discrimination, and occupation discrimination. Occupational sex discrimination (OSD) is particularly serious since other forms of sex discrimination are, to a large degree, symptomatic of a lack of female access to "male" occupations—those occupations that pay good wages, that are connected to long job ladders (that provide opportunities for vertical mobility via job promotion), and that offer positions of responsibility. (p. 22)

From the Social Sciences: Delph (2005),* An Integrative Approach to the Elimination of the "Perfect Crime"

Janet B. Delph introduces the growing problem of unsolved homicides, which she calls "perfect crimes," in these stark terms:

Modern day criminal investigation techniques do not eliminate the possibility of the "perfect crime". . . . A "perfect crime" is one that will go unnoticed and/or for which the criminal will never be caught (Fanton, Tilhet, & Achache, 1998). The public is all too aware of these likely outcomes and consequently feels unsafe and vulnerable. Parents experience silent fear each time their child wanders beyond their reach. While "men are afraid women will laugh at them, women are afraid that men will kill them" (DeBecker, 1997, p. 77). Deviant minds should not be allowed to think that they can commit murder without suffering the gravest consequences. (p. 2)

From the Humanities: Bal (1999), "Introduction," The Practice of Cultural Analysis: Exposing Interdisciplinary Interpretation

Mieke Bal's introduction serves two purposes: to expose the complex meaning of a yellow graffito found on a red brick wall in Amsterdam, Netherlands and, in the process of doing this, to introduce the reader to the school of cultural analysis of which she is a leading practitioner.

Cultural analysis as a critical practice is different from what is commonly understood as "history." It is based on a keen awareness of the critic's situatedness in the present, the social and cultural present from which we look, and look back, at the objects that are already of the past, objects that we take to define our present culture. . . .

This graffito, for example, has come to characterize the goals of the Amsterdam School for Cultural Analysis (ASCA). . . . In the most literal translation the text means:

> Note
>
> I hold you dear
>
> I have not
>
> thought you up

This piece of wall writing fulfills that function because it makes a good case for the kind of objects at which cultural analysis would look, and—more importantly—how it can go about doing so. (pp. 1–2)

From the Humanities: Silver* (2005), Composing Race and Gender: The Appropriation of Social Identity in Fiction

Lia Silver writes an informal personal narrative of how she became interested in her subject, the appropriation of social identity in fiction writing. Her story begins with her trip to Mexico during spring break of her junior year. When she returned, she had a story due in her creative writing class, so she tried writing about the people she met in the mountain villages in Oaxaca, Mexico.

And that's when the interdisciplinarity kicked in. . . .

In Mexico. We'd learned . . . it would be offensive for us, as outsiders, to assume we could fix their problems. What could we, carrying our Nalgene bottles, comprehend of the effects of water privatization and pollution? How could we listen to the plight of maquiladora workers while wearing Nikes and stonewashed jeans? How could I understand the lives of the indigenous Oaxacan villagers enough to write about them—especially from their own points of view? I couldn't separate the sociological and political lessons I'd learned in Mexico from my fiction. I ended up writing my story from the first-person peripheral perspective of a white college-aged female looking in at the village. I got good critiques in class, but was never personally satisfied with the story. It felt like I'd written a nonfiction piece. I wanted to create characters with backgrounds unlike my own, but suddenly didn't know how. (p. 2)

Each of these examples conforms to the above criteria: They are *appropriate* to interdisciplinary inquiry, they carefully *define* the scope of the problem, and they *avoid the three tendencies* that run counter to the interdisciplinary process: disciplinary bias, disciplinary jargon, and personal bias. They also *follow the three guidelines* for introducing the problem: The problems are stated clearly and concisely, are sufficiently narrow in scope to be manageable (depending on the scale of the writer's project), and appear in a context that explains why the problem should interest us.

Preparedness to Revisit The Initial Step

As further Steps are taken, students are likely to encounter new information, receive new insights (including intuitive flashes), or encounter unforeseen problems that will require revisiting the initial Step and modifying the topic. This is a normal part of the research process, especially for interdisciplinary work.

Step 2: Justify using an interdisciplinary approach

Not every problem or question is appropriate to interdisciplinary inquiry. From the field's literature, it is possible to identify at least five criteria that interdisciplinarians commonly use to justify using an interdisciplinary approach:

- The problem or question is complex
- Important insights into the problem are offered by two or more disciplines
- No single discipline has been able to address the problem comprehensively
- The research problem or focus question is at the interfaces of disciplines
- The problem is an unresolved societal need or issue (National Academy of Sciences et al., 2005, pp. 30–35)

The Problem or Question Is Complex

In our context, **complexity** can be defined as the study of the behavior of systems. A **system** is any group of interacting components or agents around which there is a clearly defined boundary between the system and the rest of the world, but also clearly definable inputs from the world and outputs to the world that cross the boundary (Boyd, 2006, p. 27).[4] As applied to interdisciplinary research, complexity means that the problem has several components and that each component has a different disciplinary character.

Complexity is a keyword in contemporary descriptions of interdisciplinarity. Chapter 1 states that interdisciplinarity is necessitated, *in part,* by complexity, specifically by the structure and behavior of complex systems and problems such as global warming, fresh water scarcity, and illegal immigration. Indeed, the nature of complex systems provides a strong rationale for interdisciplinarity. Interdisciplinarians who embrace complexity as the primary or sole justification for interdisciplinarity reason that if the question being investigated is not complex, then it may just as well be investigated in a multidisciplinary manner by merely adding disciplinary insights (Newell, 2001, p. 2).[5] The criteria of complexity also extends to problems that those in the humanities typically examine, such as the contextual meaning of an object or text.[6]

Examples of complex questions include these: What is consciousness? What is freedom? What is a family? What does it mean to be human? Why does hunger persist? Admittedly, these problems are so fundamental and complex, requiring sophisticated analysis from so many disciplines, that they are beyond the capacity of most undergraduates to address comprehensively. Nevertheless, movement toward an interdisciplinary understanding of these questions is possible even if students are limited to using only a few relevant disciplines.

Confirmation of complexity will be forthcoming as students take additional Steps, especially Step 4, which involves conducting a full-scale literature search.

Important Insights Have Been Produced by at Least Two Disciplines

A problem that is controversial, such as global warming, has likely generated interest from two or more scholarly communities, with each community offering its own insights in the form of peer-reviewed monographs and journal articles. This condition makes the problem researchable. Indeed, students should be looking for instances of **border disciplinarity**, which exists when at least two disciplines focusing on the same problem create an overlapping area between them. These disciplines, each with its own perspectives, insights, assumptions, concepts, theories, and methods, make a productive contribution to understanding the problem because each has studied the problem (Fischer, 1988, p. 37).

Sometimes, however, scholarly work on a controversial problem has not yet extended to *some* of the disciplines on which the student wishes to draw. A common problem that students encounter is this: Students identify disciplines potentially relevant to the problem using the tables appearing in Chapter 4, only to find in the course of their literature search (Step 4) that the problem has not yet attracted the attention of some of these disciplines. This situation does not necessarily mean that the problem is not researchable. As long as more than one discipline has produced important insights into the problem, the problem is researchable (i.e., appropriate for interdisciplinary inquiry).

No Single Discipline Has Been Able to Explain Comprehensively or Resolve the Problem

A problem is appropriate for interdisciplinary inquiry if (a) no single discipline has been able to explain it comprehensively or resolve it, or if (b) each discipline offers a more or less misleading understanding of it. For example, several disciplines consider terrorism within their respective domains, but no one discipline has been able to create a single comprehensive theory explaining terrorism in all of its complexity, let alone propose a holistic solution to it. Political scientists typically use rational choice theory to explain terrorist behavior, but the theory fails to address religious and cultural variables. Other problems that no single discipline has been able to address comprehensively include the causes of illegal immigration, human cloning, genetically engineered food, and the effects of the No Child Left Behind legislation. The value of using an interdisciplinary approach is that it can address complex problems in a more comprehensive way than is possible using a single disciplinary approach.

The Research Problem or Focus Question Is at the Interfaces of Disciplines

Using an interdisciplinary approach is appropriate when the research problem or focus question is at the **interfaces of disciplines,** meaning the points at which they converge because of their common interest in a particular problem. The National Academy of Sciences, the National Academy of Engineering, and the Institute of Medicine's Committee on Facilitating Interdisciplinary Research (2005) explain the high value of these interfaces:

> some of the most interesting scientific questions are found at the *interfaces* between disciplines. . . . Exploring such interfaces . . . leads

investigators beyond their own disciplines to invite participation of researchers in adjacent or complementary fields and even to stimulate the development of a new interdisciplinary field. (p. 33, italics added)

New interdisciplinary fields developed at these interfaces include bio-chemistry, cognitive science, genomics, proteomics, epidemiology, structural biology, ecology, and ecologic economics.

The Problem Is an Unmet Societal Need or Unresolved Question

Societal/public policy problems necessitate what interdisciplinarians call **problem-focused research**. Such research is distinct from what is called basic research or pure theoretical research because it focuses on unresolved societal needs and practical problem solving. According to Klein (1990), problem-focused research "emphasizes the pursuit of knowledge, and that of informed action . . . usefulness, efficiency, and practical results" (p. 122). Large-scale complex projects include "the Apollo Space project, a systematic investigation of the ecology of Lake Tahoe, attempts to harness resources from the oceans, international efforts to increase rice productivity, [and] engineering transportation studies" (p. 122). Obviously, large-scale and expensive projects such as these are beyond the resources of the individual, much less the undergraduate interdisciplinarian. However, a multitude of other societal problems and public policy issues are researchable by individuals or small teams. Here are some examples of topics successfully researched (though not comprehensively) by students: Should the FDA allow prescription drugs to be imported from Canada? Should federal tax dollars be given to faith-based organizations for social purposes? Should the public fund expensive sports complexes? Can the need for homeland security be achieved without undermining First Amendment rights? Should illegal immigrants be granted some form of amnesty?

Justifying Using an Interdisciplinary Approach: Examples From the Natural Sciences, the Social Sciences, and the Humanities

It is important to make explicit the rationale for using an interdisciplinary approach. This is, after all, what differentiates truly interdisciplinary research from multidisciplinary, not to mention disciplinary, research. Making the rationale explicit early on in the interdisciplinary process, even in cases where students do not have topic choice, has the added benefit of alerting the student to possible problems with the topic. Spending extra time in carefully screening a potential topic according to these criteria will save the student from investing in an enterprise that later may prove unprofitable.

Satisfied that the proposed problem or topic meets one or more of the above criteria, the student is then able to present a clear rationale for using an interdisciplinary approach. This rationale should ideally be included in the introduction to the study, as shown in these examples of professional work and student projects (noted by an asterisk) from the natural sciences, the social sciences, and the humanities.

From the Natural Sciences: Dietrich (1995), Northwest Passage: The Great Columbia River

Dietrich is struck by how narrowly people continue to look at the Columbia River. This narrowness of perspective and the lack of systems thinking provide his justification for taking an interdisciplinary approach, as follows:

My work as a writer on environmental issues, particularly the old-growth forests of the Pacific Northwest, had introduced me to the idea of ecosystems and the interrelationships of many parts to a greater whole. I wanted a comprehensive understanding of the river embracing history, geology, biology, hydrology, economics, and contemporary politics and management. (pp. 23–24)

From the Natural Sciences: Smolinski* (2005), Fresh Water Scarcity in Texas

Smolinski is concerned that after years of study, disciplinary experts have not been able to reach agreement on the cause and effect of the worsening problem of fresh water scarcity. This failure provides ample justification for taking an interdisciplinary approach.

The causes and effects of fresh water scarcity across Texas are beyond the ability of any single discipline to explore. A review of the professional literature in political science, geology, and biology shows that these disciplines are most relevant to the problem. Each has produced its own well-defined theories about how the shortages impact the state of Texas and its communities. While each of these theories reflects the perspective of its particular discipline, none of these explanations comprehensively addresses the issues posed by the statewide shortage of fresh water. (p. 3)

From the Social Sciences: Fischer (1988), "On the Need for Integrating Occupational Sex Discrimination Theory on the Basis of Causal Variables"

Fischer provides an example of professional work from the social sciences that presents a clear rationale for taking an interdisciplinary approach.

It appears that the problem of OSD is a good candidate for an IR [interdisciplinary] approach. OSD is a problem that a number of disciplines have separately analyzed, yet it is a problem of such complexity and breadth that its division among individual disciplines leads to incomplete and naïve views.

Another important advantage of IR is that it can ... lead to [a] more complete understanding by providing a dynamic, holistic view of the problem. (p. 37)

From the Social Sciences: Delph* (2005), An Integrative Approach to the Elimination of the "Perfect Crime"

Having introduced the topic and explained its importance, Delph justifies using an interdisciplinary approach.

To achieve the level of expertise necessary to solve more crimes, the criminal justice system must integrate a wide range of skills from multiple disciplines. This synthesis of skills and insights could serve as a strong deterrent to crime and result in safer communities. (p. 2)

From the Humanities: Bal (1999), "Introduction," The Practice of Cultural Analysis: Exposing Interdisciplinary Interpretation

The topic of the graffito is not a societal problem; it is an intellectual one that cries out for interdisciplinary understanding or meaning. Bal (1999) sees cultural analysis as an interdisciplinary practice and the field as a counterweight to critics who charge that interdisciplinarity makes objects of inquiry "vague and methodically muddled" (p. 2). Seeking to correct this mistaken view, she justifies using cultural analysis, an interdisciplinary approach, to find meaning in the graffito.

As an object, it requires interdisciplinarity [and calls for] an analysis that draws upon cultural anthropology and theology [and] reflection on aesthetics, which makes philosophy an important partner. ... [T]he humanistic disciplines ... brutally confront scholars with the need to overcome disciplinary hang-ups. ... Museum analysis requires the integrative collaboration of linguistics and literary, of visual and philosophical, and of anthropological and social studies. ... Instead of speaking of an abstract and utopian interdisciplinarity, then, cultural analysis is truly an interdiscipline, with a specific object and a specific set of collaborating disciplines. (pp. 6–7)

From the Humanities: Silver* (2005), Composing Race and Gender: The Appropriation of Social Identity in Fiction

From her fiction class experience, Silver (2005) discovered that she did not know how to write authentically about the people in the Mexican village whose backgrounds were very different from her own. Frustrated and disappointed with the artificial characters she had created for her fiction piece, she decided to use the topic of character appropriation for her senior project. Character appropriation refers to a writer's attempt to write about, or an actor's attempt to assume, another person's identity. As Silver read, she developed "a sense of what different disciplines—sociology, psychology, cultural studies, and creative writing—[said] about the matter" (p. 2). Finding that each of these disciplines offered an important perspective on an important subject, she determined that an interdisciplinary approach was clearly called for (pp. 1–6).

Each of these examples conforms to one or more of the above criteria. In most cases, the writer also identifies the disciplines relevant to the problem.

CHAPTER SUMMARY

This chapter introduces the interdisciplinary research process and examines its initial Steps. It explains the importance of the research process to interdisciplinarity, describing it as a decision-making process that is heuristic, iterative, reflexive, and that involves creativity. It introduces an integrated model of the interdisciplinary research process and notes the importance of providing students with clear guidelines for conducting research. The first Step in the interdisciplinary research process is to define the problem or focus question. Criteria for developing a good interdisciplinary question for students at any level include these: (1) It should be open-ended and too complex to be addressed by one discipline alone, (2) it should be researchable, and (3) it should be verified using appropriate research methods. The chapter alerts students to three tendencies that run counter to interdisciplinarity: privileging a particular discipline, using disciplinary jargon without defining it, and allowing personal bias to shape the project.

The second Step, ideally, is to justify using an interdisciplinary approach. Such justification should meet one or more of the following criteria: (1) It should be complex; (2) important insights into the problem should have been produced by at least two disciplines; (3) no single discipline has been able to comprehensively explain or resolve the problem; (4) the research problem or focus question is at the interfaces of disciplines; (5) the problem is an unresolved societal need or unresolved question.

Even after subjecting the proposed problem to these criteria, it is still too early in the research process to know with any certitude that the problem is researchable. This question can be resolved only by taking subsequent Steps in the interdisciplinary process.

NOTES

1. Nikitina (2005) also uses "step" to describe the interdisciplinary process (p. 405).

2. These models include the following: Hursh et al. (1983); Klein (1990), pp. 192–193; Newell (2001), pp. 14–22; Szostak, (2002). Klein has moved away from her earlier model, finding it "too linear" (personal communication, April, 2005).

Comparing these models reveals that scholarly consensus exists on the following steps: The problem or focus question should be defined, relevant disciplines and other resources must be identified, information from these disciplines (concepts, theories, methods, etc.) must be gathered, adequacy in each relevant discipline must be achieved, the problem must be studied and insights into the problem must be generated, conflicts between insights must be identified and their sources revealed, disciplinary insights must be integrated, and a new understanding must be constructed or new meaning achieved.

The models disagree on the number, order, and identity of steps, leaving students and instructors alike without a clear road map of the overall interdisciplinary research process. Of special concern is the lack of consensus on how many steps are involved in the integrative part of the process. When the participants in a Delphi Study recommended that students be provided "basic integrational methods," the question arose as to which model and/or which particular steps within these models should be provided (Welch, 2003, p. 185).

3. On the other hand, the interdisciplinarian need not be as concerned about maintaining a neutral vocabulary when the relevant disciplines are closely related, as are, for example, physics, chemistry, and Earth sciences.

4. In his controversial essay, "A Theory of Interdisciplinary Studies," Newell (2001) argues that "complex systems and phenomena are a necessary condition for interdisciplinary studies," and that "an interdisciplinary approach is justified *only* by a complex system" (p. 1, italics added).

5. However, some interdisciplinarians object to Newell's theory that interdisciplinarity is required by the complexity of its subject. See Bailis (2001).

6. See Klein (2001, pp. 47–48) for her list of interdisciplinary theories that have been put forward at various levels. Postmodernists, who are skeptical of any unifying theory such as complexity theory, object that it amounts to a modernist attempt to unify the field theoretically (Mackey, 2001). Newell (2007) states, "Certainly, no consensus definition of complexity has yet emerged, and the various subliteratures have grown out of diverse disciplines (e.g., computer science, meteorology, mathematics, biology, chemistry) that lead theorists in different directions" (p. 246).

REVIEW QUESTIONS

1. How is the interdisciplinary research process different from disciplinary methods of research?

2. How is the interdisciplinary research process heuristic, iterative, and reflexive?

3. On what points do the various models of the interdisciplinary research process agree?

4. What are the steps of the integrated model of the research process?

5. What cautions should one be mindful of when using these steps?

6. What are two tendencies that run counter to the interdisciplinary research process?

7. What are three guidelines for stating the interdisciplinary problem or question?

8. What are the justifications for using an interdisciplinary approach?

9. How does Dietrich justify using an interdisciplinary approach to studying the Columbia River system? How does his justification differ from Bal's?

7

Identifying
Relevant Disciplines

Chapter Preview

The student faces two challenges in the early phase of the interdisciplinary research process. The first is to decide which disciplines and their perspectives are *potentially* relevant to the problem and then which of these are *most* relevant (Step 3). Narrowing the number of disciplines is necessary when, for instance, course requirements limit the student to using only a few disciplines. Even so, students typically are asked to decide *which* disciplines should be mined for insights. The second challenge is to undertake a thorough literature search (Step 4). This involves making decisions that, if made correctly, serve to validate the selection of disciplines as most relevant and may even reveal additional relevant disciplines.

How to Select Relevant Disciplines

> **Step 3: Identify relevant disciplines and choose those most relevant to the problem**

In selecting disciplines from which to draw insights, the challenge to students is to decide which disciplines contribute substantially to the problem or overall pattern of behavior they wish to study. This challenge can be met by first identifying the disciplines potentially relevant to the problem before attempting to decide which of these are the most relevant. A **potentially relevant discipline** is one whose research domain includes the phenomenon that the problem represents and whose community of scholars may or may not have recognized the problem and published their research. How to identify the disciplines that are the most relevant is discussed elsewhere in this chapter.

Identify Potentially Relevant Disciplines

Students should attempt to identify the disciplines potentially relevant to the problem before conducting the full-scale literature search (Step 4), starting with the tables in Chapters 3 and 4. Why? Disciplinary research usually emphasizes conducting the literature search at the very outset of the research process. Disciplinarians are concerned that they not duplicate previous scholarship. By contrast, many interdisciplinarians do not want to be unduly influenced by what disciplinary experts have already said (or have failed to say) about the problem, and therefore they want to think through the problem themselves before conducting a full-scale literature search. Once the potentially relevant disciplines are identified, their literatures can be systematically searched for insights into the problem.

Practically, how does one go about identifying the disciplines potentially relevant to the problem? Here are some suggestions:

• *Think through the problem and attempt to identify its various components.* Some problems are more complex than others. In any case, the student needs to identify the various parts of the problem and understand how they interact with each other. Mapping the problem helps develop this understanding.

• *Refer to Table 3.3 on Disciplinary Perspectives in Chapter 3 and ask this question of each: How does this discipline illuminate some aspect of the problem or question?* This questioning process should enable the student to decide which disciplines are *potentially* relevant to the problem and explain how each illuminates some aspect of the problem.

• *Confirm the disciplinary selections made by referring to the disciplines and their phenomena surveyed in Chapter 4, Table 4.1, "The Disciplines Linked to Phenomena."* For example, Table 7.1 identifies selected disciplines that are *potentially* relevant to the problem of human cloning and how each illuminates some aspect of it. The characterization of these disciplines as potentially relevant is based on the inclusion of some aspect of human cloning within their research domains. However, just because the problem falls within a discipline's perspective and research domain does not mean that the discipline's community of scholars has addressed the problem. (Note: As Step 3, this exercise should be done before conducting the full-scale literature search called for in Step 4.)

• *Consult disciplinary research aids,* including bibliographies, encyclopedias, dictionaries, handbooks, companions, and databases *after* drawing up a list of potentially interested disciplines. For example, an indispensable source of disciplinary references for students working in the social sciences is *Social Science Reference Sources* (2000).

Table 7.1   Disciplines *Potentially* Relevant to the Problem of Human Cloning and How They Illuminate Some Aspect of It (*Before* the In-Depth Literature Search)

Discipline, Interdiscipline, and Applied Fields	How Each Illuminates Some Aspect of the Problem
Biology	The biological process of human cloning and rates of success or failure
Psychology	Possible psychological impact on the cloned person of a sense of personhood
Political Science	Role of the federal government
Philosophy	Ethical implications of cloning a human life
Religious Studies	Sanction in sacred writings against the creation of a new form of human life
Law[a]	Legal rights and relationships of the cloned child and its "parents"
Bioethics[b]	Ethical implications of the technical procedures required to clone a human, particularly in the event of failure

a. Law is an applied field in many taxonomies.

b. Bioethics is an interdisciplinary field in many taxonomies.

• *See whether experts in the disciplines have published research on the problem.* It is better to err on the side of inclusiveness in the early steps than to conclude prematurely that a discipline is not relevant. If later steps reveal that a discipline is not as useful as first supposed, it can be easily removed from the study.

• *Consult disciplinary experts for insights into the problem for further confirmation of the selections made.* After thinking through the problem and consulting disciplinary research aids, but before undertaking an in-depth literature search, ask experts in what appear to be relevant disciplines whether their discipline has published research on the problem. For example, the student might not immediately think of anthropology as having much to offer a study of acid rain. But an anthropologist, or even a student majoring in that discipline, will know that cultural materialism provides a general framework for thinking about the human-environment interface, especially the ways economic practices and technology lead to changes in the ecosystem (Newell, 2001, p. 17). Also, librarians specializing in various disciplines are an excellent source of this information.

As noted in Chapter 6, the kinds of problems ideally suited for an interdisciplinary approach are complex. The fable of building a house for an elephant, referenced in Chapter 1, shows the importance of taking into account all relevant disciplines and perspectives when trying to understand complex systems or solve complex problems. Interdisciplinary studies tends to focus on individual complex problems or systems, such as the impact of the system of dams on the salmon populations of the Columbia and Snake Rivers, the causes of acid rain, or the causes of terrorism. Because these problems are complex, they have many variables, each of which is typically studied by a different discipline.

Map the Problem

After detailing how each discipline explains the behavior of the overall problem, the student's next task is to decide how the disciplinary parts of the problem relate to each other and to the problem as a whole. Mapping the problem facilitates this understanding.[1] Maps that are profitable to interdisciplinary students include the research map, the concept/principle map, the system map, and the theory map. Mapping the problem should occur before the in-depth literature search. The results of the search should confirm the completeness and accuracy of the map.

A Research Map

The purpose of creating a **research map** is to help visualize the problem or question in its complexity. Performing this task may at first appear as a diversion from the more important business of "getting on" with the project. However, experience shows that investing time in formulating the problem and identifying its various components is helpful in performing the latter steps of the research process. An example of a research map is shown in Figure 7.1.

A Concept/Principle Map

A **concept/principle map** is a particularly good way to organize information about a problem because it shows meaningful relationships between the parts of the problem. Constructing a concept/principle map requires that we think through all the parts of the problem and understand how these behave or function, as shown in Figure 7.2.

Constructing a map is a valuable exercise because it may reveal a gap in our understanding of the problem or that we are placing too much emphasis on a few disciplinary components at the expense of other equally important components. The interdisciplinarian is concerned with achieving an interdisciplinary understanding of the problem as a whole, whereas the disciplinarian is often satisfied to focus on a single part or on a few "neighboring" parts of the problem.

A System Map

A good example of a system is a city. Understanding a system or complex problem requires that the student be able to describe what the system

Research Map

To fully understand a piece of research, the student must understand the purpose of the research, the particular methods used in the investigation, and the findings. The student should also understand the implications of the study: How do the findings fit with existing scientific knowledge, what impact did the study have on subsequent research on the particular topic, and what impact did the findings have on society? Finally, the student should also know about any alternative interpretations of the study.

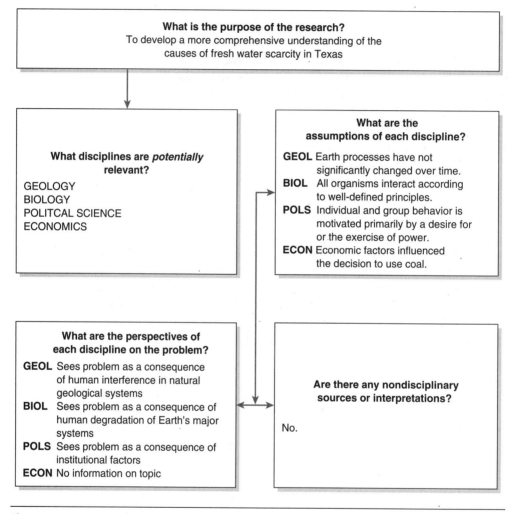

Figure 7.1   Research Map

SOURCE: Based on Motes, Bahr, Atha-Weldon, and Dansereau (2003).

does and know how it functions. The student must also be able to identify the parts of the system or problem, describe what each part does, and explain how each part relates to the other parts of the system.

A **system map** is a highly useful analytical tool that can help one visualize the system or problem as a complex whole. The purpose of constructing a system map is to show all the components of the system or

Concept/Principle-Map

Concepts and principles are ubiquitous in science. To fully understand a concept or principle, the student must be able to describe it and must also know how the concept or principle fits with existing theories and what research has been conducted on the concept or principle. Additionally, the student should know how and why the concept or principle is important to science and society, as well as any related concepts or principles.

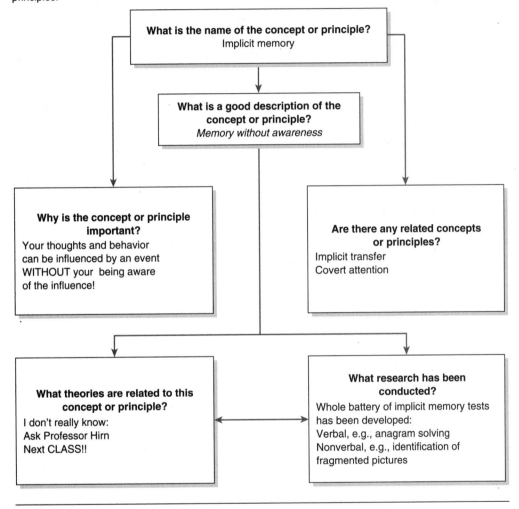

Figure 7.2   Concept/Principle Map

SOURCE: Based on Motes et al. (2003).

problem and see the causal relationships among them. Generally, each part of the complex system is studied by a different discipline. Newell (2007) points out that it may not be fully apparent to those in a discipline how the subsystem they study contributes to the overall pattern of behavior of a system or problem that is truly complex. Constructing a system map will also help the student to discover missing parts of disciplines or disciplines that were not initially obvious (p. 246).

Even if the project is limited to only two or three disciplines, the student still needs to understand where each of them fits into the overall system. Also, drawing a system map and locating the disciplines that one believes are relevant allows the student to more easily identify other relevant disciplines that may have been overlooked (see Figure 7.3).

Constructing a system map helps the student to understand not only how the system operates the way it does but also *why* the system behaves the way it does. For example, simply knowing *how* coal contributes to acid rain does not explain *why* coal was chosen over other materials to fuel electric utilities to begin with. The student should be as concerned with knowing the *why* of the problem as knowing the *how*. The system map enables one to see how the disciplinary components of the complex system or problem relate to each other and to the system as a whole (Motes et al., 2003, pp. 240–242).

Viewing the complex system of acid rain through the lens of economics, for example, reveals that economic factors drive decisions about the use of coal in power plants. And looking at the same problem through the lens of political science and its subfield of public policy reveals linkages that connect the political and economic systems (Newell, 2001, p. 18).

Perceiving these kinds of linkages and cause-and-effect relationships when dealing with complex problems is not possible by using a traditional single-discipline approach. It is in dealing with complex real-world problems that interdisciplinary process proves its analytical power and demonstrates its unmatched ability to produce a more comprehensive understanding of complex problems. The Step of identifying potentially relevant disciplines and then reducing these to only those that are most relevant requires, among other things, that students have a clear understanding of the overall behavioral pattern of the problem they are studying.[2]

A Theory Map

Theory is an inescapable part of conducting research in any discipline on an advanced undergraduate and graduate level and is therefore important to interdisciplinary inquiry. In the following chapters, some of the professional work and student projects used to illustrate aspects of the interdisciplinary research process use theory. For example, a student investigating the causes of fresh water scarcity in Texas discovered that the insights from each of the relevant disciplines are couched in terms of well-known (i.e., within these disciplines) theories. If one or more theories are involved in an inquiry, the student must develop adequacy in each one. How to develop adequacy is the subject of Chapter 8. The theory map on Piaget's theory of cognitive development can easily be modified to focus on additional aspects of any theory (see Figure 7.4).

System Map

A system is an assemblage or working combination of parts or procedures with a specific function or set of functions. To understand a system, the student must be able to describe what the system does. The student must also be able to identify the parts of the system, what each part does, and what can go wrong with a given part and the entire system. Because system functions and failures are discovered through empirical testing, the student should also know what research has been done on the system.

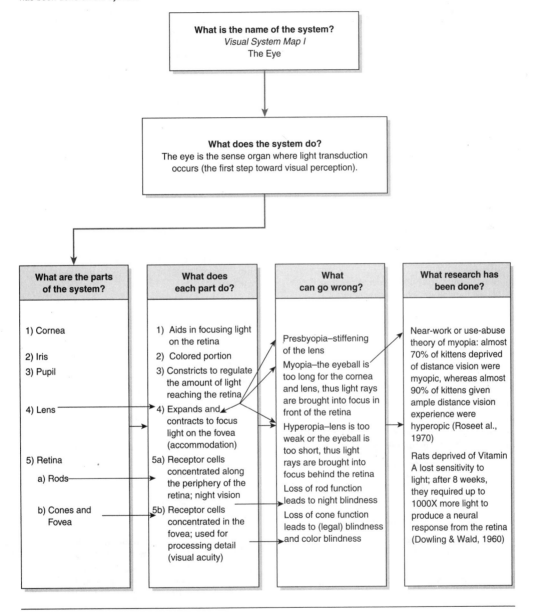

Figure 7.3   System Map

SOURCE: Based on Motes et al. (2003).

Theory Map

To fully appreciate a scientific theory, the student should be able to describe the theory, know the history of the theory, know evidence for and against the theory, know why the theory is important, and know whether there are any similar and competing theories.

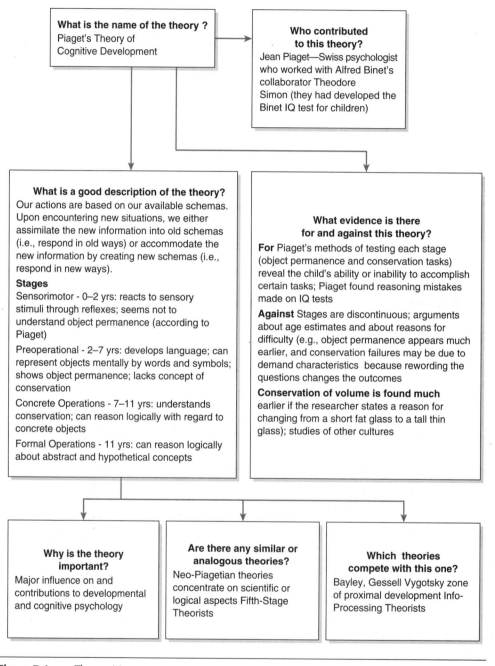

What is the name of the theory ?
Piaget's Theory of
Cognitive Development

**Who contributed
to this theory?**
Jean Piaget—Swiss psychologist who worked with Alfred Binet's collaborator Theodore Simon (they had developed the Binet IQ test for children)

What is a good description of the theory?
Our actions are based on our available schemas. Upon encountering new situations, we either assimilate the new information into old schemas (i.e., respond in old ways) or accommodate the new information by creating new schemas (i.e., respond in new ways).
Stages
Sensorimotor - 0–2 yrs: reacts to sensory stimuli through reflexes; seems not to understand object permanence (according to Piaget)
Preoperational - 2–7 yrs: develops language; can represent objects mentally by words and symbols; shows object permanence; lacks concept of conservation
Concrete Operations - 7–11 yrs: understands conservation; can reason logically with regard to concrete objects
Formal Operations - 11 yrs: can reason logically about abstract and hypothetical concepts

**What evidence is there
for and against this theory?**
For Piaget's methods of testing each stage (object permanence and conservation tasks) reveal the child's ability or inability to accomplish certain tasks; Piaget found reasoning mistakes made on IQ tests
Against Stages are discontinuous; arguments about age estimates and about reasons for difficulty (e.g., object permanence appears much earlier, and conservation failures may be due to demand characteristics because rewording the questions changes the outcomes
Conservation of volume is found much earlier if the researcher states a reason for changing from a short fat glass to a tall thin glass); studies of other cultures

**Why is the theory
important?**
Major influence on and contributions to developmental and cognitive psychology

**Are there any similar or
analogous theories?**
Neo-Piagetian theories concentrate on scientific or logical aspects Fifth-Stage Theorists

**Which theories
compete with this one?**
Bayley, Gessell Vygotsky zone of proximal development Info-Processing Theorists

Figure 7.4   Theory Map

SOURCE: Based on Motes et al. (2003).

Narrow the Number of Potentially Relevant Disciplines to Those That Are Most Relevant

Once the student has drawn up a list of disciplines potentially relevant to the problem (i.e., those disciplines that include the problem in their research domains and whose experts have written about the problem), the student's next task is to decide which of these are most relevant.

Identify the Most Relevant Disciplines

The student who works alone and labors under time and other constraints must somehow reduce the number of potentially relevant disciplines to those that are the most relevant to the problem, and do so in a way that does not compromise the integrity of the end product. This process of narrowing must also occur in collaborative research, where interdisciplinary teams engage in a form of reduction by necessity. Identifying the most relevant disciplines may involve revisiting the formulation of the research question (Step 1) and undertaking the in-depth literature search (Step 4).

"Most" Relevant Defined

The **most relevant disciplines** are those disciplines, often three or four, which are most directly connected to the problem, have generated the most important research on it, and have advanced the most compelling theories to explain it. More specifically, these disciplines, or parts of them, provide information about the problem that is essential to developing a comprehensive understanding of it (Newell, 1992, p. 213). Students must exercise great care when reducing the number of disciplines to those that are most relevant so as to not neglect important research and thus negatively affect the final product.[3]

Ask Three Questions to Distinguish Between Potentially Relevant Disciplines and Those That Are Most Relevant

What is needed is some way to make the important distinction between the potentially relevant disciplines and those that are most relevant as sharp as possible. To this end, students should ask three questions of each of the disciplines identified as potentially relevant (in the most general sense) to the problem:

- Does the discipline have a well-defined *perspective* on the problem? (Note: Perspective in this context refers to the discipline's general view of reality, which is expressed as expert insights into the problem.)

- Has the discipline produced a *body of research* (i.e., insights) on the problem of such significance that its published insights and supporting evidence cannot be ignored?
- Has the discipline generated *one or more theories* to explain the problem?

Answering these questions early in the research process will require conducting an initial literature search (but not necessarily the in-depth literature search of Step 4).

Apply These Questions to the Disciplines Relevant to Human Cloning

These three questions are now applied to each of the disciplines earlier identified as having some relevance to the problem of human cloning.

Question #1: Does the discipline have a well-defined perspective on the problem?

Here, the focus is on understanding how each discipline views the problem in a general sense. Chapter 3 explains that each discipline focuses on only one facet of reality and, thus, on only one facet of a problem (assuming that it is within the discipline's research domain). Each discipline views the problem (if it even recognizes that there is a problem) in its own distinctive way.

Answering this question, "Does the discipline have a well-defined perspective on the problem?" will require consulting Table 3.2 on the disciplines and their overall perspectives. In the event that these tables and their references prove incomplete, disciplinary handbooks, introductory textbooks, and disciplinary experts may also need to be consulted.

At this early phase of the research process, the student should be able to explain how each discipline's overall perspective illuminates the problem or some facet of it. One way to do this (and perhaps gain new insight into the problem) is to state the perspective of each discipline (noted in Table 7.1) in the form of a question, as shown in Table 7.2. **Perspective**, in an interdisciplinary sense, is used in one of two ways when approaching a problem: (1) in a general sense, in terms of how a discipline views the problem in an overall way or (2) in a more particular sense, in terms of how one or more of the discipline's defining elements pertain to the problem. As used here, *perspective* means how the discipline views, illuminates, or understands the problem in a general sense.

This same approach is applied to three of the professional works introduced in Chapter 6 to link the relevant disciplines to how each illuminates the problems, as shown in Tables 7.3 through 7.5.

There are several advantages to creating a table that links each relevant discipline to its perspective on the problem, as illustrated in the example of human cloning (Table 7.2).

Table 7.2   Disciplines and How They Illuminate Some Aspect of the Problem of Human Cloning (Before the In-Depth Literature Search)

Discipline, Interdiscipline, and Applied Field	Perspective Stated in Terms of the Kind of Overarching Questions Asked About Human Cloning
Biology	What are the scientific consequences of human cloning?
Psychology	How will the discovery of being cloned affect the cloned person psychologically and the perceptions of others who know this about the person?
Political Science	What should be the role of government concerning this issue?
Philosophy	How will human cloning affect humanity and what it means to be human?
Religious Studies	Does the science of human cloning conform to sacred writings and, more particularly, to the notion of what it means to be human?
Law[a]	What are the legal implications of human cloning, and what are the rights of those who are participants in human cloning experiments?
Bioethics[b]	What are the ethical implications of the biotechnology used in human cloning?

a. Law is an applied field in many taxonomies.

b. Bioethics is an interdisciplinary field in many taxonomies.

Table 7.3   Disciplines and How They Illuminate Some Aspect of the Columbia River Ecosystem

Discipline	Perspective Stated in Terms of the Kind of Overarching Questions Asked About the Columbia River Ecosystem
Biology	What are the consequences of the dam system to native salmon populations?
Economics	What are the economic benefits and liabilities of the dam system on the people living in the region?
Geology	What are the implications of the dams on the region's hydrological system?
History	What does the damming of the Columbia River system tell us about the nation's confidence at this period of history?
Political Science (Politics)	What should be the role of government at all levels concerning the future of the dam system?

Table 7.4   Disciplines and How They Illuminate Some Aspect of Occupational Sex
               Discrimination (OSD)

Discipline and School of Thought	Perspective Stated in Terms of the Kind of Overarching Questions Asked About Occupational Sex Discrimination
Economics	What is the economic motivation for OSD?
History	What is the historical context that would help explain OSD?
Sociology	How is OSD a reflection of broader social relationships in society?
Psychology	How does the behavior of the perpetrators and victims of OSD reflect the psychological constructs individuals develop to make sense of their situations?
Marxism[a]	How is OSD a necessary act of preserving capitalism?

a. Marxism is a school of thought.

Table 7.5   Disciplines and How They Illuminate Some Aspect of the Graffito

Discipline and Subdiscipline	Perspective Stated in Terms of the Kind of Overarching Questions Asked About the Graffito
Anthropology (Cultural)	Is the graffito an expression of contemporary "popular" Dutch culture?
Art History	Is the graffito merely illustrative of the text about it?
Linguistics (Narratology)	What does the graffito represent?
Philosophy (Epistemology)	What does the graffito suggest is real and unreal?
Literature	What can the graffito be compared to in Dutch poetry?
Psychology	Is the graffito a text of psychic mourning for love lost?

NOTE: Cultural anthropology, narratology, and epistemology are subdisciplines.

1. *The table reveals an instance of* apparent *overlap of perspectives.* There is obviously some overlap in perspective between bioethics and philosophy but not enough to warrant ignoring the insights from either scholarly community. Underlying what *appears* as similar disciplinary perspectives are differing assumptions, epistemologies, concepts, theories, and methods.

2. *The table shows gaps or dissimilarity among perspectives.* The wide gaps in perspective between all of the other disciplines are not surprising because they reflect underlying differences in disciplinary assumptions and epistemologies. The lack of scholarly consensus surrounding the problem of human cloning is, after all, what constitutes the object of the interdisciplinary research process.

3. *The table may prompt shifting the focus of the problem or redefining it.* Instead of focusing on the problem of human cloning in general, we may wish to narrow the topic to "What should be the role of government in the development of human cloning technology?" Once again, we see the nonlinearity of the interdisciplinary process— performing one Step may prompt us to revisit an earlier Step.

Question #2: Has the discipline produced important insights into the problem?

Here, the focus is on the significance of each discipline's research. Since the goal of any interdisciplinary research effort is to achieve the most comprehensive understanding of the problem possible, it is advisable to include those disciplines producing important insights into the problem. In the example of human cloning, these include biology, psychology, political science, philosophy, religion, law, and bioethics. However, given the usual constraints of time and course requirements, the student may need to limit the number of disciplines used to only three or four, based on the comparative importance of their insights. Ways to evaluate the importance of insights include (1) seeing how often the insight is cited by other experts, (2) consulting disciplinary experts, and (3) noting the date of publication. The latter factor is particularly important when dealing with time-sensitive issues involving, for instance, rapidly evolving reproductive technologies.

Students should focus on research that is published in peer-reviewed journals and by academic presses and some commercial publishing houses. There is an abundance of material on the Internet, some of which is scholarly, but much is not. Great caution must be exercised when using Internet materials unless these are obtained from a recognized academic Web site.[4] Library-based computer search techniques and problems that are distinctive to interdisciplinary research are discussed as part of Step 4.

Students frequently encounter the problem of disciplines using different keywords to describe some aspect of the problem. In the example of human cloning, keywords include "control," "legislation," and "impact" to describe the concept of "power" as it relates to the problem. Disciplinary handbooks, dictionaries, encyclopedias, introductory textbooks, and other sources are tools useful to developing familiarity with the terminology commonly used by each discipline.

An interdisciplinary network or field, not just disciplines, may also have generated insights into a particular problem or question. Discovery of such networks or unfamiliar fields is not uncommon as students read the published literature and discuss the topic with experts.

When determining the relevance of a discipline and its insights, students should not be influenced by the quantity of a discipline's research on the problem. If a discipline has just begun to address the problem, or if the problem is of recent origin, then it is not uncommon to find that its experts have published only a few insights. But those few may be extremely important because they are based on the latest research and may advance an important theory. It is not uncommon to find a single treatment of the problem by a leading scholar in a discipline that impacts the discussion in such a forceful way that one cannot ignore it. In this event, the student must ask additional questions about the research, and the discipline as a whole, before drawing any conclusions.

Question #3: Has the discipline generated one or more theories relevant to the problem?

Theories about the causes or consequences (real or possible) of a problem should be part of developing adequacy in each relevant discipline (Step 5) and may be among the possible sources of conflict between disciplinary insights (Step 7). Chapter 4 noted that theories are of two types: narrow range and grand. Narrow-range theories are produced by a discipline to address particular phenomena of interest to it. Grand theories or schools of thought, such as feminist theory, postcolonial theory, and rational choice theory, inform the literatures of two or more disciplines and, like narrow-range theories, produce insights into particular problems.

Whether or not theories of either the narrow or grand variety have generated insights into the problem can be answered only by conducting an in-depth literature search. Concerning the example of human cloning, reading the literature on this problem with this question in mind heightened student awareness of not only the amount of disciplinary activity among the relevant disciplines but also the *differing* insights in and among these disciplines.

Identifying Disciplines That Appear to Be "Most" Relevant to the Issue of Human Cloning

By asking these three questions of each relevant discipline, students should be able to identify those disciplines that are *most* relevant to the problem of human cloning. These are listed here along with an explanation for their selection:

- *Biology:* The literature search found that more biologists are writing about human cloning than are scholars from any other discipline. This is understandable because human cloning is itself a biological procedure. Students also found that biologists are advancing some of the most important theories on human cloning and are expressing the greatest diversity of opinion on this issue.
- *Bioethics:* Essays written by bioethicists contain important bridging concepts and methods. The essays written by bioethicists may appear to be similar to those written by philosophers but differ from them in one important respect: they are science based.

- *Philosophy:* Though essays written by philosophers *appear* to overlap those written by bioethicists, there are important differences. For one thing, the essays are not science based but are grounded in humanistic ethics, thus offering a perspective that contrasts sharply with that of bioethicists on this issue. For another, philosophers tend to exclude important bridging concepts and methods that bioethicists tend to include.
- *Religious Studies:* Religion and the world's major faith traditions are among the most powerful influences in our society today. This explains why congressional hearings conducted on "hot button" social issues such as human cloning always include substantial testimony from representatives of the major faith traditions. Therefore, including the perspective of religion seemed appropriate given the amount of attention religious studies scholars have devoted to this issue, the popular interest in their views, and the need to understand value systems that are faith based rather than empirically based.
- *Law:* Though the amount of legal scholarship on the issue is far smaller than that from the other disciplines, the discipline offers insights that approach the issue from the unique perspective of law and is therefore pertinent.

In the end, course constraints required limiting the number of disciplines to three. The decision to consider biology, philosophy (i.e., humanistic ethics), and religion as "most" relevant to the problem of human cloning was made on the basis of the criteria noted earlier. If students are not limited by the numbers of disciplines that they can use, they must exercise great care as they seek to limit the number of disciplines because this increases the risk that the integrative result will be less than comprehensive. Whether these criteria or others are used to differentiate between disciplines that initially *appear* to be relevant and those that are indeed *most* relevant, the essential thing is to develop some means by which to identify and justify the disciplines ultimately used and *make this decision-making process explicit*. Later Steps in the interdisciplinary process will validate whether the disciplines selected are indeed the *most* relevant.

The Literature Search

Step 4: Conduct a literature search

Basic to any research effort is the literature search.[5] An **in-depth literature search** involves identifying all expert insights relevant to the problem. The literature search may also involve gathering information on the problem that is not of interest to the disciplines or is overlooked by them but is nevertheless relevant to the inquiry. This information, called "other sources of knowledge" (i.e., nondisciplinary), is discussed at the end of this chapter. The search for disciplinary and other knowledge sources is based on the assumption that knowledge accumulates and that people learn from and build upon what others have done (Neuman, 2006, p. 111). Today's knowledge is the product of yesterday's research, and tomorrow's knowledge will be based on today's research.

The integrated model of the interdisciplinary research process introduced in Chapter 6 places the full-scale literature search at Step 4. While there is no "right time" to take this essential Step, it must be taken very early in the research process, and it is often conducted in phases, beginning with Step 1, defining the problem. This chapter discusses the purposes of the literature search and identifies the special challenges facing the interdisciplinarian in conducting it.

Purposes of the Literature Search

There are several purposes of the literature search that apply to disciplinary as well as interdisciplinary research. One purpose is simply to save time. By revealing what is known about the problem at the outset, the literature search will prevent unwitting duplication of work that has already been done.

A second purpose is to narrow the topic, sharply focus the research question, and state the problem clearly. In practice, the literature search (or at least its initial phase) overlaps with Step 1, defining the problem. One may be interested in the topic of terrorism, for example, but quickly discover that the topic is too broad and the amount of literature on it is too vast to be approached during the time allotted. A literature search on terrorism will help to narrow the topic to something more manageable, say, the causes of suicide terrorism. However, too narrow a focus may remove the topic from an interdisciplinary approach in some academic contexts because of insufficient literature on the topic from two or more disciplines. The literature search will help students decide whether the topic is researchable using an interdisciplinary approach.

A third purpose of the literature search is to understand the background of the problem by tracing its development over a period of time and by establishing the immediate context of the problem. Every problem has a history and a context. Often, interdisciplinary writing introduces the problem by situating it within a **historical background.** Along with explaining how and why the problem developed, the historical background may also include explaining how the disciplines have approached the problem over time; how they developed concepts, theories, and methods to understand it; but how these have failed to provided either a comprehensive understanding of the problem or a solution to it, thus necessitating an interdisciplinary approach. One such treatise is that of James Watson (1968), who describes in the early chapters of his book *The Double Helix: A Personal Account of the Discovery of the Structure of DNA* a brief history of how the disciplines of chemistry and physics had approached DNA research.

Another purpose of the literature search is to **situate or contextualize the problem**. This refers to providing information describing how the problem is connected to other similar problems. In general, situating or contextualizing the problem involves identifying the web of interrelationships in which the problem is embedded. These connections often surface in the process of drawing a system map.

A fifth purpose of the literature search is to show the paths of prior disciplinary research and how the interdisciplinary project is linked to these and may extend them. Reading the literature of each discipline pertaining to the problem establishes the outlines of that discipline's perspective (in a general sense) on the problem and deepens the student's understanding of its insights (books, journals, etc.) into the problem.

A further purpose of the literature search is to demonstrate a familiarity with a body of knowledge and establish academic credibility. Interdisciplinarians call this developing adequacy in the relevant disciplines, which is Step 5 and the subject of Chapter 8. Developing adequacy includes identifying the literature from the relevant disciplines pertaining to the problem and becoming knowledgeable of the major issues concerning it.

A seventh purpose of the literature search is to identify the concepts, assumptions, theories, methods, and data used by each discipline's experts in their writing on the problem. Students should be alert to how the scholarship produced by the relevant disciplines often uses differing terminology (i.e., concepts) and differing explanations (i.e., theories) to describe the same problem. It is critical, therefore, to identify the relevant disciplines early on and to investigate their terminology, looking for differences and similarities in meaning.

Special Challenges Confronting the Interdisciplinary Student

Conducting a literature search is more difficult for interdisciplinary students than for disciplinary students, for several reasons. For one thing, the interdisciplinary student is faced with the challenge of surveying the insights of each relevant discipline's literature, whereas the disciplinary student is responsible for surveying the literature of just a single discipline. After all, an interdisciplinary research project addresses a problem that requires integration of insights that come from several disciplines, interdisciplines, or schools of thought. In fact, the term "literature search" is actually a misnomer because an interdisciplinary research project typically requires several separate literature searches, one for each of the potentially relevant disciplines (Klein & Newell, 1997, pp. 406–407).

A second challenge confronting the interdisciplinary student is the current method of cataloguing in libraries that serves the interdisciplinarian poorly because it is grounded in the disciplines rather than in a universal list of phenomena, theory types, methods, and so on. Library catalogues are not set up to connect different parts of the problem (or to connect related problems) studied by different disciplines, nor are they set up to identify the same or similar problems that are given different labels by different disciplines. The present system of classification also makes it difficult to search by the phenomenon name. One way to overcome this limitation is to identify which disciplines are likely to be interested in the problem and then use resources—bibliographies and guides, dictionaries, encyclopedias, handbooks, and databases—specific to each discipline. In this way, the student can work systematically and productively across the relevant disciplines.

A third challenge the interdisciplinary student faces is becoming seduced by the existing literature. This seduction may involve accepting a particular discipline's perspective or understanding of the problem to the exclusion of others. Students must avoid allowing the existing literature and the views of others, even if they are experts, to shape their understanding of the problem. Relying on what others have said at the very outset of the research enterprise short-circuits objective and creative thinking that is essential to good interdisciplinary work.

This seduction may also involve being tempted in the early phase of the interdisciplinary research process to begin reading the disciplinary literature on the problem before first developing a clear understanding of how the problem should be approached in an interdisciplinary way. Immersing oneself in the existing literature prior to thinking through the problem in all of its aspects to the best of one's ability increases the risk that the student will ignore relevant phenomena just because certain disciplinary scholars have. Focusing on only what disciplinary experts "see" (i.e., write) will limit one's ability to see (Szostak, 2002, p. 106). Interdisciplinary research involves, among other things, looking for what disciplinarians have failed to see.

Suggestions for the Initial Phase of Interdisciplinary Research

Following are suggestions about what to do in the initial phase of the research process:

- Identify the disciplines that are *potentially* relevant to the topic by referring to Table 4.2, "Overall Perspective of Disciplines Stated in General Terms."
- Begin reading published insights that provide an *overview* of the problem.
- Read *cursorily* on the topic in each of the identified disciplines to see whether there is sufficient literature on it to warrant further inquiry. Reading cursorily, part of the process of developing adequacy (Step 5), will minimize the tendency to be unduly influenced by the literature.

- *Narrow* the topic, if necessary, so that it is manageable, and then state it as a problem or question (Step 1). One student transitioned from a broad topic to an interdisciplinary problem this way: "The issue of crime is broad, and solving more crimes is a pressing social need. Solving cases that heretofore have proven unsolvable can be achieved provided that high-level cooperation between investigatory agencies that typically represent various disciplinary approaches to crime-solving is achieved" (Delph, 2005, p. 1).
- *Reflect* on the topic and be able to *justify* using an interdisciplinary approach (Step 2).

The Disciplines in the Literature Search

The disciplines assuredly form the foundation of interdisciplinarity and provide much of the information used in the research process. In order to engage in interdisciplinary research, students must develop adequacy in disciplines relevant to the problem (Wolfe & Haynes, 2003, p. 132). As explained in Chapters 3 and 4, disciplines are distinguished from one another by their concentration on different kinds of problems; by the questions they ask about the world; by their perspectives and their defining elements expressed as insights, concepts, assumptions, theories, and methods; and by the kind of evidence they consider valid when studying a problem.

Initially, students need to look at each discipline's perspective as a whole, not just at how this perspective has been applied so far to the problem. As one reads, one should look for possible applications of each discipline's perspective to the problem, and be alert to what scholars have overlooked, not just what they have learned. Discovering scholarly silence on a problem is often as important as discovering an important published insight.

A successful literature search will confirm that the problem is researchable and is indeed appropriate to interdisciplinary inquiry. Students should always err on the side of inclusiveness in conducting the literature search, but inclusive does not mean open-ended. **Inclusive** refers not to the quantity of disciplinary insights but to the quality and diversity of these published insights. The challenge for the student is to keep these to a manageable number.

Mistakes Commonly Made in the Early Phase of the Literature Search

Those new to the interdisciplinary research process commonly make two mistakes. First, students often fail to pay close attention to the disciplinary source of the insights they are gathering. One unintended consequence of this oversight is to end up with a large number of insights drawn from one or two disciplines at the expense of other equally important disciplines.

Interdisciplinary research cannot succeed on this basis. It is important to keep track of which discipline produced which insight. Rigorous interdisciplinary research involves striking a balance between depth and breadth. In practical terms, this means identifying the important disciplinary insights and categorizing them according to disciplinary perspective. This ideal is seldom realized in undergraduate education, however, where students are typically limited to gathering a few insights from only two or three disciplines.

Another mistake commonly made is to be unduly influenced by the quantity of literature generated by a discipline. For example, if a careful search of the literature reveals that sociology has contributed only one or two essays on the problem, one may wrongly conclude that sociology is not as relevant to the investigation as other disciplines, each of which has produced several essays. *Quantity of material produced by a discipline should never decide disciplinary relevance.* Why? It may be that the one essay by a cultural anthropologist (and the *only* essay on the problem by any cultural anthropologist) contains information of such importance that an interdisciplinary understanding of the problem would not be possible without it. But what about when, for example, sociology has not addressed the specific topic, say, of rave music? Can one conclude that sociology has nothing to contribute to the discussion? Not necessarily. Sociology may have addressed house music or punk rock or musical subcultures preceding rave. Students should be open to possibilities that are not initially apparent. Many topics turn out to be subsets of a larger topic. Rather than giving up on sociology upon discovering that it has not examined rave, the student should look at the larger context—in this case, what preceded rave. If a discipline has treated a more general category of which a topic is a part, it would be quite surprising if that treatment does not have some direct applicability to the narrower topic. Indeed, if the more general treatment has no bearing on the narrower topic, then the student should reexamine the choice of general category. Also, students should look to see whether core concepts or theories from a particular discipline might usefully be applied to the topic, even though no one in the discipline has gotten around to making the application.

Students are sometimes surprised to learn that a discipline that initially appears not to be relevant has produced insights into the problem after all. These discoveries are possible only by conducting an in-depth literature search. In this effort, students can profitably use Szostak's (2004) "Categories of Phenomena About the Human World" (Table 4.2) in Chapter 4 to cross check traditional disciplinary searches.

Two Challenges in the Latter Phase of the Literature Search

The student faces two major challenges in the latter phase of the literature search: (1) collecting relevant information and (2) organizing this information. Relevant information is information about the problem or question that pertains directly to the problem and that the student will draw upon in the subsequent steps of the research process to perform integration and produce the new understanding. Having decided which disciplines are the most relevant to the problem, students should then engage in close reading of each insight with a particular agenda in mind. At a minimum, students should look for the following basic information in each source:

- The writer's name and date of publication
- The writer's disciplinary perspective on the problem
- The writer's insight, view, or understanding of the problem
- The theory the writer uses (if identified) and its description
- The concept(s) that the writer uses to express the theory or insight

More advanced students conducting research projects of greater sophistication may wish to gather additional information:

- The research method used by the writer
- The kind of data that the writer uses to support his/her theory or argument
- The assumptions underlying the writer's approach to the problem
- The writer's epistemology

Note: Students should generally approach interdisciplines, schools of thought, and the applied fields in the same way as they approach disciplines.

This close reading agenda shows that a literature search involving selecting just three or four disciplines and reading three or more insights produced by each one entails gathering a considerable amount of information. To avoid becoming overwhelmed as the reading proceeds, the student should organize the information so that it can be easily accessed when performing subsequent steps of the research process. Though there is no "right way" to organize this information, some students are profitably using "data management" tables similar to the ones used in this book. Table 7.6 is an example of such a table.

A data management table can be expanded to include more granular information about any one insight and any number of insights. Their utility for interdisciplinary work will be increasingly evident as the interdisciplinary research process unfolds.

Library-Based Computer Search Techniques and Problems Distinctive to Interdisciplinary Research

The intellectual challenges of the interdisciplinary research process are matched by the scholarly challenges of using library-based computer searches.

Table 7.6   Theory-Based Insights Into the Problem of Suicide Terrorism

Theory	Insight of Theory Stated in General Terms	Insight Into the Problem	Concept	Assumption
Terrorist Psycho-logic	Political violence is not instrumental but an end in itself. The cause becomes the rationale for acts of terrorism the terrorist is compelled to commit (Post, 1998, p. 35).	"Individuals are drawn to the path of terrorism to commit acts of violence . . . as a consequence of psychological forces, and that their special psycho-logic is constructed to rationalize acts they are psychologically compelled to commit" (Post, 1998, p. 25).	Special Logic (Post, 1998, p. 25)	Humans organize their mental life through psychological constructs.

Identification of Sources

Students need to start broadly and then narrow their search to more specialized sources. Starting broadly generally means reading books and articles cursorily to develop a general understanding of the problem and then consulting the more specialized journal literature. Books often provide more context and history than articles can.[6] There are various kinds of books: monographs, reports of major research studies, and series of chapters on the problem by different experts. The usefulness of each type of book in interdisciplinary work depends on the problem the student is investigating, the disciplines involved, and the required depth of the research. Experts also report their findings in periodical literature, including peer-reviewed scholarly journals such as *Social Science Quarterly* and semischolarly professional publications such as *American Demographics*. Experts may report their findings as papers delivered at professional meetings, dissertations, government documents, or policy reports. Encyclopedia articles may or may not be authoritative, depending on the scholarly credentials of the writer. Like Internet sources, they should be used with great care. Students may profitably consult Chart 5.1, "Types of Publications," in W. Lawrence Neuman's (2006) *Social Research Methods* (6th ed.), which identifies publication types, examples of each type, types of writer, purpose, strengths, and weaknesses of each type of publication.

With time-sensitive topics such as those noted earlier, the material in books may be dated because books require more time to research and publish. Even so, book material often provides pertinent background information that is an important component in research and writing. In starting broadly, one may profitably use Szostak's (2004) "Categories of Phenomena About the Human World" (Table 4.2 in Chapter 4). This table conveniently moves (left to right) from the more general to the more narrow. It also helps to establish links to neighboring concepts that may be relevant and might otherwise be overlooked. A good way to develop a list of possible sources is to consult the sources used in a recently published book or journal article on the problem, paying attention to which ones are most frequently cited by experts.

Using the Library of Congress Classification System in Interdisciplinary Work

Students new to interdisciplinary research will likely encounter the Library of Congress (LOC) classification system when they use the library or the online catalogue and should be aware of its characteristics. The LOC system is commonly used by major research libraries, though the Dewey system (also grounded in disciplines) continues to be used by many smaller libraries and, indeed, all general systems of library classification. The LOC system reflects the way knowledge has developed and is based on the number of books written in each discipline. The system is designed to serve the needs of the disciplines by organizing knowledge according to disciplinary categories. Each category moves from the general to the specific, enabling disciplinarians to easily find books on their specialty. Although many disciplinary books contain information that falls outside disciplinary lines, it is not presently reflected in the LOC system of classification. Knowing this basic information about the LOC system should prompt students to either browse the physical shelves in the library or conduct a call number search in the online catalogue. Browsing is very useful in the early phase of the literature search, especially when the student knows the most basic information about the relevant disciplines (provided in Chapters 3 and 4) but has not yet developed adequacy in them.

The Usefulness of Relying on LOC Subject Headings

Students need to identify not only books that address their topic but also books that reference it cursorily. These latter books are important to the interdisciplinary research process because they may bring out contrasts in disciplinary perspectives that might not otherwise exist. These books and their lists of sources may also identify, or at least provide hints regarding, important linkages to other concepts, theories, or information relevant to the topic.

Fortunately, catalogue entries for books assigned LOC call numbers often list more than one LOC subject heading to reflect the contents of the book. These subject headings, though far from exhaustive, at least reflect *some* of the topical diversity within the book (Searing, 1992, p. 14). Once the subject headings relevant to the problem are identified, these subject headings may be used to conduct more advanced searches that will yield additional references on the topic.[7]

The purpose of subject headings is to bring together books on the same topic whose authors use different terminology or jargon, including works from different disciplines (Klein & Newell, 2002, p. 152). Conducting a keyword search on the terms used in a relevant book will likely identify other books on the same topic written from a similar perspective (Newell, 2005, p. 2). The LOC subject headings and thesauri also provide a bridge between the terminologies of different disciplines. Interdisciplinarians seeking a wide range of perspectives on a topic use the subject headings instead of trying to think of all the disciplinary jargon.

Indexes, Databases, and Other Collections

Topical databases (see list in Appendix A) are now available that cut across disciplines, and referencing these provides a critical source of disciplinary scholarship upon which interdisciplinarians must draw, especially for articles. Some databases are discipline based, each having its own thesaurus or classification system using the terminology of that discipline. Some databases are more apt to cross disciplinary lines, using terminology to connect works from the contributing disciplines. As interdisciplinarians move from discipline to discipline in search of different insights on the same topic, they need to check the thesaurus or classification system for that collection to find the term(s) to search for. Starting with a good keyword and Boolean Search Strategy (described in Appendix A) helps locate appropriate descriptors—as subject headings in indexes are often called. Thesauri and subject headings are most useful, says Joan B. Fiscella (1989), where a recognized scholarly community has been established (p. 83). In the discipline of psychology, for example, a keyword search for "gender differences" in *Psych Info* will yield thousands of hits, but a check of the *Psych Info* thesaurus will reveal that it is not a valid subject heading and that one should use "human sex differences" instead, which will yield even more hits (Newell, 2005, p. 3).

Other Sources of Knowledge Available to the Interdisciplinarian

Broadly speaking, there are two kinds of knowledge available to interdisciplinary students:

1. *Scholarly knowledge.* This knowledge is generated by a discipline's community of scholars in the form of various literatures and data and is peer-reviewed. Sources of scholarly literature include the Internet, where an increasing number of scholars and scholarly organizations are posting their research. The disciplinary nature of much of this literature is easy to identify. However, the growing number of interdisciplines and their journals is

complicating the task of neatly dividing scholarly sources by discipline. Students are advised to consult disciplinary experts to assess the credibility of any site. An excellent Web site for interdisciplinary research in philosophy, cognitive science, and social science is *interdisciplines* (http://www.interdisci plines.org), which posts interdisciplinary papers and scholarly criticism of them along with threaded discussions on various topics. The interdisciplinary peer-reviewed journal *Issues in Integrative Studies,* published by the Association for Integrative Studies, is making its back issues available online at http:// www.units.muohio.edu/aisorg/pubs/issues/toclist.html.

2. *Other knowledge or knowledge formations.* This knowledge is not produced by trained disciplinary scholars. It may include oral histories, eye-witness testimonies, statistics and tables, artifacts, and artistic creations. Interdisciplinarians do not assume that *all* relevant knowledge has been generated by the disciplines. Chapter 1 identifies the broad range of knowledge outside the disciplines that one may wish to consult.

Interdisciplinarians know that relevant information sometimes comes from unexpected sources that are disciplinary as well as nondisciplinary. Carp (2001), pointing to Klein's (1990) injunction to determine "all knowledge needs" (p. 188), urges interdisciplinarians not to limit their search for relevant information to the disciplines, for the simple reason that their knowledge formations are incomplete (Carp, 2001, p. 98).[8] Nonscholarly knowledge may have important contributions to make in some interdisciplinary research projects, although concepts and theories may be less explicit in it (p. 84). Historians, sociologists, anthropologists, and other disciplinary experts are constantly mining these diverse sources of knowledge for their own disciplinary purposes and often go on to publish their findings. In this way, nonscholarly knowledge finds its way into the Academy. Oral histories of migrant workers is a good example of the kind of nonscholarly knowledge that is gathered and presented in a way that disciplinary scholars can accept. Investigating the high cost of health care may include the testimony of health care providers as part of one's study. Students should not hesitate to include nonscholarly knowledge in their work, provided that it is clearly identified as such and is collected and used in a scholarly way.

CHAPTER SUMMARY

This chapter focused on Steps 3 and 4 of the interdisciplinary research process.

Step 3 involves identifying disciplines potentially relevant to the problem and from these, determining which are most relevant. Narrowing the number of disciplines is not as necessary in professional work as it is in undergraduate or even graduate work. Course requirements generally determine how many disciplines and how much reading in their literatures students can reasonably be expected to handle. Students should consider using maps in the initial phase of their research. A simple research map, for example, can help students new to interdisciplinary research visualize the process from beginning to end. More advanced students working with more complex problems can benefit from using concept, system, and theory maps to break down the problem into its constituent parts and see how the parts relate to the whole. Students are well advised to use the two simple tests to help identify the appropriateness of a discipline and ask the three questions of each potentially relevant discipline to help to identify the most relevant disciplines.

Step 4 pertains to conducting the in-depth literature search. There is no substitute for thorough research. Identifying potentially relevant disciplines, to say nothing of the more demanding task of narrowing these to just the most relevant disciplines, may require extending the literature search until the student is confident that all of the relevant disciplines and their important insights are identified. Students must avoid limiting their reading to familiar disciplines while ignoring unfamiliar ones. They must also check each discipline to see whether it has literature on the topic. If it does, then the discipline is relevant. Students should categorize insights by discipline, interdiscipline, or school of thought and devise some method of storing this information for easy retrieval later in the research process. While conducting a literature search is common to the scholarly process of all disciplines, categorizing this material by discipline is distinctive to interdisciplinary studies.

If the literature search is hurried, it may not reveal all the relevant disciplines. Students unfamiliar with the interdisciplinary research process are sometimes tempted to end the literature search prematurely after finding a handful of sources produced by a few disciplines or a few experts. Subsequent steps in the interdisciplinary process will expose incomplete or careless work done in earlier steps. The next chapter advances the research process by explaining how to develop adequacy in the relevant disciplines.

Notes

1. The mental representation of the internal organization of a problem or system may be expressed in a text format or depicted by a visual-spatial technique called concept or knowledge mapping (Czuchy & Dansereau, 1996, pp. 91–96). The knowledge map is composed mainly of nodes of various shapes, sizes, and colors with meaningful links that are labeled to designate the relationships among the nodes. Succinct statements are incorporated in each node, and the links are identified by a letter abbreviation. The links may indicate characteristics, components, consequences, direction of action, outcomes, predictions, subsets, or subtopics; therefore, a legend is included to explain the meaning of the labels for the links. The spatial arrangements of the nodes on the map may be hierarchical, radial (spider), chain, flowchart, or even multidimensional; some map designers have positioned the nodes as trees, ladders, bridges, rockets, or other symbolic shapes for the theme of the map. The most significant purpose of the map's configuration is to depict relationships among the various aspects of the concepts in each node; consequently, the

nodes may also be arranged to designate inclusions, exclusions, overlapping concepts, or chronological sequences (C. Atha-Weldon, personal communication, March, 2005). Szostak (2004) speaks of mapping the causal links among relevant phenomena to show which phenomena are implicated in a particular research question and how they are related. The researcher might even map which theories are implicated along different links. A useful base from which to sketch such a map when doing work in the social sciences or humanities is his list of phenomena reproduced as Table 4.1 in Chapter 4.

2. Useful Internet sites for concept mapping include http://users.edte.utwente .nl/lanzing/cm home.htm, http://www.graphic.org/concept.html, http://classes.aces .uiuc.edu/ACES100/Mind/CMap.html, and http://www.fed.cuhk.edu.hk/~johnson/ misconceptions/concept_map/air_pollution.html.

3. Limiting the number of disciplines is often necessary in undergraduate courses or even graduate courses where time and other constraints are operative.

4. An excellent discussion of the problem of sources, reliability of sources, and finding and evaluating sources on the Internet is in Chapter 5 of Booth, Colomb, and Williams (2003).

5. The social sciences conduct a literature review to demonstrate familiarity with the literature, show the path of prior research and how the current project is linked to it, and integrate and summarize what is known. A thorough discussion of the literature review is in Neuman (2006) and in Hart (1998). The term *literature review* is an umbrella term that refers to specialized reviews including context review, historical review, integrative review, methodological review, self-study review, and theoretical review (Neuman, 2006, p. 112). Social scientists typically conduct the literature review at the beginning of their research.

6. The disciplines vary in the importance that they attach to books compared to peer-reviewed journal articles. Scholars in the humanities are as likely to publish their research in book form as they are to publish in peer-reviewed journals. This is less so in the social sciences and far less so in the natural sciences.

7. The best treatment of this topic from an interdisciplinary perspective is Chapter 6 in Fiscella and Kimmel (1999).

8. Carp appears to be reading too much into this phrase, the immediate context of which is Klein's (1990) second step that reads as follows: "*determining* all knowledge needs, including appropriate disciplinary representatives and consultants, as well as relevant models, traditions, and literatures" (pp. 188–189).

REVIEW QUESTIONS

1. Practically, how does one go about identifying the disciplines relevant to the problem?

2. What, in general terms, are the benefits of mapping the problem?

3. How does constructing a system map help in working with a very complex problem?

4. How can students distinguish between disciplines that are relevant and those that are most relevant?

5. What are two simple tests to help identify the relevance of a discipline?

6. What are the three questions students should ask of each relevant discipline?

7. What is the practical benefit of constructing a table such as Table 7.2 when researching a complex issue involving multiple disciplines?

8. Why do interdisciplinary students bear a heavier responsibility for performing a thorough literature search than do disciplinary students?

9. What is the goal of the literature search?

10. What mistakes are commonly made in the literature search?

11. What two challenges do interdisciplinary students face during the literature search?

12. What is the purpose of the student providing in-text evidence of disciplinary adequacy?

13. How is the Library of Congress system useful to interdisciplinarians?

14. What is the difference between scholarly knowledge and "other knowledge," and how might the latter also be useful to interdisciplinarians?

8 Developing Adequacy in Relevant Disciplines

Chapter Preview

Chapter 8 explains how to develop adequacy in relevant disciplines. By *adequacy* is meant knowing enough about the discipline to have a basic understanding of how it approaches the problem and how it illuminates and characterizes the problem. The two parts of the interdisciplinary research process—drawing on disciplinary insights and integrating insights—cannot be conducted unless adequacy is first achieved. Performing Step 5 of the interdisciplinary research process enables the student to study the problem from the perspective of each relevant discipline and evaluate each insight into the problem.

> Step 5: Develop adequacy in each relevant discipline

Once students have identified the disciplines that are the most relevant to the problem, they must develop adequacy in each of these disciplines. By contrast, disciplinary students typically develop **mastery** of their discipline by majoring in it so that they can practice it professionally. There is a critical distinction between adequacy and mastery, says Klein (1996). Adequacy shifts the focus to the task at hand and means comprehending enough of the discipline to decide which of its defining elements bear on the problem most directly (p. 212).

Developing Adequacy Involves Making Decisions

Developing adequacy in each discipline most relevant to the problem is demanding, yet achievable. It requires that we make decisions about the following:

- How much knowledge is required from each discipline
- What kind of knowledge is required from each discipline

- Whether the problem can be adequately illuminated using a handful of insights and introductory-level concepts, assumptions, theories, and methods from each discipline
- Whether the disciplines that we identified in Step 3 as most relevant are still appropriate

How Much Knowledge Is Required From Each Discipline?

This question concerns both depth and breadth in disciplinary knowledge. "How much" refers to the *depth of knowledge* in the disciplines most relevant to the problem. "How much" also refers to the *breadth of knowledge* across relevant disciplines. Concerning depth, Newell (2007) asks, "Is it even possible to do responsible interdisciplinary work as an individual, or must one collaborate with an expert from each of the other contributing disciplines?" (p. 253).[1]

The Required Depth and Breadth of Knowledge

Fortunately, Newell's answer to his own question is that the required depth and breadth is usually quite modest and depends on the length and sophistication of the study undertaken (p. 253). Two examples from published interdisciplinary work bear this out. The first example is James D. Watson's (1968) personal account of the discovery of the structure of DNA, for which he, Francis Crick, and Maurice Wilkins were awarded the Nobel Prize in Physiology in 1962. Watson reveals that at the start of his research on DNA he had been unable to interpret Linus Pauling's X-ray diffraction pictures of the a-helix, which, it was supposed, would unlock the secret of the structure of DNA. Watson, a biologist, had little training in mathematics or physics, the two disciplines most relevant to his research. Consequently, Watson was unable to determine if Pauling's just-proposed a-helix model was right. If Pauling was right, then the race to discover the structure of DNA would go to Pauling. Watson, referring to himself as "a mathematically deficient biologist," naturally began "worrying about where [he] could learn to solve X-ray diffraction pictures" (pp. 38–39). He quickly developed adequacy in disciplines and subfield specialties that bore directly on his research by spending time with disciplinary experts, working in various laboratories, reading scholarly publications, and attending conferences at which experts read papers.[2]

The second example is William Dietrich's (1995) interdisciplinary study of the Columbia River system. Dietrich, a science reporter for the *Seattle Times*, received the Pulitzer Prize in 1990 for coverage of the Exxon Valdez oil spill. To study the vast and complex Columbia River system comprehensively required Dietrich to develop adequacy in several disciplines and disciplinary specialties, including environmental science (an interdisciplinary field), chemistry, physics, political science, Native American history and culture (an interdisciplinary field), and economics as it relates to his questions about that river system, and integrate their diverse and often conflicting insights.

Students researching much more modest problems can follow the examples of Watson and Dietrich by identifying relevant disciplines, reading their literatures, evaluating their insights, and asking questions of experts.

Examples of the Need for Varying Degrees of Disciplinary Depth and Breadth

What is true for professional interdisciplinarians concerning the need for varying degrees of depth and breadth is also true for students, as the following examples of undergraduate work illustrate. The first example required the least depth and breadth in relevant disciplines. A sophomore-level course introducing the field of interdisciplinary studies required students to identify relevant disciplines and their perspectives on the topic of human cloning. Though none of the students had previously researched this particular topic, all the students had access to Table 3.2 of disciplinary perspectives stated in general terms. This table enabled them to identify three potentially relevant disciplines, the number required for the assignment. Applying these disciplinary perspectives to the topic, however, proved more challenging as it required them to read two peer-reviewed articles in each discipline, and on the basis of these, ferret out the defining elements relevant to the topic. Their instructor served as a facilitator and coach rather than "the sage on the stage."

The second example is from a junior-level theme-based course on the interdisciplinary research process. Topics included suicide terrorism, euthanasia, and illegal immigration. Students, working in small research groups, were required to identify three disciplines they considered most relevant to the problem. Most students had some depth in the form of formal coursework (12 hours or more) in one of the three disciplines they chose, but they had to develop adequacy in the other two disciplines in order to apply the interdisciplinary research process to the problem and produce an interdisciplinary understanding of it.

The third example is from an interdisciplinary senior paper course. Students entered the course with an approved research proposal on a problem or question that related to their professional or academic goal. Students had completed several advanced courses in at least two of the three disciplines that they would be mining for scholarly insights. Many of them had also had a research methods course in one of those disciplines. Developing adequacy in relevant disciplines at the senior level required students to read more deeply in the scholarship of each discipline. They also had to develop adequacy in relevant concepts, assumptions, epistemologies, research methods, and (in some cases) theories.

At every level, from introductory to mid-level to senior project, students, like professionals, must develop adequacy in those disciplines, subdisciplines, interdisciplines, or schools of thought that are relevant to the problem. The depth and breadth at each level naturally varies considerably, depending on the complexity of the problem and the requirements of the course.

Interdisciplinary knowledge production, though challenging, is manageable at all academic levels. What is required is for students to follow a research process that brings them from initial idea to integration of insights to interdisciplinary product. This and later chapters will provide numerous examples of interdisciplinary research oriented toward the natural sciences, the social sciences, and the humanities that illustrate this process.

Interdisciplinary Research Involves Borrowing

Conducting interdisciplinary research, for most undergraduates, involves **borrowing** from each discipline relevant to the problem. Borrowing, however, is not indiscriminate; it requires what one practitioner calls the **burden of comprehension**. This means having a minimum understanding of each relevant discipline's cognitive map. A discipline's **cognitive map** is synonymous with its overall perspective and its defining elements including its assumptions, epistemology, basic concepts, theories, and research methods (Klein, 2005a, p. 68). The level of comprehension depends on what level of course the student is taking and its requirements. Borrowing also calls for careful evaluation of the material borrowed in terms of its credibility (Is it peer-reviewed?), timeliness (Is it time-sensitive?), and relevance (Does it illuminate some part of the problem?).

Undergraduates do not need to start out with much specialized knowledge to engage in interdisciplinary research. Just how much depth and breadth is necessary depends, as it does for disciplinarians, on the characteristics of the problem, the goal of the research, and the availability of collaborators and their role. If the problem requires sophisticated manipulation of data, or the mastery of highly technical language, or knowledge whose mastery requires formal coursework, then more depth and reliance on disciplinary experts is required. But, says Newell (2007),

> if the problem can be illuminated adequately using a handful of introductory-level concepts and theories from each discipline, and modest information readily and simply acquired, then a solo interdisciplinary researcher or even a first-year undergraduate student can handle it. Luckily, one can get some useful initial understanding of most complex problems using a small number of relatively basic concepts and theories from each discipline. (p. 253)

Some of this foundational disciplinary information is provided in Chapters 3 and 4 in the survey of the disciplines and their defining elements. Knowing this most basic information establishes a basic "feel" for each relevant discipline.

What Kind of Knowledge
Is Required From Each Discipline?

The kind of knowledge required from each discipline centers, primarily, on how one answers these questions:

- *Which disciplinary elements are applicable to the problem?* This question can be answered satisfactorily only by engaging in Step 6, in which the problem is analyzed from the perspective of each discipline.
- *What are the characteristics of the problem?* Previous Steps have shown that the problem is complex and researchable. And, if the student has taken the time to map the problem (see Chapter 7), the student is able to identify the parts or subsystems of the problem. Once these are known, the student can determine which disciplines, and which elements of each discipline, focus on each part of the problem.
- *What is the goal of the research project?* The rule of thumb is that the more ambitious the goal, the more knowledge is required.

Can the Problem Be Adequately Illuminated
Using a Handful of Introductory-Level Elements
From Each Relevant Discipline?

In general, the answer to this question is "yes." If far more depth is required, the student will have to consult discipline-specific research aids referenced in Chapters 3 and 4. When dealing with theories and schools of thought, students often need guidance from experts to determine which theories or schools of thought pertain to the problem.

Databases useful for interdisciplinary research are listed in the Appendix of this book. These databases are typically available in major research libraries. Students can find out what resources each database offers by referencing its Web site. For example, the Oxford Reference Online database Web site (http://www.oxfordreference.com/pub/views/home.html) provides an online tour of its "premium collection product demonstration."

Are the Disciplines Identified in Step 3
as Potentially Relevant Still Appropriate?

A discipline that initially looked promising may not prove useful when the student discovers that the insights it provides appear to "overlap" with those of another discipline. **Overlap,** in an interdisciplinary sense, means that the discipline neither adds much to understanding the problem (possibly because the insights are informed by the same theory) nor offers a new way of thinking about the problem. For example, if scholars from two

different disciplines use rational choice theory to explain the same phenomenon, it is likely that their insights will be similar and thus "overlap." Their
insights will have to be scrutinized for differences other than theoretical
approach. If a discipline does not provide the anticipated illumination of a
particular aspect of the problem, then the student will need to look for
another discipline that does, revisiting Step 3.

Developing Adequacy May Include Identifying Relevant Theories

Step 5 shows how the interdisciplinarian identifies the discipline's insights,
some of which are produced by its theories. The focus here is on disciplinary
theories and theory-based insights.

Theories help scholars understand the natural or human world. They
explain certain phenomena, how they are related, and how they are supported by data and research. Theories produce insights on a specific problem
of interest to the discipline. For example, Charles C. Fischer (1988) begins his
interdisciplinary investigation of the causes of occupational sex discrimination
(OSD) by identifying four theories of OSD advanced by economists (p. 22).
He then examines other relevant disciplines and a school of thought (i.e.,
Marxism) and from these identifies additional theories on the causes of OSD.

Identifying all theories relevant to the problem is absolutely essential to
maintaining scholarly rigor and producing an interdisciplinary understanding. The easiest way to do this is to first identify theories within a single discipline and then repeat this process in serial fashion with the other relevant
disciplines until all the important theories are identified.

First, Identify Theories Within a Single Discipline That Seek to Explain the Problem

Step 4 (the literature search) urges categorizing insights by discipline, interdiscipline, or school of thought. Taking time to do this makes it easier to link,
as the following writers do, a discipline with specific theories. Identifying
theories is achieved by reviewing (or reviewing again, if necessary) the important literature with this question in mind: "What explanation or theory does
each writer advance to explain the problem I am investigating?" The value of
this question is that one can ask it of almost any topic. What explanation or
theory does each writer advance to explain, for example,

- the increase in teenage obesity?
- opposition to same-sex unions?
- public funding of professional sports stadiums?
- affordability of prescription drugs?

- the development of visual perspective in Renaissance art?
- declining salmon populations in the Columbia and Snake Rivers?
- illegal immigration?

The following examples of theories advanced by the same discipline on a particular topic are drawn from published work and student projects. The latter are identified by an asterisk after the surname.

From the Natural Sciences: Smolinski* (2005), Fresh Water Scarcity in Texas

Smolinski finds multiple theories within the discipline of geology relevant to the problem of fresh water scarcity in Texas, as shown in Table 8.1.

Geologists embrace one of three primary theories to explain the growing scarcity of fresh water in Texas: global warming theory, overexploitation theory, or infiltration theory. Deciding that these are the most relevant theories was possible only after Smolinski had thoroughly grounded himself in the published geology literature on the topic. To insure that his research was current and complete, Smolinski worked with a geology professor and consulted with geologists employed in the public and private sectors for additional and confirming insights.

From the Social Sciences: Fischer (1988), "On the Need for Integrating Occupational Sex Discrimination Theory on the Basis of Causal Variables"

In introducing his interdisciplinary essay on OSD, Fischer (1988) writes, "A review of the literature in the fields of psychology, sociology, economics, philosophy and history reveals a wide variety of explanations of OSD, each reflecting the relevant 'looking glass' of the particular discipline (or school of thought)" (p. 22). This statement is appropriate to an interdisciplinary essay for two reasons: (1) it informs the reader that the researcher has conducted an in-depth literature search, and (2) it identifies the disciplines *most* relevant to the problem.

Fischer found that four disciplines and one school of thought had produced important insights into the problem. From these, he began with economics, identifying four important economic theories on OSD, as shown in Table 8.2

Later steps explain how Fischer integrates these theories.

Table 8.1   Important Theories on Fresh Water Scarcity in Texas

Relevant Disciplines	Theories on the Causes of Fresh Water Scarcity
Geology	1. Global warming theory
	2. Overexploitation theory
	3. Infiltration theory

From the Humanities: Fry (1999), Samuel Taylor Coleridge: The Rime of the Ancient Mariner

Paul H. Fry identifies five literary theories that explain the meaning of Samuel Taylor Coleridge's complex and ambiguous classic romantic poem. These theories are identified in Table 8.3.

These theories within the discipline themselves represent significant interdisciplinary approaches that have changed the nature of interdisciplinary practice. In this example, these theories are treated almost like disciplines in that they are based on certain assumptions, express themselves in certain concepts, and use certain methods.

Students often have to work with multiple insights generated by one or more theories. The temptation at this early stage of the research process is to reduce the number of these theories prematurely.

Second, Identify Theories Within Each of the Other Most Relevant Disciplines

From the Natural Sciences: Smolinski (2005)*, Fresh Water Scarcity in Texas

Smolinski applied the same research process that he used to identify and understand the important geology theories to the disciplines of biology and political science, as shown in Table 8.4.

Table 8.2   Important Theories From Economics Concerning OSD

Relevant Disciplines	Theories on the Causes of OSD
Economics	1. Monopsony Exploitation Theory
	2. Human Capital Theory
	3. Statistical Discrimination Theory
	4. Prejudice Theory

Table 8.3   Important Theories From Literature That Explain the Meaning of the *Rime*

Relevant Disciplines	Theories That Explain the Meaning of the Rime
Literature	1. Reader-Response Criticism
	2. Marxist Criticism
	3. The New Historicism
	4. Psychoanalytic Criticism
	5. Deconstruction

Table 8.4   Important Theories From the Relevant Disciplines Concerning Fresh
                  Water Scarcity

Relevant Disciplines	Theories on the Causes of Fresh Water Scarcity
Geology	1. Global Warming Theory
	2. Overexploitation Theory
	3. Infiltration Theory
Biology	4. Single-System Theory
	5. Encroachment Theory
Political Science	6. Market Theory
	7. Border Theory

As students take additional steps in the interdisciplinary research process, they will modify and expand this table to keep track of the rapidly proliferating pieces of information that normally accumulate as the research process proceeds.

From the Social Sciences: Fischer (1988), "On the Need for Integrating Occupational Sex Discrimination Theory on the Basis of Causal Variables"

Fischer examines the literature from each of the other relevant disciplines to identify additional theories on the causes of OSD, as shown in Table 8.5.

It is not unusual for relevant disciplines to advance two or more theories concerning a particular problem. When this occurs, students would be wise

Table 8.5   Important Theories From the Relevant Disciplines Concerning OSD

Disciplines or Schools of Thought Most Relevant to OSD	Theories on the Causes of OSD
Economics	1. Monopsony Exploitation Theory
	2. Human Capital Theory
	3. Statistical Discrimination Theory
	4. Prejudice Theory
Psychology	5. Male Dominance Theory
Sociology	6. Sex Role Orientation Theory
History	7. Institutional Theory
Marxism[a]	8. Class Conflict Theory

a. Marxism is a school of thought.

to adopt Fischer's strategy of first identifying the discipline advancing multiple theories before dealing with the other disciplines, each of which may advance only one or two theories. Why is this? Theories from the same discipline are often easier to integrate than are theories from different disciplines, as will become evident in a later step.

From the Humanities: Bal (1999), "Introduction," The Practice of Cultural Analysis: Exposing Interdisciplinary Interpretation

Mieke Bal, professor of cultural analysis at the Amsterdam School for Cultural Analysis (ASCA), the Netherlands, is one of the leading practitioners of this interdisciplinary approach to understanding the meaning of cultural objects. Cultural analysis seeks to overcome the "separation" of the humanities "from real social issues that were relegated to the social sciences." Central to the study of a culture, for Bal, is what she calls "acts of exposure"—of presenting, revealing, and laying bare the "truth" of the cultural artifact on public view, whether it is a museum display, a poem, a painting, a postcard, or a graffito (wall writing). This act of exposure also involves analyzing the effects of the display on the viewer and the different sorts of looking it prompts (Bal, 1996, p. 2).

In her study of a yellow graffito that appears on a red brick wall in Amsterdam, Bal draws on several disciplines to decipher its enigmatic meaning and show how it may inform our understanding of modern Dutch culture. These include linguistics, philosophy, literature, psychology, and the new interdiscipline of cultural analysis, of which she is a leading practitioner. Bal does not reference particular theories as applied to the graffito, but only each discipline's perspective on the object.

In these examples of research conducted *inductively* (except for Bal), interdisciplinarians were working on problems that had already attracted considerable attention from disciplinary scholars. But what about when the student is working on a problem on which little scholarly research has been done (or the more common case, when research of only some of the possible types has been done), and thus the student needs to point to avenues of future research? What may be needed in this circumstance is a *deductive* approach to theory selection. Szostak (2004) suggests that interdisciplinarians ask the following questions about the kind of theory type that may be needed: Who (agency)? What (action)? Why (decision making)? When (time path)? Where (generalize)? (See Table 8.6.)

According to Szostak (2004), **nomothetic theory** posits a general relationship among two or more phenomena, and nomothetic researchers are concerned with showing a broad applicability. **Ideographic theory** posits a relationship only under specified conditions, and ideographic researchers wish to explain the relevance of a theoretical proposition in a constrained set of circumstances (pp. 68, 108). Asking these "5 W" questions about the

Table 8.6   Szostak's Typology of Selected Theories

| Theory Type | Questions to Ask of Each Theory | | | | |
	Who? Agents	What? Action	Why? Decision Making	When? Time Path	Where? Generalize
Most natural science, outside of biological science	Nonintentional agents	Passive	No active decision-making process	Various	Various
Evolutionary biology	Nonintentional generally individuals	Active	Inherent	Not the same equilibrium	Nomothetic
Evolutionary human science	Intentional individual (group)	Active	Various	Not the same (any equilibrium)	Nomothetic
Complexity (Describes systems of interaction among phenomena; applied across natural and human sciences)	Catastrophe, chaos	Active and passive	Not strictly rational but must involve adaptive elements	Varies by version	Generally nomothetic
Action (Including theories of praxis)	Intentional individual (relationship)	Intersection of action and attitude	Often rational, but may be subconscious and unpredictable	Various	Generally idiographic
Systems (recognition that patterns in social life are not accidental)	Various	Action and attitude	Various; emphasize constraints	Various	Generally nomothetic
Psychoanalytic	Intentional individual	Attitudes	Intuition; others possible	Various	Implicit nomothetic
Symbolic Interactionism	Intentional relationships	Attitudes	Various	Stochastic	Idiographic; some nomothetic
Rational Choice	Individual	Action	Rational	Usually equilibrium	Nomothetic
Phenomenology	Relationships (individuals)	Attitudes (actions)	Various	Various	Various

SOURCE: Szostak (2004), pp. 82–94.

theory type needed to address the problem at hand may well reveal what has been missed in disciplinary research. Even where many conflicting theories exist, these questions can usefully identify the sources of different insights. The utility of Szostak's typology of selected theories is that it places an important analytical tool in the hands of students who may find themselves working with theories.

Developing Adequacy Involves Identifying Disciplinary Methods Appropriate to the Problem

The disciplinary research methods discussed here are not to be confused with the interdisciplinary research process that may draw on one or more of these disciplinary methods to produce an interdisciplinary understanding of a problem. Interdisciplinarians use these disciplinary methods as they engage in the interdisciplinary research process.

The Definition of Disciplinary Method

Disciplinary method means the procedure or process or technique used by the discipline's practitioners to conduct, organize, and present research. Method implies an orderly and logical way of doing something. In the natural and social sciences, methods are the means by which to obtain evidence of how some aspect of the natural or human world functions (Szostak, 2004, p. 100). Using methods appropriate to the problem, then, serves to bind the interdisciplinary project together.

The Methods Used in the Natural Sciences, the Social Sciences, and the Humanities

Fortunately, the number of methods used by the disciplines is quite small compared to the number of theories they favor. Most methods used by the major disciplines in the natural sciences, the social sciences, and the humanities fall into one of the following categories.

The Natural Sciences

The natural sciences generally emphasize quantitative research strategies:[3]

- Experiments (usually in a laboratory setting)
- Mathematical models
- Classification (of natural phenomena)
- Mapping
- Simulations (often on a computer)

The Social Sciences

The social sciences use both quantitative and qualitative research strategies:[4]

- Experiments (usually in an applied setting)
- Statistical analysis
- Surveys (qualitative)
- Interviews (qualitative)
- Ethnography/unobtrusive measures (qualitative)
- Physical traces (as in archeology or paleontology)
- Experience/intuition (as used in interpretation of data) (qualitative)
- Classification (of human phenomena)
- Triangulation or mixed methods[5]

The Humanities

The humanities typically emphasize qualitative research strategies:[6]

- Textual analysis (content analysis, discourse analysis, and historiography)
- Hermeneutics/semiotics (study of symbols and their meaning)
- Experience/intuition (as used in interpretation/appreciation of creative works)
- Classification (of periods, schools of thought, etc.) (Berg, 2004, p. 4; Szostak, 2004, pp. 66–130)
- Cultural analysis (as developed by Bal and which is a central methodology of the humanities examined in Chapter 9)

This list of methods raises important questions. What is the interdisciplinary position on disciplinary research methods? Should quantitative methods be privileged over qualitative methods? What are the theoretical implications of using qualitative strategies? How does the interdisciplinarian choose among these? What criteria should be used to make these choices? How many methods are needed in an interdisciplinary research project? These are the questions that are now addressed.

The Interdisciplinary Position on Disciplinary Methods

The interdisciplinary position on disciplinary methods is that there are many methods, each with different strengths and weaknesses, and that no one method or overall approach should be privileged over any other in interdisciplinary work. This view follows from the belief that each discipline relevant to a problem has something to contribute to producing an integrative understanding of the problem. The interdisciplinary position is mainstream, in that there is now philosophical, if not scientific, consensus that no one method, or broad scientific approach such as positivism, animates knowledge formation today (Szostak, 2004, p. 100).

The Relative Importance of Methods
to Undergraduate and Graduate Students

Generally speaking, most undergraduate research will involve integration of insights from published research, though some interdisciplinary courses and senior projects do conduct field work. The main point in paying attention to methods is to include (insofar as it is possible in the published literature) insights generated through different methods. Some advanced undergraduates may also be interested in understanding how disciplines can and do choose methods that are good at (and biased toward) their favored theories, which, in turn, influence the insights produced. Students should contemplate how different methods might yield different insights. While undergraduates should be aware of the importance of the methods used to produce relevant research, attention to method becomes most important in graduate study or in professional research.

The Interdisciplinary Position on the
Quantitative Versus Qualitative Debate

Interdisciplinary students should be conversant with the issues involved in the quantitative versus qualitative methods debate because research methods on humans affect how these persons will be viewed (Bogdan & Taylor, 1975). Historically, disciplinary scholars have been divided over the value of qualitative versus quantitative methods. Though this debate is dying down, it is not over. David J. Hall and Irene Hall (1996) write, "Nowadays most writers on methodology avoid such a distinction and stress instead the strategy of mixing methods" (p. 35). Abbas Tashakkori and Charles B. Teddlie (1998) argue that scholars, and hence students, should accept both quantitative and qualitative approaches because each has been long used, accepted, urged, and useful. Practitioners recognize that the relative importance of the two broad approaches may, nevertheless, vary according to the characteristics of the research problem (p. 11). This methodological inclusiveness now characterizes many of the leading books on methods in the social sciences, including Bruce L. Berg's (2004) *Qualitative Research Methods,* which is written for students as much as for scholars. He urges researchers "to consider the merits of both quantitative and qualitative research strategies" (p. 3).[7] This is sound advice for interdisciplinary students who are concerned to identify the perspectives of various writers on a problem. Students should recognize that the chosen methods impose certain perspectives on reality.

Berg (2004) differentiates between quantitative and qualitative approaches by saying that the notion of *quantity* is about the amount of something whereas *quality* is essential to the nature of things. **Quantitative research strategies** emphasize evidence that can be quantified, such as the number of atoms in a molecule, the flow rate of water in a river, or the amount of energy derived from a windmill. **Qualitative research strategies** focus on the what, how, when, and where of a thing—its essence and its ambiance. Qualitative research, then, refers to meanings, concepts, definitions, characteristics, metaphors, symbols, and descriptions of things or people that are not measured and expressed numerically (pp. 2–3). Whereas most of quantitative research relies on numbers, qualitative research tends to rely on words, images, and descriptions.[8]

Two Misconceptions About Qualitative Research

There are two common misconceptions about qualitative research, according to Berg (2004). The first is that reliance on numbers results in a more certain and more valid result than qualitative research can provide. Interdisciplinary studies students working in the social sciences are well aware of the tendency to give quantitative orientations more respect. However, students should know that qualitative methods are not only fruitful, but they can provide greater depth of understanding than can be achieved by relying on quantitative methods alone. Though some qualitative research projects have been poorly done, says Berg, one need not dismiss the entire qualitative approach just because some studies inadequately applied the method. He adds that qualitative methods can and should be extremely systematic and have the ability to be reproduced by subsequent researchers. "Replicability and reproducibility, after all, are central to the creation and testing of theories and their acceptance by scientific communities" (p. 7). Interdisciplinarians, no less than disciplinarians, should be concerned that their research stand the test of having subsequent researchers examine the same problem using the same disciplines, insights, concepts, theories, and methods and achieve the same results.

The second misconception is the tendency of some to associate qualitative research with the single technique of participant observation, while others extend their understanding of qualitative research to include interviewing as well (Berg, 2004, pp. 2–3). However, qualitative research strategies also include methods such as "observation of experimental natural settings, photographic techniques (including videotaping), historical analysis (historiography), document and textual analysis, sociometry, sociodrama and similar ethnomethodological experimentation, ethnographic research, and a number of unobtrusive techniques" (p. 3).

The Theoretical Implications of Using Qualitative Research Methods

Research is conducted to discover answers to questions through the application of systematic procedures called research methods or research strategies. Qualitative research focuses on questions concerning various social settings and the persons who occupy those settings. Qualitative researchers, says Berg (2004), "are most interested in how human beings arrange themselves and their settings, and how inhabitants of these settings make sense of their surroundings through symbols, rituals, social structures, social roles, and so forth" (p. 7).

If humans were studied using just quantitative methods, the danger would arise that conclusions—although arithmetically precise—might fail to fit reality, or worse, distort that reality. Qualitative methods provide a way to evaluate and understand unquantifiable facts about actual people or artifacts left by them, such as art, literature, poetry, photographs, letters, newspaper accounts, diaries, and so on. Qualitative techniques explore how people structure their daily lives, learn, and make sense of themselves and others. Researchers using qualitative methods are thus able to understand and give meaning to humans and their activities.[9]

The interdisciplinary position on the quantitative/qualitative debate is this: Interdisciplinarians should not be bound by the theory/method combinations that disciplinarians find convenient.

A Criterion for Choosing Methods

An important decision that students have to make early on in interdisciplinary research is which disciplinary method or methods are appropriate to the problem and will best hold the research together. *These methods should not be equated with or substituted for but should be used in conjunction with the interdisciplinary research model described in this book. The interdisciplinary research process subsumes whichever disciplinary methods are used.*

Disciplines consider certain phenomena or problems within their research domains and advance theories to generate insights into these phenomena. *There is a direct correlation between a discipline and the theories it favors and between a discipline and the insights it produces to illuminate a particular problem.* In general, when interdisciplinarians identify a discipline as being relevant to the problem, they use one or more of that discipline's theories that address the problem.

Along with the discipline's insights and theories, one is likely (but is not obligated) to use the methods of the discipline. "There are complementarities such that borrowing a theory from one discipline will encourage use of its methods, study of its phenomena, and engagement with its worldview," observes Szostak (2002, p. 106). Berg (2004) agrees, noting that many researchers mistakenly perceive their research method(s) as having little or nothing to do with theory. Because of this, "they fail to recognize that methods impose certain perspectives on reality" (p. 4). The tendency of disciplinarians to link theory, method, and phenomena is a source of bias. Interdisciplinarians should be curious about how the theories fare when applied to different phenomena and especially when tested using different methods.

Berg (2004) illustrates this bias in the example of researchers deciding to canvass a neighborhood and arrange interviews with residents to discuss their views of some social problem. Their decision to use this method of data collection, he says, means that they have already made a theoretical assumption, namely, that reality is fairly constant and stable. Similarly, when researchers make direct observations of events, they assume reality is deeply affected by the actions of all participants, including themselves. Thus, each method—interview and unobtrusive participant observation—reveals a slightly different facet of the same social problem.

There is a direct link between the research methods a discipline uses and the insights derived from the discipline and its theories. Berg (2004) states, "Data gathering . . . is not distinct from theoretical orientations. Rather, data are intricately associated with the motivation for choosing a given subject, the conduct of the study, and ultimately the analysis" (p. 4). The trap that many researchers fall into, he says, is that as advocates of such methodological styles of research as participant observation, they "are frequently more concerned with asserting or defending their techniques than with indicating alternative ways of approaching the study subject" (p. 4).

The relevance of this discussion for interdisciplinary studies students is this: *A discipline tends to link with certain problems that in turn link with certain theories that in turn link with certain methods.* Therefore, concerning any given problem, the student is confronted not with an extensive list of possible methods but with a short list of those methods commonly used by the disciplines interested in the problem.

For example, if one of the disciplines is from one of the "harder" (i.e., quantitatively oriented) social sciences such as psychology, then methods such as experiments and statistical analysis would be appropriate for the interdisciplinarian to use. On the other hand, if one of the disciplines is from the humanities, then methods such as semiotics or discourse analysis might be chosen. For *some* scientific questions, one method clearly excels: experiments. Experiments are unrivalled for the analysis of nonhuman agents. Even for scientific questions, though, experiments are fallible. Interdisciplinarians working on a science-oriented topic should supplement experimental evidence with evidence from other methods (Szostak, 2004, pp. 27–28).

Generally speaking, deciding which methods are most appropriate to the problem should be comparatively easy, provided that one is conversant with at least the broad outlines of the various methods and the theories informing them. The touchstone examples from the natural sciences, the social sciences, and the humanities show how interdisciplinarians decide which methods to use.

From the Natural Sciences: Watson (1968), The Double Helix: A Personal Account of the Discovery of the Structure of DNA

In the natural sciences, the standard methods are limited to those noted earlier: experiments, mathematical models, classification (of natural phenomena), mapping, and simulations (often on a computer). In his personal account of the discovery of the structure of DNA, Watson reveals that the scientific process is seldom straightforward, logical, and linear.

The methods he and Francis Crick used in their quest to unlock the complex structure of DNA included conducting experiments (involving the combined techniques of chemistry and genetics), designing mathematical models, and manipulating physical models (much like tinker toys) based on which chemical elements like to sit next to each other. Their collaborative decisions about which methods to use at various stages of the project were influenced as much by politics, finances, and lab protocol as by purely scientific considerations.

From the Social Sciences: Fischer (1988), "On the Need for Integrating Occupational Sex Discrimination Theory on the Basis of Causal Variables"

This correlation between a discipline, its theories, and its methods is illustrated in Fischer's essay on OSD. Even though the particular economics method Fischer uses has been out of favor with economists for many years, he uses it anyway because he believes it enables him to produce an interdisciplinary understanding of OSD. Fischer makes an important point. Just because a particular method may be currently in or out of favor with disciplinary experts is no justification, by itself, for the interdisciplinarian to use it or not use it. Whatever methods are ultimately used, the interdisciplinarian should at least be explicit about their identity. The example of Fischer, then, shows how the various theories within the discipline of economics link to the problem of the causes of OSD. These economic theories ultimately led him to use a method drawn from economics.

From the Humanities: Bal (1999), "Introduction," The Practice of Cultural Analysis: Exposing Interdisciplinary Interpretation

To develop an interdisciplinary understanding of a text or art object, the interdisciplinarian, if grounded in the humanities, would likely choose one of the research methods or research strategies or approaches commonly used by those in the humanities.

Selecting a method in the humanities usually involves making two decisions. The first is to think in "both/and," not in "either/or," terms concerning modern and postmodern (including Cultural Analysis and New History) approaches. This holds for choice of methods as well as perspectives. Key distinctions between these two very distinct approaches—i.e., modernism and postmodernism—are summarized here in the most general terms.

Modernism

- investigates available written documents about the object and its creator to provide an accurate description or account of them (Fernie, 1995, p. 327)
- examines the object using visual techniques

Postmodernism/Cultural/New History

- investigates the social context of the object and its creator
- critically evaluates the relevance of prevailing modernist theories of art to the object or text

The interdisciplinarian working in the humanities should be aware of the advantages and disadvantages of using either a modern or postmodern approach, as shown in Table 8.7. This also applies to the qualitative social sciences and the interdisciplinary fields of environmental studies and science, technology, and society (STS) studies.

Table 8.7   Advantages and Disadvantages of Using a Modern or Postmodern Approach

Approach	Advantages	Disadvantages
Modernist	1. Boundaries of inquiry are clearly defined.	1. Boundaries imply exclusion.
	2. Meaning of the object can be clearly stated.	2. Meaning assumes adherence to some universal standard.
	3. The focus of inquiry is the object.	3. Focusing on the object tends to exclude the complex network of political, economic, social, and other cultural factors that provide the context of the object.
Postmodernist/ Social/New History	1. No boundaries	1. The absence of boundaries may mean an open-ended investigation.
	2. Inclusive of scholarly and nonscholarly evidence	2. These approaches show lack of scholarly consensus on what constitutes "nonscholarly evidence."
	3. Opposes "high" definitions of culture and takes seriously popular cultural forms	3. Focusing on popular culture forms may exclude other cultural forms.

Modernism and postmodernism provide insights into the humanities that are not only different but potentially complementary. In art history, for example, modernism connects work to earlier works (i.e., aesthetic traditions) and to universal and timeless aesthetic principles, while postmodernism connects work and the artist who produced the work to the larger society and culture, especially to its politics (Barnet, 2008, p. 260). Both approaches, if used together, are useful in producing a more integrative understanding of the art object than would be possible if only one of these approaches were used. This suggests that the student, who is the integrator of insights drawn from existing scholarship, ought to look for both modern *and* postmodern insights.

The second decision concerns which of the newer (i.e., postmodern) approaches to use: reader response, Marxist criticism, the New Historicism, psychoanalytic criticism, deconstruction, or Cultural Analysis. For the interdisciplinary student, no one postmodern approach is preferable to any other. Why? Because none of these approaches is either inclusive or integrative of *all* of the relevant perspectives. The interdisciplinarian should choose a combination of approaches—modern and postmodern—with an eye to being inclusive of the major relevant perspectives. Only this degree of inclusiveness will enable the interdisciplinarian to achieve the new meaning of the object or text that is truly interdisciplinary.

The method chosen for the first touchstone humanities example is **cultural analysis**. As a critical practice, it draws on a specific set of collaborating disciplines that include history, psychology, philosophy, literature, linguistics, and art history in seeking to understand a text or object of inquiry. Though cultural analysis is inclusive of the perspectives of several disciplines (and thus particularly valuable to the interdisciplinarian), it is dominated by postmodernism and thus misses the advantages of the modernist approach while suffering the disadvantages of the postmodernist approach, as shown in Table 8.7. Furthermore, within postmodern scholarship, a particular postmodernist approach typically fails to take into account the scholarship coming out of another postmodernist approach. Thus, *by itself,* cultural analysis does not produce an understanding that is truly comprehensive but one that is, nevertheless, interdisciplinary.[10]

Cultural analysis, according to Bal (1999), is based on a keen awareness of the viewer's situatedness in the present, the social and cultural context from which the viewer looks back at the object, and the fact that the object is part of how we define our present culture. Cultural analysis differs from the historian's attempt to reconstruct the past objectively or to view the past as the culmination of an evolutionary—and thus inevitable—line of development. Instead, cultural analysis seeks to understand "the past as *part* of the present, as what we have around us, and without which no culture would be able to exist" (p. 1).

Cultural analysis demands methodological exactness by requiring the object of inquiry to meet two criteria: that it be specific, meaning that it be a recognizable object or text; and that it have precise starting points. Bal (1999) uses the graffito (introduced in Chapter 6) to illustrate the method of cultural analysis that she sums up in the verb "to expose." Exposition refers to the action of making public the deepest held views and beliefs of someone or of someone's deeds that deserve to be made public (pp. 4–5).

The Number of Methods Needed in an Interdisciplinary Research Project

Most disciplinary researchers in the social sciences, says Berg (2004), "have at least one research strategy or methodological technique they feel most comfortable using, which often becomes their favorite or only approach to research" (p. 4). This is likely true for researchers in the natural sciences as well as the humanities. Interdisciplinarians, however, should not emulate disciplinarians in this regard. There are important outcome-shaping implications of selecting any research method, and interdisciplinarians must be aware of these implications when they make decisions about which research methods to use.

The Concept of Triangulation in Research Methodology

The question of how many methods to use in a given research project is directly related to the concept of triangulation in research methodology. Though this term is more commonly associated with surveying, map making, navigation, and military practices, it is also appropriate for conducting research. Each research method reveals slightly different facets of the same reality, and every method provides a different line of sight directed toward the same point or research problem. By combining several lines of sight, researchers can produce an integrated picture of the problem and have more ways to verify theoretical concepts. Social scientists call the use of multiple lines of sight *triangulation* (Berg, 2004, p. 5).[11]

Triangulation of research methodology involves using multiple data-gathering techniques (usually three) to investigate the same phenomenon. In this way, findings can be crosschecked, validated, and confirmed. The important feature of triangulation, explains Berg (2004), "is not the simple combination of different kinds of data but the attempt to relate them so as to counteract the threats to validity identified in each" (p. 5). Triangulation involves using varieties of data, theories, and methods. The research literature supports using triangulation or multiple methods in a single research project. Norman K. Denzin (1978) also suggests using multiple data-collection procedures, multiple theoretical perspectives, and multiple analysis techniques (p. 101). The use of multiple methods and theories, Berg (2004) contends, "increases the depth of understanding an investigation can yield" (p. 6).

Regarding the question of how many methods should be used in an inter-disciplinary research project, the answer is, "It depends on the problem, how it is stated, and how ambitious the investigation is." Ultimately, the number of disciplinary research methods used in a given project depend on many factors, not the least of which is the scope and complexity of the problem.

Deciding Which Research Methods Should Be Used

Once the student has narrowed the number of possible methods to a few, the next task is to decide which of these should be used. Consider, for example, the interdisciplinary analysis of the economic and environmental impacts of hydropower dams on the Columbia River system for a paper titled "Declining Salmon Populations in the Columbia and Snake Rivers." A topic, as noted earlier, may take any number of research directions. In this instance, the writer has at least two options:

A. Explain the 80% reduction of the salmon populations that has occurred since the system of dams was built.

B. Examine the current state of the salmon populations in the Columbia and Snake Rivers.

For each option, the researcher decided that the disciplines most relevant are biology, economics, and history (assuming one is limited to three disciplines). The student can easily associate each discipline with the research methods it typically uses by referring to the information provided in Chapter 4 and reproduced here in Table 8.8.

Table 8.8   Research Methods Typically Used by Each Discipline

Relevant Disciplines	Research Methods
Biology	• Experiments • Mathematical models • Classification of natural phenomena • Mapping • Simulations (computer)
Economics	• Mathematical models • Statistical analysis of empirical data • Critical thinking that includes components of logic, problem solving, and abstraction
History	• Identification of primary source material from the past in the form of documents, records, letters, interviews, oral history, archeology, etc. or secondary sources in the form of books and articles • Critical analysis in the form of interpretation of historical documents into a picture of past events or the quality of human and other life within a particular time and place

Each option defines the topic in a way that influences the choice of methods. The researcher must next decide which research methods are most appropriate for each option. Option A seeks to explain how the problem developed and who or what was responsible. Having identified the methods most commonly used by the disciplines of biology, economics, and history, the next task is to decide which of the methods typically used by each discipline are most appropriate to Option A. Table 8.9 aids making this decision.

Table 8.9 shows that the methods most appropriate to Option A are mapping (biology), statistical analysis and critical thinking (economics), and identification and interpretation of historical documents (history).

Option B seeks a more comprehensive understanding of the current state of the salmon population in the Columbia and Snake Rivers. Table 8.10 shows which methods are potential candidates for inclusion in Option B.

The Option B version of the topic results in a greatly expanded number of possible methods available to the interdisciplinarian.

Table 8.9   Possible Methods to Use in Option A

Relevant Disciplines	Research Methods	Potential Candidate for Inclusion and Justification
Biology	Experiments	No. The focus of the topic is on what happened in the past.
	Mathematical models	No. It is inappropriate for a historical explanation of how the problem developed.
	Classification of natural phenomena	No. There is nothing concerning the topic that requires classification.
	Mapping	Possibly. This method can show the progressive impact of past decisions on salmon.
	Simulations (computer)	No. Computer simulations are not appropriate for explaining past decisions.
Economics	Mathematical models	No. It is inappropriate for a historical explanation of how the problem developed.
	Statistical analysis of empirical data	Yes, provided that the statistical information was used to justify the original decision to build the dams.
	Critical thinking	Yes.
History	Identification of primary source materials	Yes. Those supporting and opposing the building of the dams could be interviewed. Original studies and past and present government hearings could be analyzed.
	Critical analysis in the form of interpretation of historical documents	Yes. The historical documents must be interpreted to answer the research questions: "How did the problem develop, and who was responsible?"

Table 8.10   Possible Methods to Use in Option B

Relevant Disciplines	Research Methods	Potential Candidate for Inclusion and Justification
Biology	Experiments	Possibly. Experiments recently concluded or in progress may illuminate how the system of dams is impacting various salmon populations.
	Mathematical models	Possibly. Modeling seasonal migrations of salmon under varying conditions would be useful.
	Classification of natural phenomena	No. There is nothing concerning the topic that requires classification.
	Mapping	Possibly. This method can show the progressive impact of past decisions on salmon populations.
	Simulations (computer)	Possibly. Computer simulations are useful to predict various outcomes under variable conditions.
Economics	Mathematical models	Possibly. For reasons stated.
	Statistical analysis of empirical data	Yes. An abundance of recent or current statistical data are likely available.
	Critical thinking	Yes.
History	Identification of primary source materials	Yes. Those presently supporting or opposing the dams could be interviewed. Original studies and past and present government hearings should be analyzed to provide background information and immediate context.
	Critical analysis in the form of interpretation of historical documents	Yes. Documents and sources must be interpreted to answer the research question: "What is the current state of the salmon populations in the Columbia and Snake Rivers?"

Deciding which research methods should be used depends on the problem, on the disciplines interested in it, on the theories producing insights into it, as well as on the time and resource constraints. The student will decide which methods are most relevant based on the requirements or limitations of the interdisciplinary project.

Providing In-Text Evidence of Disciplinary Adequacy

Finally, students are well advised to provide in-text evidence that they have developed adequacy in the disciplines they are using. **In-text evidence of disciplinary adequacy** may be expressed in many ways, such as statements about the disciplinary elements that pertain to the problem, the disciplinary affiliation of leading theorists, and the disciplinary methods used. It is relatively easy to weave this evidence into the narrative if the student has collected and organized this information in an easily retrievable way.

Another way to demonstrate adequacy is to use the most current scholarship pertaining to the problem. Interdisciplinary work tends to focus on complex and real-world problems and on intellectual problems that are not necessarily real-world. Some problems are time-sensitive. In the case of human cloning, for example, scholarship is being produced from multiple disciplines and interdisciplines in response to procedural breakthroughs, scandals, and legislative attempts to control this reproductive technology. Each of these developments raises new questions and prompts a new round of scholarly comment, often rendering earlier analysis less useful or even obsolete. When working with time-sensitive topics, student should consult the most recent scholarship.

There are two practical reasons for providing in-text evidence of disciplinary adequacy. First, it demonstrates academic rigor. Interdisciplinary students bear a heavier responsibility than disciplinary students do in their research because they have to establish adequacy in two or more disciplinary domains. Students should be concerned to counter possible criticisms of dilettantism and superficiality by doing what more and more professional interdisciplinary writers are doing: identifying those disciplinary elements that pertain to the problem. These writers are concerned to demonstrate disciplinary adequacy by weaving into their narratives explanations for using certain methods and applying certain theories.

The second practical reason for providing in-text evidence of disciplinary adequacy is to remind the student throughout the research project of its distinctive character compared to that of disciplinary research with which the student may be more familiar. *Paying attention to the interdisciplinary research process involves not just moving through its various Steps; it also involves being self-consciously interdisciplinary.* This means reflecting on one's biases (disciplinary and personal), serving as an honest broker when confronting conflicting viewpoints, and all the while keeping in view the end product that prompted the research in the first place.

CHAPTER SUMMARY

For students, developing adequacy in the disciplines relevant to the problem is usually sufficient. Adequacy is knowing enough about the discipline to have a basic understanding of how it approaches the problem and how it illuminates and characterizes the problem. The way the problem is framed greatly influences which methods one is likely to use. A consequence of deciding which methods to use is that the student may have to restate the problem or reframe the question. In the end, it is the student who must make the difficult decision of which theories and which methods are most appropriate to use. The student has not only the freedom to make these choices but also the responsibility to make these choices explicit. Whether or not one chooses to use tables to store and juxtapose data, it is important to develop some way to keep track of the information gathered so that nothing important is lost or overlooked in subsequent Steps.

Clearly, the interdisciplinary student has to engage in far more preparatory analysis than does a disciplinary scholar. As tedious and time consuming as this is, it must be done in order to perform the later Steps of the interdisciplinary process that deal with actual integration. Performing the final Steps is not possible unless these preparatory Steps have been completed successfully. Step 6 of the research process concerns deciding *whether* and *how* the disciplinary elements that have been chosen (i.e., the insights and theories) adequately illuminate the problem.

NOTES

1. Some interdisciplinarians, such as Hal Foster (1998), believe that to be interdisciplinary one must be "disciplinary first," meaning being professionally "grounded in one discipline, preferably two" (p. 162).

2. Admittedly, Watson is describing an early point in these rapidly emerging and highly technical fields when developing adequacy, though extremely difficult, was still possible. Still, the interdisciplinary point Watson is making is to be willing to pursue answers to questions even if this involves crossing into unfamiliar fields and to know when to ask experts for advice. Students today researching in fields where the density of knowledge and information is so much greater must take great care to identify a topic that is researchable and know when to ask for expert advice.

3. Introductory textbooks on the scientific method include Stephen S. Carey (2003), *A Beginner's Guide to Scientific Method* (2nd ed.), and Hugh G. Gauch, Jr. (2002), *Scientific Method in Practice*.

4. Textbooks on social science research methods include Linda E. Dorsten and Lawrence Hotchkiss (2005), *Research Methods and Society: Foundations of Social Inquiry*; W. Lawrence Neuman (2006), *Social Research Methods: Qualitative and Quantitative Approaches*; John Gerring (2001*), Social Science Methodology*; and Chava Frankfort-Nachmias and David Nachmias (2008), *Research Methods in the Social Sciences* (7th ed.). For research methods of social science-oriented fields, see Frank E. Hagan (2005), *Essentials of Research Methods in Criminal Justice and Criminology,* and William Wiersma and Stephen G. Jurs (2005), *Research Methods in Education: An Introduction.*

5. Bruce L. Berg (2004) says that triangulation was first used in the social sciences "as a metaphor describing a form of *multiple operationalism* or *convergent validation,*" meaning "multiple data collection technologies designed to measure a single concept or construct" (p. 5). For many social scientists, triangulation is usually restricted to three data-gathering techniques to investigate the same phenomenon. "The important feature of triangulation," says Berg, "is not the simple combination of different kinds of data but the attempt to relate them so as to counteract the threats to validity identified in each" (p. 5). Alan Bryman (2004) provides extensive discussion of mixed methods in Chapters 21 and 22 of *Social Research Methods.*

6. Though written for the social sciences, Berg's (2004) *Qualitative Research Methods for the Social Sciences* may be used profitably in the humanities. In contrast to the social sciences, humanities books on commonly used research methods are few. These include Catherine Marshall and Gretchen B. Rossman (2006), *Designing Qualitative Research;* John W. Creswell (1997), *Qualitative Inquiry and Research Design: Choosing Among Five Traditions;* and Matthew B. Miles and Michael Huberman (1994), *Qualitative Data Analysis: An Expanded Sourcebook.* Examples of excellent research methods textbooks used in particular humanities disciplines include those by Laurie Schneider Adams (1996), *The Methodologies of Art: An Introduction;* Hong Xio (2005), *Research Methods for English Studies;* Martha Howell and Walter Prevenier (2001), *From Reliable Sources: An Introduction to Historical Methods;* and James J. Scheurich (1997), *Research Method in the Postmodern.*

7. Berg notes that qualitative methodologies have not predominated in the social sciences (p. 2). His chapter "Mixed Methods Procedures" provides a comprehensive summary of this approach and a survey of the literature on the subject.

8. Useful books on qualitative research in all of its aspects include John W. Creswell (1997), *Qualitative Inquiry and Research Design: Choosing Among Five Traditions;* John W. Creswell (2002), *Research Design: Qualitative, Quantitative, and Mixed Methods Approaches;* and Norman K. Denzin and Yvonna S. Lincoln (Eds.) (2005), *The SAGE Handbook of Qualitative Research.*

9. The general purpose of qualitative research derives from the theoretical perspective of symbolic interaction that is one of several theoretical schools of thought associated with the social sciences. It focuses on subjective understandings and the perceptions of and about people, symbols, and objects. Human behavior depends on learning rather than on biological instinct. Humans communicate what we learn through symbols, the most common of these being language. The core task of symbolic interactionists as researchers, Berg (2004) explains, is to "capture the essence of this process for interpreting or attaching meaning to various symbols" (p. 8). By contrast, positivists use empirical methodologies borrowed from the natural sciences to investigate phenomena. Their concern is to provide rigorous, reliable, and verifiably large amounts of data and the statistical testing of empirical hypotheses. Qualitative researchers, on the other hand, are primarily interested in individuals and their so-called life-worlds. "Life-worlds include emotions, motivations, symbols, and their meanings, empathy, and other subjective aspects associated with naturally evolving lives of individuals and groups" (p. 11).

10. In fact, it rejects this posture, typical of new critical forms of interdisciplinarity.

11. Marilyn Stember (1991), among others, also makes this point in "Advancing the Social Sciences Through the Interdisciplinary Enterprise," p. 11.

REVIEW QUESTIONS

1. What decisions are involved in developing adequacy in disciplines relevant to the problem?

2. How much knowledge is required from each discipline when working on a problem?

3. What kind of knowledge is required from each discipline?

4. What role may theories play in developing adequacy in each relevant discipline?

5. What role do theories play in Smolinski's essay, *Fresh Water Scarcity in Texas?*

6. What are the differences between quantitative and qualitative methods?

7. What is the interdisciplinary position on disciplinary methods?

8. What is the relative importance of methods to undergraduate and graduate students?

9. What is the interdisciplinary position on the quantitative versus qualitative debate?

10. What are the theoretical implications of using qualitative research methods?

11. What criterion should be considered for choosing among the various disciplinary methods?

12. How is the correlation between a discipline, its theories, and its methods illustrated in Fischer's essay, "On the Need for Integrating Occupational Sex Discrimination Theory on the Basis of Causal Variables"?

13. What are some of the advantages and disadvantages of using a modernist or postmodernist approach?

14. What are the advantages and disadvantages of using the postmodernist approach of cultural analysis when attempting to find meaning in a graffito such as the one Bal describes?

15. Why should the student provide in-text evidence of disciplinary adequacy?

9

Analyzing the Problem and Evaluating Each Insight Into It

Step 3 identified the disciplines potentially relevant to the problem and then reduced these to just the most relevant. The literature search conducted in Step 4 served, among other things, to validate these choices. Then, Step 5 developed adequacy in the relevant disciplines. Now, Step 6 calls for the student to use this disciplinary-specific information and take two actions: analyze the problem from the perspective of each relevant discipline, and evaluate each insight into the problem. Evaluating insights involves identifying the strengths and weaknesses of their theories and each expert's understanding of the problem, recognizing that each expert's perspective on the problem may be skewed and understanding the implications of this, recognizing that the evidence upon which the insight and theory are based may also be skewed, and recognizing that the methods used by disciplinary experts may be skewed as well. As noted in Chapter 3, the disciplines, interdisciplines, and schools of thought provide different lenses or perspectives for viewing the same problem and illuminating its parts. The challenge is for the student to identify as many relevant perspectives as possible so that all parts of the problem are revealed and all important scholarly insights are identified.

> Step 6: Analyze the problem and evaluate each insight into it

Analyzing the Problem From Each Disciplinary Perspective

Analyzing the problem from each disciplinary perspective is the first part of Step 6. It involves moving from one discipline to another and shifting from one perspective to another. Newell (2007) describes this process of "moving" and "shifting" in rather colorful terms. The student, he says, must take

217

off one set of disciplinary lenses and put on another set in its place as each discipline is examined. A possible initial effect of doing this is "intellectual vertigo" until one's brain can refocus. Experienced interdisciplinarians have developed the mental flexibility that enables them to shift easily from one disciplinary perspective to another. They do this much in the same way that multilingual persons shift easily from English to French to German without really having to think hard about what they are doing (p. 255).

Examples of How to Analyze a Problem From Each Disciplinary Perspective From the Natural Sciences, the Social Sciences, and the Humanities

How interdisciplinarians analyze a problem from each disciplinary perspective is illustrated by drawing on published and student work (marked by an asterisk). The categorization of these examples refers to the area of the researcher's training and the orientation of the topic, more than the disciplines on which they draw.

The problem of acid rain was a classroom exercise designed to illustrate disciplinary perspective-taking. Table 9.1 views the problem from the

Table 9.1   Disciplines and Their Perspectives Stated in Terms of Overarching Questions Asked About the Problem of Acid Rain

Discipline and Interdiscipline	Perspective Stated in Terms of the Kinds of Overarching Questions Asked
Physics	What are the fundamental physical principles underlying electrical power production that lead to acid rain?
Engineering	How does the design of the power generation process lead to acid rain?
Chemistry	What molecular changes lie behind the creation of acid rain and its effects?
Biology	How does acid rain affect flora and fauna?
Economics	What public policies could encourage firms to produce less acid rain?
Political Science	How could those public policies be adopted and implemented?
Law	How could those policies be enforced?
Environmental Studies	How is the problem of acid rain part of a complex environmental system?
Science and Technology Studies	How is the problem of acid rain a reflection of the relationship between scientific and technical innovations and social, political, and cultural values of society?

NOTE: Environmental studies and science and technology studies are interdisciplines.

perspective of each relevant discipline stated in terms of an overarching "what" or "how" question that can be asked of any problem.

The overarching question posed by each relevant discipline or interdiscipline reflects its perspective (in a general sense), as noted in Chapter 3 (excluding law, environmental studies, and science and technology studies, which were not examined). There are two benefits of asking overarching "what" or "how" questions framed in each discipline's perspective: The question can deepen an existing line of inquiry and possibly initiate a new line of inquiry, and the question can help draw out interrelationships among phenomena. Table 9.1 reveals disciplinary bias in terms of the questions asked; the disciplines may also be biased in the answers they provide.

The very premise of interdisciplinary studies is that disciplines can rarely explain all aspects of a complex problem. When dealing with a problem that is complex, such as acid rain, no single discipline is equipped to approach it comprehensively. One can discover how involved a problem really is by mapping it (see Chapter 7) and by linking the problem to the perspective of each relevant discipline, as Table 9.2 does. The table shows how each discipline's unique perspective allows it to focus narrowly on only one aspect of the complex problem of acid rain.

This model is now applied to selected multi-threaded examples.

Table 9.2   Disciplinary Perspectives Relevant to the Problem of Acid Rain

Relevant Discipline	Perspective on Acid Rain in a General Sense
Physics	May see acid rain as a consequence of basic thermodynamic principles underlying the operation of an electricity-generating power plant
Engineering	May see acid rain as a power plant design problem
Chemistry	May see acid rain as the result of a series of chemical processes
Biology	May see acid rain as posing a biological problem for downwind flora and fauna
Economics	May see acid rain as the result of the behavior of that portion of the economic system that drives decisions about the use of coal in power plants
Political Science	May see acid rain as a regulatory problem
Law	May see the destructive effects of acid rain on property as a question of who is responsible and thus liable
Environmental Studies	May see acid rain as complex physical, chemical, and biological interaction caused by human activity
Science and Technology Studies	May see acid rain as an example of how embedded social, political, and cultural values affect scientific research and technological innovation and how these, in turn, affect society, politics, and culture

NOTE: Environmental studies and science and technology studies are interdisciplines.

From the Natural Sciences: Watson (1968), The Double Helix: A Personal Account of the Discovery of the Structure of DNA

Watson appropriately identifies all of the relevant disciplines early on in his study. One of his purposes in presenting this case study is to establish a historical timeline of how his work in the relevant disciplines led him to make critical decisions about which disciplinary insights to use and which to discard. These disciplines are identified and their perspectives stated in general terms in Table 9.3.

From the Natural Sciences: Smolinski (2005),* Fresh Water Scarcity in Texas

Smolinski has already identified the disciplines most relevant to the complex problem of fresh water scarcity in Texas under Step 3. These are listed in the left-hand column in Table 9.4. Using the information on disciplinary perspective provided in Chapter 3 and information gathered in the literature

Table 9.3   Disciplinary Perspectives Relevant to the Problem of the Structure of DNA

Discipline or Subdiscipline Most Relevant to the Problem	*Perspective on Problem Stated in General Terms*
Physics	Sees the problem of DNA as a structural problem solvable by using X-ray diffraction photography as the principal tool of research
Microbiology	Sees the problem of DNA as a genetic problem solvable by discovering how genes act
Biochemistry	Sees the problem of DNA as solvable by working out DNA's chemical structure

NOTE: Microbiology is a subdiscipline of biology.

Table 9.4   Disciplinary Perspectives Relevant to the Problem of Fresh Water Scarcity in Texas

Discipline Most Relevant to the Problem	*Perspective on Problem Stated in General Terms*
Geology	Sees the problem as a consequence of human interference in natural geological systems
Biology	Sees the problem as a consequence of human degradation of the Earth's major systems: atmosphere, biosphere, geosphere, and hydrosphere
Political Science	Sees the problem as a reflection of institutional and interest group factors

search, he is able to state in general terms the overall perspective of each discipline relative to the problem. This is possible even though each discipline embraces two or more conflicting theories explaining why the problem exists and offering possible solutions.

Even from these general statements of each discipline's general perspective on the problem, one can see how it will be possible to identify in a later step the common ground theory, concept, or assumption that is shared by these seemingly conflicting perspectives.

From the Social Sciences: Fischer (1988), "On the Need for Integrating Occupational Sex Discrimination Theory on the Basis of Causal Variables"

Fischer is grappling with a complex social problem involving several disciplines—and a school of thought (i.e., Marxism)—and their perspectives. While it is unlikely that undergraduate or even graduate students would be required to work with as many disciplines as Fischer does, his approach is instructive because of the way he simplifies the process for the uninformed reader by briefly describing each perspective in a narrative. From this narrative, each discipline's perspective on the problem is described in general terms, as shown in Table 9.5.

From the Social Sciences: Delph* (2005), An Integrative Approach to the Elimination of the "Perfect Crime"

Delph's senior project uses one interdiscipline (criminal justice) and two subdisciplines (forensic science and forensic psychology) in the investigation of how "perfect crimes" (i.e., the criminal is not caught) can be eliminated

Table 9.5   Disciplinary Perspectives on the Problem of OSD

Discipline or School of Thought Relevant to the Problem	Perspective on Problem Stated in General Terms
Economics	OSD is caused by rational economic decision making on the part of males and females (Fischer, 1988, pp. 27–31).
History	OSD is caused and perpetuated by longstanding institutional forces (pp. 32–34).
Sociology	OSD is caused by a process of female socialization different from men which, in turn, is directly reflected in their occupational structures (p. 34).
Psychology	OSD is caused and perpetuated by males to maintain the traditional male-female division of labor (pp. 35–36).
Marxism	OSD is a necessary act in preserving the institutions of capitalism (p. 32).

NOTE: Marxism is a school of thought.

or, at least, greatly reduced. An interdiscipline brings together aspects of other disciplines to focus on a complex phenomenon such as crime. As an interdiscipline, criminal justice brings together the subdisciplines of forensic science (biology) and forensic psychology (psychology) along with elements of sociology that focus on criminal behavior. Criminal justice generates its own theories and uses a variety of research methods borrowed from biology, psychology, and sociology. Early on in her research, Delph decided to limit her research to the discipline and subdisciplines listed in Table 9.6. Their perspectives, as they apply to the problem, are stated in general terms.

From the Humanities: Bal (1999), "Introduction," The Practice of Cultural Analysis: Exposing Interdisciplinary Interpretation

Bal, befitting an interdisciplinary approach, is able to state, in general terms, each relevant discipline's overall perspective on the meaning of the art object, a graffito, which is her focus of study. A table such as Table 9.7 is useful in keeping track of the several perspectives involved in the analysis. Juxtaposing these perspectives in this way enables the researcher to more readily identify possible areas of overlap and points of conflict among them, which is called for in later steps.

From the Humanities: Silver* (2005), Composing Race and Gender: The Appropriation of Social Identity in Fiction

Silver studies the ethics of appropriation of social identities by fiction writers, a topic that has been practically ignored, especially by fiction writers themselves. "Appropriation" refers to an attempt to take possession of another's social identity, a practice commonly used by actors, filmmakers,

Table 9.6   Disciplinary Perspectives Relevant to the Problem of Eliminating the "Perfect Crime"

Discipline or Subdiscipline Most Relevant to the Problem	Perspective on Problem Stated in General Terms
Criminal Justice	Sees the persistence of "perfect [i.e., unsolvable] crimes" as a result of inefficient investigatory processes
Forensic Science	Sees the persistence of "perfect crimes" as a result of improper application of forensic science to criminal investigations
Forensic Psychology	Sees the persistence of "perfect crimes" as a result of insufficient attention to the art of criminal profiling

NOTE: Forensic science and forensic psychology are subdisciplines.

Table 9.7   Disciplinary Perspectives on the Meaning of a Graffito

Discipline or Interdiscipline	Perspective on Problem Stated in General Terms
Art History	Sees the graffito as an autographic art object reflective of a period of Dutch culture and thus providing a window into that culture
History	Sees the graffito as a product of Flemish history and a window into Flemish culture
Linguistics	Sees the graffito as self-referential
Literature	Sees the graffito as allographic literature
Philosophy	Sees the graffito as an epistemological argument
Psychology	Sees the graffito as an expression of psychic mourning
Cultural Analysis	Sees the graffito as a "text-image" that embodies the program of cultural analysis

NOTE: Cultural analysis is an interdiscipline.

and fiction writers, although the ethics of doing so is rarely discussed. Appropriation, or "putting oneself in another's shoes," helps one to gain a more personal understanding of people who are being appropriated. Among the examples of appropriation she cites is that of John Howard Griffin, who wrote *Black Like Me* to call attention to racial injustice. By appropriating the skin of a black man, Griffin became the first white person to experience directly the kind of treatment known only to black people. Silver explores this topic from the perspectives of three disciplines: sociology, psychology, and literature, as shown in Table 9.8.

Creating tables such as these that place perspectives side by side enables the student to evaluate more easily whether or not the disciplines selected earlier as relevant to the problem are, in fact, relevant. Juxtaposing the relevant disciplines and their perspectives makes it easy to see the narrowness

Table 9.8   Disciplinary Perspectives on the Problem of the Appropriation of Social Identity in Fiction

Discipline Most Relevant to the Problem	Perspective on Problem Stated in General Terms
Sociology	Sees the problem arising from socially constructed power dynamics and guilt feelings that impact race and gender relations
Psychology	Sees the problem arising from writers attempting empathetic arousal of their audience
Literature	Sees the problem as arising from authors' need to achieve a sense of authenticity

of each perspective and the necessity to push on with the interdisciplinary process to produce a more comprehensive understanding of the problem. The disciplines, by themselves, are unable to explain comprehensively a complex problem.

If a research project is limited to three or four disciplines, the student may have to narrow the focus of the problem to one of its parts. This, in turn, will require revisiting Step 1 and rewording the problem to reflect this narrowed focus. If this limitation were to apply to the example of acid rain, deciding which part of the problem to focus on would most likely result in reducing the number of disciplines to those that are the most relevant to the narrowed focus. The progression of the research is from defining the problem to identifying its parts to identifying the disciplines that specialize in those parts.

The Problem of Personal Bias

In addition to the bias inherent in disciplinary approaches to problems, personal bias can also skew interdisciplinary work. How does the student ultimately decide which disciplinary information should be included or excluded from the study? One progresses from the topic to its parts to the disciplines that specialize in those parts. In other words, the parts of the problem that the student wants to focus on largely determine which disciplines the student ends up using. But there is an additional factor that may influence this decision.

Individual scholars, interdisciplinary as well as disciplinary, often bring their personal biases or settled prejudices to certain problems. For example, sociology, since its founding, has been more liberal than is economics, and "studies" of any sort (e.g., women's, environmental, and even religious) tend to be more liberal than are their disciplinary counterparts. It bears emphasizing that interdisciplinarians value diversity of perspective and seek out conflicting viewpoints with which they disagree. They can live with ideological diversity and tension. They also value ambiguity. The trap that students should avoid falling into is drawing disproportionately from disciplines (i.e., from their insights and theories) or schools of thought (e.g., Marxism or feminism) with which they agree or are more familiar, whether this is done consciously or unconsciously (Newell, 2007, p. 252).

Throughout the entire interdisciplinary research process, the student must keep in mind its goal: to produce an interdisciplinary understanding. If the scales of scholarship are prejudiced, then the rigor, comprehensiveness, and intellectual integrity of the project will be seriously, or even fatally, compromised.

As with previous steps, Step 6 *may* lead the student to revisit earlier steps. Here, it is important to link each part of the problem with those disciplines that are interested in it, as has been done for acid rain. Performing this Step thoroughly will enable one to identify which perspectives are the most compelling and which ones are (possibly) missing.

Evaluating Each Insight Into the Problem

Evaluating each insight into the problem is the second part of Step 6. This involves working with the information gathered thus far in the research process. This information includes an understanding of (1) the perspective of each relevant discipline and school of thought, (2) the defining elements of these perspectives (i.e., theories, concepts, and assumptions) that are relevant, and (3) the insights into the problem advanced by disciplinary experts. Here, the movement is from the general to the particular—from each discipline's perspective on the problem to the insights and theories advanced by each discipline's community of scholars. Specifically, identifying the weaknesses of insights involves the following:

1. Analyzing the problem from each disciplinary perspective *primarily* in terms of its insights and theories pertaining to the problem. Note: Insights, in an interdisciplinary sense, refer to an expert's peer-reviewed scholarship on the problem. The expert may advance a theory that explains the problem. Typically, experts are quite explicit about the theory they are advancing, and may compare and contrast it with competing theories.

2. Recognizing that each expert's way of understanding the problem may be skewed. The term **skewed understanding** means a deliberate decision or unconscious predisposition to omit certain information that pertains to a problem.

3. Recognizing that each expert's definition of the problem may also be skewed and understanding the implications of this. The way one defines the problem tends to define the way one approaches the problem.

4. Recognizing that the data or evidence upon which the insight and theory are based may also be skewed.

5. Recognizing that the methods used by disciplinary experts may be skewed as well.

Analyzing the Problem From Each Disciplinary Perspective Primarily in Terms of Its Theories and Insights

From the Natural Sciences: Watson (1968), The Double Helix: A Personal Account of the Discovery of the Structure of DNA

Watson is careful to analyze the problem from each disciplinary perspective primarily in terms of its theories and corresponding insights that bear upon the problem. These are identified in Table 9.9, an extension of Table 9.3.

Table 9.9   Disciplinary Theories and Their Insights Into the Problem of the Structure of DNA

Discipline or Subdiscipline	Theory	Insight/Hypothesis
Physics	Structure of Molecules	To learn how the genes controlled cellular heredity, the chemical structure of the virus (gene) would first have to be cracked open (pp. 15, 23).
Microbiology[a]	Phage Theory (The multiplication of bacterial viruses called bacteriophages, or phages for short)	Viruses may be a form of naked genes. Therefore, the best way to find out what a gene is and how it duplicates is to study the properties of viruses (p. 22).
Biochemistry	Molecular Theory	DNA is "the most golden of all molecules" (p. 18).[b]

a. Microbiology is a subdiscipline of biology.
b. Watson's (1968) characterization of the DNA molecule as "golden" or most important is based on two factors: (1) Avery's experiments strongly suggested that future experiments would show that all genes were composed of DNA; and (2) Linus Pauling, the greatest of all chemists, was beginning to become interested in DNA (pp. 14, 18).

From the Social Sciences: Fischer (1988), "On the Need for Integrating Occupational Sex Discrimination Theory on the Basis of Causal Variables"

While many interdisciplinarians create common ground (Step 8) using concepts (such as power) and assumptions (such as rational self-interest), Fischer, like Watson, constructs common ground through theories.

Table 9.10 analyzes the problem of occupational sex discrimination (OSD) from the perspective of each of the relevant disciplines in terms of the theories that each discipline brings to bear on the problem, with each theory illuminating the problem from its narrow perspective.

From the Humanities: Bal (1999), "Introduction," The Practice of Cultural Analysis: Exposing Interdisciplinary Interpretation

In the humanities, the object is to analyze, for instance, how Greek tragedies reflect the gender and class relations of the time as well as to explore the meaning of a text or object. Upon entering this realm of the Academy, the number and diversity of insights produced by disciplinary theories and schools of thought that are informing the disciplinary literature expands considerably. In her work in cultural analysis, for example, Bal combines interdisciplinary fields and perspectives of linguistics, epistemic philosophy, literature, art and art history, museum analysis, cultural anthropology, social studies, and theology along with various theories such as those identified in Table 9.11.

Table 9.10   Disciplinary Theories and Their Insights Into the Problem of OSD

Discipline or School of Thought	Theory	Insight
Economics	1. Monopsony Exploitation	1. OSD is caused by rational decision making that focuses on the demand for labor.
	2. Human Capital	2. OSD is caused by rational decision making that focuses on the supply of labor.
	3. Statistical Discrimination	3. OSD is caused by rational decision making that focuses on the higher turnover "costs" associated with female employees.
	4. Prejudice	4. OSD is the result of some employers indulging their own sexual prejudices.
History	Institutional Development	OSD is caused and perpetuated by longstanding institutional forces.
Sociology	Sex Role Orientation	OSD is caused by a process of "female socialization different from men which, in turn, is directly related in their occupational structure" (p. 34).
Psychology	Male Dominance	OSD is caused and perpetuated by males to maintain the traditional male-female division of labor.
Marxism	Class Conflict	OSD is a necessary act in preserving the institutions of capitalism.

NOTE: Marxism is a school of thought.

Table 9.11   Theories and Their Insights Into How to Understand a Graffito

Theory	Insight on How to Understand a Graffito
Reader Response	The reader of the graffito is to cite direct references in the text to show that the world of the text corresponds to the one in which the reader is situated.
Marxist Criticism	The graffito is a product of work and, as such, is to be understood as the product of a complex web of social and economic relationships as well as the prevailing ideology to which the majority of people uncritically subscribe.
New Historicism	The critic/reader of the graffito is to be highly conscious of and even discuss preconceived notions before situating the text in its historical/literary context.
Psychoanalytic Criticism	The graffito, as an invention of the mind, provides a psychological study of the writer, and of the reader.
Deconstruction	The graffito is an ambiguous text consisting of words from the many discourses that inform it, the meaning of which is ultimately undecidable.
Cultural Analysis	The graffito heightens one's awareness of one's situatedness in the present, the social and cultural present from which one looks at the graffito.

The student has to consider the perspectives of relevant disciplines on the problem as well as the theories and schools of thought that inform them. For example, if the student wants to produce a disciplinary understanding of *The Rime of the Ancient Mariner,* the student would naturally mine the discipline of English literature for insights. However, if the student wants to produce an interdisciplinary understanding of this text, the student would search for insights generated by scholars in a mix of disciplinary and interdisciplinary fields who approach the text from different theoretical positions such as reader response, Marxist criticism, New Historicism, psychoanalytic criticism, Cultural Analysis, and deconstruction (e.g., Fry, 1999). When working in the humanities, one works typically with a mix of disciplinary and interdisciplinary fields.

The humanities example of Bal's graffito raises the issue of how to handle a large number of insights. The possible insights from just one discipline have to be multiplied by the number of disciplines relevant to the topic. This means six disciplinary literatures multiplied by the number of insights generated by each discipline relating to the graffito—a formidable challenge even for advanced students. One solution is to focus *not* on each discipline—since the relevant disciplines have already been identified using the perspectival approach—but on the theories themselves, as shown in Table 9.11.

The example of the graffito shows that when it comes to conducting interdisciplinary work in the humanities, the student must be flexible in developing research strategies that balance disciplinary depth with theoretical breadth while keeping in clear view the ultimate goal of the enterprise—an interdisciplinary understanding of the meaning of the graffito.

Evaluating the Strengths and Weaknesses of Each Disciplinary Expert's Understanding of the Problem

When a discipline focuses on a complex problem such as occupational sex discrimination, it immediately redefines the problem in a way that allows the discipline to make use of its distinctive elements. The result is that experts offer powerful but limited (and sometimes skewed) insights and theories on the problem. This is not surprising because, as noted elsewhere, disciplines specialize in different kinds of problems and on certain parts of the problem.

Newell (2007) observes, "each discipline has it own distinctive strengths" and "the flip side of those strengths is often its distinctive weaknesses."

A discipline such as psychology that is strong in understanding individuals is thereby weak in understanding groups; its focus on parts means that its view of wholes is blurry. A discipline such as sociology that focuses [primarily] on groups doesn't see individuals clearly; indeed, at the extreme it sees individuals as epiphenomenal—a little more than the product of their society. Empirically based disciplines in the social and natural sciences cannot see those aspects of human reality that are spiritual or imaginative, and their focus on behavior that is lawful, rule-based, or patterned leads them to overlook human behavior that is idiosyncratic, individualistic, capricious and messy, or to lump it into unexplained variance. Humanists, on the other hand, are attracted to those aspects and tend to grow restive with a focus on behavior that is predictable, feeling that it misses the most interesting features of human existence. (p. 254)

In order to analyze a problem and identify the weaknesses of insights into it, therefore, the student must appreciate the strengths and corresponding limitations of each discipline's perspective (in a general sense) and be aware that these strengths and limitations flow primarily from differences in phenomena studied and theories and methods used. Only then is it possible to evaluate the insights and theories generated by each discipline's community of scholars and assess the relevance of these to the problem.

From the Natural Sciences: Watson (1968), The Double Helix: A Personal Account of the Discovery of the Structure of DNA

Watson's account of the discovery of the structure of DNA provides a good example of the importance of recognizing the strengths and limitations of the relevant disciplines. In this case, the disciplines are biology and its subdiscipline of genetics, chemistry, biochemistry, and physics and its subdiscipline of X-ray crystallography. Each brought what initially appeared to be certain strengths to the problem of the structure of DNA, but each strength was counterbalanced by critical weaknesses.

For example, geneticists had supposed that the best way to learn how genes control cellular heredity was to study viruses because they are a form of naked gene and thus might provide important clues to the structure of DNA. Watson discovered, however, that genetics was unable to describe the structure of a gene and therefore unable to describe its behavior (Watson, 1968, p. 23). Watson realized that working out DNA's chemical structure might be the essential step in learning how genes duplicated. This realization forced him to turn to biochemistry for answers.

Watson (1968) soon learned that the solid chemical facts known about DNA were meager and that the chemists who did work on DNA were almost always organic chemists with no interest in genetics. So he went to a lab in Copenhagen that was combining techniques of chemistry with genetics (p. 24). There, he began to consider the possibility that physics and the new field of X-ray diffraction photography could provide a three-dimensional picture of DNA and thus reveal important clues about its structure. Watson also learned from Maurice Wilkins, a physicist who had turned to biochemistry to understand the structure and properties of genes (p. 33).

Watson's work illustrates the importance of the researcher knowing the strengths and weaknesses of each relevant discipline. Once limitations are discovered, the researcher can overcome them, as Watson did, by quickly developing alternative strategies.

From the Social Sciences: Fischer (1988), "On the Need for Integrating Occupational Sex Discrimination Theory on the Basis of Causal Variables"

Fischer's study of occupational sex discrimination points up the strengths and weaknesses of each of the most relevant disciplines that Fischer identifies in his study (see Table 9.12). The information on strengths and weaknesses is obtained from a careful reading (or, if necessary, rereading) of the scholarly literature produced by each discipline, interdiscipline, or school of thought (Step 4).

Table 9.12   Strengths And Weaknesses of Each Discipline's Perspective on OSD

Most Relevant Discipline or School of Thought	Strength of Perspective	Weakness of Perspective
Economics	1. Economic motivation of employers	1. Economists have not decided upon a single explanation of OSD.
		2. Economic motivation fails to account for prejudice, sex role socialization, and "tastes" adverse to hiring women.
		3. It assumes that individuals are rational and self-interested.
History	1. Able to identify historical trends that may have produced the problem	1. It is unable to analyze the behavior of groups.
	2. Able to place problem in a broad context	2. It is unable to account for psychological motivation of individuals.
Sociology	1. Conflict among social groups, institutions	1. Its focus on groups fails to account for individual behavior motivated by complex psychological factors or genetic predisposition.
	2. Differences between how men and women are raised	
Psychology	1. Individual behavior, decision making	1. It is unable to study group behavior.
Marxism	1. Explains macro trends and developments	1. Economic considerations fail to explain behavior of all groups or individuals.

NOTE: Marxism is a school of thought.

Simply because a discipline, interdiscipline, or school of thought has weaknesses does not disqualify it from being used. However, these weaknesses do mean that the insights of the discipline are skewed by the way it defines the problem, and the student should acknowledge this, as Fischer does in his analysis.

After surveying the four major economics theories in his study of OSD (see Table 10.10), Fischer (1988) concludes that economists define the problem largely (but not exclusively) in terms of the economic motivation of employers. Each of these economic theories, he says, "offers a highly restrictive and incomplete explanation of the causes of OSD." Therefore, says Fischer, it is important to "broaden the analysis to include other prominent theories of OSD" (p. 31). This phrasing alerts the reader to the overall weakness of the economic theories and explains why he finds it necessary to examine theories advanced by the other relevant disciplines.

From the Humanities: Bal (1999), "Introduction," The Practice of Cultural Analysis: Exposing Interdisciplinary Interpretation

The disciplines that Bal considers relevant to understanding the meaning of the graffito include art history, history, linguistics, literature, philosophy, and psychology. Each of these, however, is limited in its ability to provide the sought-after interdisciplinary understanding. Of these, art history, literature, and psychology are examined to show how to evaluate the strengths and limitations of relevant disciplines.

The strength of art history (which is increasingly interdisciplinary in orientation) is its ability to study an art object in terms of concepts such as quality, its visual appeal, how the artist fits into the canon of great artists, the social context of the object, the uses and misuses of stylistic analysis, and the relationship of art history and movements such as postmodernism and feminism (Fernie, 1995). Though there is much that art history can contribute to one's understanding of the graffito, there is much that it is not equipped to deliver. For one thing, the graffito is unique and the author is unknown, making it impossible to fit it into the canon of great art and artists. Nor can art history comment on the graffito's philosophically profound message, evaluate its poetic structure, or explain how it embodies the concept of "culture."

Literature's strengths in evaluating Bal's graffito are its enabling one to approach it from different theoretical perspectives and situate it biographically, critically, and historically. These strengths, however, are balanced by literature's weaknesses: its inability to situate such an evaluation culturally, understand it as an art object, explain it semantically, and probe it epistemologically and ontologically.

The strength of psychology is to probe the recesses of a person's psyche, whether artist or viewer of the art object. However, psychology is not equipped to situate an art object in a cultural and historical context, examine its poetic form and narrative mode, or understand it as an aesthetic and ethical expression.

Unfortunately, some scholars do not talk as self-consciously about their methodology as Bal does. One way to fathom a writer's methodology is to read reviews of the writer's book(s). Another way is to read the writer's article on the topic closely, paying particular attention to the footnotes that may contain important methodological clues. A third way is to consult disciplinary experts, who should be called upon in any event to confirm one's understanding.

Recognizing That Each Expert's Definition of the Problem May Be Skewed and Understanding the Implications of This

The student must be keenly aware that the insights offered by disciplinary experts are skewed by the way they define the problem (i.e., those parts of the problem they overlook). These insights are also biased in the way that they look at what they *do* see. This is due to their choice of phenomena, theories, and methods, and thus perspective. Familiarity with the strengths and weaknesses of different theory types (noted in Table 8.6) and methods (Chapter 4 and this chapter) is a good starting point.

From the Natural Sciences: Watson (1968), The Double Helix: A Personal Account of the Discovery of the Structure of DNA

Watson (1968) understood early on that each discipline's way of defining the problem—i.e., the structure of DNA—was skewed, and he understood the implications of this. Biology and its subdisciplines of genetics and microbiology defined the problem as a cellular problem. Geneticists and microbiologists believed that studying viruses would eventually reveal how virus genes controlled cellular heredity. This line of reasoning led biologists to overlook the importance of identifying the chemical structure of virus genes (p. 23).

The few chemists interested in the problem (most ignored the problem altogether) believed that it had something to do with the metabolism of nucleotides. The implication of this errant hypothesis was to cause scientists to focus on the chemical process of nucleotide metabolism without first knowing the three-dimensional configuration of a nucleic acid molecule (Watson, 1968, p. 31).

Physicists, principally X-ray crystallographers, were not interested in the problem of the structure of DNA specifically. However, they were interested in perfecting X-ray diffraction pictures of molecular structures in general. The implication of their pursuit of this new method of revealing structures was to point Watson in the right direction of applying this technology to solving the structure of crystallized genes.

From the Social Sciences: Fischer (1988),
"On the Need for Integrating Occupational Sex
Discrimination Theory on the Basis of Causal Variables"

Fischer, like Watson, is explicit in identifying the strengths and weakness of relevant disciplines. Rather than discuss all five disciplines that Fischer deems relevant to the problem of occupational sex discrimination, the discussion is limited to economics and history. As a trained economist, Fischer has a professional command of his discipline. The strength of economics, he says, is that it views the problem of OSD as having to do with economic behavior. But that strength is also its weakness. The problem with economics, says Fischer, is that its theories and methods are skewed. At one time, political economists, as they called themselves, believed that social, cultural, psychological, and political factors were as much a part of their discipline as were economic factors. But since 1900, the desire of orthodox economists to transform the discipline into a science has resulted in their whittling down political economy to "economics proper," meaning that economists focus narrowly on the behavior of "economic man" (or woman—sex was not an issue), the assumptions of perfect competition, and the exclusion of normative issues. "Economic man" supposedly makes economic decisions in a predictable and exact way, always acts intentionally and deliberately, never acts impulsively or altruistically, knows the consequences of her or his actions, and acts to maximize economic benefit to herself or himself (Fischer, 1988, p. 24). As a result, the discipline's theories of OSD ignore many of the key causal dimensions of OSD and offer an "incomplete and unpersuasive explanation of the problem" (p. 26). This skewed approach, says Fischer, explains why a major sex discrimination case involving Sears Roebuck and Company and its employees used expert witnesses who were historians rather than economists. Historians, Fischer notes, "understand the importance of long-run institutional forces causing and perpetuating OSD, an area neglected by most economists" (p. 26).

Fischer's explanation of how a discipline can so easily skew its approach to a problem is instructive for interdisciplinarians. A student who has only a superficial understanding of a discipline can unwittingly buy into its skewed theories. This points up the importance of developing adequacy in each relevant discipline: its perspective on the problem, the theories explaining it, and the assumptions underlying these theories.

Insights from the discipline of economics that presume individuals are rational and self-interested may need to be reassessed when the problem involves social, religious, or cultural behavior (as in the case of OSD) that is based on other motivations as well. "In using skewed insights, interdisciplinarians need to maintain some psychological distance from the disciplinary perspectives on which they draw, borrowing *from* them without completely buying *into* them" (Newell, 2007, p. 254, italics added). There is a second point that needs emphasizing. Fischer, a trained economist who knows well the strengths and weakness of his discipline, is not a trained historian. Yet, he took the time to develop adequacy in history to the extent that he knows its perspective on the subject of OSD.

From the Humanities: Bal (1999), "Introduction," The Practice of Cultural Analysis: Exposing Interdisciplinary Interpretation

Bal (1999) uses cultural analysis because it is an interdisciplinary field with its own theory and method that enables the practitioner to explain more comprehensively than traditional disciplinary approaches can the meaning of an object such as the graffito. For example, cultural analysis differs from a traditional historical approach in its focus on the viewer's situatedness in the present and its seeking to understand the past as part of the present in which the viewer is immersed (p. 1). History tends to view the past, whether person, event, or object, as the product of evolutionary trends and developments leading up to it, societal forces, and individual decisions, which it seeks to describe in rich detail. Using history as it is usually practiced, then, would skew one's understanding of the graffito by ignoring the silent assumptions that historians consciously or unconsciously impose on the past.

Cultural analysis is also different from philosophy and its subdiscipline of epistemology, which concerns how one knows what is real and what is not real. Relying on epistemic philosophy in this case, however, would skew one's understanding of the text. The text contains a statement of nonfiction— "I have not thought you up"—that is inherently contradicted by the address— "Note"—that changes a real person, the anonymous writer's beloved, into a self-referential description of the note: that is, a referential "dear" becomes a self-referential "Note" or short letter. This changes the note into fiction (Bal, 1999, p. 3). If the note is fiction, then epistemic philosophy is of little use to deepen one's understanding of the text's meaning. Instead, one would turn to literature because it quite easily suspends ontological questions (i.e., concerning the kinds of things that have existence), and it has no trouble distinguishing between fiction and reality.

Recognizing That the Data or Evidence Upon Which the Insight and Theory Are Based May Also Be Skewed

The student must be keenly aware that the data presented by disciplinary experts may also be skewed. Each discipline has an epistemology, or way of knowing, and it collects, organizes, and presents data in a certain way that is consistent with this knowing. To say that the data presented by disciplinary experts may be "skewed" is not to allege that the data are falsified or sloppily gathered or presented in a biased way (though the latter is sometimes the case). Rather, it is to say that experts *may* omit or fail to collect certain kinds of data for various reasons. This is because experts are interested in certain kinds of questions and amass data to answer these questions without consciously realizing that they may be excluding other data that would, if included in the study, modify or even contradict the study's findings. Part of the student's task in identifying conflicts in insights (Chapter 10) is to identify and evaluate the different kinds of evidence used by each relevant discipline or theory to support its insights. What one discipline counts as evidence may be discounted or considered inappropriate by another. Therefore, the student should be alert to possible conflicts arising over the different kinds of evidence used by each discipline or theory.

As noted earlier, the sciences and the harder social sciences employ the methods of experiments, models, and statistics, all of which constitute convincing and incontrovertible evidence. For Watson, experiments and models provided the convincing evidence that the DNA molecule has an a-helical structure. Different disciplines or cognitive communities consider evidence in terms of what makes one piece of knowledge persuasive and other pieces of knowledge not persuasive. In women's studies, for example, the testimonial (i.e., "lived experience") is considered persuasive, and "in native studies, traditional knowledge preserved over centuries through an oral tradition and interpreted by Elders is central" (Vickers, 1998, p. 23). Neither kind of evidence would be considered valid in cognitive communities adhering to a positivist/empiricist epistemology and using quantitative evidence.

Historians, on the other hand, count a wide array of artifacts as evidence, including diaries, oral testimony, and official documents, none of which are accepted or considered appropriate by the sciences. Evidence for literary criticism consists of the imaginative application of theory—including the five theories discussed earlier—to the text. For Bal (1999), a cultural analyst, what counts as evidence is the discovery in the text, using the technique of "close reading," of examples of the theory's distinctive elements. These may be summarized in the meaning of the verb "to expose." One example makes the point. A close reading of the word "You," with which the text of the graffito begins, "shows" a speech act in its purest form: direct address to the reader in the present but loaded with "pastness" (pp. 7–8). The student working with a theory or series of theories must be sufficiently grounded in them to identify the evidence that the writer advances to support the theory.

In reading and thinking about the sources they gather, students should ask, "What counts as evidence in this discipline?" and "What kind of evidence is this disciplinary expert omitting that would shed additional light on the problem?" The close connection between disciplinary perspective and the kind of supportive evidence typically used by practitioners in the discipline is illustrated by examining three essays by scholars from two disciplines and a profession on the question, "Should schools adopt computer-assisted education?"

Discipline: Communications/Information Technology. Clifford Stoll (1999) argues in *High-Tech Heretic: Why Computers Don't Belong in the Classroom and Other Reflections by a Computer Contrarian* that schools should not adopt computer-assisted education. His expertise in the field of information technology extends to the business aspect of it, and this is reflected in the kind of evidence he presents to support his case: the hidden financial costs of computers, reference to supportive essays in the disciplinary journal *Education Technology News*, examples of schools having to make hard choices between making needed repairs and buying technology, and careful examination of the mythical cost savings derived from automating education administration.

Discipline: Psychology (Learning Theory). The National Research Council (NRC) is the research arm of the National Academy of Sciences, a private, nonprofit scholarly society that advises the federal government in scientific and technical matters. Its study, *How People Learn: Brain, Mind, Experience, and School*, argues that computer-assisted education can enhance learning (Bradsford, Brown, & Cocking, 1999). The kind of supportive evidence used by the NRC includes references to state-of-the-art learning software and several experimental projects such as GLOBE, which gathered data from students in over 2,000 schools in 34 countries (Bradsford et al., 1999).

Profession: Education. In 1999, The Alliance for Childhood, a partnership of individuals and organizations, issued a report, *Fool's Gold: A Critical Look at Computers in Childhood,* that subsequently appeared in a leading education journal. The report argues that computer-assisted education does not benefit young children. This view, a matter of heated debate within the profession, was nevertheless included in the Education Department's own 1999 study of nine troubled schools in high poverty areas, as well as extensive references to studies by leading education experts, including Stanford professor (Education) Larry Cuban, theorist John Dewey, Austrian innovator Rudolf Steiner, and MIT professor Sherry Turkel (Alliance for Childhood, 1999).

These examples show how each discipline or profession amasses and presents evidence that reflects its epistemology. However, in all three cases, the experts omit evidence that they consider outside the scope of their discipline or profession. "Facts," then, are not always what they appear to be. They reflect what the discipline and its community of experts are interested in.

Students may be seduced by the data on the problem, mistakenly concluding that the data must surely mean that the insight of the scholar who collected the data is "correct." So students "need to be attuned to the subliminal message of facts, and keep track of the complex problem that interests them without being sidetracked by the narrower, value-laden interests of the disciplines on which they draw" (Newell, 2007, pp. 254–255). The lesson here is that one must analyze carefully the kind of evidence used by disciplinary scholars and how they use that evidence.

Recognizing That the Methods Used by Disciplinary Experts May Be Skewed as Well

Chapter 4 introduced the dozen or so distinct methods employed by disciplinary scholars (often in combination) to conduct research and produce new knowledge and explained how these methods are of interest to inter-disciplinarians. The focus here is on the importance of recognizing how these methods may be skewed. As with theories, says Szostak (2004), there are key questions that should be asked of any method used:

Who is being studied? Is the focus of the method on intentional agents or nonintentional agents? Some disciplines—and, therefore, their methods—pay more heed to individuals than to groups. For example, surveys deal with numerous people, interviews with fewer, and observation (especially participant observation) with yet fewer. The problem with these methods, Szostak (2004) says, is that if any subset (from one to many) of the relevant population is examined, researchers will face questions of sampling: "Is the sample biased, or does it represent the average of the larger population, or perhaps the most common attributes of the larger population (which can be quite different from the average)?" (p. 104).

What is being studied? "Different methods used by different schools of thought have differing strengths and weaknesses" (Szostak, 2004, p. 105). Strict interpretivists would argue that scholars should study only atti-tudes and not actions. This point of view flows from two assumptions: that there are significant differences between individuals and how they perceive apparently similar situations, and that people can only be studied in their natural environment. Flowing from these beliefs is the interpretivist emphasis on qualitative versus quantitative analysis (see Chapter 8). Strict positivists, notes Szostak, take the opposite view on all three issues (p. 105).

Why did the researcher or others make the decisions they did? As in the case of theory, the focus of this question is on the decision-making process at work, including the passive decision making of nonintentional agents. Particular methods, observes Szostak (2004), "prove to be best suited to answering one type of question, but methods are differentially applicable to different types of decision making" (p. 107).

Where is the place or setting of the phenomenon to be studied? Phenomena can be analyzed in one place or as they are in motion. Analysis can be performed in a natural setting or in an artificial setting. The latter allows the researcher to control variables and thus isolate a particular cause-effect relationship (Szostak, 2004, p. 108).

When (at what time) should the phenomena be studied? Some methods are biased toward a conclusion that a particular sort of time path is at work. Do researchers "analyze a set of phenomena at one point in time, continu-ously through time, or at several discrete points in time? Do they analyze all phenomena at the same time(s) or at different times? The advantage of con-tinuous time is that the researcher can study the process of change, but analysis at particular points of time is easier" (Szostak, 2004, p. 109).[1]

Strengths and weaknesses of selected methods (not exhaustive) noted by Szostak (2004), are shown in Table 9.13 and should be used only as a start-ing point for further study.

Table 9.13   Strengths and Weaknesses of Disciplinary Methods (Not Exhaustive)

Method	Strengths	Weaknesses
Experiments	Experiments are primarily a deductive tool whereby the subject is manipulated in a particular way and results are measured. They are potentially highly reliable because "they can be easily repeated with all sorts of subtle changes to research design." Experiments are best at identifying simple cause-effect relationships, and "can illuminate some aspects of decision making, such as the degree to which people are swayed by the views of others" (pp. 119–121).	Analysis of group behavior is generally, but not always, unfeasible. Since experiments involve control and manipulation, advocates of qualitative research, including feminists, have often been hostile to them. "With intentional agents, researchers must worry about signaling the desired result to subjects" (pp. 118, 120–121).
Surveys	Focus is on the individual level with results often broken down on a group basis. Results "speak to average tendencies of group members rather than group processes themselves" (p. 135). They can point to important differences among group members. They can provide quantitative data on attitudes at a point in time (p. 135).	They may contain too few causal variables and usually speak only directly to relationships (but network analysis can identify relationships by surveying people with whom they interact) (p. 135).
Statistical analysis (secondary data analysis)	This most popular single method in social science involves analysis of statistics collected by others, including those generated by surveys or experiments. Data are often available for huge numbers of people, can be aggregated to show group tendencies as well as differences within groups, and are available for both nonintentional and intentional agents (p. 131). This method can establish correlations extremely well.	"Secondary data cannot provide detailed insight into how any intentional agent forms attitudes." When a correlation is established, researchers must use judgment and rely on theory in inferring causation (Silverman, 2000, pp. 6–9). McKim (1997) states that statistical analysis should only be taken as evidence of a causal relationship if reinforced by plausible theory and direct evidence from other methods (p. 10). Szostak (2004) notes that researchers "must also worry about the strength of a relationship; researchers often celebrate the 'statistical significance' of a result without taking the necessary—and inherently qualitative—step of asking if the relationship is important. They may thus too easily embrace a theory with limited explanatory power, or reject a theory with great explanatory power because their sample size was small and thus statistical evidence not established" (p. 131). Researchers "must look at how data are recorded, and ask whether either those reporting or those recording had likely biases" (p. 134).

Method	Strengths	Weaknesses
Content or textual analysis	This method includes "a variety of techniques . . . often grounded in different theoretical understandings of the meaning of a text." Texts speak most directly to the intentions of the author and "can provide valuable insights into the author's perception of groups, relationships, and non-intentional agents." Authors often reveal why they or others made decisions as they did, though they may be incorrect or purposely biased (pp. 136–137).	Theorists disagree whether, and to what degree, the core message of any text can be identified. Though texts can provide a diversity of interpretations, there are limitations to the insights that can be drawn from any text. "No text can be understood fully in isolation from other texts, since language is symbolic." A further limitation is that researchers can only build upon the information that the author (consciously or not) provides (pp. 136–137). Szostak cautions researchers that authors may bias their understanding of events. "Content analysis, by which quantitative analysis is performed on how often particular ideas or phrases appear in a text, is one technique which can potentially identify intentions of which the author was not even aware" (p. 137).
Participant observation (PO) (including ethnographic field work)	PO is the most common form of observational analysis, though discreet observation is also used. PO researchers focus on intentional agents and emphasize attitudes, but may also study actions as well as constraints/incentives. PO follows subjects over a period of time as they make decisions and often ask subjects to explain why they acted as they did. PO may be the best way to study certain or unique events and identify idiosyncrasies that prevent a rule from operating (pp. 127–128). Palys (1997) notes that PO is almost always used in conjunction with interviews, surveys, and/or textual analysis, allowing researchers to compare what people say and do, and reducing the problem of researcher bias (Chapter 9).	Only a small number of individuals and relationships can be studied at one time (p. 127). Goldenberg (1992) notes that the very presence of an observer may cause participants to behave differently and feign different attitudes. He also says that many researchers believe that the method is better for exploration/induction than hypothesis testing (p. 322). Though PO research is inherently inductive, it is possible for researchers to ignore evidence that conflicts with their desired conclusions (Szostak, 2004, p. 128). Szostak notes that protocol analysis (whereby participants are asked to perform a task and describe verbally their thoughts while doing so) "effectively combines elements of PO and interviewing. It is more inductive than other types of PO. It is also more artificial, and thus raises questions of whether participants will both do and think as they would in a less artificial environment" (p. 129).

(Continued)

Table 9.13 (Continued)

Method	Strengths	Weaknesses
Interview	Interviews are more costly than surveys and thus tend to involve fewer people. Interviews are good for identifying attitudes that encouraged certain actions (but often people do not know why they act as they do). Questions can elicit insights into constraints/incentives imposed by impersonal agents (p. 122). Narrative analysis overcomes problems of researchers biasing results through their questions by asking people to tell their own stories (p. 123).	Interviews can speak only indirectly to relationships and group processes. "They are limited in their ability to identify temporal priority . . . and dependent on the researcher asking appropriate questions" (p. 122). Interviewees may mislead about why they acted/thought as they did/do, either purposefully or through faulty memory (p. 122). Because interviews necessarily involve small numbers of people, "generalizations require integration of results across many studies" (p. 123).
Case study	Case studies provide insight into a particular issue or theory in rich detail (while statistical analysis tends to seek patterns across numerous cases). Case studies can be quantitative and/or qualitative (p. 140).	"Researchers should be careful not just to report those generalizations that seem to lend themselves to generalizations; other information may encourage the development of alternative theories or the recognition of limits to existing theories" (p. 141).

SOURCE: Szostak (2004).

A Checklist by Which to Evaluate Previous Research

Students can profitably use this checklist to evaluate previous research (i.e., insights) on the problem before identifying sources of conflicts in insights (Chapter 10):

- *Reflect* self-critically on the bias that one may be bringing to the problem. Szostak's (2002) insight is worth noting here: "While disciplines are an important source of bias, human nature, individual psychologies, and the diverse roles that people play in society are also sources of bias" (pp. 112–113).
- *Identify* the disciplinary background of each scholar. The theory or method used by a disciplinary researcher will generally reflect the overall "disciplinary perspective" of the discipline. The interdisciplinarian should question how this perspective influenced the question that the researcher asked, the theory and method(s) used, and the results produced.
- *Question* whether nonscholarly information (i.e., the "other knowledge formations" discussed in Chapter 7) can possibly provide further

perspectives. Both Klein (2001) and Carp (2001) urge students to look beyond the scholarly literature, but evaluate it just as we should evaluate any source. Newell (2001), however, urges students to avoid the extreme postmodernist view that there is no difference between scholarly and nonscholarly research.

- *Determine* whether some key phenomena (i.e., parts of the problem) were excluded from previous analysis and the impact of this (Szostak, 2002, p. 112).
- *Identify* the data that each scholar's discipline typically considers as valid evidence using the information provided in Table 4.1. Analyze the data used for possible clues concerning the sources of the data the scholar is using.
- *Identify* the epistemology that each scholar's discipline typically embraces using the information in Tables 4.6, 4.7, 4.8, 4.9, and 4.10. (The challenge here may be in discovering whether the scholar is assuming a modernist stance or is embracing one of the newer critical stances.)
- *Identify* the theory that informs each writer's insight (if it is theory-based) and be familiar with its strengths and weaknesses. Ask how the expert applied the theory to the problem.
- *Identify* the research method that each scholar uses and be familiar with its strengths and weaknesses.

CHAPTER SUMMARY

In Step 6 of the interdisciplinary research process, the student may decide to replace one of the relevant disciplines with a discipline that seemed only marginally relevant in earlier Steps. Fischer (1988), for example, found that Marxism was only marginally relevant to explaining the causes of OSD compared to the more nuanced theories advanced by modern economists. At this juncture, the student may realize the need to extend the literature search to learn more about what additional insights, concepts, or theories a particular discipline or school of thought has to offer. Also, the student may decide that the wording of the problem that once looked neutral (i.e., did not appear to privilege any one discipline) now seems too much indebted to the perspective of one of the relevant disciplines. Or, the student may realize that the very conception of the problem is overly reflective of a particular discipline (Newell, 2007, p. 255).

At the end of Step 6, the student will have decided which parts of the problem to investigate and thus which disciplinary insights are most relevant to the problem. The student is now ready to engage in the integrative part of the interdisciplinary process, beginning with Step 7, which involves identifying conflicts between disciplinary insights.

NOTE

1. For a fuller discussion of these five questions, see Szostak (2004), Chapter 4.

REVIEW QUESTIONS

1. How is disciplinary perspective important to interdisciplinary inquiry?

2. What is involved in studying the problem from each disciplinary perspective?

3. In Table 9.1, how does stating the perspective of each relevant discipline in the form of an overarching question aid one's understanding of the problem of acid rain?

4. Why was it important for Watson to identify the disciplines relevant to his work on DNA?

5. How is Smolinski's stating the perspective of each discipline relevant to the problem of fresh water scarcity in Texas likely to aid him in a later step?

6. How does constructing a table such as Tables 9.5, 9.7, and 9.8 aid the researcher?

7. How can personal bias complicate the research process?

8. What role do theories play in Fischer's approach to the problem of OSD?

9. How must language change when entering the realm of the humanities, and how is Bal's study of the graffito an example of this?

10. How does Bal's work illustrate the importance of being flexible in developing research strategies that balance disciplinary depth with theoretical breadth?

11. Why is it important to analyze the strengths and weaknesses of each discipline's understanding of the problem as reflected in its scholarship? How is this point illustrated by the work of Watson, Fischer, and Bal?

12. How is it possible for each discipline's way of defining the problem to skew its understanding of the problem? What are the implications of this? How is this point illustrated by the work of Watson, Fischer, and Bal?

13. Why does Bal use cultural analysis to understand the meaning of the graffito instead of relying on specific disciplines and their perspectives?

14. What are the ways that factual information may be skewed by the very nature of disciplinarity?

15. How do the examples from communication/information technology, psychology, and education show that each discipline amasses and presents evidence that reflects its epistemology?

16. How can asking the five key questions of any disciplinary method provide important insights into an expert's analysis of a problem?

PART IV

Integrating Insights

10 Identifying Conflicts in Insights

In summation, the first part of the interdisciplinary research process involves drawing on insights from relevant disciplines and making two kinds of decisions: disciplinary and interdisciplinary. **Disciplinary decisions** include determining what disciplines are relevant to the problem, which disciplinary elements (i.e., phenomena, assumptions, epistemologies, concepts, theories, and methods) pertain to the problem,[1] how many and what kind of sources to collect, how to develop adequacy in each of the relevant disciplines, and how to analyze the problem and evaluate each insight into it. **Interdisciplinary decisions** include determining whether the disciplines have skewed their data and findings in their approach to the problem and considering the possibility that one's own disciplinary and personal bias may have crept into the work.

The second part of the interdisciplinary research process, the focus of this and the next two chapters, requires making additional interdisciplinary decisions that are step-like:

1. identifying conflicts between insights and locating the source(s) of these conflicts (this chapter);

2. creating common ground between these insights or discovering the latent commonality (i.e., at least one theory, concept, or assumption) between them (Chapter 11);

3. using this common ground to integrate the conflicting insights (Chapter 12);

4. producing an interdisciplinary understanding of the problem or question and testing it (Chapter 12).

Identifying conflicts in insights (Step 7), though demanding, is preparatory to creating common ground (Step 8), integrating insights (Step 9), and producing an interdisciplinary understanding of the problem (Step 10). This chapter explains how to identify conflicts between insights and illuminate the source(s) of these conflicts. Professional and exemplary student work is used to illustrate how this is done.

> Step 7: Identify conflicts between insights and locate their sources

Explaining the Importance of Conflicts in Insights

The immediate challenge for the student is to identify conflicts in disciplinary insights and then locate the sources of these conflicts. This is necessary because these conflicts stand in the way of creating or discovering common ground and, thus, of achieving integration. One cannot integrate two things that are exactly alike or that have identical properties. Integration can be achieved only between things that are different, whether those differences are seemingly small or impossibly large. In other words, integration arises out of conflict, controversy, and difference. Without these, integration would be unnecessary. Thus, "integration is typically seen as the litmus test of interdisciplinarity" (Wolfe & Haynes, 2003, p. 153).

The existence of conflict is not some inconvenience that somehow keeps popping up when reading the literature on a problem; rather, it is endemic, inevitable, and central to the interdisciplinary enterprise. Conflict is what one typically discovers when viewing a complex problem from the perspective of several disciplines and reading their insights. Conflict between the insights produced by scholars from different disciplines should not be surprising, explains Newell (2007), because the disciplines reflect "the irreducibly different, conflicting, or even incommensurate principles" by which that part of reality they study operates. The nature and extent of conflict in insights often depends on whether they are drawn from the natural sciences, the social sciences, or the humanities (p. 256).

Students typically encounter conflicts between insights when reading the literature on a problem that is of interest to experts from several disciplines, such as the causes of suicide terrorism. A literature search on this problem reveals that scholarship has been generated by cognitive psychology (a subdiscipline of psychology), political science, religious studies, and cultural anthropology (a subdiscipline of anthropology). (The relative importance of these insights is determined, in part, by how often other writers cite these insights and by how much scholarly debate they generate.) The questions facing the student at this juncture in the interdisciplinary research process are these: Where are these insights located? What are the sources of their conflicts (i.e., why do they conflict)?

Locations of Insights

The two possible locations of insights are within a single discipline or scattered between several disciplines. Bal's (1999) study of the enigmatic graffito, introduced in Chapter 6, reveals how insights produced by different disciplines can easily conflict and, in the absence of some integrative concept, theory, or assumption, ultimately muddle our understanding of its meaning. For example, history's focus on the graffito's "pastness" conflicts with art history's view that the writing is subservient to the image itself and the wall on which it was painted. Similarly, linguistics' focus on the graffito's utterance "Look!" (thus creating a subject/object dichotomy) conflicts with rhetorical analysis' broader focus of helping us "read" not just the graffito but the wall as well (pp. 8–9).

In the threaded example of the causes of suicide terrorism introduced here, conflicting theory-based insights are found both within the same discipline and between other disciplines, as shown in Table 10.1.

More challenging than identifying conflicts in insights *within* a discipline is identifying conflicts in insights *between* disciplines. In the former situation, conflict is generally limited because the insights typically reflect the discipline's basic assumptions. However, there is far more opportunity for conflicts to arise between insights from two or more disciplines because of their differing basic assumptions.

Table 10.1 Locations of Conflicting Insights Into the Causes of Suicide Terrorism Within the Same Discipline and Between Other Disciplines

Discipline or Subdiscipline	Insight of Expert
Cognitive Psychology	Individuals are driven to commit acts of violence that they are psychologically compelled to commit (Post, 1998, p. 25).
	Self-sanctions can be disengaged by cognitive restructuring the moral value of killing so that the killing can be done free of self-censuring restraints (Bandura, 1998, p. 164).
	"In most cases, the perpetrators sacrificed themselves in the name of a nationalistic rather than a religious idea" (Merari, 1998, p. 205).
Political Science	"Terrorism can be understood as an expression of political strategy" (Crenshaw, 1998, p. 7).
	"The principal difference in means between sacred terror and secular terror derives from the special justifications and precedents each uses" (Rapoport, 1998, p. 107).
Cultural Anthropology	Suicide terrorists act out of a universal heartfelt human sentiment of self-sacrifice for the welfare of the group/culture (Atran, 2003, p. 2).

NOTE: Cognitive psychology and cultural anthropology are subdisciplines.

Once the important disciplinary insights are identified, the next challenge is to identify the sources of these conflicts—why these insights conflict.

Sources of Conflicts Between Insights

The possible sources of conflict between insights are concepts, assumptions, and theories (discussed in Chapter 4). Concepts are technical terms that represent a phenomenon or idea and are basic components of insights. Assumptions underlie both concepts and theories. Theories, which increasingly dominate the scholarly discourse within the disciplines, determine the questions asked, the phenomena investigated, and the insights produced. Advanced students and professionals often find themselves having to deal with insights produced by one or more theories and determine why these theory-based insights conflict. Given their importance to interdisciplinary work, a more extended discussion of theories will follow in a separate section of this chapter.

Concepts

Because disciplinary insights, discussed in Chapter 4, are largely expressed in language, conflicts in insights may involve embedded terminology or concepts. (However, those in the fine and performing arts are quick to point out that insights are not exclusively expressed in language but may also be expressed in form, movement, and sound.) Interdisciplinarians commonly encounter three problematic situations concerning concepts.

The first problematic situation arises when the same concept masks different contextual meanings in the relevant disciplinary insights (Bromme, 2000, p. 127). When the same concept is used by two disciplines to describe some aspect of the problem, the student needs to look closely for differences in both implied and specified meaning. Concerning the earlier example of acid rain in Chapter 9, the alert student will discover that the concept "efficiency" has related but different meanings for biologists and physicists (energy out/energy in), economists (dollars out/dollars in), and political scientists (influence exerted/political capital expended) (Newell, 2001, p. 19). Creating common ground when the same concept masks different contextual meanings is relatively easy because the integrative concept (in this case, "efficiency") already exists and merely awaits discovery.

The second problematic situation involves semantic disagreements that arise when different concepts are used to describe essentially the same idea. In the threaded example of suicide terrorism shown in Table 10.2, the subdiscipline of cognitive psychology uses the concept of "special logic" that has a similar meaning to the political science concept of "strategic logic." Since both concepts are grounded in the assumption that the agents are rational, the disagreement can be easily overcome by using either a new technical term or an existing term that scholars agree to freight with new meaning.

The third problematic situation involves real disagreements that arise when different concepts are used that cannot be overcome by clarifying their meaning. This is the case between the concepts of "displacement" and "religious communion," as shown in Table 10.2. The former concerns an individual's psychological state of mind in a given context, while the latter concerns a communal commitment to a faith tradition. Creating common ground between these concepts by clarifying their meaning is unworkable.

Table 10.2   Differing Concepts Used by Disciplines to Address the Causes of Suicide Terrorism

Discipline or Subdiscipline	Concept
Cognitive Psychology	Special logic
	Displacement
	Indoctrination
Political Science	Strategic choice
	Strategic logic
Cultural Anthropology	Religious communion

Assumptions

Chapter 4 established that every discipline makes a number of assumptions. These assumptions include what constitutes truth, what counts as evidence or proof, how problems should be formulated, and what are the general ideals of the discipline (Wolfe & Haynes, 2003, p. 154). Disciplinary scholars seldom feel the need to make these assumptions explicit in their writings, much less justify them. Undergraduates majoring in a discipline become familiar with these assumptions by taking advanced coursework in the discipline and by becoming enculturated in the discipline (Newell, 2007, p. 256). However, interdisciplinary students who have not had much coursework in a particular discipline need to ferret out these assumptions in order to achieve integration.

Assumptions can be of three kinds:

a. *Ontological (regarding the nature of reality)*: For example, each social science makes an ontological assumption about the rationality of individuals: whether they are rational, irrational, or rationalizing. If, for example, the student is trying to develop an interdisciplinary understanding of those persons carrying out suicide bombings, the student will likely encounter a variety of scholarly opinion on the bomber's state of mind, ranging from rational to irrational to rationalizing. Other ontological assumptions by the social sciences concern whether persons act autonomously or as a product of their culture, are self-centered or other-regarding.

b. *Epistemological (regarding the nature of knowledge of that "reality")*: Epistemology basically answers the question, "How do we know what we know?" In essence, epistemology is a way of testing any belief or assertion of truth. Each discipline tests for truth in different ways. In biology, for example, the assumption that all plants need sunlight may seem obvious. However, in order to *prove* this is true, the biologist must conduct experiments to demonstrate consistently and conclusively that plants die without sunlight. Experiments often lead to new knowledge, for instance, that forms of artificial light can cause plants to grow or that some plants are not very dependent on light. In the humanities, by contrast, epistemology becomes much more subjective. A poem may acquire validity not because it is liked by a large number of people, but because its meaning has withstood the test of time.

c. *Value-laden:* The social sciences make value assumptions about diversity, justice, and truth; the humanities often deal quite directly with questions of value; and the natural sciences make value judgments about which problems are worth studying and what knowledge is worth developing.

Each discipline brings its time-tested assumptions to bear as it focuses on the part of the problem in which it specializes. While the insights into a problem generated by each discipline necessarily share some assumptions (otherwise the discipline would dissolve), they may differ on other assumptions. Where these differences are relevant to the problem at hand, they will lead to controversy within the discipline (Newell, 2007, pp. 256–257). Assumptions may vary somewhat within a discipline, but vary much more from discipline to discipline.

Examining an object like Bal's (1999) graffito that spans many disciplines illustrates how ontological, epistemological, and value-laden assumptions can easily conflict. Concerning ontological assumptions, just as disciplinary communities differ over the state of mind of a person who carries out a suicide bombing, so, too, will scholars differ over the state of mind of the person who wrote the graffito. This person's state of mind, like that of the suicide bomber, can range from rational to irrational to rationalizing. Another ontological assumption that may be disputed by scholars from the relevant disciplines concerns whether the writer was acting autonomously or merely as a product of the culture.

The epistemological assumptions brought to bear by the relevant disciplines are no less problematic. As applied to the graffito, one cannot prove that it has a singular meaning by conducting an experiment. Epistemology is much more subjective in the humanities than in the social sciences or the natural sciences.

Making value-laden assumptions about the graffito is also problematic because these, too, are likely to generate conflict. As Bal (1999) says, "an exposition is always also an argument" (p. 5). What, then, are students to do in such circumstances? They should recognize that conflicting assumptions are a natural feature of the interdisciplinary landscape.

The student should be mindful of disciplinary assumptions in order to more easily identify conflicts between them. One effective way to probe the assumptions of a discipline is to step back from the disciplinary insights on the problem and ask the simple question, "How does this writer see the problem?" By stepping back from the insights of economists on occupational sex discrimination (OSD), the student can see clearly that economics views OSD as an economic problem and the result of rational economic-based decision making. A useful resource for probing the assumptions of insights is Tables 4.3, 4.4, and 4.5 (for disciplinary assumptions). Finally, creating a table that juxtaposes these differences will prove valuable for performing the Steps involved in integration.

Picking up the threaded example of suicide terrorism, Table 10.3 shows how the basic assumption of each discipline (as noted in Chapter 4) is reflected in the conflicting insights into this problem. A scholar's assumptions are typically implicit, and identifying them requires close reading. The table also shows how it is possible for insights produced by a discipline (in this case, by cognitive psychology and political science) to share the discipline's basic assumptions even though the insights conflict somewhat.

Theories

Theories are the third possible source of conflict between insights. Theories contain embedded concepts. For example, the concept "special logic" is a technical term that describes the basic idea of Terrorist Psychologic Theory. Therefore, understanding this concept is essential to developing a full understanding of the theory. Disciplinary theories (and the insights they produce) typically share the basic assumptions of the disciplines that produced them. Interdisciplinarians are interested in theories (the focus here is on disciplinary theories) because they generate insights into problems.

Depending on the problem, the student is likely to encounter multiple theories from one or several disciplines that explain some aspect of the problem. The student should thoroughly research the problem so as not to overlook any relevant theory and insight. Such omission might skew the results of the research, calling into question its validity.

Important theories on the problem of suicide terrorism are shown in Table 10.4.

Table 10.3   Basic Assumptions of Disciplines Reflected in Insights Into the Causes of Suicide
Terrorism

Discipline or Subdiscipline	Basic Assumption of Discipline	Insight of Expert
Cognitive Psychology	Group behavior can be reduced to individuals and their interactions, and humans organize their mental life through psychological constructs (Leary, 2004, p. 9).	Individuals are driven to commit acts of violence that they are psychologically compelled to commit (Post, 1998, p. 25). Self-sanctions can be disengaged by cognitively restructuring the moral value of killing so that the killing can be done free of self-censuring restraints (Bandura, 1998, p. 164). "In most cases, the perpetrators sacrificed themselves in the name of nationalistic rather than a religious idea" (Merari, 1998, p. 205).
Political Science	Individual and group behavior are motivated primarily by a desire for or the exercise of power. "[H]uman beings, while they are undeniably subject to certain causal forces, are . . . in part intentional actors, capable of cognition and acting on the basis of it" (Goodin & Klingerman, 1996, pp. 9–10).	"Terrorism can be understood as an expression of political strategy" (Crenshaw, 1998, p. 7). "The principle difference in means between sacred terror and secular terror derives from the special justifications and precedents each uses" (Rapoport, 1998, p. 107).
Cultural Anthropology	Cultural relativism (the notion that people's ideas about what is good and beautiful are shaped by their culture) assumes that systems of knowledge possessed by different cultures are "incommensurable" (i.e., not comparable and not transferable) (Whitaker, 1996, p. 480).	Suicide terrorists act out of a universal heartfelt human sentiment of self-sacrifice for the welfare of the group/culture (Atran, 2003, p. 2).

Theories are also prominent in the story of the discovery of the structure
of DNA. Watson's (1968) account of the process by which he and Crick
discovered the structure of DNA is useful to interdisciplinarians because it
identifies the conflicting theories about how to unlock the secret of the
DNA molecule and also explains why these theories conflict. The "suspi-
cion" (i.e., theory) among geneticists, Watson recalls, was that viruses are
a form of "naked gene." If true, the best way to find out what a gene is and
how it duplicates was to study the properties of viruses, beginning with the
phages, or simplest viruses. So, Watson joined the growing number of scientists who studied phages in hopes that they would eventually learn how
the genes control cellular heredity (pp. 22–23). Soon, however, Watson

Table 10.4   Theories on the Causes of Suicide Terrorism

Discipline or Subdiscipline	Theory
Cognitive Psychology	Terrorist Psycho-logic
	Self-Sanction
	Suicidal Terrorism
Political Science	Collective Rational Strategic Choice
	"Sacred" Terror
Cultural Anthropology	Kin Altruism

began to realize "deep down" that "it is impossible to describe the behavior of something when you don't know what it is" (p. 23). This realization led him to consider Wilkins' method of X-ray crystallography (physics) that Watson hoped would provide a picture that showed DNA having a crystalline structure. Watson realized that no single discipline or theory would, by itself, solve the mystery of the structure of the DNA molecule, but that the solution would involve the combined techniques of chemistry, genetics (biology), and physics.

Identifying Theory-Based Insights and Locating the Sources of Conflicts Between Them

Theory is an important component of academic inquiry for advanced undergraduates, graduate students, and professionals. For this reason, students must identify the theory-based insights relevant to the problem and locate the sources of conflict between them. **Theory-based insights** are insights that are informed by or advance a particular theoretical perspective.

Students must develop a basic understanding of relevant theories in terms of each theory's (1) insight stated in general terms, (2) insight into the problem at hand, (3) key concept(s) expressive of the theory, and (4) its underlying assumption(s). Gathering this information is necessary whether the student is dealing with theories produced by a particular discipline or theories produced by different disciplines. In either situation, the student is trying to determine the source(s) of conflict between these theories and their insights. Knowing this information about each theory will enable the student to quickly identify the sources of conflict between theories, and thus between their respective insights into the problem. If the student has to work with several theories and their conflicting insights, it is helpful to assemble basic information about them in a table, to see more clearly the relationships and conflicts that might otherwise escape the student's notice. Basic information about the theories and insights relevant to the problem of suicide terrorism is shown in Table 10.5.

Table 10.5 Theory-Based Insights Into the Problem of Suicide Terrorism

Theory	Insight of Theory Stated in General Terms	Insight Into the Problem	Concept	Assumption
Terrorist Psycho-logic	Political violence is not instrumental but an end in itself. The cause becomes the rationale for acts of terrorism the terrorist is compelled to commit (Post, 1998, p. 35).	"Individuals are drawn to the path of terrorism to commit acts of violence . . . as a consequence of psychological forces, and that their special psycho-logic is constructed to rationalize acts they are psychologically compelled to commit" (Post, 1998, p. 25).	Special Logic (Post, 1998, p. 25)	Humans organize their mental life through psychological constructs.
Self-Sanction	"Self-sanctions can be disengaged by reconstruing conduct as serving moral purposes, by obscuring personal agency in detrimental activities, by disregarding or misrepresenting the injurious consequences of one's victims, or by blaming and dehumanizing the victims" (Bandura, 1998, p. 161).	Self-sanctions can be disengaged by cognitively restructuring the moral value of killing, so that the killing can be done free of self-censuring restraints (p. 164). See dissociative practices (Bandura, 1998, pp. 171–182).	Moral cognitive restructuring (Bandura, 1998, p. 164)	
Suicidal Terrorism	"Terrorist suicide . . . is basically an individual rather than a group phenomenon; it is done by people who wish to die for personal reasons" (p. 206). "Personality factors seem to play a critical role in suicidal terrorism. . . . It seems that a broken family background is an important constituent" (Merari, 1998, p. 207).	"Perpetrators of suicidal attacks . . . are not the exclusive domain of religious fanaticism in general. . . . In most cases the perpetrators sacrificed themselves in the name of nationalistic rather than a religious idea" (Merari, 1998, p. 205).	Indoctrination (Merari, 1998, p. 199)	
Collective Rational Strategic Choice	This approach permits the construction of a standard that can measure degrees of rationality, the degree to which strategic reasoning is modified by psychology and other constraints, and explain how reality is interpreted (Crenshaw, 1998, pp. 9–10).	Terrorism can be understood as an expression of political strategy (Crenshaw, 1998, p. 7).	Collective rationality (Crenshaw, 1998, pp. 8–9)	"Terrorism may follow logical processes that can be discovered and explained" (Crenshaw, 1998, p. 7).
"Sacred" Terror	"Holy" or "sacred" terror is "terrorist activities to support religious purposes or terror justified in theological terms" (Rapoport, 1998, p. 103).	"Sacred" or "holy" terrorists justify the means they use on the basis of sacred writings and/or on certain theological interpretations of these writings (Rapoport, 1998, pp. 107–130).	"Holy" or "sacred" terror (Rapoport, 1998, p. 103)	
Kin Altruism	A sense of religious sharing and empowerment motivates suicide terrorists (Atran, 2003, p. 6).	Suicide terrorists act out of a universal heartfelt human sentiment of self-sacrifice for the welfare of the group/culture (Atran, 2003, p. 2).	"Religious communion" (Atran, 2003, p. 6)	The notion that people's ideas about what is good and beautiful are shaped by their culture (Whitaker, 1996, p. 480).[a]

a. This expression of cultural relativism does not equate to ethical relativism (that all ethical systems are equally good because they are all cultural products), as Merrilee Salmon (1997) makes clear.

The student should note that Table 10.5 consists largely of quotations rather than paraphrases of each writer's words. The reason for this is that paraphrasing runs the risk of unintentionally distorting the writer's meaning, especially when the writer is explaining complex and unfamiliar theories or concepts. This rule of thumb pertains only to the data collection phase of the research project. Juxtaposing statements and key concepts in the words of each writer, as this table does, makes it easier for the student to identify sources of conflict and latent commonalities. Identifying these statements and locating assumptions, key concepts, and theories in each text requires skill in the technique of **close reading**. This is a fundamental method of modern criticism that calls for the careful analysis of a text and close attention to individual words, syntax, and the order in which sentences and ideas unfold (Baldick, 2004). Given the necessity of careful textual analysis across disciplinary literatures in interdisciplinary work, close reading is an indispensable skill that students must develop. Students should approach each insight with an agenda of particular things to look for and then store this information in a systematic way that is easily retrievable for future use.

Students may not use every feature of the interdisciplinary research process presented in this book on any given research project. Such is the case with the touchstone examples of Watson (1968), Fischer (1988), and Bal (1999) that use most of these features, but not all of them. Since there are no conflicting theories within the disciplines used in Watson's natural science example, a student paper, *Fresh Water Scarcity in Texas,* is introduced. To broaden coverage of approaches used in the humanities, a critique on the British Romantic poem *The Rime of the Ancient Mariner* by Samuel Taylor Coleridge is substituted for Bal.

Sources of Conflict Between Theory-Based Insights Produced by the Same Discipline

Theories generated by the same discipline are likely to have far less conflict because they typically share the discipline's basic assumptions. Nevertheless, disciplines differ considerably in their internal coherence, varying from economics, which is very unified, to English literature, which is fragmented among a host of theoretical approaches. Every theory is undergirded by one or more assumptions. Admittedly, these are more difficult for students new to a discipline and to the interdisciplinary research process to discover because they require a greater knowledge of the discipline and the skill of close reading. But the task is not impossible and may simply involve asking a disciplinary expert for help.

From the Natural Sciences:
Smolinski* (2005), Fresh Water Scarcity in Texas

Table 10.6 illustrates the conflicting insights produced by geological theories explaining the scarcity of fresh water in Texas. In the absence of

Table 10.6   Conflicting Theory-Based Insights Into the Problem of Fresh Water Scarcity in Texas
Within the Same Discipline

Discipline	Theory	Insight of the Theory Stated in General Terms	Insight of the Theory Applied to the Problem
Geology	Global Warming	The production of greenhouse gases has caused, and will continue to cause, the planet's temperature to rise, and this negatively impacts fresh water availability.	Global warming will significantly increase the rates of evaporation, exacerbating an already critical fresh water shortage in Texas.
	Overexploitation	Too much water is taken from aquifers (water-bearing rock formations), and this practice is seriously degrading the quality of the remaining volume of water in these aquifers.	Increased rates of water removal from the Ogallala Aquifer under Texas coupled with decreased rates of recharge have led to an overall draw down of the water table (the uppermost limit of the water contained in the Ogallala Aquifer).
	Infiltration	There is more than enough water in the nation's groundwater systems to satisfy demand, but saline water is increasingly contaminating it.	In Texas, saline and brackish water is infiltrating and contaminating the remaining groundwater.

prior discussion of these theoretical approaches, the insight of each theory is conveyed in general terms before applying the insight of each theory to the problem.

From the Social Sciences: Fischer (1988), "On the Need for Integrating Occupational Sex Discrimination Theory on the Basis of Causal Variables"

Table 10.7 identifies four major economics theories that provide insights into the causes of occupational sex discrimination (OSD).

For each theory, conflict between the insights is noticeably sharpened when it is applied to the problem of OSD.

From the Humanities: Fry (1999), Samuel Taylor Coleridge: The Rime of the Ancient Mariner

Coleridge's *Rime* illustrates the importance of identifying conflicting theory-based insights into a text or work of art. In literature, critical essays

Table 10.7   Conflicting Theory-Based Insights Into the Problem of OSD Within the Same Discipline

Discipline	Theory	Insight of the Theory Stated in General Terms	Insight of the Theory as Applied to the Problem
Economics	Monopsony Exploitation	"The profit-maximizing monopsonist . . . hires labor up to the point of where marginal labor costs equal marginal revenue (or marginal value) . . . [and thus] pays workers a wage less than their value contribution to the firm" (Fischer, 1988, p. 27).	Focuses on the demand side of OSD, explaining it as "the result of collusive behavior of male employers in discriminating against females" (p. 31)
	Human Capital	"Each worker [human capital] is viewed as a combination of native abilities and raw labor power plus specific skills acquired through education and training" (p. 28).	"Focuses on the supply side of OSD, characteristics of females— particularly their education and training levels" (p. 31)
	Statistical Discrimination	"Statistical discrimination exists when an individual is evaluated on the basis of the average characteristics of the group to which he or she belongs, rather than on his or her personal characteristics" (p. 29).	"Emphasizes group (rather than individual) characteristics of female job applicants. It is female group characteristics that make women a poor choice for risk adverse employers" (p. 31).
	Prejudice	This model is "based on the notion that some employers indulge their own sexual prejudices (or the prejudices, real or perceived, of their employees and customers) in making hiring and other personnel decisions" (p. 30).	Says that "the male employer doesn't hire women because of his own tastes or preferences for female discrimination" (p. 31)

on a text typically approach it using different theoretical approaches (Fry, 1999, p. v). These are of great interest to the interdisciplinarian because they are informed by a set of coherent assumptions that can be articulated and also modified and extended through comparison as the process of integration proceeds. Table 10.8 shows five theoretical approaches and their insights into the text.

Examining a text from the stance of two or more theoretical frames, while valuable, is not, by itself, interdisciplinary. What is needed for the analysis of the text to be truly interdisciplinary is the creation or discovery of a common ground theory, concept, or assumption by which these conflicting theoretical frames can be integrated and a new and comprehensive understanding produced. This is the subject of Chapter 11.

Table 10.8   Conflicting Theory-Based Insights Into the Problem of the Meaning of *The Rime of the Ancient Mariner* Within the Same Discipline

Discipline	Theory	Insight of the Theory	Insight of the Theory as Applied to the Text
Literature	Reader-Response	The meaning of a work is not inherent in its internal form but rather is cooperatively produced by the readers (what they bring to the text) and the text (Murfin, 1999c, p. 169, 1999e, p. 108).	The major issue of the poem is not its implied moral values but the process of arriving at moral values, and that process is about reading (Murfin, 1999e, p. 108; Ferguson, 1999, p. 123).
	Marxist Criticism	Literature is a material medium that reflects prevailing social and cultural ideologies and also "transcends or sees through the limitations of ideology" (Murfin, 1999b, p. 144).	*The Rime* is susceptible to an historical approach that reveals an early instance of ecological concern, an emerging interest in hypnotism, and that raises Protestant issues regarding free will, choice, election, and damnation, as well as broader, philosophical questions regarding "epistemological consensus" (Simpson, 1999, p. 152, 158).
	The New Historicism	Literature is not a sphere apart or distinct from the history that is relevant to it (Murfin, 1999c, p. 171).	Reconstructing the historical context of a literary text like *The Rime* is, by itself, treacherously difficult to achieve, and all the more so because we have been conditioned by our own place and time (Murfin, 1999c, p. 171).
	Psychoanalytic Criticism	A work of literature is a fantasy or a dream, and psychoanalysis can help explain the mind that produced it (Murfin, 1999d, p. 225).	*The Rime* is a constructed world unified by language and symbols and is, in fact, "a reaction against the horrifying loss of a boundariless, pre-oedipal world in which the infant, mother and natural world are one" (Murfin, 1999d, p. 232).
	Deconstruction	A text is not a unique, hermetically sealed space but is perpetually open to being seen in the light of new contexts and has the potential to be different each time it is read (Murfin, 1999a, p. 268).	*The Rime* should be seen in terms of its "linguistic strangeness, as a 'series of dislocations—translations, displacements, metonymies'— that 'dares its audience to make sense of it'" (Eilenberg, 1999, p. 283).

From the Natural Sciences: Smolinski*
(2005), Fresh Water Scarcity in Texas

Although theories in the same discipline tend to share the discipline's underlying assumptions, Table 10.9 shows that sometimes its theories, their insights, and their respective assumptions can still differ significantly. Such is the case with the theories explaining the reasons for fresh water scarcity in Texas. This makes more challenging the student's task of creating common ground between them.

From the Social Sciences: Fischer (1988),
"On the Need for Integrating Occupational Sex
Discrimination Theory on the Basis of Causal Variables"

Fischer's study is an example of how a professional interdisciplinarian may see the need to make explicit the conflicting assumptions of theories advanced by a particular discipline, in this case, economics. After identifying the four major orthodox or mainstream economic theories that address OSD, Fischer states the assumptions of each one. He says, for instance, that Monopsony Exploitation Theory "*assumes* that men, in their role as husbands, employers, workers, consumers, and legislators, have power over female occupational choices" (p. 26, italics added). These economic theories, their assumptions, and corresponding insights into the problem of OSD are summarized in Table 10.10.

Table 10.9   Conflicting Theory-Based Insights and Their Corresponding Assumptions on the Problem of Fresh Water Scarcity in Texas Within the Same Discipline

Discipline	Theory	Assumption of the Theory	Insight of the Theory as Applied to the Problem
Geology	Global Warming	Global warming is the result of rapid agricultural and technological advances.	Global warming will significantly increase the rates of evaporation, exacerbating an already critical fresh water shortage.
	Overexploitation	Strict conservation legislation aimed primarily at agriculture will solve the problem.	Increased rates of water removal from the Ogallala Aquifer coupled with decreased rates of recharge have led to an overall draw down of the water table (the uppermost limit of the water contained in the Ogallala Aquifer).
	Infiltration	Fresh water scarcity already exists, either as a result of global warming or overexploitation.	In Texas, saline and brackish water is infiltrating and contaminating the remaining groundwater.

Table 10.10   Conflicting Theory-Based Insights and Their Corresponding Assumptions on the Problem of OSD Within the Same Discipline

Discipline	Theory	Assumption of the Theory	Insight of the Theory as Applied to the Problem
Economics	Monopsony Exploitation	"Men, in their role as husbands, employers, workers, consumers, and legislators, have power over female occupational choices" (Fischer, 1988, p. 27).	Focuses on the demand side of OSD, explaining it as the result of "collusive behavior of male employers in discriminating against females" (p. 31)
	Human Capital	"OSD is largely the result of choices that women make regarding home responsibilities and career commitment" (p. 29).	"Focuses on the supply characteristics of females—particularly their education and training levels" (p. 31)
	Statistical Discrimination	"Statistical discrimination exists because . . . its benefits to the employer outweigh its costs" (p. 30).	Emphasizes "group (rather than individual) characteristics of female job applicants. It is female group characteristics that make women a poor choice for risk adverse employers" (p. 31).
	Prejudice	"Sex role socialization helps form [employer] tastes . . . For example, . . . employers tend to believe that women can not and/or should not do hard physical work . . . [and] 'can't handle responsibility'" (p. 31).	Says that "the male employer doesn't hire women because of his own tastes or preferences for female discrimination" (p. 31)

Since these theories are from the same discipline, they share the discipline's overall perspective that the world is a rational marketplace and its fundamental assumption that humans are motivated by rational self-interest (see Table 4.4). However, when these theories address the causes of OSD, it is clear that they conflict more than they overlap, even though they are from the same discipline. It is appropriate for the student to explain, as Fischer does, why there is need to go beyond these particular theories: Each of them, he says, offers an "incomplete explanation of the causes of OSD," requiring that the analysis be broadened to include the "relevant work in related disciplines if an interdisciplinary understanding is to be achieved" (Fischer, 1988, p. 31).

From the Humanities: Fry (1999), Samuel Taylor Coleridge: The Rime of the Ancient Mariner

The theories of reader-response, Marxist criticism, New Historicism, psychoanalytic criticism, and deconstruction shown in Table 10.11 are prevalent in

Table 10.11 Conflicting Theory-Based Insights and Their Corresponding Assumptions on the Problem of the Meaning of *The Rime of the Ancient Mariner* Within the Same Discipline

Discipline	Theory	Assumption of the Theory	Insight of the Theory as Applied to the Text
Literature	Reader-Response	*The Rime* is about its author and the deluded reader.	The major issue of *The Rime* is not its implied moral values but the process of arriving at moral values, and that process is about reading (Murfin, 1999e, p. 108; Ferguson, 1999, p. 123).
	Marxist Criticism	*The Rime* is driven by an "agenda" of remystifying the world and thus undermines the reader's confidence in rationality and rationalist theories (Simpson, 1999, p. 158).	*The Rime* is susceptible to a historical approach that reveals an early instance of ecological concern, an emerging interest in hypnotism, and that raises Protestant issues regarding free will, choice, election, and damnation, as well as broader, philosophical questions regarding "epistemological consensus" (Simpson, 1999, p. 152, 158).
	The New Historicism	*The Rime* reflects and challenges any number of ideologies or value systems, ranging from Christianity, to the radical political standpoints on the French Revolution, to the slave trade (Modiano, 1999, p. 215).	Reconstructing the historical context of a literary text like *The Rime* is, by itself, treacherously difficult to achieve, and all the more so because we have been conditioned by our own place and time (Murfin, 1999c, p. 171).
	Psychoanalytic Criticism	The "horror" at the heart of *The Rime* is a symptom of the not yet self's casting off the maternal and semiotic (loosely associational) in favor of the paternal and symbolic (Murfin, 1999d, p. 231).	*The Rime* is a constructed world unified by language and symbols and is, in fact, "a reaction against the horrifying loss of a boundariless, pre-oedipal world in which the infant, mother and natural world are one" (Murfin, 1999d, p. 232).
	Deconstruction	All texts, including *The Rime*, are ultimately unreadable (if reading means reducing a text to a single, homogenous meaning) (Murfin, 1999a, p. 269).	*The Rime* should be seen in terms of its "linguistic strangeness, as a 'series of dislocations— translations, displacements, metonymies'—that 'dares its audience to make sense of it'" (Eilenberg, 1999, p. 283).

literary criticism (Fry, 1999, pp. v–vi). They are not monolithic schools of thought but, rather, umbrella terms, each of which covers a variety of approaches to textual criticism. The insights associated with each theory, therefore, are not definitive but expressive of each critic's way of applying the theory to the text.

Sources of Conflict Between Theory-Based Insights Produced by Different Disciplines

Once the theory-based insights in one discipline are identified and the sources of conflict between them are located, the student must continue identifying the theory-based insights in the other relevant disciplines, as Fischer does in Table 10.12. Insights of theories generated by different disciplines, but focusing on the same problem, are likely to conflict even more because the basic assumptions of each discipline conflict.

Having identified all relevant theory-based insights into the problem of OSD, Fischer is ready to proceed with creating or discovering common ground, the subject of the next chapter.

From the Humanities: Bal (1999), "Introduction," The Practice of Cultural Analysis: Exposing Interdisciplinary Interpretation

At several points, Bal's (1999) discussion of the graffito reveals conflicts between theories. For one thing, by stressing the methodological explicitness of cultural analysis, Bal is implicitly challenging postmodernism, with its disdain for explicitness and method (p. 4). Also, cultural analysis' emphasis on self-reflexivity places this theory at odds with the modernist emphasis on the object and/or text as opposed to the viewer and/or reader (p. 6). For Bal, what counts as evidence is the discovery in the text of layered meanings using the technique of close reading. One example of layered meaning is the word "You" at the beginning of the graffito, which, on one level, is a direct address to the reader in the present, but, on another level, is an address to a past someone (pp. 7–8).

The student working with a theory such as cultural analysis, or even a series of theories, must be sufficiently grounded in them to identify the evidence that the writer advances to support the theory. The sciences and the harder social sciences employ the methods of experiments, models, and statistics, all of which constitute convincing and seemingly incontrovertible evidence. For Watson (1968), experiments and models provided the convincing evidence that the DNA molecule has an a-helical structure. Historians, on the other hand, count a wide array of artifacts as evidence,

Table 10.12   Conflicting Theory-Based Insights and Their Corresponding Assumptions on the Problem of OSD Within and Between Disciplines

Discipline or School of Thought	Theory	Assumption	Insight of the Theory as Applied to the Problem
Economics	Monopsony Exploitation	OSD is an economic problem.	Focuses on the demand side of OSD, explaining it as "the result of collusive behavior of male employers in discriminating against females" (Fischer, 1988, p. 31)
	Human Capital		"Focuses on the supply side of OSD, characteristics of females—particularly their education and training levels" (p. 31)
	Statistical Discrimination		"Emphasizes group (rather than individual) characteristics of female job applicants. It is female group characteristics that make women a poor choice for risk adverse employers" (p. 31).
	Prejudice		Says that "the male employer doesn't hire women because of his own tastes or preferences for female discrimination" (p. 31)
History	Institutional Development	OSD is a historical problem.	"Sex segregation at entry to firms is perpetuated over time, and done so without the need for further overt sex discrimination" (p. 34).
Sociology	Sex Role Orientation	OSD is a social problem.	"Female socialization encourages the acceptance of responsibility for domestic work, and a nurturant and helping orientation for child care. . . . Female socialization, on the other hand, discourages authoritativeness or aggressiveness, physical prowess, and quantitative or mechanical aptitude. It is argued that sex role orientation produces different traits in females, and employers use their knowledge of these traits to decide what jobs should be 'female jobs'" (p. 34).
Psychology	Male Dominance	OSD is a male problem.	"Men have socio-economic incentives to continue monopolizing their privileged status in the labor market, and that they can best do this by maintaining the traditional male-female division of household production" (p. 36).
Marxism	Class Conflict	OSD is an ideological problem.	"Some workers—women in particular—are channeled into less desirable jobs and segregated from other workers to keep workers in general from developing a class consciousness and acting collusively to overthrow capitalism. Here, OSD is seen as a necessary act in preserving the institutions of capitalism" (p. 32).

including diaries, oral testimony, and official documents, none of which are accepted or considered appropriate by the sciences. What one disciplinary scholar counts as evidence may be discounted or considered inappropriate by a scholar from another discipline. Therefore, interdisciplinarians should be alert to possible conflicts arising over the different kinds of evidence the various writers use.

Addressing Conflicting Theory-Based Insights _____

Once the student has identified all of the relevant theory-based insights and located the sources of conflict between them, the next task is to present this information as part of the student's analysis of the problem. There are multiple ways to do this, as evidenced in the touchstone examples by Watson (1968), Fischer (1988), and Bal (1999). These examples offer three different types of interdisciplinary literature, each of which is aimed at a somewhat different audience.

From the Natural Sciences: Watson (1968), *The Double Helix: A Personal Account of the Discovery of the Structure of DNA*

Watson (1968) has written a book-length recollection to inform the general reader of how he and Crick made one of history's greatest scientific discoveries. Ever the scientist, Watson is careful to identify each theory as he and Crick encountered it, explain each one in language that the general reader can easily understand, and show how it conflicted with other major theories about the DNA molecule. Two of these conflicting theories are Avery's gene theory and Bragg's theory of X-ray diffraction. Concerning Avery's theory and the role that scientists supposed DNA played in passing on hereditary traits from one cell to another, Watson writes,

> Given the fact that DNA was known to occur in the chromosomes of all cells, Avery's experiments strongly suggested that future experiments would show that all genes were composed of DNA. If true, this meant to Francis [Crick] that proteins would not be the Rosetta Stone for unraveling the true secret of life. Instead DNA would have to provide the key to enable us to find out how the genes determined, among other characteristics, the color of our hair, our eyes, most likely our comparative intelligence, and maybe even our potential to amuse others. (p. 14)

Watson introduces Bragg's theory of X-ray diffraction with equal clarity:

> For almost forty years Bragg, a Nobel Prize winner and one of the founders of crystallography, had been watching X-ray diffraction methods solve structures of ever-increasing difficulty. The more complex the molecule, the happier Bragg became when a new method allowed its elucidation. Thus in the immediate postwar years he was especially keen about the possibility of solving the structures of proteins, the most complicated of all molecules. (p. 8)

Later, the reader learns that it is not the structure of proteins that holds the key to unlocking the mystery of the complex helical structure of DNA, but X-ray crystallography.

From the Social Sciences: Fischer (1988), "On the Need for Integrating Occupational Sex Discrimination Theory on the Basis of Causal Variables"

Fischer (1988) has written a peer-reviewed journal article on the topic of occupational sex discrimination to illustrate the interdisciplinary research process to a professional audience. Theory is central to his purpose and his discussion of it dominates the essay, but in clearly defined ways. First, Fischer is concerned to describe concisely each theory and its underlying assumption. Consider, for example, his description of human capital theory:

> The human capital theory of OSD focuses on the relatively high mobility and intermittent nature of employment women tend to experience. . . . Because of domestic responsibilities, women tend to be in and out of the labor force more frequently than men and thus acquire less on-the-job training (OJT) than their male counterparts. This, it is argued, adversely affects female occupational opportunities in two ways. First, fewer women than men acquire sufficient human capital for jobs which require substantial previous experience. Second, while women are out of the labor force, their job skills depreciate. It is thus rational for women who anticipate intermittent employment to choose occupations which require relatively little time to acquire the necessary job skills and which require job skills that do not depreciate rapidly from nonuse. The combined impact of reduced job experience and the incentive to minimize depreciation of job skills results in women being concentrated in service, sales, clerical and labor jobs and underrepresented among operators, managers, and professionals. (pp. 28–29)

Second, Fischer contrasts each theory with the theory that precedes it. Contrasting differences precedes comparing differences. In what follows,

Fischer contrasts monopsony theory (the first economic theory) with human capital theory (the second economic theory):

> While monopsony theory focuses on the demand side of OSD, human capital theory offers a supply-side explanation of OSD. Each worker is viewed as a combination of native abilities and raw labor power plus specific skills acquired through education and training. The latter is commonly referred to as human capital. (p. 28)

Third, Fischer applies the theory specifically and clearly to the problem of OSD. He concludes: "In summary, the human capital theory of OSD holds that economic incentives lead women to segregate themselves into female occupations. It is economically rational for women to continue to pursue traditional female jobs" (p. 29).

Finally, Fischer briefly critiques each theory. Concerning human capital theory as applied to the problem of OSD, he says that "it is bound to be controversial since it implies that OSD is largely the result of choices that women make regarding home responsibilities and career commitment; that is, it tends to 'blame the victim' for OSD" (p. 29).

From the Humanities: Bal (1999), "Introduction," *The Practice of Cultural Analysis: Exposing Interdisciplinary Interpretation*

Bal's (1999) interdisciplinary essay differs from Watson and Fischer's works in two ways. First, unlike Watson and Fischer, who assume that the reader has little prior knowledge of the topic or theories relevant to it, Bal assumes that the reader is already familiar with the theory and concepts of cultural analysis. Second, Bal, in contrast to Watson and Fischer, privileges the theory of cultural analysis over other approaches. Watson is concerned to show how he and Crick avoided the trap of privileging any particular theory, as most scientists investigating DNA were doing. Fischer tries not to privilege one discipline over the others, but he nonetheless ends up organizing them in a framework that is essentially economic and that uses economic concepts such as demand, supply, and labor market. Bal, however, privileges cultural analysis because "it is an interdisciplinary practice" (p. 1). She uses the graffito to demonstrate what cultural analysis can and should be, and to answer critics who fault cultural analysis for its lack of "methodological explicitness" (p. 4).

She contrasts other approaches with cultural analysis, beginning with history:

> Cultural analysis as a critical practice is different from what is commonly understood as "history." It is based on a keen awareness of the

critic's situatedness in the present, the social and cultural present from which we look, and look back, at the objects that are always already of the past, objects that we take to define our present culture. (p. 1)

Once she explains this basic contrast, Bal (1999) is able to expand the contrast, emphasizing three differences. The first is that cultural analysis probes "history's silent assumptions in order to come to an understanding of the past that is different" (p. 1). The object, of course, is not merely to have an understanding that is just different but that is different because it is integrative and, thus, interdisciplinary. Her second point is that cultural analysis does not attempt to project on the past, and thus on the object in question, what she calls "an objectivitist 'reconstruction'" (p. 1). She means that cultural analysis accepts that there will remain, even after one has undertaken the most comprehensive examination of the moment in time and of the object in it that is possible, an element of ambiguity and mystery. Bal's third point of contrast is that cultural analysis, in contrast to much history writing, does not seek to impose on the past "an evolutionist line," meaning that the object was an inevitable product of knowable historical "developments."

These examples by Watson, Fischer, and Bal show how interdisciplinarians, writing for different audiences, approaching different problems, and using different methods, go about describing conflicting theories. Fischer's four actions can profitably be applied to theories relating to almost any problem.

CHAPTER SUMMARY

Step 7, which begins the integrative process, identifies conflicts in insights and locates the sources of conflict. One important insight of this chapter is the great diversity of interdisciplinary work, as is evident in the touchstone examples by Watson (1968), Fischer (1988), and Bal (1999). Different audiences, different problems, and different purposes for writing are inevitably reflected in different approaches to the interdisciplinary task. Using a combination of narrative and tables is helpful when dealing with many variables. While professionals may not use every feature of the interdisciplinary process described in this book, they typically deal with conflicting insights and theories. Identifying these conflicts and their sources is foundational to the next step of the integrative process: creating common ground by discovering latent commonalities in the conflicting insights, or creating a commonality.

NOTE

1. The extent to which students engage in this work depends on the level of difficulty of the course.

REVIEW QUESTIONS

1. What are the two possible locations of insights, as illustrated in Table 10.1?

2. What are the three possible sources of conflict between insights?

3. Why should the student be mindful of disciplinary assumptions when locating the sources of conflict between insights, and how does the problem of suicide terrorism (as shown in Table 10.3) illustrate this point?

4. How is Table 10.5 helpful in explaining the importance of theory-based insights and locating the sources of conflict between them?

5. How are the theory-based insights (stated in general terms) dealt with by Smolinski (Table 10.6), Fischer (Table 10.7), and Fry (Table 10.8) reflected in the problem-specific theory-based insights?

6. Why is examining a text, such as *The Rime of the Ancient Mariner* (Table 10.8), from the stance of multiple theoretical frames from within the same discipline not, by itself, interdisciplinary?

7. How is the assumption of each of the theories used by Smolinski in Table 10.9 reflected in the insight of each theory as it is applied to the problem of fresh water scarcity in Texas?

8. Why are the theory-based insights generated by different disciplines but focusing on the same problem more likely to conflict?

9. Why should the student be alert to possible conflicts arising over the different kinds of evidence each writer uses?

10. How do the three types of interdisciplinary literature written by Watson, Fischer, and Bal differ in their approach to discussing conflicting theories?

11

Creating
Common Ground

The integrative part of the interdisciplinary research process began with Step 7 and continues with Step 8, creating common ground, the focus of this chapter. Careful attention to this step will make integration possible (Step 9), moving us closer to producing an interdisciplinary understanding of the problem or question (Step 10).

Creating common ground is undoubtedly the most difficult task that students face, probably because it requires original thought that draws on both close analytical reasoning and creative thinking. But it is achievable if the student takes a systematic approach, pays attention to the nature of the challenge, and chooses an appropriate integrative technique. This chapter defines common ground, examines the theory of common ground, explains the importance of common ground to the integrative process, identifies the cognitive processes required to create common ground, and explains how to create common ground.

Deciding in Step 7 which insights conflicted and why was basically a descriptive process, meaning that we simply identified and contrasted conflicts between the perspectives, theories, concepts, and assumptions of the relevant disciplines. We worked with information that was already known to us and did not modify it in any way. Now, in Step 8, we use these findings to create or discover common ground.

> Step 8: Create or discover common ground

Definition of Common Ground

From the earliest conceptions of interdisciplinarity, interdisciplinarians have recognized the need for a common or collaborative language to integrate conflicting disciplinary insights, theories, and concepts. Joseph J. Kockelmans

(1979) was the first to use the term *common ground,* seeing it as a basis for collaborative communication—a common ground—among research scientists from different disciplines working on large government and industry projects. Common ground, he says, is the fundamental element of all interdisciplinary investigation because without it, "genuine communication between those who participate in the discussion would be impossible" (p. 141). Kockelmans was also the first to connect integrating relevant disciplinary "insights" with developing common ground (pp. 142–143).

Newell and William J. Green (1982) link common ground to what they call "the interdisciplinary method" of conducting research (pp. 25, 29). This method, they explain, "requires an appreciation of the full complexity of the disciplines involved, especially an awareness of their often unconscious assumptions, in order to discern the underlying *common ground* or conflict between their insights" (p. 25, italics added). The key to performing integration and producing an interdisciplinary understanding, they say, is creating or discovering the underlying common ground between conflicting insights.

Interdisciplinary common ground is one or more theories, concepts, and assumptions by which conflicting insights can be reconciled and integrated. Creating common ground involves bringing out potential commonalities underlying the conflicting disciplinary and theory-based insights so that these can be reconciled and ultimately integrated. These conceptions of common ground contain three ideas developed in this chapter:

1. Common ground is something that one must create, except between the natural sciences, where it can often be discovered.

2. Creating or discovering common ground calls for (ideally) identifying a theory, concept, or assumption to serve as the "common ground integrator" that applies only to the problem at hand.

3. Integrating disciplinary and theory-based insights generally involves using one or more integrative techniques.

The Theory of Common Ground

In everyday communication, we encounter people who have different perspectives than we have on a wide range of matters. Our everyday perception of facts and events depends on the categories we bring to a certain situation, raising the question of how we are able to comprehend so many different perspectives. Common ground theory advanced by cognitive psychology tries to answer this question.

The Findings of Cognitive Psychology

Cognitive psychology explains successful communication between individuals having different perspectives by exploring the way our brain subjectively constructs perceiving, seeing, and acting. **Common ground theory** postulates that "every act of communication presumes a common cognitive frame of reference between the partners of interaction called the common ground." The theory postulates further that "all contributions to the process of mutual understanding serve to establish or ascertain and continually maintain this common ground" (Bromme, 2000, p. 119). This theory applies to both oral and written communication.

The theory assumes that any verbal encounter represents an act of cooperation by both parties. When we communicate, we do so to attain a certain goal or to respond to a certain question, whether verbalized or unspoken. According to cognitive psychologist Rainer Bromme (2000),

> All contributions to communication are formulated and understood on the basis of background assumptions we make about the situation in question, the object of conversation and its goal: "Two people's common ground is, in effect, the sum of their mutual, common, or joint knowledge, beliefs, and suppositions" (Clark, 1996, p. 93). . . . One's own assumptions on which the conversation is based are designated as *one's own perspective* and that of the other person as [the] *perspective of the other*. (p. 120, italics added)

Though common ground theory was developed to explain everyday interactions, cognitive psychology is now applying it to communication across academic disciplines, especially the natural sciences.

As noted in Chapter 3, the distinctiveness of disciplinary and theoretical perspectives is foundational to interdisciplinarity. A significant finding of cognitive psychology is that in **interdisciplinary communication,** differences in common ground are frequently "discovered" only when the partners of cooperation—the relevant disciplines or theories—"find out that they use the same concepts with different meanings, or that they use different codings (terms, symbol systems) for [similar] concepts" (Bromme, 2000, p. 127).

Other Significant Findings of Cognitive Psychology

Other significant findings of cognitive psychology as applied to interdisciplinarity and to the integrative process include the following:

- Common ground can be in the form of *terminology common to two or more disciplines*. (However, interdisciplinarians are also interested in different concepts that appear to have the same or similar meanings.)
- Common ground in the form of *common terminology does not dissolve all the differences between disciplinary perspectives*. (How to modify conflicting disciplinary assumptions and concepts are addressed under "Techniques Commonly Used to Create Common Ground.")
- Common ground can be composed of *knowledge that is distributed among or is common to disciplines*.

- Common ground can also comprise *agreement on what is* not *part of the shared knowledge* (Bromme, 2000, pp. 128–129).

Common ground theory helps us to establish the basis for identifying disciplinary theories, concepts, and assumptions that will enable us to combine or integrate insights and thus produce an understanding that is interdisciplinary.

Common Ground Theory in Contexts of Narrow Versus Wide Interdisciplinarity

Common ground theory plays out differently in contexts of narrow versus wide interdisciplinarity, as defined by Kelly (1996) and discussed in Chapter 5. The epistemological presuppositions of the natural sciences have this in common: They tell us what the facts are. Scientific presuppositions do not allow us to assign value (in a moral or ethical sense) to facts as do the epistemological presuppositions of the humanities that give us access to moral reality. This means that it should be easier to discover common ground between insights produced by the natural sciences concerning a problem (given their more narrow epistemological focus) than it is to create common ground between insights produced by disciplines spanning the natural sciences and the humanities, whose epistemologies differ widely. In general, *the greater the epistemological differences between disciplines, the more difficult it is to create common ground between their insights.*

The Interdisciplinary Studies Project (Project Zero), Harvard Graduate School of Education

The theory of common ground as it relates to integration receives additional support from a report by the Interdisciplinary Studies Project (Project Zero), Harvard Graduate School of Education. It examines exemplary practices of interdisciplinary work at the collegiate, precollegiate, and professional levels. The theoretical premise of the study, reports Nikitina (2005), is that

> there exists an important similarity—and possibly a fundamental connection!—between the interdisciplinary efforts and other mental operations that involve internal or external dialogue such as metaphoric thought, collaborative work, and other forms of negotiating differences and merging of ideas. (p. 392)

Interdisciplinary thinking, she explains, occurs as the mind performs a complicated chain of cognitive operations integrating disciplinary ideas. At the juncture of disciplines, the mind is involved in at least three cognitive activities: overcoming internal **monodisciplinarity** (i.e., the preference for a single disciplinary perspective), attaining integration, and recognizing that the resultant integration is only provisional. An important finding of the study is the possibility that there exists "a central cognitive process," expressive of the dialogical tendency of the human mind, that manifests itself in interdisciplinary thinking (Nikitina, 2005, p. 414).

The Harvard study provides useful support for the integrative process as described in this and the following chapter. For one thing, it validates a process approach to achieving integration. The key to this process is creating common ground. Integration is not, as one might suppose, achieved by having an "instantaneous flash of imagination that intuitively and inseparably blends ideas and creates a striking new synthesis" (Nikitina, 2005, p. 389). Rather, synthesis or integration *is the result of a cognitive process.* Second, interdisciplinary cognition is a natural tendency of the human mind. This means that we can overcome monodisciplinarity (though not without difficulty because our educational system reinforces it) by creating common ground and thereby achieve integration.

An Example of Common Ground

The story of Helen Keller provides an example, albeit imperfect, of common ground and its importance in establishing effective communication across an apparent unbridgeable divide, in this case between two persons. Helen, after an illness in infancy, was left unable to see or hear, and thus unable to speak or communicate with anyone. Though everyone had given up on Helen, her young teacher, Anne Sullivan, did not, believing that she could find a way to communicate with Helen. For some time, Anne's best efforts proved fruitless, and Helen grew more and more incorrigible—until one day when they were at the well outside the cabin where they were staying, and Helen knocked over the bucket of drinking water that Anne had just drawn. In that instant, water became more than water. In an intuitive flash, Anne realized that she could use the spilled water to make the sign for "water" in the palm of Helen's wet hand. It worked. Helen understood. Anne had achieved common ground with Helen. Water became the key that ended Helen's terrible isolation and enabled her to comprehend and communicate with her world. The result was a new and an amazingly productive life.

This example overlooks the fact that one usually has to redefine disciplinary concepts to create or even discover common ground. And without using redefinition or some other integrative technique discussed in this chapter, common ground, and thus integration, can seldom be achieved.

The Importance of Common Ground to the Integrative Process

Many interdisciplinarians agree that creating common ground is essential to achieving integration (Newell, 2001, pp. 14–15). This creation or discovery of common ground prepares us for the actual combining of disciplinary and theory-based insights that is Step 9. Creating common ground is like building a bridge in order to span a deep chasm. The near side is the place of identifying the sources of conflicts between insights (Step 7); the opposite side is the place of combining as many insights as possible (Step 9). Unless the interdisciplinarian builds the bridge of common ground to connect the two sides, the integrative process cannot occur. As Kockelmans (1979) emphasizes, "*The search for a common ground is the fundamental element of all [interdisciplinary] investigation*" (p. 141, italics added).

Achieving common ground may test how well the student has performed previous Steps, especially Step 6, which calls for analyzing the problem and evaluating each insight into it. To the extent that this task is thoroughly completed, the student may be reasonably confident that creating, or even discovering, common ground is achievable. Perhaps the student has overlooked points of conflict between the disciplinary insights that were examined in Step 7. Perhaps the student needs to reread the relevant insights and their theories to see which causal variable each emphasizes and which theory addresses these variables comprehensively. Or, it may be that no matter how hard the student looks, a point of commonality that will allow integration of at least some insights remains elusive. The latter case, though theoretically possible, is unlikely. If the student looks hard enough, it is likely that a way to create common ground will be found.

The Cognitive Processes Required to Create or Discover Common Ground

Chapter 1 emphasizes that interdisciplinary study requires that students alter the way they think about thinking. Achieving common ground, and indeed the whole interdisciplinary process, requires that students engage in unconventional thinking about how to approach problems and their solutions and about finding new meaning in objects and texts. In this connection, it is worth contrasting our *natural* thinking process with our *learned* thinking process.

Our Natural Thinking Process Versus Our Learned Thinking Process

Psychologists tell us that the human brain is designed to process information integratively. This is evident from the many complex activities that a person engages in every day. People seldom even realize the extent to which they are thinking and acting in an integrative way when they play an instrument, plant a garden, cook a meal, or drive to work. A person's ability to make a series of complex decisions without consciously reflecting on all the parts of those decisions is an example of a person's natural capacity to process information integratively.

But a person's *natural* thinking process stands in sharp contrast to a person's *learned* thinking process. Much of modern education teaches students to think in nonintegrative ways. From kindergarten onward, students are taught to think in disciplinary categories. They are told that knowledge is found in clearly marked "boxes" or disciplines called math, social studies, English, and art (though this is changing). Learning, students discover, occurs through a process of knowledge fragmentation and compartmentalization.

Another nonintegrative way to think is to emphasize that answers are either right or wrong. According to educational psychologists, students commonly experience frustration when they read a novel like *Tom Sawyer* and are forced to choose, for example, whether Huck Finn is a good or bad influence on Tom.

A third nonintegrative way to think is to argue a point of view. Though debates on controversial topics are effective ways to engage students, they reinforce the idea that the point of it all is to win and that the purpose of confronting alternative perspectives is to choose one and reject the rest. However, the interdisciplinary enterprise is not like prosecuting a case, defending a client, or just adding another scholarly opinion to the many opinions already offered on the problem. Rather, the interdisciplinary enterprise is about producing an interdisciplinary understanding of the problem that is more comprehensive than single-discipline approaches. And this requires a different kind of thinking and mode of analysis, one that draws (critically but sympathetically) on most, if not all, available perspectives and their insights.

The Interdisciplinarian's Responsibility

There is an abundance of opinion (scholarly and otherwise) but a scarcity of integrative understanding of the many complex problems that bedevil our society and characterize our world. *Interdisciplinary study and the integrative process are not about who can win the argument but about who can bring together the best ideas of all stakeholders to get the job done.* The task of the interdisciplinarian is to achieve this much-needed understanding in a way that is similar to the role played by a marriage counselor.

The marriage counselor knows that nothing lasting will be achieved if the parties remain focused on the issues that divide them, much as the interdisciplinarian knows that no integration will be achieved if the focus remains on the conflicting disciplinary insights. Marriage counselors try to get behind the conflicting positions of the parties to find out what the underlying issues are, much as the interdisciplinarian tries to get behind each conflicting insight to identify the assumptions on which it is based. Marriage counselors try to find common ground by identifying interests that are

- shared or overlapping (analogous to common meaning revealed through *redefinition*, explained later in this chapter)
- similar or related (analogous to common ground achieved through *extension*, explained later in this chapter)

- compatible (analogous to common ground achieved through *organiza-tion,* explained later in this chapter)
- negotiable (analogous to common ground achieved through *transfor-mation,* explained later in this chapter)[1]

Examples of each of these integrative techniques are applied to the threaded examples later in this chapter. **Integrative techniques** are ways to create common ground among conflicting insights, theories, and concepts.

Greater understanding of the causes and nature of complex problems will hopefully result in finding solutions to them. The interdisciplinarian's responsibility is to think about these problems in a way that is integrative and that transcends the absolutist, fragmented, and biased thinking so common in the Academy.

Traits and Skills Involved in Creating Common Ground

This discussion brings up the traits and skills of interdisciplinarians iden-tified in Chapter 2. The interdisciplinarian will need to draw upon several of these in creating or discovering common ground, especially the following:

- Enterprising
- Love of learning
- Reflective
- Tolerance for ambiguity and paradox in the midst of complexity
- Receptivity to other disciplines and to the perspectives of those disciplines
- Ability to communicate competently
- Ability to think abstractly
- Ability to think dialectically
- Ability to engage in nonlinear thinking
- Ability to think creatively
- Ability to think integratively
- Ability to recognize the limits of what is knowable

Creative thinking is closely connected to intuition. **Intuition** is the natural ability to know or perceive something immediately without using rational thought or inference. Though method and process are emphasized over all, adherence to method cannot automatically resolve all problems, including the challenging problem of creating common ground. That is why students are well advised to leave room, in some cases a great deal of room, for an "intu-itive leap" or a "eureka moment" when, after a period of struggle, reflection, and analysis, they suddenly discover how to create common ground.

How Common Ground Is Created: An Illustration

An illustration of how common ground is created in a concrete setting is the Admission, Review, and Dismissal (ARD) meeting in special education.

The purpose of this meeting is to formulate a comprehensive approach to providing individualized instruction for a student with learning disabilities. Those attending the meeting include administrators, various specialists, the student, the student's parents, and the facilitator whose job it is to move the discussion toward an integrated plan for the student's educational needs for the coming year. The facilitator asks each person—the speech pathologist, the social studies teacher, the neurologist, an assistant principal—to propose a solution designed to meet the student's educational needs for the coming year. The specialists commonly use highly technical language to describe the student's disability. Perhaps sensing that the parents do not understand what the specialists are saying, the facilitator asks the specialists to "translate" the technical jargon into language that the parents, and indeed all in attendance, can understand. The facilitator attempts to find common ground among the various proposals offered by the specialists and the parents. Then, building on that, the facilitator proposes an integrative solution.

The facilitator's role in the ARD meeting is similar to that of the interdisciplinary student who is attempting to produce an integrative understanding of and a more comprehensive solution to a problem. Each participating discipline brings its perspective to the table. The task of the student is, like that of the ARD facilitator, to allow each perspective to be expressed, compare and contrast their insights, and then, by asking certain questions, encourage one or more points of agreement to surface.

Two lessons can be drawn from the above narrative. The first is the role of technical language in establishing common ground. The second is the importance of recognizing that underneath the technical language used by the various professionals are disciplinary perspectives on how to treat a child with learning disabilities. The student must take into account not only disciplinary terminology but also disciplinary perspectives.

What Common Ground Is Created From

Common ground is created not by modifying insights directly, but by modifying the theories, concepts, or assumptions from which the conflicting insights were produced. As pointed out in the example of the marriage counselor, one needs to focus elsewhere than on the conflicting insights (i.e., expert views) themselves in order to integrate them: One has to get *behind* the conflict itself to bring out the source of the conflict. These modified theories, concepts, and assumptions are used to reconcile the insights and form the common ground on which a more comprehensive understanding is constructed using those insights.

Students have a choice of what to create common ground from: theories, concepts, or assumptions. One option is to focus directly on the theories that produced the insights. Theories, as noted in Chapter 4, are generalized scholarly explanations of an entire class of phenomena and explain why and how the concepts of the discipline are related. Applied to a specific problem, object, or text, a theory provides an insight into a problem.

A second option is to look behind the theories at the concepts used to build the theories. Concepts are technical terms used by a discipline to describe specific ideas developed by that discipline.[2] A third option is to look behind the concepts at their underlying assumptions that are the accepted truths upon which a discipline's theories and concepts are based.

The nature of the challenge of integration varies with what is being integrated and the context in which the integration takes place. As noted in Chapter 10, theory-based insights are found across the disciplines but are more prominent in the natural sciences and in the harder social sciences. The creation of common ground by modifying theories appears easiest in the natural sciences, more problematic in the social sciences, and least promising in the humanities.

With the exception of redefinition, which is often required no matter what the context, the creation of common ground by modifying concepts appears easiest in the social sciences, more problematic in the humanities, and least promising in the natural sciences. And creating common ground by changing assumptions is workable in the humanities, more problematic in the social sciences, and least promising in the natural sciences. The choice of strategy is also dependent on whether the interdisciplinarian has a more theoretical, conceptual, or philosophical turn of mind. In the end, it's up to the individual.

Common ground, however, is not created from disciplinary perspectives. Perspective, as explained in Chapter 3, is a discipline's overall view of any problem or question. An insight is what is produced when that perspective is applied to a specific problem, as illustrated in Chapter 9 in the example of acid rain. If the student attempted to integrate disciplinary perspectives, the student would be taking on the considerable task of formulating an overarching or mega approach that replaces those of the contributing disciplines. It would be an approach that could then be applied to *any* specific question to generate insights into it. This is a formidable intellectual challenge, and one that is far beyond the interdisciplinary process described in this book. The interdisciplinarian tries to solve a specific problem, not all problems or even a class of problems. All the interdisciplinarian needs to do is integrate the insights produced by disciplines into a single problem that is limited in time and space, if not also in culture (Klein, 1996, p. 3; Newell & Green, 1982, p. 24).

The next section examines the techniques available to students to modify theories, concepts, and assumptions in order to create common ground.

Techniques Available to Create Common Ground _____

Possible Challenges

Students face three possible challenges in attempting to create common ground.[3] Each concerns the nature and extent of the conflict between insights.

- There is *no apparent conflict among insights* but commonality is nonetheless obscured by differences in the concepts used by the different disciplines to describe similar ideas.
- The *conflicting insights are different but not opposing;* they merely reflect alternatives.
- The *insights are diametrically opposed.*

Students should first ask what the nature of the challenge is to creating common ground and then select one of five integrative techniques that are useful for that purpose: theory expansion, redefinition, extension, organization, and transformation, or possibly some combination of these. Students, especially those new to the interdisciplinary research process, will almost always use redefinition (whether it takes the form of a new term or a new meaning for an old term). But whether they also use the technique of theory expansion, extension, organization, or transformation depends on the challenges posed by those conflicting theories, concepts, or assumptions.

Examples of each technique are drawn from a problem-based course project (the causes of suicide terrorism), published literature, and student papers that are explicitly interdisciplinary. An asterisk after the surname identifies the student papers. As with the touchstone examples written by professional interdisciplinarians, the problem-based course project and student papers illustrate many, but not all, of the possible features of an interdisciplinary research paper. A minimum requirement is that these must demonstrate at least one of the integrative techniques. In the absence of a student paper using the technique of organization (the least commonly used integrative technique), Kenneth Boulding's integrative study of differing conceptions of human nature is used to illustrate this technique. Finally, the categorization of these examples refers to the area of the researcher's training and the orientation of the topic more than to the disciplines from which insights were drawn.

1. The Integrative Technique of Theory Expansion

The integrative technique of theory expansion is used to modify a theory so that it can address all of the causation factors pertaining to the problem. **Theory expansion** may involve merely adding a factor or factors (e.g., a variable or variables) from any of the sources of alternative perspectives, including different fields within the same discipline, different disciplines, schools of thought that cut across disciplines, interdisciplines, or even folk knowledge. Of the possible sources of conflicts between insights, conflicts between theory-based insights are the most common situation the student, especially in graduate work, is likely to encounter. An example of using the integrative technique of theory expansion is the problem of the causes of suicide terrorism (introduced in Chapter 10) that was the focus of a junior-level course on the interdisciplinary research process.

Students used close reading to query the six relevant theories to determine their views on the primary causes of suicide terrorism. These causes were then grouped under three broad headings, as shown in Table 11.1: cultural factors, political/economic factors, and psychological factors. Cultural factors include the external influences of religion, social mores, and the family (immediate and extended). Political/economic factors include the external influences of institutions (including those of terrorist organizations) and the individual's socioeconomic status. Psychological factors include those internal cognitive processes by which individuals make decisions such as "mental accounting" (i.e., that people tend to think about their gains and losses as if these were separate accounts), "justification" (an even stronger, more compelling, moral claim that overrides one's natural repugnance to engage in suicide terrorism), and "emotion" (e.g., traumatic memory, or regret for not exacting vengeance on an enemy) (Reisberg, 2006, pp. 465–470). Once these broad categories of causation factors were identified, the next task was to determine which of the six theories came closest to addressing each of these causal factors. The result of this evaluative process is shown in Table 11.1.

Table 11.1   Theory-Based Causes of Suicide Terrorism (ST) Showing Key Causation Factors

	Theory-Based Causes of ST		
Theory of ST	Cultural Factors (External)	Political/ Economic Factors (External)	Psychological Factors (Internal)
Terrorist Psycho-logic (Cognitive Psychology)	No	No	Yes
Self-Sanction (Cognitive Psychology)	Yes	Yes	Yes, if expanded
Martyrdom (Cognitive Psychology)	No	No	Yes
Collective Rational Choice (Political Science)	No	Yes	Yes
Sacred Terror (Political Science)	Yes	Yes	No
Kinship Altruism (Cultural Anthropology)	Yes	Yes	No

Table 11.1 shows that Self-Sanction Theory comes closest to addressing all three causal factors and, if expanded, can satisfactorily address all of them. The theory explains how "socialized people" are converted into dedicated combatants by the terrorist organization "cognitively restructuring the moral value of killing, so that the killing can be done free from self-censuring restraints" (Bandura, 1998, p. 164). According to Albert Bandura (1998), the process of moral cognitive restructuring includes (a) using religion to justify such acts by invoking "situational imperatives," (b) using the

political argument of self-defense to show how the group is "fighting ruthless oppressors" who are threatening the community's "cherished values and way of life," and (c) using the psychological device of dehumanization to justify killing "the enemy" (pp. 174, 180–182). This theory already incorporates material from outside the discipline (psychology) that produced it by its inclusion of cultural and political factors that inform individual decision making. However, the theory excludes those individual personality factors in the would-be terrorist's decision-making process that the theories of personality and psycho-logic address in detail. This limitation can be overcome quite easily by using the technique of theory expansion. Since the theory already addresses individual behavior, it is relatively easy to expand the theory's focus on moral cognitive restructuring to include the role of mental accounting and emotion without distorting the theory.

2. The Integrative Technique of Redefinition

The integrative technique of **redefinition** involves modifying or redefining concepts and assumptions used by the relevant disciplines to bring out a common meaning. As noted earlier, each discipline has developed its own technical vocabulary to describe the phenomena it prefers to study. Embedded in the curricula of many disciplinary "majors" is a course that introduces students to the discipline's peculiar language. Some biology programs, for example, offer a course on medical terminology so that students entering the health care professions, or intending to pursue graduate study in the field, will be able to communicate effectively within the profession. Indeed every profession, and almost every job, has its specialized or technical vocabulary. People in the profession understand it, but people outside the profession seldom do.

An Illustration of How Our Particularized Disciplinary Training and Attitudes Prevent Our Appreciating the Approaches of Other Disciplines

Problems arise, however, when one discipline—say, social psychology—wants to communicate with other disciplines that are far removed from it—say, the creative arts. Eugenia P. Gerdes, Dean of Liberal Arts at Bucknell University, tells a story about the validity of intuition, illustrating how our particularized disciplinary training and attitudes prevent our appreciating the approaches of other disciplines and how our ignorance of other disciplines prevents us from seeing because we are narrow-minded.

When Gerdes (2002) tried to re-energize the stalled general education program at her university by finding common ground among faculty and making the case for multiple perspectives, she "inadvertently stepped on discipline toes" by using language appropriate to her discipline but "discordant" to some in the creative arts. She wrote, "I want our students to be able to get outside their own intuitive perspective—to recognize where they are situated in nature, in history, among the world's cultures, and in a pluralized American society" (p. 50).

To Gerdes (2002), a social psychologist, "'intuition' represents the unexamined biases of self-interest, stereotypes, prejudices, etc." To her shock and embarrassment, a studio artist informed her, "a professor in the arts not only values, but also seeks to put students in touch with, the intuitive." Unfortunately, she confesses, "in attempting to espouse all students being exposed to a variety of disciplinary perspectives, I excluded one type of perspective as legitimate because of my ignorance of other disciplines" (pp. 49–50).

It is the responsibility of the interdisciplinarian to connect ideas from different disciplines about a complex problem—in Gerdes's case, reform of general education—so we can all understand it more fully. This should be of concern to everyone who cares about the problem.

The Need to Create a Common Vocabulary

Since every discipline has its own vocabulary expressed as concepts, it is sometimes necessary for the interdisciplinarian to create a common vocabulary. This new vocabulary may amount to only a few key terms, but just enough of them to enable the disciplinary specialists to communicate effectively with each other (Wolfe & Haynes, 2003, p. 155). The trick is to modify terms as little as possible while still creating common ground on which to construct a coherent understanding (Newell, 2001, pp. 19–20).

The Importance of Concepts

Concerning concepts, then, the student is well advised to do two things. First, pay close attention to how concepts are used differently in different disciplines within the context of the problem and how different disciplinary concepts are used to describe similar ideas (Wolfe & Haynes, 2003, pp. 155, 165). As mentioned before, "efficiency" has quite different meanings for economists (money out/money in), biologists (energy out/energy in), and political scientists (influence exerted/political capital expended) (Newell, 2001, p. 19).

Second, carefully redefine specific concepts (Wolfe & Haynes, 2003, p. 165). This is essential and preparatory to creating common ground. Students should avoid using terminology that tacitly favors one disciplinary approach at the expense of another.

The technique of redefinition, then, can reveal commonalities in concepts or assumptions that may be obscured by discipline-specific language. Since most disciplinary concepts and assumptions are obscured in this way, the technique of redefinition is involved in most efforts to create common ground, sometimes in conjunction with other integrative techniques, as shown in these examples.

From the Natural Sciences: Nagy* (2005), Anthropogenic Forces Degrading Tropical Ecosystems in Latin America: A Costa Rican Case Study

Nagy (2005) draws as much in this example from the social sciences as from the natural sciences. She examines the various theories from biology, anthropology, and economics that explain the ecological and environmental problems facing Latin America in general and Costa Rica in particular. She finds a dichotomy between theories dealing with the environment and those dealing with economics. Nagy explains that the region's economic and environmental problems are linked in a mutual feedback loop: Growing population requires increased economic development, which causes environmental degradation of tropical ecosystems such as Costa Rica's, which worsens living conditions for the poor and widens the income gap between the rich and the poor. Purely disciplinary approaches (of which there have been many) suggest that the choice is between economics or environmental science. That is, a nation like Costa Rica must choose between either increasing economic development to help raise living standards (and thereby worsen environmental degradation) or restricting development to protect fragile tropical ecosystems (and thereby reduce living standards).

The challenge for the student is to create common ground between these irreconcilable disciplinary stances. When Nagy reexamined the assumptions of these disciplinary approaches, she saw that the basic values of the two perspectives are at odds with one another. These conflicting values express themselves in how each discipline defines "wealth." For environmental scientists, wealth refers to the health of an ecosystem (excluding humans) and to the diversity of species within it. For economists, wealth is accumulated assets derived from development. For Nagy (2005), creating common ground involves redefining "wealth" to include economic development *and* ecosystem health (pp.104–108). She also extends the redefined meaning of wealth from assets valued solely by the marketplace (the result of development) to assets valued by society as a whole (a healthy and diverse environment). By freeing herself from the marketplace, she can extend "wealth" from a short-term (economic) to a long-term (environmental) concept.

From the Sciences and the Social Sciences: Delph* (2005), An Integrative Approach to the Elimination of the "Perfect Crime"

Delph (2005) questions whether advances in criminal investigatory techniques are able to eliminate the possibility of the "perfect crime." She defines a "perfect crime" as one that goes unnoticed and/or as one for which the criminal will never be caught (p. 2). Of the several disciplines and subdisciplines that are relevant to crime investigation, the three that Delph finds most relevant are criminal justice, forensic science, and forensic psychology. Delph identifies the current theories of these rapidly evolving subdisciplines and finds that the source of conflict between them is their preference for two different investigatory methods and reliance on two kinds of evidence. Forensic science analyzes physical evidence, whereas forensic psychology analyzes behavioral evidence. Each approach constructs a "profile" of the criminal, with forensic science using physical evidence and forensic psychology using a combination of intuition informed by years of experience and information collected from interviews and other sources.

Delph creates common ground between the conflicting approaches by redefining the meaning of profiling to include both forensic science, with its emphasis on physical evidence, and forensic psychology, with its emphasis on "intuition" born of extensive experience and insights derived from crime scene analysis. This redefinition of criminal profiling enables her to bridge the physical (i.e., forensic science) and the behavioral sciences (i.e., forensic psychology and criminal investigation). Forensic scientists do not need to use profiling as long as they have adequate evidence to analyze. But in the absence of such evidence, profiling can move the investigation forward by using a combination of "intuition" born of extensive experience and insights derived from crime scene analysis (p. 29). In this way, profiling integrates the specialized knowledge that criminal investigation, forensic science, and forensic psychology offer.

From the Humanities: Silver (2005),* Composing Race and Gender: The Appropriation of Social Identity in Fiction

After demonstrating that there is much written from psychology and sociology on what goes into appropriating a social identity, Silver (2005) integrates these insights with what has been written separately on fiction from the perspective of literature. Silver did this by redefining the term "appropriation" to include fiction writing as well as acting and filmmaking.

The key to creating common ground among these differing perspectives on appropriation, she discovered, is the term *implicature*. This is the notion that underlying all humans, regardless of their differences, is a universal state of being—emotion (Silver, 2005, p. 63). Implicature is the ultimate level of empathy. It is what makes appropriation ethical and not hypocritical. Appropriation cannot be successful, she argues, until the fiction writer has achieved implicature with the person being written about. Appropriation is ethical when there is no psychic difference between the author and the character.

3. The Integrative Technique of Extension

The technique of **extension** addresses conflict between disciplinary concepts or assumptions by extending the meaning of an idea beyond the domain of one discipline into the domain of another discipline. Robert H. Frank (1988) illustrates this integrative technique by extending the concept of altruistic behavior over time, so that it embraced the insights of the relevant disciplines. These included sociology, evolutionary biology, and economics. Whereas economics focuses on short-term self-interested behavior and tends to reject claims of altruism as disguised self-interest, sociology and evolutionary biology take a much longer term view of self-interest. Frank learned that some behavior that is self-interested in the short run (such as economic behavior) actually undermines long-run self-interest because it discourages others from entering into contracts with a person who has developed a reputation for placing short-run material self-interest ahead of his long-run material self-interest. In the same way, behavior that is characterized as altruistic in the short run can actually enhance long-run self-interest. Common ground among the insights offered by these disciplinary literatures, Frank discovered, could be achieved by extending the meaning of the economic concept of self-interest where it has a short-term context to the longterm, so as to embrace the insights of sociology and evolutionary biology.

A second way to apply the technique of extension is across individuals, as Kenneth Boulding (1981) does. Boulding uses utility analysis from the subdiscipline of microeconomics to develop a new understanding of altruistic behavior. He achieves this by extending the concept of self-interest. Under his reformulation of the concept, a person's utility, or amount of satisfaction, extends beyond the goods and services the person consumes to include the well-being of others toward whom the person feels benevolence or malevolence. Thus, if A feels benevolent towards B and gives B a gift, A's utility will rise if A perceives that B is better off.

The integrative technique of extension, then, can be used to create common ground by extending a concept or assumption not only in time (as Frank did) and across individuals (as Boulding did), but also across the boundaries of cultures, races, ethnicities, genders, ideologies, nations, regions, classes, or any other classification (Newell, 2007, pp. 258–259). How this technique is used is illustrated in the examples below.

From the Natural Sciences: Watson (1968), The Double Helix: A Personal Account of the Discovery of the Structure of DNA

Watson and Crick illustrate how one can use the integrative technique of extension when facing conflicts that are apparently irreconcilable. They supposed that they could quickly solve the problem of the structure of DNA by taking the unorthodox step of building a helical model of it before they knew the details of its structure. They based their model on the theory that it had a sugar-phosphate core at its center. When their attempt failed, Watson and Crick were ordered to give up on DNA. Watson (1968) explains why they did not appeal the verdict: "We were up the creek with models based on sugar-phosphate cores" because these models "forced atoms closer together than the laws of chemistry allowed. A fresh start would be necessary to get the problem rolling again" (p. 99). The fresh start involved Watson and Crick making two decisions. The first was to find the exact sizes of inorganic ions by rereading Pauling's *The Nature of the Chemical Bond*. This knowledge was crucial to any new attempt at model building. Unfortunately, the book offered no clue about how the ions were arranged so tightly in 3-D. The second decision was to approach the problem of DNA from a new angle by working on the tobacco mosaic virus (TMV), a vital component of which was a nucleic acid known as RNA. "If we solved [the structure of] RNA," Watson and Crick reasoned, "we might also provide the vital clue to DNA" (p. 110). After several days of work, the idea came to Watson "that each TMV particle should be thought of as a tiny crystal growing like other crystals through the possession of cozy corners [i.e., spaces that would accommodate all of the ions]. Most important, the simplest way to generate cozy corners was to have the subunits helically arranged [in 3-D]. The idea was so simple that it had to be right" (p. 114). By extending the concept of cozy corners in TMV to DNA, Watson and Crick moved one step closer to proving that DNA had helical symmetry.

From the Social Sciences: Schoenfeld* (2005), Customer Service: The Ultimate Return Policy

Karen Schoenfeld (2005) draws from the disciplines of psychology, sociology, and management to address an all-too-often overlooked and underappreciated aspect of consumerism, customer service. She defines customer service as "anything we do for a patron that embraces their experience" (p. ii). The goal of her study is to probe "the deeper levels of providing customer service," which is another way of saying "to develop a holistic approach to the customer experience" (pp. 3–4). Schoenfeld distinguishes between the concept of customer service (any steps that are taken to satisfy and retain customers' loyalty while they are in the store) and the concept of customer relationship management, or CRM (any steps taken to satisfy and retain customers when they are not in the store), and seeks to create common ground between them (p. 6). Her approach is to apply theories generated by psychology, sociology, and anthropology—including social exchange theory, expectancy theory, reasoned action, role theory, and attribution theory—to explain customers' expectations, behaviors, and habits. These disciplinary theories enable her to extend the concept of customer service from what the company considers excellent service to what the customer thinks it is. In this way, she creates common ground between the conflicting theories and concepts of customer service and CRM.

From the Humanities: Bal (1999), "Introduction," The Practice of Cultural Analysis: Exposing Interdisciplinary Interpretation

The problem Bal (1999) faces with the graffito is to expose its meaning by analyzing it from three perspectives simultaneously: from the perspective of its author, from the perspective of the subject (i.e., the author's beloved), and from the perspective of one who is reading the graffito and pondering its meaning. Bal uses the integrative technique of extension to create a common vocabulary centered on the verb "to expose," to which she connects three nouns: exposition, exposé, and exposure. These are the three meanings or insights that this close reading of the graffito brings together. The verb refers to making a public presentation or to "publicly demonstrating"; "it can be combined with a noun meaning opinions or judgments and refer to the public presentation of someone's views; and it can refer to the performing of those deeds that deserve to be made public" (pp. 4–5). The graffito, as an exposition, brings out into the public domain the deepest held views and beliefs of the author. Exposition, says Bal, "is also always an argument. Therefore, in publicizing these views the author objectifies, exposes, himself as much as the subject. This makes the graffito an exposure of the self. Such exposure is an act of producing meaning, a performance" (Bal, 1996, p. 2).

4. The Integrative Technique of Organization

The technique of **organization** does two things: (1) it identifies an underlying commonality in meaning of different disciplinary concepts or assumptions and redefines them accordingly, and (2) it organizes the redefined concepts or assumptions to bring out a relationship among them (Newell, 2007, p. 259). Since this technique is more complex than the other three techniques discussed here, it is used sparingly by most interdisciplinarians. An example of the effective use of this technique is Kenneth Boulding's study of grants.

From the Social Sciences: Boulding (1981), A Preface to Grants Economics: the Economy of Love and Fear

Boulding's study of grants involved him probing the complexities of human behavior that motivates grant bequests. More particularly, Boulding sought a way to transform the debate about whether human nature in general is selfish or altruistic. So clear is Newell's (2007) description of Boulding's use of the technique of organization that it is reproduced here:

Boulding recognized that benevolent behavior (studied by sociologists) and malevolent behavior (studied by political science) can both be understood as other-regarding behavior (positive and negative, respectively). He then arrayed them along a continuum of other-regarding behavior. The self-interested behavior studied by economists became the midpoint on that continuum since its degree of other-regarding behavior is zero. Thus, he set out a way to transform the debate about whether human nature in general is selfish or altruistic into a choice of where on the continuum of motivations people are likely to fall in the particular complex problem under study. By combining into a single continuum with self-interest the motivations of love and hate/fear that support or threaten the integrative mechanisms binding together societies and politics, Boulding used the technique of organization to integrate the differing conceptions of human nature underlying economics, sociology, and political science. (p. 259)

5. The Integrative Technique of Transformation

The integrative technique of **transformation** uses continuous variables in contexts where concepts or assumptions are not merely different (e.g., love, fear, selfishness) but opposite (e.g., rational, irrational; Newell, 2007, p. 259). For example, Amitai Etzioni (1988) addresses the problem of how to overcome opposing disciplinary assumptions about the rationality (economics) or irrationality (sociology) of humans by placing them on opposite ends of a continuous variable called "the degree of rationality." By studying the factors that influence rationality, it is possible to determine in principle the degree of rationality exercised in any given situation.

The value of using continuous variables as an integrative technique is that determinative influences can be explored and estimated in any particular context, rather than as dichotomous assumptions to accept or reject. Transforming opposing assumptions into variables allows the interdisciplinarian to move toward resolution of almost any dichotomy, as illustrated in these examples.

From the Social Sciences: Englehart* (2005), Organized Environmentalism: Towards a Shift in the Political and Social Roles and Tactics of Environmental Advocacy Groups

Laura Englehart is concerned that anti-environmentalism is becoming institutionalized in the Republican-dominated political system. To ensure that environmental responsibility becomes an integral part of our society, she proposes that environmental advocacy groups integrate their social and political agendas. These groups assume various active roles in society: They challenge and pressure the government with an environmental ethic; they are actors in the political arena who influence policy making by lobbying and campaigning in election cycles; and they are what sociologists call "social movement organizers" who mobilize the public to take action on pressing environmental issues. To better understand the roles and tactics of environmental groups, Englehart examines them in light of relevant theories, including social movement theory (in its several variations), rational choice theory, collective identity theory, and structural network theory. By comparing these theories and the insights they have generated, she finds that for environmental groups to grow and recapture the political initiative, they must change their approach to what they do and how they do it.

Integrating the various theories and insights requires that she use the technique of transformation. This involves transforming opposing theoretical assumptions so as to expand the scope of social movement theory. This will result in transforming the "I" of self-interested economics and political advocacy and the "We" of collective identity in social movements into a jointly maximized "I" and "We" for environmental advocacy. Englehart (2005) advocates using face-to-face relationships within an environmental organization to shift members along the continuum from "I" to "We," and then to extend the "We" (for the purposes of interorganizational networking) to include those with differing environmental values. In practical terms, this will cause environmental organizations to concentrate their efforts on educating and politicizing the social arena and creating their own political opportunity structures through innovative mobilization strategies so as to challenge current anti-environmental political action. Integration via transformation of these theoretical and disciplinary insights, says Englehart, will result in a bottom-up, grassroots, coalition-driven social emphasis that, when combined with the traditional top-down, legislative-driven political pressure, will help environmental advocacy groups recapture the political initiative (pp. 58–63).

From Science and the Humanities: Arms* (2005), Mathematics and Religion: Processes of Faith and Reason

Leslie Arms (2005) compares faith and reason, which are often seen as polar opposites. "People think," she says, "that religion finds its home in the heart and faith, while mathematics belongs in the brain and reason" (p. i). The disciplines of her focus are mathematics, philosophy (i.e., logic), and religion. Logic, she finds, is the fulcrum discipline for mathematics *and* religion because both rely on it. Religion employs logic, albeit according to its own rules and within its own frame of reference. Logic is also used in determining the provability of mathematics, and this requires that one employ deductive reasoning. Godel shows us in his Incompleteness Theorems, she writes, that we cannot prove necessary truths in mathematics. But by his Completeness Theorem, we know that first-order logic, sometimes called mathematical logic, is complete, and therefore at least trustworthy (p. 5). She also draws upon sociology and Durkheim's theory of religion and extracts from the latter his definition of religion as a socially constructed belief system, which she employs in her study.

The belief in the existence of a Christian God and the belief in the completeness and consistency of mathematics are not only belief systems, she says, but faith-based belief systems, and very different ones at that (Arms, 2005, pp. 66–67). Arms uses the concept of faith to continue the idea that mathematics and religion still have the possibility of certainty. Her reasoning runs as follows:

> We take it on faith that reason is a good thing. Since reason is an object of faith, it is reasonable to assume than an object of reason can become

an object of faith. Faith is justifiable in keeping belief in the certainty of mathematics. Mathematics has made it clear to us that we cannot depend on it purely through reason. And even if Godel and his Incompleteness Theorems had never come about, there would still be things in mathematics that are not provable. There are plenty of problems that have never been solved, and many that may never be solved. It took mathematicians over 300 years to solve Fermat's Last Theorem, but they had faith that it was true and that they would find a solution. In mathematics, it is common to prove something using an idea that we do not know is true, but assume it is. (p. 76)

To integrate faith and reason, Arms (2005) transforms the dichotomies of faith and reason and, by implication, the dichotomies of mathematics and religion. In the end, she confesses that she had been under the impression that her logic could "go anywhere"; that "science trumped religion, and [that] logic trumped science." Therefore, logic was obviously stronger than faith. Then she learned that her "dear logic," while complete, could not prove even mathematics. This rude awakening kept faith "afloat" and enabled her to accept "the complementary nature of reason and faith" (p. 80).

The Value of These Integrative Techniques

The value of these integrative techniques is that they are proven ways to create common ground. These techniques achieve that objective by replacing the either/or thinking characteristic of the disciplines with both/and thinking characteristic of interdisciplinarity. Inclusion, insofar as this is possible, is substituted for conflict. As Newell (2007) expresses it, "Intellectual flexibility and playfulness are more useful than logic at this step in the integrative part of the interdisciplinary process" (p. 260).

CHAPTER SUMMARY

Creating or discovering common ground involves getting behind the conflicting insights themselves to the source of conflict. Possible sources of conflict are disciplinary theories, concepts, and assumptions. Depending on the problem and the characteristics of the literature involved, some students may need to focus on theory-based insights. Other students, focusing on different kinds of problems, may need to work with conflicting concepts or even assumptions. In any case, creating common ground calls for identifying the theory, concept, or assumption that can be used to integrate the relevant insights. Based on the characteristics of the problem, the student will select one of the available integrative techniques of theory expansion, redefinition, extension, organization, and transformation to modify the theory, concept, or assumption. Having completed this step of the research process, the student is now ready to integrate or combine insights (Step 9) and then produce the interdisciplinary understanding of the problem (Step 10), the focus of the next chapter.

NOTES

1. I am indebted to Bill Newell, who gave me the idea to link the four interests in marriage counseling to the integrative techniques (personal communication, April, 2005). Though instructive, the example is not truly interdisciplinary in that the conflicting issues straining the relationship cannot be neatly categorized in disciplinary or theoretical terms.

2. Szostak rightly points out that "concepts are often incredibly vague." Consequently, "the interdisciplinarian must often struggle to narrow the range of meaning" and cites as an example the many definitions of "culture" in the literature (personal communication, May 7, 2007). In his *Classifying Science: Phenomena, Data, Theory, Method, Practice* (2004), he shows that most cultural arguments referred to, at most, a handful of the cultural phenomena listed in his table of phenomena (reproduced in my Chapter 4).

3. Critics of interdisciplinary studies, such as Fish (1991), are concerned that integration is too challenging for undergraduates or even graduate students. Their concern may have been valid at a time when interdisciplinarians were uncertain about what exactly they were attempting to integrate and when they had not yet developed the techniques of integration currently available. Today, however, there is general agreement on what integration consists of and how to achieve it. This book reflects these developments, refines them further, and illustrates how professionals and students are using these techniques to achieve common ground and integration.

REVIEW QUESTIONS

1. How does common ground theory, as developed by cognitive psychology, explain how we are able to comprehend so many different perspectives?

2. How do the findings of cognitive psychology concerning common ground theory pertain to interdisciplinary communication and the interdisciplinary research process?

3. How does the report from the Interdisciplinary Studies Project at Project Zero support the theory of common ground as it relates to integration?

4. How is the story of Helen Keller an example of creating common ground, and in what way is the example imperfect?

5. Why is creating common ground essential to integrating conflicting disciplinary insights?

6. What are three nonintegrative ways to think?

7. How is the role of a marriage counselor similar to the interdisciplinarian's responsibility?

8. What particular skills and traits does one need to draw on to create common ground?

9. How is the role that the facilitator plays in an Admission, Review, and Dismissal (ARD) meeting in special education similar to the role played by the interdisciplinarian in attempting to create common ground among conflicting disciplinary insights?

10. What is common ground created from?

11. What five techniques are available to interdisciplinarians to create common ground?

12. How can one create common ground from among conflicting theory-based insights, and how is the problem of the causes of suicide terrorism illustrative of this approach?

13. How does Gerdes's story about the validity of intuition illustrate how our particularized disciplinary training and attitudes prevent our appreciating the approaches of other disciplines?

14. What role do concepts play in the integrative technique of redefinition, and how is the work of Nagy, Delph, and Silver illustrative of this role?

15. What role do concepts and assumptions play in the integrative technique of extension, and how is the work of Watson, Schoenfeld, and Bal illustrative of this role?

16. What role do concepts and assumptions play in the integrative technique of transformation, and how is the work of Englehart and Arms illustrative of this role?

12 Integrating Insights and Producing an Interdisciplinary Understanding

The focus on integration has progressed from identifying the relevant disciplines and their insights, to tracing connections and conflicts between them, and to creating common ground among them. Next to creating common ground, the most critical and most demanding Step of the entire interdisciplinary process is using the common ground theory, concept, or assumption to integrate disciplinary insights. Nikitina (2002) admits that attempting "any kind of synthesis" on the undergraduate level "is no small task" (p. 40). Klein (1990) speaks of the "complex actuality of doing interdisciplinary work" (p. 184). And Gordon F. Vars (2002) says that the words "integrate" and "synthesize" describe "an extremely complex mental process" (p. 66). Nevertheless, though admittedly difficult, integration is achievable. Integrating disciplinary insights is Step 9 of the interdisciplinary research process.

Step 10 explains the purpose of the research process: how to produce an interdisciplinary understanding of the problem and then test it.[1] Achieving this intended outcome depends on the quality of the decisions the researcher makes at each of these last Steps of the process.

Defining Integration

Commonly, integration is defined as "the combining of the constituent elements of separate materials or abstract entities into a single or unified entity" (*Random House Dictionary*). Similarly, Benjamin S. Bloom (1956) and his committee of college and university examiners defined synthesis as "the putting together of elements and parts so as to form a whole." The committee also distinguished among various types of synthesis, primarily on the basis of the characteristics of the end product. The two characteristics that are most relevant to the focus on integration are these:

- The end product shall be derived from a set of abstract relations (that interdisciplinarians call the common ground or integrating theory, concept, or assumption).
- The end product shall reflect the results of an investigation that are integrated into an effective plan to form a unified entity (i.e., a comprehensive understanding of the problem). (pp. 168–184)

Bloom's (1956) committee recognized that all thought involves some elements of synthesis or integration: "*Every* experience involves a combination of parts of previous experience with the present in such a way that the organism is permanently changed, however slightly" (italics added). The committee also recognized that integration "is the category in the cognitive domain which most clearly provides for creative behavior on the part of the learner" (pp. 168–184).

Four salient concepts offered by Bloom's (1956) committee contribute to a more comprehensive definition of interdisciplinary integration than was offered in Chapter 5. Interdisciplinary integration is an activity or process that

- is the result of an "investigation" or research effort.
- involves using a "set of operations" (hence, the interdisciplinary research process).
- enables the creative "putting together of elements and parts so as to form a whole." (However, the committee emphasized that this is not completely free creative expression because generally the student is expected to work within the limits set by particular problems, materials, or some theoretical and methodological framework.)
- yields "an effective plan or solution to solve a problem." (pp. 168–184)

Conclusively, integration (as defined in Chapter 5) is the cognitive activity of critically evaluating and creatively combining ideas and knowledge to form a new whole.

Cognitive Qualities and Internal Dispositions Needed to Engage in Integration

Along with the traits and skills of interdisciplinarians identified in Chapter 2, there are several cognitive qualities and internal dispositions of learners essential to perform integrative work successfully.

Cognitive Qualities and Internal Dispositions

- Ability to isolate analytically the defining elements of the perspective of each discipline, interdiscipline, or school of thought
- Ability to compare and contrast different insights to generate an integrative understanding or meaning of the problem
- Desire to find commonalities among disciplinary insights and explain how the differences in insights relate to the problem[2]
- Provocation to find a better theory or approach when encountering difficulty in reconciling dissimilar elements (Nikitina, 2002, pp. 39–40)
- Engagement in a higher level of analysis and multilevel thinking about complex problems or questions
- Development of a critical stance toward scholarly claims of completeness and willingness to suspend disciplinary certainty[3]
- Awareness that any integration achieved is likely to be limited and/or that other approaches may well result in a more comprehensive understanding. It is unlikely that the undergraduate student will arrive at a conclusive or all-inclusive understanding of the problem.

The Role of Intuition

Interdisciplinarians are of two minds concerning intuition. Some see interdisciplinarity as primarily a step-based process versus an intuition-based one. The division over this issue, however, is not as deep as the rhetoric may imply. One prominent advocate of a step-based process, for instance, also includes language in his model of the interdisciplinary research process such as "*creating* common ground" and "*producing* a model (metaphor, theme) that captures the new understanding" (Newell, 2001, p. 15). Intuition is involved when attempting to create common ground among several apparently disparate theories, concepts, or assumptions and devising a metaphor that comprehensively describes the new understanding or model.

The interdisciplinary process must leave room for, and indeed encourage, intuition, reflection, and creative imagination. The interdisciplinary research process is not strictly a linear or step-based or rule-based procedure; it is a combination of step taking and intuition.

In the middle of the twentieth century, post-positivist philosophers of science moved away from a step- or rule-based view of scientific research toward one that incorporated an intuitive view in which hypotheses could emerge from hunches, intuition, and even dreams. Subsequent research in learning theory and cognitive science increasingly supports the importance of intuition. "If this is true for science," says J. Linn Mackey (2002), "it must certainly be true for interdisciplinary work" (p. 127).

The Necessity of Creativity

In his recent study of creativity and its relation to the interdisciplinary process, Marc Spooner (2004) has found that the choice of term used to describe creative activity "appears largely to be a function of the discipline with which one is associated." The natural sciences typically prefer discovery, the applied sciences prefer invention, business and high technology prefer innovation, and the social sciences and the humanities prefer creativity (pp. 87–88). Nevertheless, there is considerable consensus on the following definition of creativity, from P. E. Vernon (1989):

> [Creativity is the] capacity to produce new or original ideas, *insights*, restructurings, inventions, or artistic objects, which are accepted by experts as being of scientific, aesthetic, social, or technological value. In addition to novelty as our major criterion, we must incorporate in our definition the acceptability or appropriateness of the creative product, even though this valuation may change with the passage of time. (p. 94, italics added)

Creativity, says Klein (1996), starts with partial information. It develops through exploration and experimental application of familiar techniques to new situations (p. 222). "Excellence" of the creative result, she says,

> is measured in terms not of fidelity to disciplinarity but of interdisciplinary originality. Disciplinary accuracy and clarity are important, but . . . the creation of new meaning [is] of primary importance. . . . Interdisciplinarity is most successful when it is most creative. (pp. 222, 224)

Creativity and the Integrative Process

Recent research has identified the connections between creativity and integrative thinking. Creativity, says David Sill (1996), draws from the richness of the subconscious in relying on nonlogical and nonlinear thought processes (i.e., intuition), not mechanical rules. Our subconscious provides the raw material for creative combinations in the form of ideas, images, or concepts. The ripeness of these ideas, images, or concepts encourages creative insights that tend to be ambiguous, novel, meaningful, incongruent, and divergent (pp. 140–141).

Sill (1996) notes that creativity is an apt analogue for integrative thought, and he points out that research into creativity suggests that it occurs in stages (p. 130). For example, Gary A. Davis (1992) finds that the "creative process typically refers to (1) steps or stages, (2) perpetual change or transformation, or (3) techniques and strategies that are used to inform or produce the creative act" (p. 5).

Sill (1996) also notes, "Without the initial idea or impetus, without saturation in the ideas, the background, the culture, and the social order, and without time to allow creativity to occur, creativity cannot occur" (p. 129). Sill makes four important points about creativity that warrant the attention of interdisciplinarians:

- Creativity occurs in stages.
- Creativity begins with an initial idea.
- Creativity results from saturation in the insights and theories relevant to the problem.
- Creativity takes time. (pp. 145–149)

Just as some theorists argue that creativity progresses in stages, adds Deborah Vess (2004), "the ability to think in an integrative fashion may also occur in stages" (p. 5).

According to Spooner (2004), a basic set of tools undergirds and guides creative thinking. Each tool may enter into the interdisciplinary process at various steps and make a useful contribution to the end goal of developing interdisciplinary integration or synthesis.

For example, in order to draw on various disciplinary perspectives, observation and abstraction are useful tools. Likewise, in order to integrate disciplinary insights, the ability to *recognize patterns*, to *form patterns*, to *analogize*, to *think dimensionally*, to *develop models*, to *transform*, and finally to *synthesize* information is very valuable. (p. 98)

The result of the creative and integrative process is "the production of something that is both new and useful"(Houtz & Patricola, 1999, p. 1). Creativity combined with using the research process described in this book should result in an interdisciplinary understanding of the problem.

How Integration Is Achieved

What Is Integrated

Chapter 5 noted that what must be integrated are disciplinary insights, including those that are theory based. This is achieved by creating common ground from the theories, concepts, and assumptions embedded in these insights.

The Importance of Integration to the Interdisciplinary Research Process

The previously recounted stories of the blind men and the elephant and of building the elephant house illustrate the primary importance of integrating insights. Like the blind men in the first story, scholars each represent a separate discipline earnestly attempting to explain a complex phenomenon represented by the elephant. The result of their combined efforts is merely setting various disciplinary perspectives side by side, represented by their description of various parts of the elephant (i.e., a complex phenomenon). More fundamentally, their fragmented views of the elephant prevented them from achieving a comprehensive understanding of what they were investigating, leaving them the poorer for their efforts.

A similar failure occurs in the story of the elephant house. Once again, each disciplinary specialist uses a method and contributes an insight appropriate to that discipline. But their collective failure to combine and integrate their disciplinary insights results in a product that fails the ultimate test: the product's utility.

Both stories point up the importance of integration in solving a complex problem, designing a complex product, or answering a complex question. The interdisciplinary effort will prove a hollow exercise unless some measure of integration is achieved.

Paying Attention to Process

Achieving integration requires that students pay careful attention to process. In practical terms, this means three things:

1. Examine how the insights to be combined are obtained and interrelated. Achieving integration to produce an interdisciplinary understanding must be grounded in the commonalities but still take into account the differences (Klein & Newell, 1997, pp. 404, 406).

2. Reconcile the conflicting theories, concepts, or assumptions of the conflicting insights, some of which may appear to be identical but may be merely similar and some of which may deceptively appear to be so dissimilar as to render integration difficult or even impossible.

3. Leave room for nonlinear thinking. "The progression of integrative strategies from learning the disciplines, tracing connection and disconnection among them, to pointing out the limitations of any single view and attempting a synthesis is not to be viewed linearly" (Nikitina, 2002, p. 41).

Devotion to process is not the end but merely the means to an end. The interdisciplinary process must remain flexible to leave room for creativity and intuition. *The interdisciplinary research process, then, is a combination of step taking, decision making, intuition, process, and creativity.*

Step 9: Integrate insights

The Basis of Integration

Insights cannot be integrated until common ground among them is first established. This means deciding which common ground theory, concept, or assumption is the one that addresses all or most of the conflicting insights.

The objective of creating common ground is not to eliminate tension altogether between the insights of different disciplines, but to reduce the level of tension. Tension, even conflict, will remain, reflecting the differing assumptions and epistemologies by which the disciplines and their theories operate (Newell, 2007, p. 260).

Once common ground is created, the student can confidently proceed to Step 9, which calls for integrating the insights identified earlier. The common ground that undergirds these insights should reflect the most basic theory, concept, or assumption upon which the problem or object rests. This theory, concept, or assumption operates much like a magnet, pulling all of the known variables toward itself. It is—to use another, though imperfect, metaphor—the glue that enables the interdisciplinarian to begin the process of integrating the known variables or causal factors of the different insights, setting the stage for producing the interdisciplinary understanding.

The Interdisciplinarian's Work

In integrating insights, the interdisciplinary student is doing work that disciplinary students seldom do. Disciplinary majors typically focus on only those parts of a problem that fall within the discipline's research domain. The interdisciplinary student, however, has the responsibility of studying the problem comprehensively, of studying those parts of the problem that fall between the disciplines, or of studying the linkages between all the parts. The disciplines use a divide and conquer strategy of **disciplinary reductionism** that simply ignores what is not of interest to them. Unless the interdisciplinarian addresses these ignored linkages and conflicting insights into a given problem, there will be no overall problem, merely "smaller" and separate problems, each one studied separately by those disciplines interested in it. Worse, the reductionist strategy of the disciplines would prevail, leaving us ignorant of the possibilities of integrative thinking and problem solving (Newell, 2007, pp. 260–261). Though students working in multidisciplinary programs are trained to study the parts of the problem from various disciplinary viewpoints, they are not charged with the responsibility of integrating them.

When Integration Occurs

When exactly does integration occur? According to Szostak (2002), "Integration occurs when the insights of each particular theory and method are delineated, and it is shown how, in combination, they yield a better explanation than any in isolation" (p. 115). Klein (1996) adds that because achieving a working relationship between differentiation and combination is an ongoing task, the boundaries between stages also blur. "Synthesis is not reserved for a final step. The possibilities are tested throughout, moving in zigzags and in fits and starts as new knowledge becomes available and new possibilities and limits arise" (p. 223).

How do we know when integration has occurred? Practitioners offer these criteria:

- When an interdisciplinary understanding is achieved (Klein, 1996, p. 223)
- When the integrated result is greater than the sum of its disciplinary parts (Shin, 1986, p. 99)
- When "a new object that belongs to no one" is created (Carp, 2001, p. 85)

Examples of Integrating Insights

In each of the following examples drawn from a problem-based course project, published work, and undergraduate student papers, interdisciplinarians are careful to identify the insights that they are seeking to integrate. The integrative techniques used in each case to achieve integration are in italics.

From a Problem-Based Course Project: The Causes of Suicide Terrorism

In the problem-based course project on the causes of suicide terrorism, common ground among the six conflicting theory-based insights was achieved by *expanding* Self-Sanction Theory so that it can address all of the causal factors of this phenomenon. Once expanded, the theory is able to integrate the other five theories. Integrating these theories proceeds serially, as follows.

- The focus of Terrorist Psycho-logic Theory is on individuals who are drawn to the path of terrorism to commit acts of violence. Their behavior is explained "as a consequence of psychological forces," and more specifically by "their special psycho-logic" that enables them to construct rationalizations for their actions that they are "psychologically compelled to commit" (Post, 1998, p. 25). Expanding Self-Sanction Theory to include the moral cognitive restructuring of individuals allows it to integrate Terrorist Psycho-logic Theory with its similar focus. The common ground between the two theories is the rationality of individual decision making, which is influenced by multiple factors that are internal and external to the individual.

- The focus of Martyrdom Theory is on individuals who are ready to die while committing violence against others. According to Ariel Merari (1998), these persons "wish to die for personal reasons" that include "personality factors" and "broken family backgrounds" (pp. 206–207). Though a product of cognitive psychology, the theory takes into account factors that one does not readily associate with this subdiscipline, such as cultural factors (including the influence of religion), indoctrination (which may include charismatic political, military, or religious leaders, as well as family members), and situational factors (which may include a variety of social, political, and economic circumstances).

- Expanding Self-Sanction Theory to include the moral restructuring of individuals allows it to integrate Martyrdom Theory, with its intense focus on individual personality factors that influence a rational decision-making process.

- Collective Rational Strategic Choice Theory, a product of political science, takes a "big picture" view of suicide terrorism, understanding it as an expression of a sophisticated political strategy, whether that strategy involves secular or religious goals. For Martha Crenshaw (1998), terrorism follows logical processes that are discoverable and explainable (p. 7). The theory, she says, is unlike conventional rational choice theories of individual participation in political rebellions because it focuses on (a) "collective behavior" and (b) the "strategic reasoning" driving this behavior. The theory also addresses the degree to which "strategic reasoning" may be "modified by psychological and other constraints" (p. 9). The common ground between this theory and the expanded theory of Self-Sanction is that the decision-making process used by suicide terrorists is a rational one (whether it is "strategic" in a secular sense or intensely personal in a religious sense). The rational decision-making (or "strategic reasoning") aspect of Collective Rational Choice Theory, along with its emphasis on the psychological modification that occurs in the process of transforming a person into a suicide terrorist, allows it to be integrated with Self-Sanction Theory.

- "Sacred" Terror Theory, also a political science theory, focuses on the "special justifications and precedents" that religiously motivated terrorists use (Rapoport, 1998, p. 107). These "special justifications," designed to dispel the doubts of recruits, concern the religious importance of martyrdom that is based on sacred writings and commentaries on these (both oral and written; p. 122). The common ground between this theory and Self-Sanction Theory is the belief that terrorists engage in a rational process of decision making despite this process being heavily influenced by religion. The expansion of Self-Sanction Theory to include the role of mental accounting and emotion (as defined in Chapter 11) allows it to integrate "Sacred" Terror Theory with its particular focus on the influence of religion on the process of moral cognitive restructuring.

- Kin Altruism Theory, a cultural anthropology theory, holds that suicide terrorists act out of a universal heartfelt human sentiment of self-sacrifice for the welfare of the group or culture (Atran, 2003, p. 2). Scott Atran rejects the notions that suicide terrorists have a special psychopathology, that religion "or even religious-like motivation" can explain this phenomenon, or that "utility" (i.e., transitive preferences) motivates terrorist behavior. Rather, Atran argues that Kin Altruism Theory offers the best way to understand suicide terrorist behavior because it addresses psychological and cultural relationships and shows how these, rooted in rationality, are "luring and binding thousands of ordinary people into terrorist organization's martyr-making web" (p. 8). This theory, he says, explains "why nonpathological individuals respond to novel situational factors in sufficient numbers for recruiting organizations to implement [their] policies" (p. 3). The expansion of Self-Sanction Theory to include the role of emotion and mental accounting as part of the process of moral cognitive restructuring allows it to integrate Kin Altruism Theory, with its emphasis on how cultural factors inform the terrorist's psychology and decision-making process.

Clearly, the common ground theory in this example does not erase all differences between the conflicting theories but instead focuses on their fundamental commonality, namely, that terrorists' decision-making processes are rational, complex, and influenced by factors both internal and external to the individual.

From the Natural Sciences: Watson (1968), The Double Helix: A Personal Account of the Discovery of the Structure of DNA

Watson (1968) is careful to identify each insight and decision point that ultimately led him and Crick to solve the complex structure of the DNA molecule. These insights and decisions about research pathways include the following:

- The insight that X-ray crystallography was the key to genetics and that Bragg's law could be applied to studying DNA in 3-D (p. 8)
- The insight of Avery's theory that genes are the key components of living cells, pointing to the need to understand how genes act and that future experiments could show that all genes are composed of DNA (p. 14)
- The insight that working out DNA's chemical structure might be the essential step in learning how genes duplicate (p. 23)
- The decision by Watson to study viruses to get at genes, hoping that the combined techniques of chemistry and genetics would yield biological dividends in the form of unlocking the secret to the structure of DNA (p. 22)
- The decision to use Wilkins's theory that genes could crystallize and thus must have a regular structure that could be solved in a straightforward fashion (p. 33)

- The decision to use Crick and Cochran's mathematical model of diffraction of X-rays, proving that DNA has a helical structure, and confirming Pauling's a-helical model developed through manipulating physical models (much like tinker toys) based on which chemical elements like to sit next to each other (p. 50)
- The insight from astronomer Tommy Gold's "The Perfect Cosmological Principle" that far-out ideas could be applied to the problem of the structure of DNA (p. 126)
- The insight (i.e., hypothesis) by Watson that the TMV structure was helical and comprised of a central RNA core surrounded by a large number of identical small protein subunits (pp. 112, 124)
- The decision to apply to DNA the principle that important biological objects come in pairs (p. 171)

These insights could not be integrated and a model of DNA produced, however, until Watson and Crick determined the angle and radii at which the DNA strands twisted about the central axis. The specific problem they faced was finding spaces large enough along the length of the helix that would accommodate clusters of atoms without forcing them closer together than the laws of chemistry allowed. As Watson explains, "Positioning one atom the proper distance from its neighbor often caused a distant atom to become jammed impossibly close to its partners" (p. 99). This problem was solved when Watson *extended* the concept of "cozy corners" in the chemical structure of the similar tobacco mosaic virus (TMV) to DNA, as noted in Chapter 11. This breakthrough allowed Watson and Crick to begin rapidly integrating their research.

The first major integrative breakthrough came from Rosalind Franklin, the lab's expert on X-ray crystallography, who developed a new 3-D form of DNA (called the B structure), which occurred when the DNA molecules were surrounded by a large amount of water. This new structure produced much sharper black cross reflections via X-ray crystallography than the A form Watson and Crick had been working with. The black cross reflections confirmed the Stokes-Cochran-Crick theory that such an image could arise only from a helical structure (p. 169). The remaining critical problem was arriving at a structural hypothesis that would allow them to pack the bases regularly in the inside of the helix. This problem was ultimately overcome when Watson and Crick abandoned two long-held assumptions: that the helix could be either a three-chain or a two-chain model, and that the backbone of the helix was in the center of the helix. Knowing that they did not have time to explore both a three-chain and a two-chain hypothesis, Crick urged Watson to focus on two-chain models. Watson agreed and also decided to relocate the backbone of the helix on the outside. Doing so showed that there was "no difficulty in twisting an externally situated backbone into a shape compatible with the X-ray evidence" (pp. 178–179).

The remaining integrative breakthrough, and the key to ultimately revealing the atomic structure of the helix, was figuring out the composition of the bases or clusters of atoms that held the two chains together. Watson describes the problem like this:

> There was the vexing problem of how the intertwined chains might be held together by hydrogen bonds between the bases. Though for over a year Francis [Crick] and I had dismissed the possibility that bases formed regular hydrogen bonds, it was now obvious to me that we had done so incorrectly. . . . The crux of the matter was a rule governing hydrogen bonding between bases. (p. 183)

One day, Watson recalls, "a nontrivial idea" emerged.

> It came while I was drawing. . . . Suddenly, I realized the potentially profound implications of a DNA structure in which the adenine residue formed hydrogen bonds similar to those found in crystals of pure adenine. If DNA was like this, each adenine residue related to it by a 180-degree rotation. Most important, two symmetrical hydrogen bonds could also hold together pairs of guanine, cytosine, or thymine. I thus started wondering whether each DNA molecule consisted of two chains with identical base sequences held together by hydrogen bonds between pairs of identical bases. (p. 184)

Watson's insight provided the final integrative element that unlocked the secret of the structure of DNA. The only remaining task was to model their integrative understanding of the DNA molecule to show that it conformed to all the known rules of chemistry.

From the Natural Sciences: Nagy* (2005), Anthropogenic Forces Degrading Tropical Ecosystems in Latin America: A Costa Rican Case Study

In her study of anthropogenic forces degrading the tropical ecosystems of Latin America, and Costa Rica in particular, Nagy (2005) achieves common ground by *redefining* "wealth" in a way that addresses the need both for economic development and for ecosystem health. Wealth, in an environmental sense, can refer to biological diversity and ecosystem health. By contrast, wealth, from an economic perspective, usually means financial prosperity, often derived from exploiting natural resources. The way Nagy integrates these diametrically opposed positions is instructive. The lines between these conflicting positions begin to blur when she places them on a continuum that stretches from "anti-development" (the natural science/ environmental position) to "pro-development" (the social science/economics position). On the end opposing development are the environmentalists who focus primarily on conserving natural resources and who seek to minimize human interaction with the environment. At the opposite end of the continuum is economic activity that seeks to exploit natural resources for human benefit and that promotes capitalist activity (p. 106). Across the continuum is a universal focus on meeting basic needs. On the anti-development end, the primary needs of the ecosystem are included for all organisms, as well as the physical features of the community. A healthy ecosystem, she says, allows exchange and regulation of both the abiotic and the biotic communities. The basic needs of humans on the pro-development end are derived from the same basic needs of ecosystems. Both require food, water, shelter, and sanitation. These needs can be derived only from a healthy environment. Human life and development is directly related to meeting the most basic needs of the environment.

Essentially, she says, the problem becomes how to maximize jointly human and ecosystem needs. Her integrative insight is that one can look at the problem like this: the needs of the human species alone ("I") versus the needs of *all* living species ("We"). Seeing where their needs overlap on the continuum is a starting point for addressing the problem in a comprehensive way. Armed with this broadened definition of wealth, and using the integrative technique of the continuum, Nagy is able to integrate the conflicting insights produced by environmental science and economics.

From the Social Sciences: Delph* (2005), An Integrative Approach to the Elimination of the "Perfect Crime"

Delph's (2005) study is an example of some insights conflicting while others do not. Whenever there is conflict, common ground must be created to overcome it, at least to the extent possible. On the one hand, Delph found "no apparent contradiction" between the insights generated by forensic psychology and criminal investigation, making the integration of these insights relatively easy to achieve. On the other hand, she found substantial conflict between the approaches of the physical sciences and the behavioral sciences concerning the standard practice of criminal profiling, meaning recreating the criminal act so as to obtain insights into the personality of the criminal. The physical sciences privilege empirically derived insights of investigative profiling, whereas the behavioral sciences prefer intuitively derived insights. Delph argues that many more crimes could be solved if the disciplines of criminal justice, forensic science, and forensic psychology "better understood each other's needs and integrated their theories and methods" (p. 29).

Integration of these very different approaches to profiling, of course, is predicated on creating common ground between the conflicting insights. More specifically, integration is predicated on creating common ground between the conflicting physical science and behavioral science views on profiling. Delph (2005) accomplishes this by *redefining* the meaning of profiling used by each field so that the broadened term integrates the specialized kind of knowledge that criminal investigation, forensic science, and forensic psychology each privileges. What is actually integrated is "the unique knowledge possessed by each of these areas of expertise" (p. 30). She proceeds to describe each kind of knowledge so that she can show how their integration provides the "more comprehensive solution" of so-called perfect crimes (discussed later in this chapter).

From the Humanities: Bal (1999), "Introduction," The Practice of Cultural Analysis: Exposing Interdisciplinary Interpretation

Bal's (1999) objective is to expose the full meaning of an enigmatic graffito that appeared on a brick wall in Amsterdam:

Note

I hold you dear

I have not

Thought you up (p. 2)

As noted in an earlier chapter, Bal uses the interdiscipline of cultural analysis to arrive at new and more comprehensive understandings of cultural artifacts and texts. As applied to the graffito, this approach centers on the verb "to expose," which refers to the action of "making a public presentation" or "publicly demonstrating." The verb, says Bal (1996) in *Double Exposures: the Subject of Cultural Analyses*, "can be combined with a noun meaning opinions or judgments and refers to the public presentation of someone's views; or it can refer to the performing of those deeds that deserve to be made public" (p. 2). Bal creates common ground by *extending* the meaning of the verb "expose" from a specific and literalized definition to a broader, more ambiguous, and metaphorical one by combining it with the nouns "exposition," "exposé," and "exposure." The graffito is a particular form of discursive behavior that is characterized by the posture or gesture of exposing. She integrates the various gestures of exposing, gestures that point to things like the graffito that seems to say, "Look!"—often implying, "That's how it is." The "Look!" aspect involves the visual availability of the exposed graffito as a bright yellow handwriting on the red bricks of the city wall. The "That's how it is" aspect involves the authority of the author, who knows from experience the heartbreak of loss. The concept of exposing, she says, integrates the two gestures. "The possible discrepancy between the object [i.e., the graffito] that is present and the statement about it creates the ambiguities" that she examines (p. 2). Armed with these analytical tools, Bal attempts to expose the meaning of the graffito by integrating not only the insights of cultural analysis but also the insights of other relevant disciplines.

Bal's study of the graffito generally conforms to the integrative process outlined in these chapters. She identifies the problem, identifies the relevant disciplines and their insights, identifies those that conflict, and creates common ground among them using the technique of *extension*.

From the Humanities: Silver (2005),* Composing Race and Gender: The Appropriation of Social Identity in Fiction

Creative writing, says Silver (2005), like all other disciplines, sees the world through its own "peephole" or perspective. "I love this peephole deeply," she confides, "but I also want to see the entire truth [because] *truth is fundamental to fiction*" (p. 75). For Silver, seeing the "entire truth" as a writer of fiction involves boundary crossing. One way fiction writers cross boundaries is by appropriating social identities, which are reflected in their characters. Silver uses the integrative technique of *redefinition* to resolve an ethical dilemma that exists when fiction writers, actors, and filmmakers regularly and uncritically appropriate a person's identity. That dilemma is how to engage in this practice in an ethical, by which Silver means truthful or authentic, way. The disciplines that Silver finds most relevant to the problem are sociology, psychology, cultural studies, and creative writing. The challenge for Silver was finding common ground among the conflicting disciplinary insights concerning this problem. Silver redefines the concept of "implicature" to mean the ultimate level of empathy that one person can have with another. Implicature, she says, is what makes appropriation ethical rather than hypocritical. What she integrates are "'the rules of fiction' with the social and historical implications of appropriation" (p. ii). These rules include characterization, point of view, and trusting the author. Silver's discussion of the historical and social implications of appropriating a social identity is informed by "the power dynamics and guilt feelings of race and gender relations" (p. 15).

The integration of insights is foundational to Silver's (2005) ultimate objective, "a cohesive set of guidelines" for writers, actors, and filmmakers that would govern their fictional appropriation of race and gender (p. ii). These guidelines express her integrative understanding of the topic (discussed later in this chapter).

Summary

The concern in this part of the chapter is not so much with the specific theories, concepts, and assumptions that are being integrated but with the principle of integration at work. This principle is that the student must have an adequate grasp of the disciplinary insights and the corresponding theories, concepts, and assumptions that are to be combined. As has been emphasized, the most relevant disciplines and their perspectives usually produce the most relevant insights.

The portion of an interdisciplinary essay that identifies the relevant theories, concepts, and assumptions performs two critical functions: It validates the

choice of disciplines, and it lays the groundwork and provides the raw data
for the integrative portion of the study. To the extent that the student has
been thorough and balanced in identifying and examining these important
disciplinary data, the integrative effort should proceed relatively smoothly,
as these examples demonstrate. At the very least, the integrative phase of
the project will most certainly reveal any oversights in the interdisciplinary
process that need to be addressed. The integrative phase itself provides an
internal assessment of the research and analysis that has occurred up to this
critical point.

Producing an Interdisciplinary Understanding_____

> **Step 10: Produce an interdisciplinary understanding of the problem and test it**

In this Step of the integrative process, the student is working with information already known from having successfully performed earlier Steps,
particularly 8 and 9. Step 10 affords the student an opportunity to review
and validate decisions made in earlier Steps.

A Definition of Interdisciplinary Understanding

Interdisciplinary understanding is "the capacity to integrate knowledge
and modes of thinking in two or more disciplines to produce a cognitive
advancement" that would not be possible using single disciplinary means.
This advancement includes "explaining a phenomenon, solving a problem, creating a product, or raising a new question" (Boix Mansilla, 2005,
p. 16).

The interdisciplinary understanding and its application is the end product of the interdisciplinary enterprise. Boix Mansilla (2005) identifies four
core premises that underlie this concept:

1. "It builds on a performance view of understanding—one that privileges the capacity to *use* knowledge over that of *having* or *accumu-
   lating* it [emphasis added]."

2. It "is 'disciplined'—i.e., deeply informed by disciplinary expertise."

3. "It involves the integration of disciplinary views."

4. It "is purposeful" leading to "*cognitive advancement*—e.g., a new
   insight, a solution, an account, an explanation." (pp. 16–18)

Ways to Express the Interdisciplinary Understanding

The remaining Step in the research process is to produce the interdisciplinary understanding of the problem and test it. This Step may take one of several forms, or some combination of these, but there may well be others.

- Introduce a *metaphor* (a figure of speech in which a word or phrase literally denoting one kind of object or idea is used to describe another to suggest an analogy between them) that illustrates how the common ground or integrating theory, concept, or assumption actually provides an integrative understanding of the problem.
- Create a *model* (an example, pattern, archetype, or prototype that can be set before one for guidance or imitation) that shows how the common ground theory, concept, or assumption provides an interdisciplinary understanding.
- Write a *narrative* (a written or spoken account or story) that explains how the common ground theory, concept, or assumption provides an understanding that is more comprehensive than using single disciplinary approaches.
- Pose a *new question* or develop a new avenue of research.
- Create a *new process or physical product* that is derived from the practical application of the new understanding.
- Apply the new understanding to the problem to (1) explain the implications of the interdisciplinary understanding for an existing policy, plan, program, or schema; and (2) propose a *new policy, plan, program, or schema*.

The interdisciplinary understanding is the product of, but distinct from, the various disciplinary insights into the problem. The resultant "interdisciplinary 'whole,'" says Boix Mansilla (2005), "stands as more than the sum of its disciplinary 'parts'" (p. 17). The metaphor, model, narrative, new question or avenue of research, new physical product, new policy, plan, program, or schema each expresses the integration between the parts and whole of the problem established in Step 9.

Testing the New Understanding

Advanced undergraduate or graduate courses typically encourage or even require using metaphors, models, and narratives to capture creatively the new understanding in all of its richness. This final Step in the research process affords the student an opportunity to review and validate decisions made in earlier Steps.

However one chooses to express the new understanding, it should be inclusive of each discipline's insights but beholden to none of them. That is, each relevant insight, theory, or concept should contribute to that understanding but not dominate it. The objective of this Step is to achieve unity, coherence, and balance among those disciplinary influences that have contributed to the interdisciplinary understanding (Newell, 2007, p. 261).

In effect, the new understanding and its various expressions tests whether it is coherent, unified, and balanced, and thus, truly interdisciplinary. A metaphor, for example, "brings out the defining characteristics of that understanding without denying the remaining conflict that underlies it" (Newell, 2007, p. 261). Metaphors are particularly useful in the humanities, where meaning cannot be adequately expressed using quantitative and empirical approaches. However, the social sciences and even the natural sciences make use of metaphors (Lakoff & Johnson, 1980). An interdisciplinary understanding has been reached when the metaphor is consistent with (1) the contributing disciplinary insights as modified to create common ground, (2) the interdisciplinary linkages found, and (3) the patterns observable in the overall behavior of the complex system (Newell, 2007, p. 261).

A model also may capture the unity, coherence, and balance contained in the interdisciplinary understanding. The model may be a tinker toy-like model of a molecule, such as the model of the DNA molecule that Watson and Crick built or Nagy's model of sustainable development for Costa Rica.

Narratives are essential components to integrative learning, thinking, and research. The narrative expressing the new understanding or new meaning should explain how it is, in fact, new and more comprehensive than the understandings offered by the participating disciplines or how the meaning is new compared to the meanings offered by the disciplinary insights examined. This may involve comparing the new understanding to each insight in serial fashion, insight by insight or discipline by discipline, to show how the insight, because of its narrow perspective, is unable to capture the more comprehensive nature or meaning of the new understanding.

Creating a new process or product is another way to test the new understanding. One of the drivers of interdisciplinary research in the sciences and engineering is the stimulus of generative technologies "whose novelty and power not only find applications of great value but also have the capacity to transform existing disciplines and generate new ones" (National Academy of Sciences et al., 2005, p. 35). A recent example is the development of the Internet and the cyberinfrastructure that is rapidly transforming the economy. Other examples of interdisciplinary products are buildings that incorporate the principles of aural architecture (an emerging interdisciplinary field) and the use of "green" building materials to improve energy efficiency. Products may also be a play, poem, sculpture, or painting. These products are the result of extracting relevant information from disciplines and applied fields and integrating their contributions (Blesser & Salter, 2007, p. x).

Application of the new understanding may be in the form of a critique of an existing policy to show how it is failing to meet a societal need because of its disciplinary or conceptual narrowness. This may be followed by a proposed new policy, program, or schema that, because of its inclusiveness, is more likely to solve the problem.

Examples of Interdisciplinary Understandings

In each of the following examples drawn from professional works and undergraduate student projects, interdisciplinarians are careful to articulate the understanding derived from their integration of the relevant insights. The forms used to express this understanding—metaphor, model, narrative, or conclusion—are in italics.

From the Natural Sciences: Watson (1968), The Double Helix: A Personal Account of the Discovery of the Structure of DNA

For Watson and Crick, the final step in their quest to solve the mystery of the structure of DNA was building a *model* of this complex molecule. This required knowing its atomic structure and particularly the composition of the bases or clusters of atoms that held the two chains in the helix together. Once they figured out this rule, they were able to build the model.

Watson's *narrative* of the integrative steps taken and the critical decisions reached is instructive for interdisciplinarians, particularly those working in the natural sciences. For one thing, the scientific process, like the interdisciplinary research process, is not straightforward, logical, and linear, as is commonly supposed. Working with complex problems is messy. One may encounter dead ends and follow false leads, as Watson and Crick did. Trial and error and following "hunches" is inexorably part of many research processes. Second, and this applies to most interdisciplinary work, Watson and Crick did not need much expertise in unfamiliar fields in order to draw upon them effectively. They drew insights from specialized disciplinary literature and from disciplinary experts. Their experience shows the importance of achieving adequacy in the discipline one is working in, to at least know what is not known and be able to ask disciplinary experts appropriate questions, as Watson did repeatedly. Third, solving complex problems often requires that one break with conventional wisdom, as Watson and Crick did when, for example, they decided to build a scale model of the DNA molecule before knowing all of its atomic components and how they were arranged. Finally, Watson and Crick carefully considered every insight that appeared to be relevant to the problem. Inclusiveness, especially early in the research process, is preferable to excluding insights that may later prove useful.

Watson and Crick's discovery conforms to the overall approach of the interdisciplinary process described in this book. They focused on a complex problem (the structure of DNA) and drew insights from disciplines they knew (physics and biology) as well as from disciplines they knew nothing about (biochemistry, chemistry, X-ray crystallography, and even astronomy) in order to produce an integrative model that expressed their new understanding of DNA. Though model building preceded new understanding, it nevertheless expressed this understanding when it was successfully completed. Indeed, it was through the tedious, technical, and slow process of model building that the new understanding eventually came.

From the Natural Sciences: Nagy* (2005), Anthropogenic Forces Degrading Tropical Ecosystems in Latin America: A Costa Rican Case Study

Nagy (2005) characterizes her interdisciplinary understanding as "sustainable development." It amounts to an integrative *model* that is designed to meet the needs of people now, but in a way that will not mortgage the ability of future generations to get their basic needs met. Sustainable development, she says, considers not just the environment and economic development, but social and cultural aspects as well. The components of her model include "resource conservation, ecosystem protection, economic motivation, cultural celebration and protection, and social considerations" (p. 107). Nagy believes that her integrative model makes it easier to incorporate cultural diversity and protection of indigenous peoples, for the simple reason that the practices of these groups, often linked myopically to endangered ecosystems, are also in need of economic development to ensure their survival. Within her continuum, cultural science (and thus the needs of indigenous peoples) would fall between economic development and environmental protection. Perhaps, she says, by focusing on conservation rather than preservation, sustainability could be achieved for these people as well. This insight is drawn from recognizing that it is unlikely that countries like Costa Rica, which need more economic development in order to meet the needs of their growing populations, will continue to set aside large tracts of land for these small groups as they have been doing. "Rather than emphasizing the preservation of land in a pristine and untouched condition, it is more realistic that activities allowing for multi-purpose land use (for ecosystem and cultural protection *and* economic development) will progress towards sustainability" (p. 108).

Nagy's work conforms in almost every respect to the integrative research process discussed in these chapters. She identifies a complex problem, avoids the pitfall of siding with either the extreme environmental or development camp, dispassionately identifies and evaluates all of the relevant disciplines and their conflicting insights, creates common ground among them by using one of the integrative techniques discussed in this chapter, integrates these insights, and then constructs an integrative model that proposes a realistic solution to the problem.

From the Social Sciences: Delph* (2005), An Integrative Approach to the Elimination of the "Perfect Crime"

Having created common ground and integrated conflicting disciplinary insights and approaches to criminal profiling, Delph (2005) offers her integrated understanding of the problem in *narrative* form. Criminal profiling, she writes, could achieve its greatest potential if profilers from forensic psychology and forensic science integrate their analytical techniques and share them with local criminal investigators. If achieved, this integrated approach will produce four likely outcomes: (1) quickly reduce the list of possible suspects, (2) predict the prime suspect's future behavior, (3) offer investigative avenues that have been overlooked by police, and (4) empower local law enforcement agencies to use these integrated profiling techniques themselves (p. 32).

Delph's study of criminal profiling meets all three criteria noted earlier. First, the understanding is interdisciplinary because it is based on the insights offered by the three disciplines most concerned with this topic. In fact, Delph's new understanding fills an important gap in the literature on profiling from forensic psychology that, surprisingly, is virtually silent on how it can interface with forensic science. Second, the integrated result is greater than the sum of its disciplinary parts, meaning that the four outcomes transcend purely disciplinary approaches and are achievable only if these approaches are transcended. Third, Delph models good interdisciplinary practice by carefully keeping conflicting perspectives in balance. Her understanding belongs to "no one," in the sense that it does not privilege one discipline or one insight over another.

Delph's study illustrates two important practices urged in this book. First, she is clear about the disciplinary knowledge she is integrating. Second, by her detailing this knowledge, the reader can appreciate both the challenge of the integrative task and the importance of the integrative achievement.

From the Humanities: Bal (1999), "Introduction," The Practice of Cultural Analysis: Exposing Interdisciplinary Interpretation

Cultural analysis, as noted earlier, stands for an interdisciplinarity that is primarily analytical. Bal (1999) uses *narrative* to express her integrative understanding of the graffito's meaning. It is, she says, "a good case for the kind of objects at which cultural analysis looks, and—more importantly—how it goes about doing so" (p. 2). The graffito is a letter both visually and linguistically. Though the literal translation of the opening from the Dutch is "Note," the more usual address that comes to Bal's mind is "Dearest" or "Sweety" (p. 3). "This implied other word fits in with the beginning of the rest of the text that says something like 'I love you'" (p. 3). With the "discourse of the love letter" firmly in place, the graffito shifts to epistemic philosophy by continuing with "I did not invent you" or "I did not make you up." "The past tense, the action negated, the first-person speaking," observes Bal, "all indicate the discourse of narrative only to make a point about what's real and what is not" (p. 3). What is striking is that the address changes a real person, the anonymous writer's beloved, into a self-referential description of the note: A referential "Dearest" becomes a self-referential "Note" or short letter. "This turns the note into fiction," says Bal,

> and the addressee into a made-up "you," after all. Yet, by the same token, this inscription of literariness recasts the set of characters, for the identity of the "you" has by now come loose from the implied term of endearment that personalized him or her. So, the passerby looks again, tripping over this word that says "YOU!" . . . Addressed as beloved and not as a guilty citizen, the city dweller gets a chance to reshape her or his identity, gleaming in the light of this anonymous affection. But is it real? (p. 3)

One possible meaning, and one Bal (1999) considers plausible, is that the addressee is real if the beloved cannot be found; "she or he is irretrievably lost, and the graffito mourns that absence" (p. 4). For Bal, the graffito is an autographic poem. "Moreover, it is publicly accessible, semantically dense, pragmatically intriguing, visually appealing and insistent, and philosophically profound. Just like poetry" (p. 4).

Bal's understanding extends to linking the graffito to the interdiscipline of cultural analysis itself. It is the interest in more than the public self-exposure of the subject (author) and object (the lost beloved) of the poem that makes the exposition an exposure of the self. Such exposure, says Bal, is an act of producing meaning (1996, p. 2). Cultural analysis is also interested in moving from a literal meaning of the poem to its broader and metaphorical meaning. Exposing meaning, as Bal does, creates a subject/object dichotomy. The dichotomy enables the subject (in this case, the author of the poem) to make a statement about the object (in this case, the lost beloved). The object is there, explains Bal, to substantiate the statement and enable the statement to come across (p. 3). There is an addressee for the statement: the reader. In expositions like the poem, a "first person," the exposer, tells a "second person," the reader, about a third person, "the object" or lost beloved, who does not participate in the conversation. But, Bal says, "unlike many other constative speech acts, the object, although mute, is present" (1996, p. 4). In this sense, the poem is a *sign*. A sign stands for a thing or idea in some capacity, or for someone. In this instance, the poem is a sign for the writer's beloved, who is now lost. It is also a sign for the culture that produced it, the reader that reads it, and the field that examines it.

Bal follows the usual interdisciplinary process. She identifies all relevant disciplinary perspectives on the poem, creates common ground among their insights, integrates them within the framework of cultural analysis, and presents a multi-layered meaning of the poem that is integrative, new, and more comprehensive.

Bal's understanding of the meaning of the graffito meets the three criteria for integration identified earlier. Her understanding is indeed comprehensive, far more comprehensive than would be possible relying on a single-discipline approach. The integrated result is greater than the sum of its disciplinary parts, and the new understanding belongs to no one discipline.

From the Humanities: Silver* (2005), Composing Race and Gender: The Appropriation of Social Identity in Fiction

Silver uses a brief case study to communicate her integrative understanding of appropriation and its importance beyond the realm of fiction writing, acting, and filmmaking. An example of appropriation is when a person in the social majority takes on the character of a person in the minority. Silver's understanding is in the form of an extended discourse, in which she presents three general principles that are necessary to achieve implicature.

Before proceeding with appropriation, she says, a person must consider the element of implicature. "It is only through implicature that one's work will be able to reach a level rewarding for both themselves and society. Reaching this high level," she cautions, "is a very challenging process" (Silver, 2005, p. 61). The key is emotion. Emotion is the universal tie and the universal state of being. "Through emotionally implicating oneself within a given social identity—writers should potentially be capable of appropriating a voice within that identity" (p. 63).

The most striking example of implicature, Silver (2005) finds, is not from the world of fiction as one might suppose, but from the world of biography. Dr. Paul Farmer, the subject of Tracy Kidder's Pulitzer Prize-winning biography *Mountains Beyond Mountains,* revolutionized the health care systems of Haiti and other developing nations. Kidder (and Silver) see Farmer as the ideal "global man" who believes in the universality of humankind and sees all the people of the world as having the same emotions. Silver describes Farmer's unique ability to identify emotionally with the people he is trying to help. Reflecting on how he is able to love the poor children of the area as much as he loves his own daughter, Farmer wonders whether it may be the result of the unique childhood his eccentric father imposed on him. His home was either a bus or a boat dock, so he never developed a sense of place. This experience, Kidder (and Silver) suspect, accounts for Farmer's ability to engage in hyper-connective thinking, meaning that he is able to function without being influenced by limiting considerations of time and national identity (pp. 63–65, 218).

Silver's (2005) understanding, expressed in an extensive narrative that includes two illustrative case studies, reflects the three criteria for integration noted earlier. It is more comprehensive because it is based on insights from all the principle disciplines interested in the topic. Second, the integrated result is greater than the sum of its disciplinary parts because her three "general principles of implicature," the core finding of her study, clearly transcend disciplinary boundaries. These include awareness of ethnocentric feelings, extended exposure to social identities outside one's own, and hyper-connective thinking (p. 65). Third, the study models the interdisciplinary practice of avoiding advocacy of disciplinary points of view by keeping these views at a professional distance. Silver's study truly belongs to "no one" because it keeps conflicting perspectives in balance and does not privilege one disciplinary insight over another. Her conclusions are her own.

CHAPTER SUMMARY

This chapter explains the last two Steps of the interdisciplinary research process: integrating insights (Step 9) and producing an interdisciplinary understanding of the problem and testing the understanding (Step 10). What is integrated are insights produced by the disciplines. Integration, a distinguishing characteristic of interdisciplinarity, requires paying close attention to process. A key insight concerning the interdisciplinary research process is that all practitioners do not apply it in the same way. In fact, one is struck by the variety of integrative approaches that published work and student projects use.

The last Step in the research process is producing the interdisciplinary understanding. Throughout this book, the phrases "interdisciplinary understanding," "more comprehensive understanding," "integrative understanding," and "new meaning" are used interchangeably to describe the goal or product of the research process. This goal is to arrive at a result that is new and "more comprehensive" compared to available disciplinary insights. The student should explain how the integrative result, even if only partially achieved, is, in fact, new and more comprehensive and thus interdisciplinary. For Watson, it was to narrate the construction (at least initially) of a model of the DNA molecule to show that it conformed to all the known rules of chemistry. For Bal, it was using the graffito as a metaphor to express the theory and methods of cultural analysis.

Students need awareness that any integration achieved is likely to be limited and that methods other than those demonstrated here may well produce a more comprehensive understanding of a particular problem.

NOTES

1. For a detailed discussion of the term "understanding" from a social science perspective, and an explanation of the difference between the *verstehen* (and the more recent interpretive) approach and the predictive approach, see Frankfort-Nachmias & Nachmias (2008), pp. 10–11.

2. To some, these differences are frustrating, while to others, they are acceptable or even invigorating.

3. Examining the insights, concepts, and theories advanced by various disciplines relevant to the problem will develop an awareness of the limits of a single expert view. Interdisciplinarians are prone to skepticism of "expert views"—and indeed, should be—because in their regular crossing of disciplinary boundaries they are uniquely positioned to see the limits of expert views on particular topics. Skepticism is intellectually healthy and can embolden students to challenge traditional or well-entrenched views, freeing them to explore new lines of inquiry. Skepticism is the wellspring of new understanding.

REVIEW QUESTIONS

1. What is integration in interdisciplinary terms?

2. What cognitive qualities and internal dispositions aid integrative work?

3. What is the role of intuition in integration?

4. What role does creativity play in Steps 9 and 10 of the research process?

5. Why is creativity necessary in research, whether disciplinary or interdisciplinary?

6. What does research by Spooner, Vess, and Sill suggest about creativity and the integrative process?

7. What exactly is integrated?

8. What is the importance of creating common ground and integration to the interdisciplinary research process?

9. When exactly does integration occur?

10. When does integration occur in the example of the problem of suicide terrorism?

11. How is Watson's narrative of the integrative steps taken instructive for interdisciplinarians?

12. How does Bal's study of the graffito conform to the integrative model of the interdisciplinary research process used in this book?

13. What exactly is "an interdisciplinary understanding"?

14. What are some of the ways that one can express an interdisciplinary understanding?

15. How may proposing a new policy constitute a test of whether the new understanding is unified, coherent, and balanced?

16. How does Delph and Silver's integrative work meet all three integrative criteria?

Conclusion _____

Interdisciplinarity for the New Century

This book invites students and academicians to think about, and hopefully practice, interdisciplinary studies and interdisciplinarity in a more explicit, knowledgeable, rigorous, and nuanced way. It also asks them to think about six interrelated issues: (1) the definition of interdisciplinary studies, (2) interdisciplinary studies as an emerging academic field, (3) the role of the disciplines in interdisciplinary work, (4) the importance of integration, (5) the product and purpose of integration, and (6) the cognitive abilities associated with interdisciplinarity.

_____ The Definition of Interdisciplinary Studies

The book dwells heavily on defining interdisciplinary studies and interdisciplinarity for two practical reasons. If interdisciplinary programs are fuzzy in their conception of what interdisciplinarity is, then their curricula are unlikely to provide the proven educational outcomes for students that interdisciplinarity promises. Interdisciplinary courses and programs should develop a local conception of interdisciplinary studies that is informed by the national conversation and craft clearly stated outcomes for student learning, at the course and program level, that are consistent with this understanding. This makes comprehensive and rigorous assessment possible.

The second reason for dwelling at length on definition is that interdisciplinary studies is still widely misunderstood. Indeed, it is commonplace to hear well-meaning but uninformed academics claim, "We are already doing it." Perhaps this is true, but according to what standard? Accompanying this claim is the occasional call to fold the local interdisciplinary program into disciplinary units now that interdisciplinarity is supposedly occurring in various disciplinary contexts on campus. These academics, it seems fair to say, are obliged to show how their discipline-based conception of interdisciplinarity, their approach to interdisciplinary research, and their understanding of the field's underlying theory are sufficiently grounded in the field's literature. Without such grounding, their claim of doing interdisciplinarity is suspect.

One of the most promising developments in the Academy is the increase in border-crossing activity. This makes interdisciplinary programs more necessary than ever because they can provide the intellectual center of gravity for interdisciplinary learning, thinking, and research on campus. Even a cursory reading of the field's extensive literature shows that interdisciplinarity in all its breadth and complexity cannot be ignored or folded into narrow disciplinary structures. At a minimum, there is a need for a core of interdisciplinary courses whose express purpose is to do the following: (1) define interdisciplinary studies and identify its key concepts, (2) trace the intellectual origins of the field, (3) explain the theory undergirding the field, (4) lay out the research process, and (5) introduce students to the field's important literature.

The Emergence of Interdisciplinary Studies as an Academic Field

The book attempts to show that interdisciplinary studies can rightfully stake its claim as an academic field that deserves its place in the Academy alongside the disciplines. The criteria necessary to substantiate this claim are already in place: There is a consensus understanding of what interdisciplinarity is; there is an integrated model of the research process; there is a body of theory underlying its approach to learning, thinking, and producing knowledge; there is a growing community of interdisciplinary experts; and there is an extensive and growing body of literature that is explicitly interdisciplinary. This literature includes theory, program administration, curriculum design, research process, pedagogy, assessment, student learning, and research on specific problems. Those claiming the mantle of interdisciplinarity should familiarize themselves, at least cursorily, with this literature.

The Role of the Disciplines

The book addresses the sometimes contentious issue of what role the disciplines should play in interdisciplinary work. The disciplines provide the depth while interdisciplinarity provides the breadth and the integration.

Interdisciplinarity stands as a counterweight to the reductionist tendencies of the disciplines. This book is one way that interdisciplinarians can communicate to their disciplinary colleagues that interdisciplinarity is not about competing with the disciplines, or about replacing them, but rather about working with them. On this point, the literature is clear: interdisciplinarity needs the disciplines, and the disciplines, by their growing involvement in interdisciplinary research, need interdisciplinarity. This mutual dependence warns against an interdisciplinarity that is overenthusiastic, overconfident, and overwhelming.

The Role and Nature of Integration

The book discusses the role and nature of integration and comes down on the side of the "integrationists," who argue that integration is a key characteristic of interdisciplinary studies. The objects of integration are the defining elements of disciplinary perspectives—i.e., theories, concepts, and assumptions—that are expressed in disciplinary insights pertaining to a particular problem or question. Minimizing, obscuring, or eliminating integration from a conception of interdisciplinarity hollows out the concept of interdisciplinarity and makes it far easier for critics to argue that interdisciplinarity "is whatever we say it is." It also makes problematic the production and assessment of interdisciplinary work.

The Product and Purpose of Integration

The book especially explains the product of integration, which is the interdisciplinary understanding or cognitive advancement produced by integration. The development of this concept and its underlying theory is of major importance to interdisciplinary research for three reasons. First, it makes possible a more rigorous and more granular assessment of interdisciplinary work through the use of rubrics based upon course and program learning outcomes. Second, the enlarged conception of interdisciplinary understanding effectively connects interdisciplinary work to the real world in new and creative ways because the products of the research effort include work that is practical, purposeful, and performance oriented. Third, the creative development of the concept of interdisciplinary understanding on the local level has important implications for service learning, internship experiences, and student projects.

The Cognitive Outcomes of Interdisciplinarity

Lastly, the book briefly discusses the cognitive abilities, outcomes, and underlying theory associated with interdisciplinary thinking and research.

Students, academics, and administrators should be aware of how the interdisciplinary approach to problem solving and decision making involved in the research process differs from the learning that occurs in many traditional disciplinary contexts. A major recent finding of learning theory, for example, shows that with repeated exposure to interdisciplinary thought, students develop more mature epistemological beliefs, enhanced critical thinking ability, metacognitive skills, and an understanding of the relations among perspectives derived from different disciplines. These are critical cognitive abilities that students need when entering the professions or pursuing graduate study.

For interdisciplinary studies, or interdisciplinarity, to fulfill its potential to advance knowledge in the new century, several developments need to occur, each of which this book encourages. One of these is the design of an introductory course that provides students with a clear understanding of what interdisciplinary studies is: its distinctive approach to learning, thinking, and producing knowledge; its intellectual origins and present manifestations; how it is an academic field; some of its key concepts; the cognitive abilities that interdisciplinary study fosters; and how these abilities are of practical value to the student in the Academy and in real-world settings. A course with these objectives stated as student learning outcomes will enhance students' identity as interdisciplinarians early on and provide critical foundational information needed in subsequent courses in the major.

A second need is the development of a course on how to do interdisciplinary research. This course should be included in each program's required core, to be taken immediately *after* completing an introduction to interdisciplinary studies course and *before* taking advanced courses requiring substantive research. Such a course on the interdisciplinary research process (and its underlying theory) would show students how their interdisciplinary work differs from disciplinary work and prepare them for doing research and writing in advanced theme-based or problem-based courses. It would allow later courses to go into more depth about the nature of interdisciplinarity in various contexts and address conceptual, theoretical, and methodological issues with greater sophistication. Adding such a course would enhance the program's academic standing among disciplinarians who highly value research methods courses. At a minimum, focusing more intently on how to do interdisciplinary research would mute disciplinary criticism of interdisciplinary work for its lack of rigor and achieve much-needed balance between disciplinary depth and interdisciplinary breadth.

A third need is to inform faculty, undergraduate and graduate, who are new to the field or who have been doing interdisciplinarity on their own but have not had time to immerse themselves in the literature or to keep up with that literature. With a few exceptions (e.g., American studies), most graduate faculty teaching in interdisciplinary programs were themselves trained in a discipline and picked up an interdisciplinary approach later in their careers. Moreover, they typically developed their own idiosyncratic style of interdisciplinary research because the professional literature, until recently, had little to offer them. Some may not have reexamined the professional literature in recent years, and thus have missed its dramatic increase in sophistication, depth of analysis, and thus, utility. In part, the burgeoning of the professional literature has been made possible by a growing consensus on the definition and nature of interdisciplinarity itself. Their graduate students, however, are likely to seek out the professional literature in conducting interdisciplinary research. Consequently, some graduate faculty may be increasingly directing the research of students who are more familiar with the professional literature on interdisciplinarity than they are. This gap needs to close.

Finally, there is need for more research that is explicitly interdisciplinary. A wide range of complex problems require the combined efforts of many disciplines. Indeed, breakthroughs of lasting importance are increasingly the product of cross fertilization between different knowledge formations and research cultures. What the interdisciplinarian brings to a complex problem is the recognition that multiple perspectives are needed, the knowledge of which tools to apply, and an understanding of how best to use them. It is hoped that the integrated research model described in this book will inform and challenge a new generation of students and academicians to engage in this much-needed work.

Appendix _____

Interdisciplinary Resources

_____ **Associations**

Association for Integrative Studies, http://www.units.muohio.edu/aisorg/

The Association for Integrative Studies (AIS) is an interdisciplinary professional organization founded in 1979 to promote the interchange of ideas among scholars and administrators in all of the arts and sciences on intellectual and organizational issues related to furthering integrative studies. The Web site has materials that may be downloaded at no charge, including the AIS journal, course syllabi, a directory of doctoral programs, guidelines for accreditation in interdisciplinary general education, interdisciplinary writing assessment profiles, and detailed information on the core AIS list of recommended publications at http://www.units.muohio.edu/aisorg/pubs/aisbib.html. The AIS journal *Issues in Integrative Studies* publishes articles on a wide range of interdisciplinary topics such as assessment, program development, theory, pedagogy, the research process, special reports on the status of and challenges to interdisciplinary studies programs, and topics of current interest such as euthanasia.

_____

AUTHOR'S NOTE: The information in this Appendix is adapted from Klein, J. T. (2003), Thinking about interdisciplinarity: A primer for practice, *Colorado School of Mines Quarterly, 103*(1), 101–114; Klein, J. T., & Newell, W. H. (2002), Strategies for using interdisciplinary resources across K–16, *Issues in Integrative Studies, 20,* 139–160. I have also drawn on Joan B. Fiscella and Stacey E. Kimmel (Eds.) (1999), *Interdisciplinary education: A guide to resources,* New York: College Board. I thank Julie Thompson Klein for making available her "Interdisciplinary Searching Module," and C. Diane Shepelwich, Interdisciplinary Librarian at the University of Texas at Arlington, for providing the information on databases and online resources.

New Directions: Science, Humanities, Policy, http://www.ndsciencehumanitiespolicy.org/

This site focuses on interdisciplinary approaches to problems in research, education, and society.

Association for General and Liberal Studies, http://www.bsu.edu/web/agls/

AGLS is a community of learners—faculty, students, administrators, alumni—intent upon improving general and liberal education at two-year and four-year institutions. AGLS identifies and supports the benefits of students' liberal education attained through general education programs. As an advocate, AGLS tracks changes in general education and liberal studies and sponsors professional activities that promote successful teaching, curricular innovation, and effective learning.

Databases

Academic Search Complete

The world's largest scholarly, multidiscipline, full text database, Academic Search Complete offers critical information from many sources found in no other database, including peer-reviewed full text articles for almost 4,600 periodical titles in more than 100 scholarly journals dating back to 1965, or the first issue published (whichever is more recent). Areas of study include social sciences, humanities, education, computer sciences, engineering, language and linguistics, arts and literature, medical sciences, ethnic studies, etc.

ERIC

The ERIC (Educational Resources Information Center) database is sponsored by the U.S. Department of Education to provide extensive access to education-related literature. The database corresponds to two printed journals: *Resources in Education* (RIE) and *Current Index to Journals in Education* (CIJE). Both journals provide access to some 14,000 documents and over 20,000 journal articles per year. In addition, ERIC provides coverage of conferences, meetings, government documents, theses, dissertations, reports, audiovisual media, bibliographies, directories, books and monographs.

H-NET

A self-described "international interdisciplinary organization" that provides teachers and scholars forums for the exchange of ideas and resources in the arts, humanities, and social sciences. The database includes over 100 free edited Listservs and Web sites that coordinates communication in a wide variety of disciplinary and interdisciplinary fields as well as subject and topic.

JSTOR

JSTOR (Journal Storage) is an archive collection of over 620 full text scholarly journals primarily from university presses and professional society publishers. Subject areas include African American studies, anthropology, Asian studies, botany, ecology, economics, education, finance, folklore, history, history of science technology, language literature, mathematics, philosophy, political science, population studies, public policy administration, science, Slavic studies, sociology, statistics.

ProQuest Dissertations and Theses

The Dissertations Abstracts database contains citations for dissertations and theses from institutions in North America and Europe. Citations for dissertations published from 1980 forward also include abstracts. Citations for master's theses from 1988 forward include abstracts. Titles published from 1997 forward have 24-page previews and are available as full text PDF documents.

Web of Knowledge

Abstracts and citations in ISI's Science Citation Index Expanded, Social Sciences Citation Index, and Arts & Humanities Citation Index. Searches by subject term, author name, journal title, or author affiliation, also for articles that cite an author or work. Along with an article's abstract, its cited references (bibliography) are listed for further searching.

WorldCat

Books and other materials in libraries worldwide. WorldCat contains more than 32 million records describing items owned by libraries around the world.

Online Resources

CISMI Carleton Interdisciplinary Science and Math Initiative

http://serc.carleton.edu/cismi/literature/index.html

This site has compiled literature and resources to support interdisciplinary and integrative teaching activities, with an emphasis on science and math. Areas include research on expert interdisciplinary thinking and practice, assessing interdisciplinary work in college, strategies for interdisciplinary teaching, integrative learning, national reports, and books.

Integrative Learning: Opportunities to Connect

*http://www.carnegiefoundation.org/files/elibrary/
integrativelearning/index.htm*

Integrative Learning: Opportunities to Connect is a national project sponsored by the Association of American Colleges and Universities (AAC&U) and The Carnegie Foundation for the Advancement of Teaching. Aimed at promoting integrative learning in undergraduate education, this three-year project worked with 10 campuses to develop and assess advanced models and strategies to foster students' abilities to integrate their learning over time.

Interdisciplinary Studies Project

http://www.pz.harvard.edu/interdisciplinary/index.html

The project examines the challenges and opportunities of interdisciplinary work carried out by experts, faculty, and students in well-recognized research and education contexts. Building on an empirical understanding of cognitive and social dimensions of interdisciplinary work, the project develops practical tools to guide quality interdisciplinary education.

Interdisciplines

http://www.interdisciplines.org/

Interdisciplines is a project aimed at enhancing interdisciplinary research and exchanges in the social sciences and the humanities.

Journals

There are many interdisciplinary journals, a few of which appear here. Articles on interdisciplinary topics such as interdisciplinary resources and interdisciplinary curriculum design are scattered across professional journals, some of which periodically devote special issues to interdisciplinarity. Locating these requires searching databases using keyword searching and Boolean Search Strategy.

Ecology and Society, http://www.ecologyandsociety.org/

Issues in Integrative Studies, http://www.units.muohio.edu/aisorg/pubs/issues/toclist.html

Journal of Interdisciplinary History, http://www.jstor.org/journals/00221953.html

Sustainability: Science, Practice, and Policy, http://ejournal.nbii.org/index.html

Search Strategies

Locating resources for interdisciplinary purposes is typically not a straight-forward process for interdisciplinary studies students. A metaphor descriptive of the challenge of identifying and locating relevant resources is suggested in the title of a special issue of *Library Trends, 45*(2), "Navigating Among the Disciplines: The Library and Interdisciplinary Inquiry." Students must "navigate" across multiple knowledge forums to locate relevant information. Before using the following approaches, students must state the problem or question they are investigating as clearly and as concisely as possible.

There are three approaches or strategies to navigation. The first is to use the traditional method of keyword searching. The typical search box options are author, title, keyword, or subject. This approach works well when the author and title of the article are already known. If this information is not known, then keyword and subject searching should be used. For example, if the problem under investigation is "The Causes of Childhood Obesity: An Interdisciplinary Analysis," the primary search term is "obesity." The search will identify numerous articles written by experts from several disciplines. The student must identify the disciplines these writers represent because interdisciplinary research projects typically involve analyzing a problem from three or more disciplinary perspectives.

The second approach is the Boolean Search Strategy. This strategy is useful when it is necessary to narrow the number of references to those that are most relevant to the problem. For example, a keyword search of the problem, "The Causes of Suicide Terrorism: An Interdisciplinary Analysis," would focus on "terrorism" and "suicide" because these terms are at the heart of the problem. However, navigating databases using just one, or even both, of them will yield an overwhelming number of references. The value of using the Boolean Search Strategy when faced with an abundance of resources is this: It refines the search by creating a "string" of terms that frame the search more precisely. The more one refines the search, the better the results.

The Boolean Search Strategy is based on the words AND, OR, and NOT. The basic formula for combining keyword and Boolean Search Strategy is as follows:

_____ and _____ and [or _____] *[Fill in your search terms.]*

Inserting the terms "suicide" and "terrorism" connects the two terms and narrows the number of relevant resources. A more refined search can be achieved by adding another term, say, "Islamic," to the string.

Another way to narrow the number of resources is to use the NOT feature of the Boolean Search Strategy. For example, if the problem is youth gun violence, inserting the key terms "youth" "gun" and "violence" into the string will produce a substantial number of references. Adding a restrictive term, such as the name of a city, or type of violence, such as homicide, into the string after NOT will produce a more precise result.

Klein (2003) notes that different databases respond in different ways, so students should be prepared to "play" with the terms in the search string. If a particular term is not yielding good results, use a synonym, consult the thesaurus of a particular database, or check the list of common terms in the Library of Congress (LOC) classifications. If the student encounters further problems, a librarian should be consulted.

The third approach is Federated Searching. This tool is a boon for interdisciplinarians because it enables access to multiple databases at a single keystroke. For example, the database ABI/Inform allows Federated Searching.

Regardless of the strategy used, achieving the most relevant results requires that students use precise keywords and Boolean logic, and this requires a clear statement of the problem or question.

Core Resources on Interdisciplinary Studies

Assessment and Curriculum Design

Boix Mansilla, V. (2005). Assessing student work at disciplinary crossroads. *Change, 37*, 14–21.

Kain, D. L. (1994). Designing interdisciplinary courses. In J. T. Klein & W. G. Doty (Eds.), *Interdisciplinary studies today* (pp. 35–51). New Directions for Teaching and Learning #58. San Francisco: Jossey-Bass.

Repko, A. F. (2007). Interdisciplinary curriculum design. *Academic Exchange Quarterly, 11*(1), 130–137.

Shapiro, D. F. (2003). Facilitating holistic curriculum development. *Assessment & Evaluation in Higher Education, 28*(4), 423–434.

Definitions of Interdisciplinarity

Klein, J. T. (1990). *Interdisciplinarity: History, theory and practice.* Detroit: Wayne State University Press.

Klein, J. T. (1996). *Crossing boundaries: Knowledge, disciplinarities, and interdisciplinarities.* Charlottesville: University Press of Virginia.

Klein, J. T. (1999). *Mapping interdisciplinary studies, The Academy in transition series, Vol. 2.* Washington, DC: Association of American Colleges and Universities.

Klein, J. T., & Newell, W. H. (1996). Advancing interdisciplinary studies. In J. G. Gaff, J. L. Ratcliff, & Associates (Eds.), *Handbook of the undergraduate curriculum: A comprehensive guide to purposes, structures, practices, and change* (pp. 393–415). San Francisco: Jossey-Bass.

Lattuca, L. R. (1998). Professionalizing interdisciplinarity: A literature review and research agenda. In W. H. Newell (Ed.), *Interdisciplinarity: Essays from the literature.* New York: The College Board.

Lattuca, L. R. (2001). *Creating interdisciplinarity: Interdisciplinary research and teaching among college and university faculty.* Nashville, TN: Vanderbilt University Press.

Turner, S. (2000). What are disciplines? And how is interdisciplinarity different? In P. Weingart & N. Stehr (Eds.), *Practising interdisciplinarity* (pp. 46–65). Toronto: University of Toronto Press.

Pedagogy

Davis, J. (1995). *Interdisciplinary courses and team teaching: New arrangements for learning.* Phoenix, AZ: Oryx Press.

Haynes, C. (Ed.). (2002). *Innovations in interdisciplinary teaching.* American Council on Education. Series on Higher Education. Westport, CT: Oryx Press/Greenhaven Press.

Kain, D. L. (2005). Integrative learning and interdisciplinary studies. *Peer Review,* 7(4), 8–10.

Klein, J. T. (Ed.). (2002). *Interdisciplinary education in K–12 and college: A foundation for K–16 dialogue.* New York: The College Board.

Newell, W. H. (2001). Powerful pedagogies. In B. L. Smith & J. McCann (Eds.), *Reinventing ourselves: Interdisciplinary education, collaborative learning and experimentation in higher education.* Bolton, MA: Anker Press.

Newell, W. H. (2006). Interdisciplinary integration by undergraduates. *Issues in Integrative Studies, 24,* 89–111.

Repko, A. F. (2006). Disciplining interdisciplinary studies: The case for textbooks. *Issues in Integrative Studies, 24,* 112–142.

Seabury, M. B. (Ed.). (1999). *Interdisciplinary general education: Questioning outside the lines.* New York: The College Board.

Resources

Fiscella, J. B., & Kimmel, S. E. (Eds.). (1999). *Interdisciplinary education: A guide to resources.* New York: College Entrance Examination Board.

Fiscella, J. B. & Kimmel, S. E. (1999). Interdisciplinary information searching: Moving beyond discipline-based resources. In J. Fiscella & S. Kimmel (Eds.), *Interdisciplinary education: A guide to resources* (pp. 293–309). New York: College Entrance Examination Board.

Klein, J. T. (2006, March/April). Resources for interdisciplinary studies. *Change.* Retrieved from http://research.wayne.edu/idre/articles/CHANGE_article_012007.pdf

Klein, J. T., & Newell, W. H. (2002). Strategies for using interdisciplinary resources across K–16. *Issues in Integrative Studies, 20,* 139–160.

Theory

Boix Mansilla, V. (2006). Interdisciplinary work at the frontier: An empirical examination of expert epistemologies. *Issues in Integrative Studies, 24,* 1–31.

Newell, W. H. (2001). A theory of interdisciplinary studies. *Issues in Integrative Studies, 19,* 1–25.

Newell, W. H. (2001). Reply to respondents to "A theory of interdisciplinary studies." *Issues in Integrative Studies, 19,* 135–146.

Spooner, M. (2004). Generating integration and complex understanding: Exploring the use of creative thinking tools within interdisciplinary studies. *Issues in Integrative Studies, 22,* 85–111.

Programs and Course Models

Edwards, A. F. (1996). *Interdisciplinary undergraduate programs: A directory* (2nd ed.). Acton, MA: Copley.

Research Practice

Creso, M. (2007). Interdisciplinary strategies in U.S. research universities. *Higher Education,* DOI 10.1007/s10734-007-9073-5. Retrieved from http://www.springerlink.com/content/k2186651n2147737/fulltext.pdf

National Academies. (2005). *Facilitating interdisciplinary research.* Washington, DC: National Academies Press.

Newell, W. H. (2007). Decision making in interdisciplinary studies. In G. Morçöl (Ed.), *Handbook of decision making* (pp. 245–264). New York: Marcel-Dekker.

Repko, A. F. (2005). *Interdisciplinary practice: A student guide to research and writing.* Boston: Pearson Custom.

Rhoten, D. (2004). Interdisciplinary research: Trend or transition. *Items & Issues, 5,* 6–11.

Seabury, M. B. (2004). Scholarship about interdisciplinarity: Some possibilities and guidelines. *Issues in Integrative Studies, 22,* 52–84.

Other Works

Augsburg, T. (2006). *Becoming interdisciplinary: An introduction to interdisciplinary studies* (2nd ed.). Dubuque, IA: Kendall/Hunt.

Czechowski, J. (2003). An integrated approach to liberal learning. *Peer Review, 5*(4), 4–7.

Fiscella, J. (1996, Fall). Bibliography as an interdisciplinary service. *Library Trends, 45*(2), 280–295.

Frodeman, R., Klein, J. T., & Mitcham, C. (Eds.). (in press). *Oxford handbook on interdisciplinarity.* http://www.ndsciencehumanitiespolicy.org/oup2/index.html

Graff, G. (1991, February 13). Colleges are depriving students of a connected view of scholarship. *The Chronicle of Higher Education,* 48.

Huber, M. T., Hutchings, P., & Gale, R. (2005). Integrative learning for liberal education. *Peer Review, 7*(4), 4–7.

Kain, D. L. (1993). Cabbages—and kings: Research directions in integrated/interdisciplinary curriculum. *Journal of Educational Thought/Revue de la Pensee Educative, 27*(3), 312–331.

Roberts, J. A. (2004). *Riding the momentum: Interdisciplinary research centers to interdisciplinary graduate programs.* Paper presented at the July 2004 Merrill conference.

Walker, D. (1996). *Integrative education.* Eugene, OR: ERIC Clearinghouse on Educational Management.

Glossary of
Key Terms _____

Abstract thinking: A higher order cognitive ability that enables one to understand and express an interdisciplinary understanding or meaning of a problem symbolically in terms of a metaphor, or to compare a hard to understand and complex phenomenon to a symbol that is simple, familiar, and easy to understand. [2:45]

Adequacy (disciplinary): The student borrower does not claim expertise or professional command of all the disciplines used, but rather acquires a sufficient understanding of each discipline's cognitive map and is thus able to identify the insights, concepts, theories, methods necessary to understand a particular problem, process, or phenomenon. [5:124]

Antidisciplinary: A preference for a more "open" understanding of "knowledge" and "evidence" that would include "lived experience," testimonials, oral traditions, and interpretation of those traditions by elders. [2:39]

Association for Integrative Studies (AIS): A professional organization whose purpose is to study interdisciplinary methodology, theory, curricula, and administration. [2:37]

Assumption: Something taken for granted, a supposition, a principle that underlies the discipline as a whole and its overall perspective on reality. This principle is accepted as the truth upon which the discipline's theories, concepts, methods, and curriculum are based. [4:89]

Bilingualism: A popular, but inappropriate, metaphor for interdisciplinary work that implies mastery of two complete languages that rarely, if ever, occurs. It also glosses over the challenges inherent in integrating the insight from the two disciplines using those languages. [1:24]

"Blurring of the genres": The lively trade in concepts, theories, and methods, and even subject matter, engaged in by the humanities and the social sciences. [3:72]

Border disciplinarity: Exists when at least two disciplines focusing on the same problem create an overlapping area between them. These disciplines, each with its own perspectives, insights, assumptions, concepts, theories, and methods, make a productive contribution to understanding the problem because each has studied the problem. [6:152]

Borrowing (from the disciplines): Calls for having a minimum understanding of each relevant discipline's cognitive map (i.e., its overall perspective and its defining elements including its assumptions, epistemology, basic concepts, theories, and research methods) and carefully evaluating this material in terms of its credibility (Is it peer-reviewed?), timeliness (Is it time-sensitive?), and relevance (Does it illuminate some part of the problem?). [8:192]

Boundary crossing: A process of moving across knowledge formations for the purpose of achieving an enlarged understanding. [1:22]

Boundary work: Occurs as researchers detach a subject or object from existing disciplinary frameworks, fill gaps in knowledge from lack of attention to the category, and if the research attains critical mass, redraw boundaries by constituting new knowledge space and new professional roles. [1:5]

Breadth (interdisciplinary): The ability to make connections between not only the defining elements of one discipline but also the elements of all the relevant disciplines. [5:125]

Bridge building: The borrowing of tools and methods between disciplines. [1:23]

Burden of comprehension: Having a minimum understanding of each relevant discipline's cognitive map. [8:192]

Categories of traditional disciplines: Include the natural sciences, the social sciences, the humanities, and the applied professions. [1:4]

Classical division of knowledge: The hierarchy established by Aristotle between the different academic subjects with the theoretical subjects of theology, mathematics, and physics on top; the practical subjects of ethics and politics in the middle; and the productive subjects of the fine arts, poetics, and engineering at the bottom. [2-31]

Classification approach: The linking of all phenomena to particular disciplines, provided that one knows the discipline's general perspective and the phenomena it typically studies. [4:84]

Close reading: A fundamental method of modern criticism that involves careful analysis of a text and close attention to individual words, syntax, and the order in which sentences and ideas unfold. [10:257]

Cognitive decentering: The intellectual capacity to consider a variety of other perspectives and thus perceive reality more accurately, process information more systematically, and solve problems more efficiently. The term "decentering" denotes the ability to shift deliberately among alternative perspectives and to bring each to bear upon a complex problem. [2:40]

Cognitive discord: Disagreement among the discipline's practitioners over the defining elements of the discipline. [3:56]

Cognitive fluidity: The increasing boundary crossing between disciplines. [3:57]

Cognitive map: A discipline's cognitive map is synonymous with its overall perspective and its defining elements, including its assumptions, epistemology, basic concepts, theories, and research methods. [8:192]

College: A large unit within a university consisting of a cluster of related disciplines. [3:51]

Common ground theory (cognitive psychology): Postulates that "every act of communication presumes a common cognitive frame of reference between the partners of interaction called the common ground." The theory postulates further that "all contributions to the process of mutual understanding serve to establish or ascertain and continually maintain this common ground" (Bromme, 2000, p. 119). This theory applies to both oral and written communication. [11:273]

Communicative competence: The ability to comprehend and translate terminology that is discipline-specific. [2:45]

Complexity: As applied to interdisciplinary research, complexity means that the problem has several components and that each component has a different disciplinary character. [6:152]

Concept: A symbol expressed in language that represents a phenomenon or an abstract idea generalized from particular instances. [3:61]

Concept/principle map: Shows meaningful relationships between the parts of the problem and requires that we think through all of the parts of the problem as well as understand how these behave or function. [7:163]

Conceptual bridging (or overarching conceptual framework): A single concept, principle, or law that accounts for phenomena typically studied by a broad range of disciplines. [5:126]

Conceptual interdisciplinarity: Emphasizes the integration of knowledge and the importance of posing questions that have no single disciplinary basis. This notion of interdisciplinarity often implies a critique of disciplinary understandings of the problem, as in the case of cultural studies, feminist, and postmodern approaches. [1:18]

Contested space or **contested terrain:** Problems or questions that are the focus of several disciplines. [1:6]

Creative breakthroughs: Often occur when different disciplinary perspectives and previously unrelated ideas are brought together. [2:30]

Creativity: A process that involves rethinking underlying premises, assumptions, or values, not just tracing out the implications of agreed-upon premises, assumptions, or values. Creativity involves iterative (i.e., repetitive) and heuristic (i.e., experimental) activity. [2:46]

Creole: A new first language among a hybrid community of knowers. [1:24]

Critical humanities: The newer interdisciplinary fields—feminism, critical theory, postcolonial studies, culture studies, gender studies, queer theory, postmodernism, poststructuralism, deconstructionism, etc.—focus not so much on human culture itself as on our knowledge of it and on disciplinary knowledge in general. [3:72]

Critical interdisciplinarity: Aims to transform existing structures of knowledge and education, raising questions of value and purpose. [1:17]

Critical social theory: A major theoretical perspective of sociology which looks at conflict, competition, change, and constraint within a society. [3:69–70]

Cultural analysis: A critical approach that draws on a specific set of collaborating disciplines that include history, psychology, philosophy, literature, linguistics, and art history in seeking to understand a text or object of inquiry. Though cultural analysis is inclusive of the perspectives of several disciplines (and thus particularly valuable to the interdisciplinarian), it is dominated by postmodernism and thus misses the advantages of the modernist approach while suffering the disadvantages of the postmodernist approach. [8:208]

Curriculum: A generally recognized core of knowledge that is subdivided into specific courses. [1:7]

Decision making: A uniquely human activity necessitated by the prevalence of complex problems, decision making is the cognitive ability to choose after considering alternatives. [6:137–138]

Defining elements of a discipline's perspective: The phenomena it studies, the kind of data it collects, the assumptions it makes about the natural and human world, its epistemology or rules about what constitutes evidence or "proof," its theories about the causes and behaviors of certain phenomena, and its methods (the way it gathers, applies, and produces new knowledge). [3:58]

Depth (interdisciplinary): To successfully engage in the first half of the interdisciplinary research process (i.e., drawing in disciplines and their insights) requires developing adequacy or sufficiency in each discipline relevant to the problem (the subject of Chapter 8). The depth required for engaging in the second half of the research process (i.e., integrating insights) involves identifying conflicts between insights and locating their sources, creating common ground, integrating insights, producing an interdisciplinary understanding of the problem, and testing it. [5:124]

Dialectical thinking: Any systematic reasoning or argument that places opposing ideas side by side for the purpose of seeking to resolve their conflict. It is a method of determining the truth of any assertion by testing it against arguments that might negate it. [2:45]

Disciplinarity: The system of knowledge specialties called disciplines. [3:51–52]

Disciplinary: Relating to a particular field of study or specialization. [1:5]

Disciplinary adequacy: Minimum understanding of the cognitive map or the defining elements of each of the disciplines, interdisciplines, and schools of thought relevant to a particular problem. [2:39]

Disciplinary bias: Using words and phrases that connect the problem to a particular discipline. [6:145]

Disciplinary categories: Broad categories of related disciplines that typically include the sciences, the social sciences, the humanities, and the applied professions such as engineering, nursing, education, and business. [3:52]

Disciplinary decisions: Include determining what disciplines are relevant to the problem, which disciplinary elements (i.e., phenomena, data, assumptions, epistemologies, concepts, theories, and methods) pertain to the problem, how many and what kinds of sources to collect, how to develop adequacy in each of the relevant disciplines, and how to analyze the problem, identifying weaknesses of insights into it. [10:247]

Disciplinary depth: The intensive focus on a discipline or subdiscipline. [1:9]

Disciplinary inadequacy: The view that the disciplines by themselves are inadequate to address complex problems. [2:39]

Disciplinary insights: Views of disciplinary experts on a particular problem. [1:12]

Disciplinary jargon: Terminology unique to a discipline. [6:145]

Disciplinary knowledge: Includes (1) an understanding of the overall perspective of each relevant discipline and (2) adequacy in each discipline's defining elements that pertain to the problem. These elements and the discipline's overall perspective are generally reflected in its literature, from which insights into particular problems are drawn. Disciplinary knowledge is produced in the form of books, journals, databases, and conferences—all of which are vetted by the disciplines. [5:126]

Disciplinary method: Means the procedure or process or technique used by the discipline's practitioners to conduct, organize, and present research. [8:200]

Disciplinary perspective: The ensemble of a discipline's defining elements that include phenomena and data, assumptions, epistemology, concepts, theory, and methods. [3:58]

Disciplinary perspective (in a general sense): Each discipline's characteristic view of that portion of reality that it is interested in. [3:53]

Disciplinary reductionism: Ignoring what is not of interest to the discipline. [12:301]

Disciplinary specialization: The focus on a particular portion of reality that is of interest to the discipline to the exclusion of other portions of reality. [2:28]

Disciplinary understanding: Using disciplinary knowledge and modes of thinking to create products, solve problems, and offer explanations that echo the work of disciplinary experts. [1:21]

Discipline: A particular branch of learning or body of knowledge whose defining elements distinguish it from other knowledge formations. [1:4]

Discourse: The dominant language (spoken and/or written) used by a community to discuss or transact business of any kind. The knowledge of a discourse—its vocabulary, concepts, and rules—constitutes power. [4:99]

Elements: The constituent parts of a discipline that provide its essential and formative character. [4:83]

Empiricism: Holds that all knowledge is derived from our perceptions (transmitted by the five senses of touch, smell, taste, hearing, and sight), experience, and observations. Observation is required to back up what we have perceived. [3:77]

Enlightenment: A seventeenth- and eighteenth-century Europe-wide intellectual movement that challenged the notion of the unity of knowledge and emphasized the progress of human knowledge through the powers of reason and rationality. [2:32–33]

Epistemic norms of a discipline: Agreements about how researchers should select their data, evaluate their experiments, and judge their theories. [4:94]

Epistemological pluralism: The deep divide between the modernist and newer critical approaches to knowledge formation, especially within the humanities, which makes it problematic to associate a particular epistemology with a particular discipline. [4:95]

Epistemological positivism: A "law and order" approach that views any flexibility in matters epistemological as a guise for relativism or at least a mask for being weak or lacking conviction in expressing one's views. [4:98]

Epistemological postmodernists: View epistemology as "totally arbitrary, being nothing more than a political power game to legitimize one's favored views" (Bell, 1998, p. 103). [4:98]

Epistemological self-reflexivity: Awareness of the advantages and disadvantages of a favored epistemological approach, as well as the advantages and disadvantages of other approaches with which one is perhaps less familiar. [4:95]

Epistemology: The branch of philosophy that studies how one knows what is true and how one validates truth. [4:93]

Expert interdisciplinarian: One who is able to integrate the input of others to address an issue, which may include coordinating team members. [2:44]

Extension: An integrative technique that addresses conflict between disciplinary concepts or assumptions by extending the meaning of an idea beyond the domain of one discipline into the domain of another discipline. [11:286]

Feedback: Corrective information about a decision, operation, event, or problem that compels the researcher to revisit an earlier phase of the project. This corrective information typically comes from previously overlooked scholarship or other knowledge formations. [6:143]

Feedback loop: Requires the researcher to periodically revisit earlier activity. [2:46]

Feminism: Both a social movement and a grand theoretical perspective on society. [3:75–76]

Four "posts:" Intellectual movements that have transformed modern thought, including postpositivism, poststructuralism, postmodernism, and postcolonialism. [2:28]

Functionalism (or its most recent reincarnation in systems theory): A major theoretical perspective of sociology that focuses on the functional contributions of each part of society and tends to be associated with a focus on order in society and lesser attention to conflict in society. [3:69]

General education movement: A post–World War I reform movement that sought to solve the problems of the lack of national unity and eroding cohesiveness of general education by reemphasizing the arts and the values associated with classical humanism, which emphasized wholeness of knowledge and of human nature. [2:35]

Generic skills: Cognitive functions such as recognizing and defining problems, analyzing the structure of an argument, assessing the relationship of facts, assumptions, and conclusions, and performing "hypothetico-deductive processes." [5:127]

Grand theory (or grand narratives or school of thought): A general analysis that attempts to explore and explain interrelationships between phenomena that extend beyond the borders of two or more disciplines, such as Marxism, feminism, and rational choice. Each grand theory or school of thought is like a discipline only in that it has its own perspective, assumptions, epistemology, concepts, and methods. [4:101]

Heuristic: An aid to understanding or discovery or learning. The heuristic method places the student in the role of the discoverer of knowledge with the instructor intervening only to suggest a certain methodology for approaching the problem. [6:138]

Historical background (of the problem): Along with explaining how and why the problem developed, the historical background may also include explaining how the disciplines have approached the problem over time and how they developed concepts, theories, and methods to understand, but how these have failed to provided either a comprehensive understanding of the problem or a solution to it, thus necessitating an interdisciplinary approach. [7:176]

Holistic thinking: A skill characteristic of interdisciplinarians that involves thinking about the problem as part of a complete system. Aspects of holistic thinking include inclusiveness that accepts similarities as well as differences, comprehensiveness that balances disciplinary breadth and disciplinary depth (disciplinary specialties privilege depth over breadth), ability to associate ideas and information from several disciplines and connect these to the problem, creativity that is dissatisfied with the partial insights available through individual disciplinary specialties and that produces an interdisciplinary understanding, and metaphorical thinking that visually expresses the resultant integration. [2:46]

Humanities: Express human aspirations, interpret and assess human achievements and experience, and seek layers of meaning and richness of detail in written texts, artifacts, and cultural practices. [3:71]

Hypothetico-deductive processes: Involve proposing hypotheses and testing their acceptability or falsity by determining whether their logical consequences are consistent with observed data. [5:127]

Ideographic theory: Posits a relationship only under specified conditions, and ideographic researchers wish to explain the relevance of a theoretical proposition in a constrained set of circumstances. [8:198]

Inclusive: In the context of interdisciplinary research, the term refers not to the quantity of disciplinary insights but to the quality and diversity of these insights. [7:179]

In-depth literature search: Involves identifying all expert insights relevant to the problem and may also involve gathering information on the problem that is not of interest to the disciplines or is overlooked by them but is nevertheless relevant to the inquiry. [7:175–176]

Insight: A scholarly contribution to the clear understanding of a problem. Insights into a problem can be produced either by disciplinary experts or by interdisciplinarians. [1:12]

Instrumental interdisciplinarity: A pragmatic approach that focuses on research and practical problem solving. [1:17]

Integrated insight (or interdisciplinary insight): The new understanding that is the result of the integrative process and encompasses the conflicting disciplinary insights. [5:118]

Integration of knowledge: Identifying and blending knowledge from relevant disciplines to produce an interdisciplinary understanding of a particular problem or intellectual question that is limited in time and to a particular context that would not be possible by relying solely on a single disciplinary approach. [1:19]

Integrative field: An effort to explore important dimensions of human experience and understanding in the spaces between disciplinary boundaries or the places where they cross, overlap, divide, or dissolve. [2:30]

Integrative knowledge: The ability to identify the disciplinary elements relevant to the problem, identify conflicts between disciplinary insights and evaluate their sources, apply the appropriate integrative technique(s) to create or discover common ground, integrate these conflicting insights by applying the common ground theory, concept, principle, or value to them, and produce the new understanding or cognitive advancement. [5:130]

Integrative mind-set: Cultivating these five qualities of mind: (1) seeking what is useful even if it is problematic; (2) thinking inclusively and integratively, not exclusively; (3) being responsive to each perspective but beholden to none (not allowing the student's strength in a particular discipline to influence the student's treatment of other relevant disciplines with which the student is less familiar); (4) striving for balance among disciplinary perspectives; and (5) maintaining intellectual flexibility. These five integrative qualities correspond to several of the traits and skills of interdisciplinarians identified in Chapter 2. [5:130]

Integrative skills: Include (1) familiarity with models of integration, (2) familiarity with techniques of integration, (3) self-conscious awareness of the interdisciplinary research process, and (4) critical evaluation of disciplinary insights. [5:126]

Integrative techniques: Ways to create common ground among conflicting insights, theories, and concepts. [11:278]

Intellectual "center of gravity": That which enables each discipline to maintain its identity and have a distinctive (but not undisputed) disciplinary perspective. [3:57]

Interdisciplinarity: The essence of interdisciplinary studies, which is manifested through research involving two or more knowledge domains. [1:6]

Interdisciplinary common ground: One or more theories, concepts, and assumptions by which conflicting insights can be reconciled and integrated. Creating common ground involves bringing out potential commonalities underlying the conflicting disciplinary and theory-based insights so that these can be reconciled and ultimately integrated. [11:272]

Interdisciplinary communication: Is possible when the partners of cooperation—i.e., the relevant disciplines or theories—find out that they use the same concepts with different meanings, or that they use different codings (terms, symbol systems) for similar concepts. [11:273]

Interdisciplinary decisions: Include determining whether the disciplines have skewed their data and findings in their approach to the problem, considering the possibility that one's own disciplinary and personal bias has crept into the work, identifying conflicts between insights and locating the source(s) of these conflicts, creating common ground between these insights or discovering the latent commonality (i.e., at least one theory, concept, principle, or value) between them, using this common ground to integrate the conflicting insights, and producing an interdisciplinary understanding of the problem or question. [10:247]

Interdisciplinary insight: Produced when the interdisciplinary research process (or some version of it) is used to create an integrated and purposeful understanding of the problem. [1:12]

Interdisciplinary integration: The cognitive activity of critically evaluating and creatively combining ideas and knowledge to form a new whole. It requires active triangulation of depth and breadth of disciplinary knowledge, integrative skills, integrative knowledge, and an integrative mind-set. A synonym of *integration* is the noun *synthesis*. [5:116]

Interdisciplinary learning: Developing an understanding of the limitations and biases of a discipline, the benefits and perspective of a discipline, and how a discipline works simply by forcing us to see one discipline in light of another. Interdisciplinary learning also develops the ability to integrate disciplinary insights relevant to a problem or question and produce a new and more comprehensive understanding of it than would be possible using single disciplinary means. [2:43]

Interdisciplinary question: It should be open-ended and too complex to be addressed by one discipline alone, it should be researchable, and it should be verified using appropriate research methods. [6:145]

Interdisciplinary research: A decision-making process that is heuristic, iterative, and reflexive. [6:137]

Interdisciplinary studies: A process of answering a question, solving a problem, or addressing a topic that is too broad or complex to be deal with adequately by a single discipline and draws on disciplinary perspectives and integrates their insights to produce a more comprehensive understanding or cognitive advancement. [1:3]

Interdisciplinary understanding: The capacity to integrate knowledge and modes of thinking in two or more disciplines to produce a cognitive advancement that would not be possible using single disciplinary means.

This advancement includes explaining a phenomenon, solving a problem, creating a product, or raising a new question. [12:310]

Interdiscipline: Literally means "between disciplines"—i.e., between the bodies of knowledge defined by the theories and methods of the established disciplines. An interdiscipline often begins initially as an interdisciplinary field, but over time becomes like a discipline, developing its own perspectives, journals, and professional associations. [3:52]

Interfaces of disciplines: The points at which disciplines converge because of their common interest in a particular problem. [6:153]

Interpenetration: A term Steve Fuller (1993) uses to describe his model of interdisciplinary research that questions the differences between the disciplines involved and calls for the "renegotiation of disciplinary boundaries." [5:128]

Interpretivist approaches: Theories such as postmodernism, feminism, and critical theory that are challenging the bedrock assumptions of modernism (e.g., that there is an independent reality out there that can be perceived and measured), claiming that the perceptions and interpretations of what we perceive are filtered through a web of values, expectations, and vocabularies that influence understanding. [4:100]

Interpretivists: Believe that (a) the world is socially constructed, (b) social phenomena do not exist independently of our interpretation of them, and (c) objective analysis is impossible. [4:93]

In-text evidence of disciplinary adequacy: Evidence of disciplinary adequacy may be expressed in the form of statements about the disciplinary elements that pertain to the problem, the identity of leading theorists, and the kind of data upon which experts from each discipline typically rely. [8:212]

Intuition: The natural ability to know or perceive something immediately without using rational thought or inference. [11:278]

Issues in Integrative Studies: The peer-reviewed journal of the Association for Integrative Studies (AIS), founded in 1982, and a national voice for interdisciplinary studies. [2:37]

Iterative: Procedurally repetitive; involving of a sequence of operations yielding results successively closer to the desired outcome. [6:139]

Knowledge domain: Consists of a body of facts, concepts, or ideas and generates theories and uses methods to produce new knowledge. [1:4]

Knowledge formations: Alternatives to disciplines that are both bodies of knowledge and processes of coming to know that contain within themselves dynamic patterns from which they have been generated and by which they will be transformed. [1:10]

Knowledge production: Scholarly research published in the form of peer-reviewed articles and books. [1:21]

Mapping: A metaphor based on the idea that the carving up of knowledge space is like the practice of cartography or map making. Mapping involves using a "combinational" or integrative method to map or display information that is gathered from a variety of sources. [1:23]

Mastery (disciplinary): Involves majoring in a discipline for the purpose of practicing it professionally. [8:189]

Meaning: An important concept in the humanities often equated with author or artist intent, audience reaction, and reader or viewer response. [1:16]

Metaphor: A figure of speech in which a word or phrase, a story, or a picture is likened to the idea that one is attempting to communicate. An example of a metaphor to illustrate the product of the interdisciplinary research process is the smoothie. [1:22]

Method: Concerns how one conducts research, analyzes data or evidence, tests theories, and creates new knowledge. [4:104]

Mode of thinking: The way of thinking and perceiving reality that characterizes a discipline—in other words, its perspective. [1:19]

Models of integration: Approaches to interdisciplinary work occurring inside and outside the Academy described in terms of their vision, theory, practice, and primary strength or weakness. [5:126]

Modernist approach: Belief in objective, empirically based, rationally analyzed truth that is knowable. [4:98]

Monodisciplinarity: The preference for a single disciplinary perspective. [11:274]

Most relevant disciplines: Those disciplines, often three or four, which are most directly connected to the problem, have generated the most important research on it, and have advanced the most compelling theories to explain it. More specifically, these disciplines, or parts of them, provide information about the problem that is essential to developing a comprehensive understanding of it. [7:169]

Multidisciplinarity: The placing side by side of insights from two or more disciplines without attempting integration. [1:13]

Multidisciplinary studies: Merely bringing insights from different disciplines together in some way but failing to engage in the hard work of integration. The main difference between multidisciplinary studies and interdisciplinary studies lies in the mechanism of the research process and the end product. [1:13]

Narrow interdisciplinarity: Focuses on factual situations and structures in need of modification, not on the rightness or wrongness of the activity, which is the realm of the humanities. [5:117]

Narrow-range theories: Often specific to a discipline and, thus, have limited applicability. Narrow-range theories are designed to account for a relatively small number of phenomena and produce insights into a specific problem of interest to a segment of the discipline's community of scholars. Each narrow-range theory has its own epistemology, concepts, and methods. [4:101]

Natural sciences: Tell us what the world is made of, how what it is made of is structured into a complex network of interdependent systems, and why what happened in a given localized system happened. [3:63]

New humanities: The development in the humanities of interdisciplinary identity fields and new specialties, such as film studies. [2:28]

New whole: The product of the activity of integration that is something larger and more complex than the sum of its constituent parts. The "constituent" or essential "parts" are those individual disciplinary insights into a particular problem or object. Though separate, they relate directly to the problem or question. (This statement is designed to emphasize the distinctiveness of the new whole from its constituent parts, that is, from the disciplines themselves.) [5:117]

Nomothetic theory: Posits a general relationship among two or more phenomena, and nomothetic researchers are concerned with showing a broad applicability. [8:198]

Nonlinearity (of the interdisciplinary process): Along the way the researcher should reflect on, and may need to revisit, or even revise, earlier work. [6:143]

Nonlinear thinking: The ability to approach a problem creatively, think about it "outside the box" without being influenced by solutions attempted in the past, and view it from different perspectives. [2:46]

Organization: An integrative technique that does two things: (1) it identifies an underlying commonality in meaning of different disciplinary concepts or assumptions and redefines them accordingly, and (2) it organizes the redefined concepts or assumptions to bring out a relationship among them. [11:289]

Overarching conceptual framework: See Conceptual bridging.

Overlap: In an interdisciplinary sense, overlap means that the discipline neither adds much to understanding the problem (possibly because the insights are informed by the same theory) nor offers a new way of thinking about the problem. [8:194]

Paradigm shift: A profound and transformative change in the philosophical and theoretical framework that dominates a discipline or approach to knowledge formation. [2:40]

Personal bias: One's own point of view on the problem. [6:146]

"Perspectival" approach: Relying on each discipline's unique perspective on reality. [4:84]

Perspective (in an interdisciplinary sense): In interdisciplinary usage, the term perspective is used in two ways: (1) In a general sense in terms of how a discipline views the problem in an overall way, and (2) in a more particular sense in terms of how one or more of the discipline's defining elements pertain to the problem. [7:170]

Perspective taking: Viewing some problem, object, or phenomenon from a particular dimension or viewpoint other than one's own. As applied to interdisciplinary work, perspective taking involves examining a problem from the standpoint of interested disciplines (in serial fashion), understanding how each discipline would typically view the problem, seeing the problem in terms of its constituent disciplinary parts (i.e., its defining elements), and identifying the differences between them. [5:120]

Phenomena: Enduring aspects of human existence that are of interest to scholars and are susceptible to scholarly description and explanation. [4:83]

Pidgin: A form of simplified speech used for communication between people with different languages for a limited purpose. [1:124]

Positivists: Are concerned to establish causal relationships between social phenomena through direct observation, attempting to develop explanatory, and even predictive, models. [4:93]

Postmodernism: Offers a revolutionary way of understanding society by its questioning the validity of modern science and the notion of objective knowledge. Postmodernism discards history, rejects humanism, and resists any truth claims. The postmodern challenge radiates across the disciplines. [4:99]

Postmodernist approaches: Typically operate under the assumption that there is no such thing as objective truth, or at least no objective truth available to humans. Instead, knowledge is explained sociopolitically, usually as a weapon in the hands of some individuals or groups to dominate and intimidate others. [4:98]

Potentially relevant discipline: One whose research domain includes the phenomenon that the problem represents but the discipline's community of scholars has either not yet recognized the problem or has not yet published their research. [7:160]

Pragmatic interdisciplinarity: Focused on the historically situated problems of society while holding to the notion of general education as the place where all the parts would add up to a cohesive whole. [2:35]

Premise of interdisciplinary studies: The disciplines (including interdisciplines) themselves are the necessary preconditions for and foundations of interdisciplinarity. [1:25]

Problem-focused research: Societal/public policy problems necessitate this type of research, which is distinct from what is called basic research or pure theoretical research because it focuses on unresolved societal needs and practical problem solving and emphasizes the pursuit of knowledge, informed action, usefulness, efficiency, and practical results. [6:154]

Process (integrative): Conveys the notion of making gradual changes that lead toward a particular (but often nonlinear) result. [5:123]

Proposition formation: Involves generating statements about the world or some aspect of it. [3:71]

Qualitative approach: Focuses on evidence that cannot easily be quantified, such as cultural mannerisms and personal impressions of a musical composition. [4:111]

Qualitative (or consensual) knowledge: Arrived at through contention rather than the empirical testing of theories. The humanities are organized around the production of consensual knowledge. [3:77]

Qualitative research strategies: Focus on the what, how, when, and where of a thing—its essence and its ambiance. Qualitative research refers to meanings, concepts, definitions, characteristics, metaphors, symbols, and descriptions of things or people that are not measured and expressed numerically. [8:203]

Quantification of evidence: Discovering or expressing the numerical quantity of something, as, for example, in quantitative chemical analysis where one needs to determine the exact amount of each element in a substance. [3:77]

Quantitative approach: Emphasizes that evidence can be expressed numerically over a specified time frame. [4:111]

Quantitative research strategies: Emphasize evidence that can be quantified, such as the number of atoms in a molecule, the flow rate of water in a river, or the amount of energy derived from a windmill. [8:202–203]

Rationalism: Reason aided by observation can discover basic truth regarding the world. [3:77]

Receptivity to other disciplines: Being open to information or insights from any and all relevant disciplinary perspectives as well as being willing, even eager, to learn about other fields of knowledge, gaining both an intuitive and intellectual grasp of them. [2:43]

Redefinition: An integrative technique that involves modifying or redefining concepts and assumptions used by the relevant disciplines to bring out a common meaning. [11:283]

Reductionism: An approach to understand the whole of something by examining its parts. [4:106]

Reflection: Occurs when students evaluate sources of information, demonstrate lines of reasoning from conflicting perspectives, evaluate complex problems or objects, discuss controversial issues, or justify an important decision. Reflection also occurs when students examine, perhaps in a reflective paper, their responses to an emotionally charged question. [2:42]

Reflexive: To be self-conscious or self-aware. [6:139]

Reflexive scholarship: Scholarship that exhibits self-critique. [1:12]

Research: Involves identifying problems, discovering source material, generating data, organizing and analyzing that information, and drawing conclusions substantiated by it. [2:28]

Researchable: A problem is researchable in an interdisciplinary sense (1) when it is the focus of two or more disciplines, and (2) when there is a gap in attention to a problem beyond one domain. In the second instance, a problem may be complex but for some reason has failed to generate scholarly interest outside a particular discipline. [6:144]

Research design: Involves establishing criteria for evaluating evidence, selecting appropriate methods of analysis, and choosing verification strategies. [3:71]

Research map: A way to help visualize the problem or question in its complexity. [7:163]

Rigor (interdisciplinary): Derives from attention to integrative process, the product of integration, and testing. [5:125]

Role taking: Used by interdisciplinary research teams who adopt a "set of perspectives" associated with a person, a culture, or even an animal. [5:120]

Rote learning: Occurs when the learner memorizes new information without relating it to prior knowledge and involves no effort to integrate new knowledge with existing concepts, experience, or objects. [6:140]

School of thought: See Grand theory.

Science: Claims to give us empirical information that, combined with rational thought, leads to knowledge of what exists in the universe and also claims to explain why it behaves the way it does. [3:63]

Scientific method: The method, idealized, has four steps: (1) observation and description of phenomena; (2) formulation of a hypothesis to explain the phenomena; (3) use of the hypothesis to predict the existence of other phenomena, or to predict quantitatively the result of new observations; (4) execution of properly performed experiments to test those hypotheses or predictions. The scientific method is based on beliefs in empiricism (whether the observation is direct or indirect), quantifiability (including precision in measurement) replicability/reproducibility, and free exchange of information (so that others can test or attempt to replicate/reproduce). [4:104, 106]

Scientific revolution: A seventeenth- and eighteenth-century intellectual movement that challenged the notion of the unity of knowledge and emphasized greater specialization and heightened research activity, initially in the sciences and then in all the disciplines. [2:33]

Scope: Refers to the parameters of what is included and excluded from consideration, how much of the problem will be investigated, and the limits of the investigation. [6:144]

Situate or contextualize the problem: Refers to providing information describing how the problem is connected to other similar problems. In general, situating or contextualizing the problem involves identifying the web of interrelationships in which the problem is embedded. These connections often surface in the process of drawing a system map. [7:177]

Skewed understanding: A deliberate decision or unconscious predisposition to omit certain information that pertains to a problem. [9:225]

Skills: Cognitive abilities to use one's knowledge effectively and readily in performing a task. [2:42]

Social sciences: Seek to explain the human world and figure out how to predict and improve it. [3:67]

Studies: Multidisciplinary or interdisciplinary approaches to a wide array of knowledge domains, work, and educational programs that have not yet coalesced into discrete fields. [1:8]

Subdiscipline: A branch or subunit of an existing discipline. [3:52]

Symbolic interactionism: A major theoretical perspective of sociology that focuses on the use of signs and symbols in interaction among people. [3:69]

Synthesis: A synonym of *integration* that connotes creation of an interdisciplinary outcome through a series of integrative actions. [5:116]

System: Any group of interacting components or agents around which there is a clearly defined boundary between it and the rest of the world, but also clearly definable inputs from the world and outputs to the world that cross the boundary. [6:152]

System map: A highly useful analytical tool that can help one visualize the system or problem as a complex whole. The purpose of constructing a system map is to show all the components of the system or problem and see the causal relationships among them. [7:164–165]

Taxonomy: A systematic and orderly classification. [3:62]

Theory: A generalized scholarly explanation about some aspect of the natural or human world, how it works, and why specific facts are related that is supported by data and research. [4:101]

Theory-based insights: Those insights that are informed by or advance a particular theoretical perspective. [10:255]

Theory expansion: An integrative technique that may involve merely adding a factor or factors (e.g., a variable or variables) from any of the sources of alternative perspectives, including different fields within the same discipline, different disciplines, schools of thought that cut across disciplines, interdisciplines, or even folk knowledge. [11:281]

Traditional humanities: Focus on human culture in terms of its meaning, its values, and the significance of its art, literature, music, philosophy, religion, and performing arts. [3:72]

Traditional interdisciplinarity: Focused on the classical and secular ideals of liberal culture and education while holding to the notion of general education as the place where all the parts would add up to a cohesive whole. [2:35]

Traits: Distinguishing qualities of a person. [2:42]

Transdisciplinarity: The application of theories, concepts, or methods across disciplines and sectors of society by including stakeholders in the public and private domains with the intent of developing an overarching synthesis. [1:15]

Transdisciplinary study: The focus on a mega and complex problem or theme such as "the city" or "sustainability" that requires collaboration among a hybrid mix of actors from different disciplines, professions, and sectors of society. [1:15]

Transformation: An integrative technique that uses continuous variables to transform determinative and dichotomous concepts, assumptions, and values into influences that can be explored and estimated in any particular context. Transforming opposing assumptions into variables allows the interdisciplinarian to move toward resolution of almost any dichotomy. [11:290]

Triangulation: In an interdisciplinary sense, means achieving balance between disciplinary depth, disciplinary breadth, and interdisciplinary integration. [5:124]

Triangulation of research methodologies: A predominantly social science approach to research that involves using multiple data-gathering techniques (usually three) to investigate the same phenomenon. In this way, findings can be crosschecked, validated, and confirmed. [8:209]

Tribes: An anthropological metaphor used to describe the disciplines, each having its own culture and language. [2:36]

Unifying knowledge: Blending differences out of existence in subservience to an "overarching idea." [1:20]

University: An institution of higher learning that provides teaching and research and is authorized to grant academic degrees. [2:32]

Wide interdisciplinarity: An integrative approach that enables interdisciplinary practitioners from the sciences and the humanities to work together to identify, solve, or resolve normative problems, both practical and theoretical, having to do with the satisfaction of human needs. [5:118]

References

Adams, L. S. (1996). *The methodologies of art: An introduction.* Boulder, CO: Westview Press.

Agger, B. (1998). *Critical social theories: An introduction.* Boulder, CO: Westview Press.

Alford, R. R. (1998). *The craft of inquiry: Theories, methods, evidence.* New York: Oxford University Press.

Alliance for Childhood. (1999). *Fool's gold: A critical look at computers in childhood.* Retrieved from http://www.allianceforchildhood.net.

Alvesson, M. (2002). *Postmodernism and social research.* Philadelphia: Open University Press.

Alvesson, M., & Sköldberg, K. (2000). *Reflexive methodology: New vistas for qualitative research.* Thousand Oaks, CA: Sage.

American Sociological Association. (2008). *American Sociological Association.* Retrieved from http://www.asanet.org.

Anderson, C. (2001). Knowledge, politics, and interdisciplinary education. In B. L. Smith & J. McCann (Eds.), *Collaborative learning, and experimentation in higher education* (pp. 454–465). Bolton, MA: Anker.

Anderson, L. W., Krathwohl, D. R., Airasian, P. W., Cruikshank, K. A., Mayer, R. E., Pintrich, P. R., et al. (2000). *Taxonomy for learning, teaching, and assessing: A revision of Bloom's Taxonomy of Educational Objectives* (2nd Rev. ed.). Boston: Allyn & Bacon.

Arms, L. A. (2005). *Mathematics and religion: Processes of faith and reason.* Unpublished paper.

Armstrong, F. H. (1980). Faculty development through interdisciplinarity. *The Journal of General Education, 32*(1), 52–63.

Arthurs, A. (1993). The humanities in the 1990s. In A. Levine (Ed.), *Higher learning in America, 1980–2000* (pp. 259–272). Baltimore, MD: The Johns Hopkins University Press.

Association of American Colleges. (1991). *Interdisciplinary studies. Vol 2: Reports from the field.* Washington, DC: Author.

Atran, S. (2003). *Genesis and future of suicide terrorism.* Retrieved August 14, 2006, from http://interdisciplines.org/terrorism/papers/1.

Atran, S. (2005, July 8). *Genesis and future of suicide terrorism: Discussion.* Retrieved from http://interdisciplines.org/terrorism/papers/1/14/printable/discussions/view/782

Baca, J. F. (1994). Whose monument where: Public art in a many-cultured society. In R. M. Carp (Ed.), *Saber es poder/Interventions* (n.p.). Los Angeles: Adobe LA.

Bailis, S. (2001). Contending with complexity: A response to William H. Newell's "A theory of interdisciplinary studies." *Issues in Integrative Studies, 19*, 27–42.

Bailis, S. (2002). Interdisciplinary curriculum design and instructional innovation: Notes on the social science program at San Francisco State University. In C. Haynes (Ed.), *Innovations in interdisciplinary teaching* (pp. 3–15). Westport, CT: Oryx Press.

Bal, M. (1996). *Double exposures: The subject of cultural analysis.* New York: Routledge.

Bal, M. (1999). Introduction. In M. Bal (Ed.), *The practice of cultural analysis: Exposing interdisciplinary interpretation* (pp. 1–14). Stanford, CA: Stanford University Press.

Bal, M. (2002). *Traveling concepts in the humanities: A rough guide.* Buffalo, NY: University of Toronto Press.

Bal, M., & Bryson, N. (1991). Semiotics and art history. *The Art Bulletin, 73*(2), 174–208.

Baldick, C. (2004). *The concise dictionary of literary terms* (Reissue ed.). New York: Oxford University Press.

Bandura, A. (1998). Mechanism of moral disengagement. In W. Reich (Ed.), *Origins of terrorism: Psychologies, ideologies, theologies, states of mind* (pp. 161–191). Washington, DC: Woodrow Wilson Center Press.

Barnard, A., & Spencer, J. (Eds.). (1996). *Encyclopedia of social and cultural anthropology.* New York: Routledge.

Barnet, S. (2008). *A short guide to writing about art* (9th ed.). Upper Saddle River, NJ: Pearson Prentice Hall.

Baum, J. (2002, Fall). Toward a new integrative field: "Strategic organization." *Rotman Magazine,* 21–22.

Becher, T. (1989). *Academic tribes and territories: Intellectual enquiry and the cultures of disciplines.* Milton Keynes: Open University Press.

Becher, T., & Trowler, P. R. (2001). *Academic tribes and territories* (2nd ed.). Great Britain: The Society for Research into Higher Education & Open University Press.

Bechtel, W. (1986). The nature of scientific integration. In W. Bechtel (Ed.), *Integrating scientific disciplines* (pp. 3–52). Dordrecht, The Netherlands: Martinus Nojhoff.

Bechtel, W. (2000). From imagining to believing: Epistemic issues in generating biological data. In R. Creath & J. Maienschein (Eds.), *Biology and epistemology* (pp. 138–163). Cambridge, UK: Cambridge University Press.

Bell, J. A. (1998). Overcoming dogma in epistemology. *Issues in Integrative Studies, 16,* 99–119.

Bender, T. (1997). Politics, intellect, and the American University, 1945–1995. In T. Bender & C. E. Schorske (Eds.), *American academic culture in transformation: Fifty years, four disciplines* (pp. 17–54). Princeton, NJ: Princeton University Press.

Bennington, G. (1999). Inter. In M. McQuillan, G. MacDonald, R. Purves, & S. Thompson (Eds.), *Post-theory: New directions in criticism* (pp. 103–119). Edinburgh: Edinburgh University Press.

Berg, B. L. (2004). *Qualitative research methods for the social sciences* (5th ed.). Boston: Pearson Education.

Bernard, H. R. (2002). *Research methods in anthropology: Qualitative and quantitative methods* (3rd ed.). New York: AltaMira Press.

Berthoff, A. (1981). *The making of meaning: Metaphors, models, and maxims for writing teachers.* Upper Montclair, NJ: Boynton.

Bishop, M. (1970). *The middle ages.* New York: American Heritage Press.

Blackburn, S. (1999). *Think: A compelling introduction to philosophy.* Oxford, UK: Oxford University Press.

Blau, J. R. (2001). Preface. In J. R. Blau (Ed.), *The Blackwell companion to sociology* (pp. x–xvi). Malden, MA: Blackwell.

Blesser, B., & Salter, L. R. (2007). *Spaces speak, are you listening?* Cambridge, MA: The MIT Press.

Bloom, B. S. (Ed.). (1956). *Taxonomy of educational objectives, handbook 1: Cognitive domain.* Boston: Addison Wesley.

Bogdan, R., & Taylor, S. J. (1975). *Introduction to qualitative research methods.* New York: Wiley.

Bohlman, P. V. (1996). Epilogue: Music and canons. In K. Bergeron & P. V. Bohlman (Eds.), *Disciplining music: Musicology and its canons* (pp. 197–210). Chicago: University of Chicago Press.

Boix Mansilla, V. (2002, October). *Approaches to ID inquiry.* PowerPoint presented at the Association for Integrative Studies Annual Convention, Springfield, Missouri.

Boix Mansilla, V. (2005, January/February). Assessing student work at disciplinary crossroads. *Change, 37,* 14–21.

Boix Mansilla, V., & Gardner, H. (2003). *Assessing interdisciplinary work at the frontier: An empirical exploration of "symptoms of quality."* GoodWork Project Report Series, Number 26. Retrieved August 2, 2006, from http://www.pz.harvard.edu/ebookstore/search_results.cfm.

Boix Mansilla, V., Miller, W. C., & Gardner, H. (2000). On disciplinary lenses and interdisciplinary work. In S. Wineburg & P. Gossman (Eds.), Interdisciplinary curriculum: Challenges to implementation (pp. 17–38). New York: Teachers College, Columbia University.

Booth, W. C., Columb, G. G., & Williams, J. M. (2003). *The craft of research* (2nd ed.). Chicago: University of Chicago Press.

Boulding, K. (1981). *A preface to grants economics: The economy of love and fear.* New York: Praeger.

Boyd, I. (2006). Studying complexity: Are we approaching the limits of science? In J. Atkinson & M. Crowe (Eds.), *Interdisciplinary research: Diverse approaches on science, technology, health and society* (pp. 25–40). West Sussex, England: John Wiley & Sons.

Boyer, E. I. (1981). The quest for common learning. In *Common learning: A Carnegie colloquium on general education* (pp. 3–21). Washington, DC: The Carnegie Foundation for the Advancement of Learning.

Bradsford, J. D., Brown, A. L., & Cocking, R. R. (Eds.). (1999). *How people learn: Brain, mind, experience, and school.* Washington, DC: National Academy Press.

Bressler, C. E. (2003). *Literary criticism: An introduction to theory and practice* (3rd ed).). Upper Saddle River, NJ: Pearson Education.

Briggs, A., & Micard, G. (1972). Problems and solutions. In *Interdisciplinarity: Problems of teaching and research in universities* (pp. 185–299). Paris: Center for Educational Research and Innovation.

Bromme, R. (2000). Beyond one's own perspective: The psychology of cognitive interdisciplinarity. In P. Weingart & N. Stehr (Eds.), *Practising interdisciplinarity* (pp. 115–133). Toronto: University of Toronto Press.

Bruun, H., & Toppinen, A. (2004). Knowledge of science and innovation: A review of three discourses on the institutional and cognitive foundations of knowledge production. *Issues in Integrative Studies, 22,* 1–51.

Bryman, A. (2004). *Social research methods* (2nd ed). New York: Oxford University Press.

Burke, P. (1991). Overture: The new history, its past and its future. In P. Burke (Ed.), *New perspectives in historical writing* (pp. 1–23). University Park: Pennsylvania State University Press.

Caldwell, L. K. (1983). Environmental studies: Discipline or metadiscipline? *Environmental Professional, 5,* 247–259.

Calhoun, C. (Ed.). (2002). *Dictionary of the social sciences.* Oxford: Oxford University Press.

Capps, W. H. (1995). *Religious studies: The making of a discipline.* Minneapolis, MN: Augsburg Fortress.

Carey, S. S. (2003). *A beginner's guide to scientific method* (2nd ed.). Belmont, CA: Wadsworth.

Carlisle, B. (1995, June/July). Music and life. *American Music Teacher, 44,* 10–13.

Carp, R. M. (2001). Integrative praxes: Learning from multiple knowledge formations. *Issues in Integrative Studies, 19,* 71–121.

Coppola, B. P., & Jacobs, D. C. (2006). Is the scholarship of teaching and learning new to chemistry? In M. Taylor Huber & S. P. Morreale (Eds.), *Disciplinary styles in the scholarship of teaching and learning: Exploring common ground* (pp. 197–216). Stanford, CA: The Carnegie Foundation.

Crenshaw, M. (1998). The logic of terrorism: Terrorist behavior as a product of strategic choice. In W. Reich (Ed.), *Origins of terrorism: Psychologies, ideologies, theologies, states of mind* (pp. 7–24). Washington, DC: Woodrow Wilson Center Press.

Creswell, J. W. (1997). *Qualitative inquiry and research design: Choosing among five traditions.* Thousand Oaks, CA: Sage.

Creswell, J. W. (2002), *Research design: Qualitative, quantitative, and mixed methods approaches* (2nd ed.). Thousand Oaks, CA: Sage.

Cullenberg, S., Amariglio, J., & Ruccio, D. (2001). Introduction. In S. Cullenberg, J. Amariglio, & D. Ruccio (Eds.), *Postmodernism, economics and knowledge* (pp. 3–57). New York: Routledge.

Czuchry, M., & Dansereau, D. F. (1996). Node-link mapping as an alternative to traditional writing assignments in undergraduate courses. *Teaching of Psychology, 23,* 91–96.

Dabrowski, I. J. (1995). David Bohm's theory of the implicate order: Implications for holistic thought processes. *Issues in Integrative Studies, 13,* 1–12.

Davidson, C., & Goldberg, D. (2004). *Engaging the humanities. MLA: Profession,* 42–62.

Davis, G. A. (1992). *Creativity is forever* (3rd ed.). Dubuque, IA: Kendall/Hunt.

Davis, J. R. (1995). *Interdisciplinary courses and team teaching: New arrangements for learning.* Phoenix, AZ: American Council on Education, Oryx.

Davis, W. (1978). *The act of interpretation: A critique of literary reason.* Chicago: University of Chicago Press.

Delph, J. B. (2005). *An integrative approach to the elimination of the "perfect crime."* Unpublished paper.

Denzin, N. K. (1978). *The research act.* New York: McGraw-Hill.

Denzin, N. K., & Lincoln, Y. S. (Eds.). (2005). *The SAGE handbook of qualitative research* (3rd ed.). Thousand Oaks, CA: SAGE.

Derry, S. J., Schunn, C. D., & Gernsbacher, M. A. (Eds.). (2005). *Interdisciplinary collaboration: An emerging cognitive science.* Mahwah, NJ: Lawrence Erlbaum Associates.

de Saint-Exupéry, A. (2000). *The little prince.* New York: Harcourt.

DeZure, D. (1999). Interdisciplinary teaching and learning. *Teaching Excellence, 10*(3), pp. 2–3.

Dietrich, W. (1995). *Northwest passage: The great Columbia river.* Seattle: University of Washington Press.

Dogan, M., & Pahre, R. (1989). Fragmentation and recombination of the social sciences. *Studies in Comparative International Development, 24,* 56–73.

Dogan, M., & Pahre, R. (1990). *Creative marginality: Innovation at the intersections of the social sciences.* Boulder: Westview Press.

Dölling, I., & Hark, S. (2000). She who speaks shadow speaks truth: Transdisciplinarity in women's and gender studies. *Signs, 25*(4), pp. 1195–1198.

Donald, J. (2002). *Learning to think: Disciplinary perspectives.* San Francisco: Jossey-Bass.

Dorsten, L. E., & Hotchkiss, L. (2005). *Research methods and society: Foundations of social inquiry.* Upper Saddle River, NJ: Prentice-Hall.

Dow, S. (2001). Modernism and postmodernism: A dialectical analysis. In S. Cullenberg, J. Amariglio, & D. F. Ruccio (Eds.), *Postmodernism, economics and knowledge* (pp. 61–101). New York: Routledge.

Easton, D. (1991). The division, integration, and transfer of knowledge. In D. Easton & C. S. Schelling (Eds.), *Divided knowledge: Across disciplines, across cultures* (pp. 7–36). Newbury Park, CA: Sage.

Eilenberg, S. (1999). Voice and ventriloquy in "The Rime of the Ancient Mariner." In P. H. Fry (Ed.), *Samuel Taylor Coleridge: The rime of the ancient mariner* (pp. 282–314). Boston: Bedford/St. Martin's.

Elliott, D. J. (2002). Philosophical perspectives on research. In R. Colwell & C. Richardson (Eds.), *The new handbook of research on music teaching and writing* (pp. 85–102). Oxford: Oxford University Press.

Ember, C. R., & Ember, M. (2004). *Cultural anthropology* (11th ed.). Upper Saddle River, NJ: Prentice-Hall.

Englehart, L. (2005). *Organized environmentalism: Towards a shift in the political and social roles and tactics of environmental advocacy groups.* Unpublished paper.

Etzioni, A. (1988). *The moral dimension: Towards a new economics.* New York: Free Press.

Ferguson, F. (1999). Coleridge and the deluded reader: "The rime of the ancient mariner. In P. H. Fry (Ed.), *Samuel Taylor Coleridge: The rime of the ancient mariner* (pp. 113–130). Boston: Bedford/St. Martin's.

Fernie, E. (1995). Glossary of concepts. In E. Fernie (Ed.), *Art history and its methods: A critical anthology* (pp. 323–368). London: Phaidon Press.

Fiscella, J. B. (1989). Access to interdisciplinary information: Setting the problem. *Issues in Integrative Studies, 7,* 73–92.

Fiscella, J. B., & Kimmel, S. E. (Eds.). (1999). *Interdisciplinary education: A guide to resources.* New York: The College Board.

Fischer, C. C. (1988). On the need for integrating occupational sex discrimination theory on the basis of causal variables. *Issues in Integrative Studies, 6,* 21–50.

Fish, S. (1991). Being interdisciplinary is so very hard to do. *Issues in Integrative Studies, 9*, 97–125.

Foster, H. (1998). Trauma studies and the interdisciplinary: An overview. In A. Coles and A. Defert (Eds.), *The anxiety of interdisciplinarity* (pp. 157–168). London: BACKless Books.

Frank, R. H. (1988). *Passions within reason: The strategic role of emotions.* New York: Norton.

Frank, R. (1988). "Interdisciplinarity": The first half century. In E. G. Stanly & T. F. Hoad (Eds.), *WORDS: For Robert Burchfield's sixty-fifth birthday* (pp. 91–101). Cambridge: D. S. Brewer.

Frankfort-Nachmias, C., & Nachmias, D. (2008). *Research methods in the social sciences* (7th ed.). New York: Worth.

Friedman, S. S. (2001). Academic feminism and interdisciplinarity. *Feminist Studies, 27*(2), 504–509.

Fry, P. H. (Ed.). (1999). *Samuel Taylor Coleridge: The rime of the ancient mariner.* Boston: Bedford/St. Martin's.

Fuller, S. (1993). The position: Interdisciplinarity as interpenetration. In *Philosophy, rhetoric, and the end of knowledge: The coming of science and technology studies* (pp. 33–65). Madison: University of Wisconsin Press.

Fussell, S. G., & Kraus, R. M. (1991). Accuracy and bias in estimates of others' knowledge. *European Journal of Social Psychology, 21*, 445–454.

Fussell, S. G., & Kraus, R. M. (1992). Coordination of knowledge in communication: Effects of speakers' assumptions about what others know. *Journal of Personality and Social Psychology, 62*, 378–391.

Gaff, J. G., Ratcliff, J. L., & Associates (Eds.). (1997). *Handbook of the undergraduate curriculum: A comprehensive guide to purposes, structures, practices, and change.* San Francisco: Jossey-Bass.

Gallagher, C., & Greenblatt, S. (2000). *Practicing new historicism.* Chicago and London: The University of Chicago Press.

Garber, M. (2001). *Academic instincts.* Princeton: Princeton University Press.

Gardner, H. (1999). *The disciplined mind: What all students should understand.* New York: Simon & Schuster.

Gauch, H. G., Jr. (2002). *Scientific method in practice.* Cambridge, UK: Cambridge University Press.

Geertz, C. (1980). Blurred genres: The reconfiguration of social thought. *The American Scholar, 49*(2), 165–179.

Geertz, C. (1983). *Local knowledge: Further essays in interpretative anthropology.* New York: Basic Books.

Geertz, C. (2000). The strange estrangement: Charles Taylor and the natural sciences. In C. Geertz (Ed.), *Available light: Anthropological reflections on philosophical topics* (pp. 143–159). Princeton, NJ: Princeton University Press.

Gerdes, E. P. (2002). Disciplinary dangers. *Liberal Education, 88*(3), 48–55.

Gerring, J. (2001). *Social science methodology: A critical framework.* Boston: Cambridge University Press.

Giere, R. N. (1999). *Science without laws.* Chicago: University of Chicago Press.

Giri, A. K. (2002). The calling of a creative transdisciplinarity. *Futures, 34*(1), 103–116.

Goldenberg, S. (1992). *Thinking methodologically.* New York: Harper Collins.

Goodin, R. E., & Klingerman, H.-D. (Eds.). (1996). *A new handbook of political science.* New York: Oxford University Press.

Grace, N. (1996). An exploration of the interdisciplinary character of women's studies. *Issues in Integrative Studies, 14,* 59–86.

Graff, G. (1987). *Professing literature: An institutional history.* Chicago: University of Chicago Press.

Grayling, A. C. (1995). Introduction. In A. C. Grayling (Ed.), *Philosophy: A guide through the subject* (pp. 1–6). New York: Oxford University Press.

Graziano, A. M., & Raulin, M. L. (2004). *Research methods: A process of inquiry* (5th ed.). Boston: Pearson Education Group.

Griffin, G. (2005). Research methods for English studies: An introduction. In G. Griffin (Ed.), *Research methods for English studies* (pp. 1–16). Edinburgh: Edinburgh University Press.

Gunn, G. (1992). Interdisciplinary studies. In J. Gibaldi (Ed.), *Introduction to scholarship in modern languages and literatures* (pp. 239–261). New York: Modern Language Association.

Hacking, I. (2004). *The complacent disciplinarian.* Retrieved May 19, 2004, from http://www.interdisciplines.org/interdisciplinarity/papers/7

Hagan, F. E. (2005). *Essentials of research methods in criminal justice and criminology.* Boston: Allyn & Bacon.

Hall, D. J., & Hall, I. (1996). *Practical social research: Project work in the community.* Basingstoke, UK: Macmillan.

Harris, E. (1997). The arts. In J. G. Gaff, J. L. Ratcliff, & Associates (Eds.), *Handbook of the undergraduate curriculum: A comprehensive guide to purposes, structures, practices, and change* (pp. 320–340). San Francisco: Jossey-Bass.

Harris, J. (2001). *The new art history: A critical introduction.* NewYork: Routledge.

Hart, C. (1998). *Doing a literature review: Releasing the social science research imagination.* Thousand Oaks, CA: Sage.

Haskins, C. H. (1940). *The rise of universities.* New York: Peter Smith.

Haynes, C. (2002). Introduction: Laying a foundation for interdisciplinary teaching. In C. Haynes (Ed.), *Innovations in interdisciplinary teaching* (pp. xi–xxii). Westport, CT: Oryx Press.

Hendershott, A. B., & Wright, S. P. (1997). The social sciences. In J. G. Gaff, J. L. Ratcliff, & Associates (Eds.), *Handbook of the undergraduate curriculum: A comprehensive guide to purposes, structures, practices, and change* (pp. 301–319). San Francisco: Jossey-Bass.

Hershberg, T. (1981). The new urban history: Toward an interdisciplinary history of the city. In T. Hershberg (Ed.), *Philadelphia: Work, space, family, and group experience in the nineteenth century* (pp. 3–42). New York and Oxford: Oxford University Press.

Hirst, P. H. (1974). *Knowledge and the curriculum: A collection of philosophical papers.* London: Routledge & Kegan Paul.

Holmes, F. L. (2000). The logic of discovery in the experimental life sciences. In R. Creath & J. Maienschein (Eds.), *Biology and epistemology* (pp. 167–190). Cambridge, UK: Cambridge University Press.

Hoskin, K. W. (1993). Education and the genesis of disciplinarity: The unexpected reversal. In E. Messer-Davidow, D. R. Shumway, & D. J. Sylvan (Eds.), *Knowledges: Historical and critical studies in disciplinarity* (pp. 271–304). Charlottesville and London: University Press of Virginia.

Houtz, J. C., & Patricola, C. (1999). Imagery. In M. A. Runco & S. R. Prentky (Eds.), *Encyclopedia of creativity* (Vol. 2, pp. 1–11). San Diego: Academic Press.

Howell, M., & Prevenier, W. (2001). *From reliable sources: An introduction to historical methods.* Ithaca, NY: Cornell University Press.

Huber, M. T., & Hutchings, P. (2004). *Integrative learning: Mapping the terrain.* Washington, DC: The Association of American Colleges and Universities.

Huber, M. T., & Morreale, S. P. (2002). Situating the scholarship of teaching and learning: A cross-disciplinary conversation. In M. T. Huber & S. P. Morreale (Eds.), *Disciplinary styles in the scholarship of teaching and learning: Exploring common ground* (pp. 1–24). Stanford, CA: The Carnegie Foundation.

Huffman, K., Vernoy, M., Vernoy, J. (2000). *Psychology in action* (5th ed.). New York: John Wiley & Sons.

Hursh, B., Haas, P., & Moore, M. (1983). An interdisciplinary model to implement general education. *Journal of Higher Education, 54*(1), 42–59.

Hutcheon, L., & Hutcheon, M. (2001). A convenience of marriage: Collaboration and interdisciplinarity. *PMLA, 116*(5), 1364–1376.

Hutcheson, P. A. (1997). Structures and practices. In J. G. Gaff, J. L. Ratcliff, & Associates (Eds.), *Handbook of the undergraduate curriculum: A comprehensive guide to purposes, structures, practices, and change* (pp. 100–117). San Francisco: Jossey-Bass.

Hyneman, C. S. (1959). *The study of politics: The present state of American political science.* Champaign: University of Illinois Press.

Iggers, G. G. (1997). *Historiography in the twentieth century: From scientific objectivity to postmodern challenges.* Middletown, CT: Wesleyan University Press.

Karlqvist, A. (1999). Going beyond disciplines: The meanings of interdisciplinarity. *Policy Sciences, 32,* 379–383.

Kassabian, A. (1997). Introduction: Music, disciplinarity, and interdisciplinarities. In D. Schwarz, A. Kassabian, & L. Siegel (Eds.), *Keeping score: Music, disciplinarity, culture* (pp. 1–10). Charlottesville: University Press of Virginia.

Katz, C. (2001). Disciplining interdisciplinarity. *Feminist Studies, 27*(2), 519–525.

Kelly, J. S. (1996). Wide and narrow interdisciplinarity. *The Journal of Education, 45*(2), 95–113.

Klee, R. (1999). Introduction. In R. Klee (Ed.), *Scientific inquiry: Readings in the philosophy of science* (pp. 1–4). New York: Oxford University Press.

Klein, J. T. (1990). *Interdisciplinarity: History, theory and practice.* Detroit: Wayne State University Press.

Klein, J. T. (1996). *Crossing boundaries: Knowledge, disciplinarities, and interdisciplinarities.* Charlottesville: University Press of Virginia.

Klein, J. T. (1999). *Mapping interdisciplinary studies.* Number 13 in the Academy in Transition series. Washington, DC: Association of American Colleges and Universities.

Klein, J. T. (2000). A conceptual vocabulary of interdisciplinary science. In P. Weingart & N. Stehr (Eds.), *Practising interdisciplinarity* (pp. 3–24). Toronto: University of Toronto Press.

Klein, J. T. (2001). Interdisciplinarity and the prospect of complexity: The tests of theory. *Issues in Integrative Studies, 19,* 43–57.

Klein, J. T. (2003). Unity of knowledge and transdisciplinarity: Contexts and definition, theory, and the new discourse of problem-solving. *Encyclopedia of life support systems.* Retrieved from http://www.eolss.net/

Klein, J. T. (2005a). *Humanities, culture, and interdisciplinarity: The changing America academy.* Albany: State University of New York Press.

Klein, J. T. (2005b). Interdisciplinary teamwork: The dynamics of collaboration and integration. In S. J. Derry, C. D. Schunn, & M. A. Gernsbacher (Eds.), *Interdisciplinary collaboration: An emerging cognitive science* (pp. 23–50). Mahwah, NJ: Lawrence Erlbaum Associates.

Klein, J. T., & Newell, W. H. (1997). Advancing interdisciplinary studies. In J. G. Gaff, J. L. Ratcliff, & Associates (Eds.), *Handbook of the undergraduate curriculum: A comprehensive guide to purposes, structures, practices, and change* (pp. 393–415). San Francisco: Jossey-Bass.

Klein, J. T., & Newell, W. H. (2002). Strategies for using interdisciplinary resources across K–16. *Issues in Integrative Studies, 20,* 139–160.

Kockelmans, J. J. (1979). Why interdisciplinarity. In J. J. Kockelmans (Ed.), *Interdisciplinarity and higher education* (pp. 123–160). University Park and London: The Pennsylvania State University Press.

Kuklick, B. (1985). The professionalization of the humanities. In D. Callahan, A. L. Caplan, & B. Jennings (Eds.), *Applying the humanities* (pp. 41–54). New York: Plenum Press.

Lakoff, G., & Johnson, M. (1980). *Metaphors we live by.* Chicago: University of Chicago Press.

Lasker, G. W., & Mascie-Taylor, C. G. N. (Eds.). (1993). *Research strategies in human biology: Field and survey studies.* Cambridge: Cambridge University Press.

Lattuca, L. (2001). *Creating interdisciplinarity: Interdisciplinary research and teaching among college and university faculty.* Nashville, TN: Vanderbilt University Press.

Leary, M. R. (2004). *Introduction to behavioral research methods* (4th ed.). Boston: Pearson Education.

Lenoir, T. (1997). *Instituting science: The cultural production of scientific disciplines (writing science).* Stanford: Stanford University Press.

Levin, H. L. (2003). *The earth through time.* Hoboken, NJ: John Wiley & Sons.

Long, D. (2002). *Interdisciplinarity and the English school of international relations.* Paper presented at the International Studies Association Annual Convention, New Orleans, March 25–27.

Longo, G. (2002). The constructed objectivity of the mathematics and the cognitive subject. In M. Mugur-Schachter & A. van der Merwe (Eds.), *Quantum mechanics, mathematics, cognition and action* (pp. 433–462). Boston: Kluwer Academic.

Lyman, P. (1997). Liberal education in cyberia. In R. Orrill (Ed.), *Education and democracy: Re-imagining liberal learning in America* (pp. 299–320). New York: College Entrance Board.

Lyon, A. (1992, October). Interdisciplinarity: Giving up territory. *College English, 54*(6), 681–693.

Mackey, J. L. (2001). Another approach to interdisciplinary studies. *Issues in Integrative Studies, 19,* 59–70.

Mackey, J. L. (2002). Rules are not the way to do interdisciplinarity: A response to Szostak. *Issues in Integrative Studies, 20,* 123–129.

Magnus, D. (2000). Down the primrose path: Competing epistemologies in early twentieth-century biology. In R. Creath & J. Maienschein (Eds.), *Biology and epistemology* (pp. 91–121). Cambridge, UK: Cambridge University Press.

Maienschein, J. (2000). Competing epistemologies and developmental biology. In R. Creath & J. Maienschein (Eds.), *Biology and epistemology* (pp. 122–137). Cambridge, UK: Cambridge University Press.

Manheim, J. B., Rich, R. C., Willnat, L., & Brians, C. L. (2006). *Empirical political analysis: Research methods in political science* (6th ed.). Boston: Pearson Education.

Marsh, D., & Furlong, P. (2002). A skin, not a sweater: Ontology and epistemology in political science. In D. Marsh & G. Stoker (Eds.), *Theory and methods in political science* (2nd ed., pp. 17–41). New York: Palgrave Macmillan.

Marshall, C., & Rossman, G. B. (2006). *Designing qualitative research*. Thousand Oaks, CA: Sage.

Marshall, D. G. (1992). Literary interpretation. In J. Gibaldi (Ed.), *Introduction to scholarship in modern languages and literatures* (pp. 159–182). New York: The Modern Language Association of America.

Martin, R., Thomas, G., Charles, K., Epitropaki, O., & McNamara, R. (2005). The role of leader-member exchanges in mediating the relationship between locus of control and work reactions. *Journal of Occupational and Organizational Psychology, 78,* 141–147.

Maurer, B. (2004). Models of scientific inquiry and statistical practice: Implications for the structure of scientific knowledge. In M. L. Taper & S. R. Lee (Eds.), *The nature of scientific evidence: Statistical, philosophical, and empirical considerations* (pp. 17–31). Chicago: University of Chicago Press.

Mayville, W. V. (1978). *Interdisciplinarity: The mutable paradigm*. Washington DC: The Association of American Colleges and Universities.

McCall, R. B. (1990). Promoting interdisciplinarity and faculty-service-provider relations. *American Psychology, 45,* 1319–1324.

McKeon, R. P. (1964). The liberating and humanizing arts in education. In A. A. Cohen (Ed.), *Humanistic education and western civilization* (pp. 159–181). New York: Holt, Rinehart, & Winston.

McKim, V. R. (1997). Introduction. In V. R. McKim, S. P. Turner, & S. Turner (Eds.), *Causality in crisis? Statistical methods and the search for causal knowledge in the social sciences*. Notre Dame, IN: University of Notre Dame Press.

Mehl, J., Gulick, W., & Cree, C. (1987, Fall). Open forum: Towards a functional definition of the humanities. *Humanities Education,* 3–15.

Merari, A. (1998). The readiness to kill and die: Suicidal terrorism in the Middle East. In W. Reich (Ed.), *Origins of terrorism: Psychologies, ideologies, theologies, states of mind* (pp. 192–210). Washington, DC: Woodrow Wilson Center Press.

Miles, M. B., & Huberman, M. (1994). *Qualitative data analysis: An expanded sourcebook* (2nd ed.). Thousand Oaks, CA: Sage.

Miller, R. C. (1982). Varieties of interdisciplinary approaches in the social sciences. *Issues in Integrative Studies, 1,* 1–37.

Minor, V. H. (2001). *Art history's history.* (2nd ed.). Upper Saddle River, NJ: Prentice Hall.

Modiano, R. (1999). Sameness or difference? Historicist readings of "The Rime of the Ancient Mariner." In P. H. Fry (Ed.), *Samuel Taylor Coleridge: The rime of the ancient mariner* (pp. 187–219). Boston: Bedford/St. Martin's.

Moran, J. (2002). *Interdisciplinarity*. New York: Routledge.

Motes, M. A., Bahr, G. S., Atha-Weldon, C., & Dansereau, D. F. (2003). Academic guide maps for learning psychology. *Teaching of Psychology, 30*(3), 240–242.

Murfin, R. C. (1999a). Deconstruction and "The Rime of the Ancient Mariner." In P. H. Fry (Ed.), *Samuel Taylor Coleridge: The rime of the ancient mariner* (pp. 261–282). Boston: Bedford/St. Martin's.

Murfin, R. C. (1999b). Marxist criticism and "The Rime of the Ancient Mariner."
  In P. H. Fry (Ed.), *Samuel Taylor Coleridge: The rime of the ancient mariner*
  (pp. 131–147). Boston: Bedford/St. Martin's.

Murfin, R. C. (1999c). The new historicism and "The Rime of the Ancient Mariner."
  In P. H. Fry (Ed.), *Samuel Taylor Coleridge: The rime of the ancient mariner*
  (pp. 168–186). Boston: Bedford/St. Martin's.

Murfin, R. C. (1999d). Psychoanalytic criticism and "The Rime of the Ancient
  Mariner." In P. H. Fry (Ed.), *Samuel Taylor Coleridge: The rime of the ancient
  mariner* (pp. 220–238). Boston: Bedford/St. Martin's.

Murfin, R. C. (1999e). Reader-response criticism and "The Rime of the Ancient
  Mariner." In P. H. Fry (Ed.), *Samuel Taylor Coleridge: The rime of the ancient
  mariner* (pp. 97–113). Boston: Bedford/St. Martin's.

Myers, C., & Haynes, C. (2002). Transforming undergraduate science through interdisciplinary inquiry. In C. Haynes (Ed.), *Innovations in interdisciplinary teaching* (pp. 179–197). Phoenix, AZ: American Council on Education/The Oryx
  Press.

Nagy, C. (2005). *Anthropogenic forces degrading tropical ecosystems in Latin
  America: A Costa Rican case study.* Unpublished Paper.

National Academy of Sciences, National Academy of Engineering, & Institute
  of Medicine. (2005). *Facilitating interdisciplinary research.* Washington, DC:
  National Academies Press.

National Center for Educational Statistics. (2003). *The condition of education 2003.*
  Washington, DC: Department of Education.

National Research Council. (2002, April 17). *Connecting quarks with the cosmos:
  Eleven science questions for the new century.* Washington, DC: The National
  Academies Press. Retrieved October 3, 2007, from http://www7.national
  academies.org/bpa/FrontMatterq2cprepub.pdf

Nehamas, A. (1997). Trends in recent American philosophy. In T. Bender, C. E.
  Schorske, & S. R. Graubard (Eds.), *American academic culture* (pp. 227–241).
  Princeton, NJ: Princeton University Press.

Neuman, W. L. (2006). *Social research methods: Qualitative and quantitative
  approaches* (6th ed.). Boston: Pearson Education.

Newell, W. H. (1990). Interdisciplinary curriculum development. *Issues in Integrative
  Studies, 8,* 69–86.

Newell, W. H. (1992). Academic disciplines and undergraduate interdisciplinary education: Lessons from the school of interdisciplinary studies at Miami University,
  Ohio. *European Journal of Education, 27*(3), 211–221.

Newell, W. H. (1998). Professionalizing interdisciplinarity. In W. H. Newell (Ed.),
  Interdisciplinarity: Essays from the literature (pp. 529–563). New York: College
  Entrance Examination Board.

Newell, W. H. (2000). Transdisciplinarity reconsidered. In M. Somerville &
  D. J. Rapport (Eds.), *Transdisciplinarity: Recreating integrated knowledge*
  (pp. 42–48). Oxford, UK: EOLSS.

Newell, W. H. (2001). A theory of interdisciplinary studies. *Issues in integrative
  studies, 19,* 1–25.

Newell, W. H. (2005). *Distinctive challenges of library-based interdisciplinary
  research and writing.* Unpublished paper.

Newell, W. H. (2007). Decision making in interdisciplinary studies. In G. Morçöl
  (Ed.), *Handbook of decision making* (pp. 245–264). New York: Marcel-Dekker.

Newell, W. H., & Green, W. J. (1982). Defining and teaching interdisciplinary studies. *Improving College and University Teaching, 30*(1), 23–30.

Newman, D. M. (2004). *Sociology: Exploring the architecture of everyday life* (5th ed.). Thousand Oaks, CA: Pine Forge Press.

Nikitina, S. (2002). "Navigating the disciplinary fault lines" in science and in the classroom: Undergraduate neuroscience classroom in mind, brain, and behavior at Harvard. *Issues in Integrative Studies, 20,* 27–44.

Nikitina, S. (2005). Pathways of interdisciplinary cognition. *Cognition and Instruction, 23*(3), 389–425.

Nissani, M. (1995). Fruits, salads, and smoothies: A working definition of interdisciplinarity. *Journal of Educational Thought, 29,* 119–126.

Novak, J. D. (1998). *Learning, creating, and using knowledge: Concept maps as facilitative tools in schools and corporations.* Mahwah, NJ: Lawrence Erlbaum Associates.

Novick, P. (1998). *That noble dream: The "objectivity question" and the American historical profession.* New York: Cambridge University Press.

Nussbaum, M. C. (1985). Historical conceptions of the humanities and their relationship to society. In D. Callahan, A. L. Caplan, & B. Jennings (Eds.), *Applying the humanities* (pp. 3–28). New York: Plenum Press.

Organization for Economic Cooperation and Development. (1972). *Interdisciplinarity: Problems of teaching and research in universities.* Paris: Author.

Palmer, C. L. (2001). *Work at the boundaries of science: Information and the interdisciplinary research process.* Boston: Kluwer Academic.

Palys, T. (1997). *Research decisions: Quantitative and qualitative perspectives.* Toronto: Harcourt Brace.

Pasler, J. (1997). Directions in musicology. *Acta Musicologica, 69*(1), 16–21.

Peck, J. M. (1989). There's no place like home? Remapping the topography of German studies. Special issue interdisciplinary theory and methods. *German Quarterly, 62*(2), 178–187.

Peterson's four year colleges. (2006). Florence, KY: Thompson Peterson's.

Petrie, H. (1976). Do you see what I see? The epistemology of interdisciplinary inquiry. *Journal of American Education, 10,* 29–43.

Pinnock, C. (1994). Feminist epistemology: Implications for philosophy of science. *Philosophy of Science, 61,* 646–657.

Polkinghorne, J. (1996). *Beyond science: The wider human context.* Cambridge: Cambridge University Press.

Post, G. M. (1998). Terrorist psycho-logic: Terrorist behavior as a product of psychological forces. In W. Reich (Ed.), *Origins of terrorism: Psychologies, ideologies, theologies, states of mind* (pp. 25–40). Washington, DC: Woodrow Wilson Center Press.

Preziosi, D. (1989). *Rethinking art history: Meditations on a coy science.* New Haven, CT: Yale University Press.

Quinn, G. P., & Keough, M. J. (2002). *Experimental design and data analysis for biologists.* Cambridge, UK: Cambridge University Press.

Rapoport, D. C. (1998). Sacred terror: A contemporary example from Islam. In W. Reich (Ed.), *Origins of terrorism: Psychologies, ideologies, theologies, states of mind* (pp. 103–130). Washington, DC: Woodrow Wilson Center Press.

Rashdall, H. (1936). *The universities in Europe in the middle ages, Vol. 1.* London: Oxford University Press.

Reese, W. L. (1980). *The dictionary of philosophy and religion*. New York: Prometheus Books.

Reisberg, D. (2006). *Cognition: Exploring the science of the mind* (3rd ed.). New York: W.W. Norton & Company.

Repko, A. F. (2005). *Interdisciplinary practice: A student guide to research and writing*. Boston: Pearson Custom.

Repko, A. F. (2006). Disciplining interdisciplinarity: The case for textbooks. *Issues in Integrative Studies, 24,* 112–142.

Richards, D. G. (1996). The meaning and relevance of "synthesis" in interdisciplinary studies. *The Journal of Education, 45*(2), 114–128.

Rogers, Y., Scaife, M., & Rizzo, A. (2005). Interdisciplinarity: An emergent or engineered process? In S. J. Derry, C. D. Schunn, & M. A. Gernsbacher (Eds.), *Interdisciplinary collaboration: An emerging cognitive science* (pp. 265–285). Mahwah, NJ: Lawrence Erlbaum Associates.

Rosenau, P. M. (1992). *Post-modernism and the social sciences: Insights, inroads, and intrusions*. Princeton, NJ: Princeton University Press.

Rosenberg, A. (2000). *Philosophy of science* (2nd ed.). New York: Routledge.

Saffle, M. (2005). The humanities. In M. K. Herndon (Ed.), *An introduction to interdisciplinary studies* (pp. 11–27). Dubuque, IA: Kendall/Hunt.

Salmon, M. H. (1997). Ethical considerations in anthropology and archeology: Or, relativism and justice for all. *Journal of Anthropological Research, 53,* 47–63.

Salter, L., & Hearn, A. (1996). Introduction. In L. Salter & A. Hearn (Eds.), *Outside the lines: Issues in interdisciplinary research* (pp. 3–15). Montreal: McGill-Queen's University Press.

Saxe, J. G. (1963). *The blind men and the elephant*. New York: McGraw-Hill.

Scheurich, J. J. (1997). *Research method in the postmodern*. Washington, DC: The Falmer Press.

Schoenfeld, K. (2005). *Customer service: The ultimate return policy*. Unpublished paper.

Schulman, L. S. (2002). Foreword. In M. Taylor Huber & S. P. Morreale (Eds.), *Disciplinary styles in the scholarship of teaching and learning: Exploring common ground* (pp. v–ix). Menlo Park, CA: American Association for Higher Education.

Seabury, M. B. (2002). Writing in interdisciplinary courses: Coaching integrative thinking. In C. Haynes (Ed.), *Innovations in interdisciplinary teaching* (pp. 38–64). Westport, CT: Oryx Press.

Seabury, M. B. (2004). Scholarship about interdisciplinarity: Some possibilities and guidelines. *Issues in Integrative Studies, 22,* 52–84.

Searing, S. E. (1992). How libraries cope with interdisciplinarity: The case of women's studies. *Issues in Integrative Studies, 10,* 7–25.

Seipel, M. (2002). *Interdisciplinarity: An introduction*. Retrieved from http://www2.truman.edu/~mseipel/

Sewell, W. H. (1989). Some reflections on the golden age of interdisciplinary social psychology. *Social Psychology Quarterly, 52*(2), 88–97.

Shin, U. (1986). The structure of interdisciplinary knowledge: A polanyian view. *Issues in Integrative Studies, 4,* 93–104.

Silberberg, M. S. (2006). *Chemistry: The molecular nature of matter and change* (4th ed.). Boston: McGraw-Hill.

Sill, D. (1996). Integrative thinking, synthesis, and creativity in interdisciplinary studies. *Journal of General Education, 45*(2), 129–151.

Silver, L. (2005). *Composing race and gender: The appropriation of social identity in fiction*. Unpublished paper.

Silverman, D. (2000). *Doing qualitative research: A practical handbook*. London: Sage.

Simpson, D. (1999). How Marxism reads "The rime of the ancient mariner." In P. H. Fry (Ed.), *Samuel Taylor Coleridge: The rime of the ancient mariner* (pp. 148–167). Boston: Bedford/St. Martin's.

Sjoberg, G., & Nett, R. (1968). *A methodology for social research*. New York: Harper & Row.

Smelser, N. J., & Swedberg, R. (Eds.). (2005). *The handbook of economic sociology* (2nd ed.). Princeton, NJ: Princeton University Press.

Smolinski, W. J. (2005). *Fresh water scarcity in Texas*. Unpublished paper.

Snow, C. P. (1964). *The two cultures*. London: Cambridge University Press.

Society for Industrial and Organization Psychology. (1998). *Perspective-taking*. Retrieved from http://siop.org/Instruct/LMXTheory/sld009.htm

Sokolowski, R. (1998). The method of philosophy: Making distinctions. *The Review of Metaphysics, 51*(3), 1–11.

Somerville, M. A., & Rapport, D. J. (Eds.). (2000). *Transdisciplinarity: Recreating integrated knowledge*. Oxford, UK: EOLSS.

Somit, A., & Tanenhaus, J. (1967). *The development of American political science*. Boston: Allyn & Bacon.

Spooner, M. (2004). Generating integration and complex understanding: Exploring the use of creative thinking tools within interdisciplinary studies. *Issues in Integrative Studies, 22*, 85–111.

Squires, G. (1975). *Interdisciplinarity: A report by the group for research and innovation*. London: Group for Research and Innovation, Nuffield Foundation.

Steffen, W., Sanderson, A., Jager, J., Tyson, P. D., Moore, B., Matson, P. A., et al. (2004). *Global change and the earth system: A planet under pressure*. Netherlands: Springer.

Stember, M. (1991). Advancing the social sciences through the interdisciplinary enterprise. *The Social Science Journal, 28*(1), 1–14.

Stoddard, E. R. (1991). Frontiers, borders, and border segmentation: Toward a conceptual clarification. *Journal of Borderlands Studies, 6*(1), 1–22.

Stoker, G., & Marsh, D. (2002). Introduction. In D. Marsh & G. Stoker (Eds.), *Theory and methods in political science* (2nd ed., pp. 1–16). New York: Palgrave Macmillan.

Stoll, C. (1999). *High-tech heretic: Why computers don't belong in the classroom and other reflections by a computer contrarian*. New York: Doubleday.

Stoller, P. (1997). *Sensuous scholarship*. Philadelphia: University of Pennsylvania Press.

Stone, J. R. (1998). Introduction. In J. R. Stone (Ed.), *The craft of religious studies* (pp. 1–17). New York: St. Martin's Press.

Struppa, D. C. (2002). The nature of interdisciplinarity. *Perspectives: The Journal of the Association of General and Liberal Studies, 30*(1), 97–105.

Sturgeon, S., Martin, M. G. F., & Grayling, A. C. (1995). Epistemology. In A. C. Grayling (Ed.), *Philosophy 1: A guide through the subject* (pp. 7–60). New York: Oxford University Press.

Swoboda, W. W. (1979). Disciplines and interdisciplinarity: A historical perspective. In J. J. Kockelmans (Ed.), *Interdisciplinarity and higher education* (pp. 49–92). University Park: Pennsylvania State University Press.

Szostak, R. (2002). How to do interdisciplinarity: Integrating the debate. *Issues in Integrative Studies, 20,* 103–122.

Szostak, R. (2004). *Classifying science: Phenomena, data, theory, method, practice.* Netherlands: Springer.

Szostak, R. (2005). *Modernism, postmodernism, and interdisciplinarity.* Unpublished paper.

Szostak, R. (2006, August). Economic history as it is and should be: Toward an open, honest, methodologically flexible, theoretically diverse, interdisciplinary exploration of the causes and consequences of economic growth. *Journal of Socio-Economics,* 727–750.

Taffel, A. (1992). Physics: Its methods and meanings (6th ed.). Upper Saddle River, NJ: Prentice-Hall.

Taper, M. L., & Lele, S. R. (2004). The nature of scientific evidence: A forward-looking synthesis. In M. L. Taper & S. R. Lele (Eds.), *The nature of scientific evidence: Statistical, philosophical, and empirical considerations* (pp. 527–551). Chicago: University of Chicago Press.

Tashakkori, A., & Teddlie, C. B. (1998). *Mixed methodology: Combining quantitative and qualitative approaches.* Thousand Oaks, CA: Sage.

Trow, M. (1984). Interdisciplinary studies as a counterculture: Problems of birth, growth and survival. *Issues in Integrative Studies, 4,* 1–15.

Vars, G. (2002). Educational connoisseurship, criticism, and the assessment of integrative studies. *Issues in Integrative Studies, 20,* 65–76.

Vernon, P. E. (1989). The nature-nurture problem in creativity. In J. A. Glover, R. R. Ronning, & C. R. Reynolds (Eds.), *Handbook of creativity* (pp. 93–110). New York: Plenum Press.

Vess, D. (2004). *Explorations in interdisciplinary teaching and learning: A collection of portfolios by Dr. Deborah Vess Carnegie scholar 1999–2000* (pp. 1–10). Retrieved April 9, 2004, from http://www.faculty.de.gcsu.edu/~dvess/ids/course-portfolios/overview.htm

Vess, D., & Linkon, S. (2002). Navigating the interdisciplinary archipelago: The scholarship of interdisciplinary teaching and learning. In M. Taylor Huber & S. P. Morreale (Eds.), *Disciplinary styles in the scholarship of teaching and learning: Exploring common ground* (pp. 87–106). Washington, DC: American Association for Higher Education and the Carnegie Foundation for the Advancement of Teaching.

Vickers, J. (1998). "[U]framed in open, unmapped fields": Teaching the practice of interdisciplinarity. *Arachne: An Interdisciplinary Journal of the Humanities, 4*(2), 11–42.

Wallace, R. A., & Wolf, A. (2006). *Contemporary sociological theory: Expanding the classical tradition* (6th ed.). Upper Saddle River, NJ: Pearson.

Watson, J. D. (1968). *The double helix: A personal account of the discovery of the structure of DNA.* New York: Simon & Schuster.

Weingart, P. (2000). Introduction. In P. Weingart & N. Stehr (Eds.), *Practising interdisciplinarity* (pp. xi–xvi). Toronto: University of Toronto Press.

Welch, J., IV. (2003). Future directions for interdisciplinarity effectiveness in education. *Issues in Integrative Studies, 21,* 170–203.

Wentworth, J., & Davis, J. R. (2002). Enhancing interdisciplinarity through team teaching. In C. Haynes (Ed.), *Innovations in interdisciplinary teaching* (pp. 16–37). Westport, CT: Oryx Press.

Wheeler, L., & Miller, E. (1970). *Multidisciplinary approach to planning*. Paper presented at Council of Education Facilities Planners 47th Annual Conference in Oklahoma City, OK, 6 Oct 1976. (ERIC Document Reproduction Service No. ED044814)

Whitaker, M. P. (1996). Relativism. In A. Barnard & J. Spencer (Eds.), *Encyclopedia of social and cultural anthropology* (pp. 478–482). New York: Routledge.

White, L. M. (1997). The humanities. In J. G. Gaff, J. L. Ratcliff, & Associates (Eds.), *Handbook of the undergraduate curriculum: A comprehensive guide to purposes, structures, practices, and change* (pp. 262–279). San Francisco: Jossey-Bass.

Wiersma, W., & Jurs, S. G. (2005). *Research methods in education: An introduction*. Boston: Allyn & Bacon.

Wolfe, C., & Haynes, C. (2003) Interdisciplinary writing assessment profiles. *Issues in Integrative Studies, 21*, 126–169.

Xio, H. (2005). *Research methods for English studies*. Edinburgh: Edinburgh University Press.

Zeki, S. (2000). *Inner vision: An exploration of art and the brain*. New York: Oxford University Press.

Zetterberg, H. L. (1967). *On theory and verification in sociology* (3rd ed). Totowa, NJ: Bedminster Press.

Author Index _____

Adams, L. S., 109, 215
Agger, B., 57, 103
Alford, R. R., 108
Alliance for Childhood, 236
Alvesson, M., 12, 91, 100–101
Amariglio, J., 68
American Sociological Association, 56, 70
Anderson, C., 35
Anderson, L. W., 115
Aristotle, 31
Arms, L. A., 291–292
Armstrong, F. H., 43
Arthurs, A., 28
Association for General and
    Liberal Studies, 328
Association for Integrative Studies, 37, 327
Association of American Colleges,
    39, 125, 330
Atha-Weldon, C., 164
Atran, S., 249, 254, 256, 304
Augsburg, T., 334

Baca, J. F., 10
Bahr, G. S., 164
Bailis, S., 101–102, 122, 158
Bal, M.:
    analysis of problem, 226
    on art, 109
    choice of method, 206
    conflicting theory-based insights, 264–266,
        268–269
    on cultural analysis, 113, 119, 208–209
    on disciplinary perspective, 222
    expert's understanding of problem,
        231–235
    on graffito, 252–253
    integration of insights, 288–289, 308
    on interdisciplinary studies, 16, 61
    interdisciplinary understanding, 315–316

justification of interdisciplinary
    approach, 156
statement of problem, 150
theories, identification of, 198
Baldick, C., 257
Bandura, A., 249, 254, 256, 282
Barnard, A., 68, 80
Barnet, S., 97, 109, 208
Baum, J., 30
Becher, T., 36, 56, 58
Bechtel, W., 64, 105
Bell, J. A., 95, 98, 340
Bender, T., 35
Bennington, G., 16
Berg, B. L., 201–205, 209, 214–215
Bernard, H. R., 91, 96, 106–107
Berthoff, A., 46
Bishop, M., 32
Blackburn, S., 92
Blau, J. R., 70, 80
Blesser, B., 312
Bloom, B. S., 115–116, 295–296
Bogdan, R., 202
Bohlman, P. V., 74
Boix Mansilla, V.:
    on disciplinary perspective, 53–54
    on integration of knowledge, 19, 123, 126
    on interdisciplinary understanding,
        11–12, 21, 310–311
    resources on interdisciplinary
        studies, 332, 333
Booth, W. C., 187
Boulding, K., 281, 287, 289–290
Boyd, I., 152
Boyer, E. I., 35
Bradsford, J. D., 236
Bressler, C. E., 110
Brians, C. L., 91
Briggs, A., 32

371

Bromme, R.:
  on common ground theory, 273–274, 337
  on disciplinary insights, 250
  on disciplinary perspective, 58
  on interdisciplinarians, traits of, 42
  theory of, studies supporting, 80
Brown, A. L., 236
Bruun, H., 52, 56
Bryman, A., 113, 214
Burke, P., 73

Caldwell, L. K., 7
Calhoun, L. K., 70, 76, 80–81, 95, 101
Capps, W. H., 76, 81
Carey, S. S., 214
Carlisle, B., 43
Carnegie Foundation for the
    Advancement of Teaching, 38
Carp, R. M., 10–11, 16, 59, 185, 241
Charles, K., 121
Cocking, R. R., 236
Columb, G. G., 187
Columbia University, 35
Coppola, B. P., 64
Cree, C., 81
Crenshaw, M., 249, 256, 303
Creso, M., 334
Creswell, J. W., 215
Cullenberg, S., 68, 90–91
Czechowski, J., 334
Czuchry, M., 186

Dabrowski, I. J., 46
Dansereau, D. F., 164, 186
Davidson, C., 72
Davis, G. A., 46, 298
Davis, J. R., 25, 44, 123, 132, 333
Davis, W., 46
Delph, J. B.:
  on crime investigation disciplines, 285–286
  on criminal profiling, 307, 315
  interdisciplinary crime investigation,
      119, 156, 221–222
  on interdisciplinary research, 179
  on perfect crimes, 149
Denzin, N. K., 209, 215
Derry, S. J., 80
DeZure, D., 38
Dietrich, W., 29, 131, 148, 155, 190–191
Dogan, M, 56–57, 74
Dölling, I., 15
Donald, J., 63, 65, 90, 102, 105–106
Dorsten, L. E., 77, 108
Dow, S., 96, 106–107, 111

Easton, D., 34
Edwards, A. F., 334
Eilenberg, S., 260, 263
Elliott, D. J., 92–93, 97, 100, 110
Ember, C. R., 67
Ember, M., 67
Englehart, L., 290–291
Epitropaki, O., 121
Etzioni, A., 290

Farmer, P., 317
Ferguson, F., 260, 263
Fernie, E., 207, 231
Fiscella, J. B., 184, 327, 333, 334
Fischer, C. C.:
  on application form, 257
  on interdisciplinary integration, 258–259,
      261–262
  interdisciplinary investigation, 194–195,
      197–198
  interdisciplinary problems, 149, 153, 155
  interdisciplinary research, 257
  on occupational sex discrimination theory,
      226, 230–231, 233, 265
  on sex discrimination as basis of causal
      variables, 206
  theory-based insights,
      conflicting, 266–269
Fish, S., 39, 293
Foster, H., 214
Foucault, M., 36
Frank, R., 27
Frank, R. H., 286–287
Frankfort-Nachmias, C.:
  on assumptions, 89, 100
  on social sciences, 67, 77
Friedman, S. S., 40
Frodeman, R., 334
Fry, P. H., 196, 228, 258–259, 262–264
Fuller, S., 22–24, 31, 128
Furlong, P., 93, 95–96
Fussell, S. G., 121

Gaff, J. G., 57
Gale, R., 334
Gallagher, C., 103
Garber, M., 7, 79
Gardner, H., 19, 58
Gauch, H. G., 214
Geertz, C., 28, 41, 79
Gerdes, E. P., 283–284
Gernsbacher, M. A., 80
Gerring, J., 71, 81, 99, 214
Giere, R. N., 113

Giri, A. K., 39–40
Goldberg, D., 72
Goldenberg, S, 239
Goodin, R. E., 91, 96, 107, 254
Grace, N., 52
Graff, G., 35, 334
Grayling, A. C., 92
Graziano, A. M., 107
Green, W. J., 4, 40, 117, 123, 272, 280
Greenblatt, S., 103
Griffin, G., 97, 110
Gulick, W., 81
Gunn, G., 30, 41, 43, 74

Haas, P., 40–42
Hacking, I., 55
Hagan, F. E., 214
Hall, D. J., 202
Hall, I., 202
Hark, S., 15
Harris, E., 73
Harris, J., 92, 93, 97
Hart, C., 187
Harvard University, 35, 247–275, 330
Haskins, C. H., 32
Haynes, C.:
    on common vocabulary, 284
    on conflicts in insights, 248, 251
    on defining scope, 145
    *Innovations in Interdisciplinary
        Teaching*, 333
    on interdisciplinary research,
        140, 144–145, 179
    on traits, 42
Hearns, A., 9, 18, 79
Hendershott, A. B., 67
Hershberg, T., 34
Hirst, P. H., 31
Holmes, F. L., 105
Hoskin, K. W., 33, 36
Hotchkiss, L., 77, 108
Houtz, J. C., 299
Howell, M., 92, 97, 215
Huber, M. T.:
    on interdisciplinary studies, 4, 38, 79
    resources on interdisciplinary
        studies, 334
Huberman, M., 215
Huffman, K., 69
Hursh, B., 40–42, 120, 127–128,
    138–139, 143
Hutcheson, P. A., 35
Hutchings, P., 38, 334
Hyneman, C. S., 107

Iggers, G. G., 92, 109
Innocent III, Pope, 32
Institute of Medicine, 11, 63

Jacobs, D. C., 64
Johnson, M., 22, 312
Jurs, S. G., 214

Kain, D. L., 332, 333, 334
Karlqvist, A., 52
Kassabian, A., 74
Katz, C., 36–37
Keller, H., 275
Kelly, J. S., 95, 117–118, 274
Keough, M. J., 90
Kimmel, S. E., 333
Klee, R., 63
Klein, J. T.:
    on adequacy *vs.* mastery, 189
    on American studies, 73
    on borrowing, 192
    on boundary crossing, 22, 57, 74–75
    on bridge building, 23
    on communicative competence, 24
    on concepts and theories, 102–103, 158
    on creativity, 298
    on decision making, 139
    on disciplinary perspective, 59
    on disciplines, 30, 32–35, 122
    on epistemological self-reflexivity, 95
    on grand theory, 101
    on integration of knowledge,
        123–125, 128, 280, 295
    on integration process, 302
    on interdisciplinary assumptions, 38–39
    on interdisciplinary process, 300
    on interdisciplinary research, 140, 154, 241
    on interdisciplinary student, 177
    on interdisciplinary studies, 25–26
    interdisciplinary studies, defining, 5–8, 11,
        15, 17–20
    on interdisciplinary studies, history of, 28
    on mapping, 24
    resources on interdisciplinary studies, 332,
        333, 334
    on skills, 45
    on social sciences, 70
    on subject headings, 184
    on synthesis, 116
    on traits, 42–43
Klingerman, H.-D., 91, 96, 107, 254
Kockelmans, J. J., 126–127, 271–272
Kraus, R. M., 121
Kuklick, B., 5

Lakoff, G., 22, 312
Lasker, G. W., 63
Lattuca, L.:
  on epistemology, 95
  on grand theory, 104
  integration, assessing, 132–133
  interdisciplinary resources, 332–333
  on interdisciplinary studies,
      15, 18, 25
  on modern disciplines, 33
  on modernist approach, 98
Leary, M. R., 90–91, 96, 107, 254
Lele, S. R., 64, 113
Lenoir, T., 56
Levin, H. L., 64
Lincoln, Y. S., 215
Linkon, S., 74
Long, D., 8
Longo, G., 94
Lyman, P., 138
Lyon, A., 23

Mackey, J. L., 158, 297
Magnus, D., 94
Maienschein, J., 94, 105
Manheim, J. B., 91
Marsh, D., 93, 95–96, 99
Marshall, C., 215
Marshall, D. G., 92
Martin, M. G. F., 92
Martin, R., 121
Mascie-Taylor, C. G. N., 63
Maurer, B., 65, 89–90
Mayville, W. V., 36
McCall, R. B., 40
McKeon, R. P., 35
McKim, V. R., 238
McNamara, R., 121
Mehl, J., 81
Merari, A., 249, 254, 256, 303
Micard, G., 32
Miles, M. B., 215
Miller, E., 14
Miller, R. C., 53
Minor, V. H., 72
Mitcham, C., 334
Modiano, R., 263
Moore, M., 40–42
Moran, J., 4, 13, 16–17, 31–34, 36
Morreale, S. P., 4, 79
Motes, M. A., 164–168
Murfin, R. C., 260, 263
Myers, C., 42, 145

Nachmias, D.:
  on assumptions, 89, 100
  on social sciences, 67, 77
National Academies, 334
National Academy of Engineering, 11, 63
National Academy of Sciences, 11, 28, 63,
      151, 153, 236, 312
National Research Council, 65, 236
Nehamas, A., 75
Nett, R., 77
Neuman, W. L., 12, 176, 187
Newell, W. H.:
  on assumptions, 251–252
  on borrowing, 192
  on causal variables, 233, 236
  on collaboration, 190
  on common ground theory, 275, 280
  on common vocabulary, 284
  on concepts and theories, 284
  on conflicts in insights, 248, 250
  on disciplinary perspective, 59, 217
  on extension, 287
  on humanities, 72
  on integration of knowledge, 117, 119,
      123–124, 128, 130
  on integration process, 300, 301
  on integrative techniques, 292
  on interdisciplinary
      assumptions, 38–40
  on interdisciplinary method, 272
  on interdisciplinary research,
      138–139, 141, 143, 241
  on interdisciplinary student, 177
  on interdisciplinary studies, 4, 6, 10
  interdisciplinary studies, defining,
      11, 13, 17, 79
  on intuition, 297
  on mapping, 165–166
  new understanding, testing, 312
  on organization, 289
  on personal bias, 224
  on problem complexity, 152
  on relevant disciplines, 162, 169
  resources on interdisciplinary studies,
      332, 333, 334
  strengths/weaknesses, evaluating, 228
  on subject headings, 184
  on traits, 43–44
  on transdisciplinarity, 113
  on transformation, 290
Newman, D. M., 56
Ngay, C., 285, 306–307, 314
Nietzsche, F., 34

Nikitina, S.:
  on common ground, 274–275
  on integration of knowledge, 295, 297
  on integrative work, 80
  on interdisciplinary studies, 15
  on nonlinear thinking, 46
  on process, 300
  on provisional integration, 118
Nissani, M., 13, 120
Novak, J. D., 61, 101, 140
Novick, P., 97
Nussbaum, M. C., 31

Organization for Economic Cooperation and
      Development, 17, 44
Ortega y Gasset, J., 34

Pahre, R., 56–57, 74
Palmer, C. L., 3
Palys, T., 239
Pasler, J., 74
Patricola, C., 299
Peck, J. M., 128–129
Petrie, H., 79
Pinnock, C., 99
Polkinghorne, J., 113
Post, G. M., 182, 249, 254, 256, 302
Prevenier, W., 92, 97, 215
Preziosi, D., 56

Quinn, G. P., 90

Rapoport, D. C., 249, 254, 256, 303
Rapport, D. J., 25
Rashdall, H., 32
Ratcliff, J. L., 57
Raulin, M. L., 107
Reese, W. L., 75
Reisberg, D., 282
Repko, A. F.:
  categories of disciplines, 78
  interdisciplinary research process
      model, 142
  resources on interdisciplinary studies,
      332, 333, 334
Rhoten, D., 334
Rich, R. C., 91
Richards, D. G., 123
Rizzo, A., 7
Roberts, J. A., 334
Rogers, Y., 7, 13, 79, 105
Rosenau, P. M., 93, 99–100, 103, 104
Rosenberg, A., 95, 113

Rossman, G. B., 215
Ruccio, D., 68

Saffle, M., 32
Salmon, M., 91
Salter, L., 9, 18, 79
Salter, L. R., 312
Saxe, J. G., 55
Scaife, M., 7
Scheurich, J. J., 215
Schoenfeld, K., 288
Schulman, L. S., 4
Schuun, C. D., 80
Seabury, M. B., 45, 131, 138, 333, 334
Searing, S. E., 183
Seipel, M., 123, 131
Sewell, W. H., 5
Shapiro, D. F., 332
Shin, U., 302
Silberberg, M. S., 105
Sill, D., 30, 298–299
Silver, L., 150, 157, 222–223, 286, 309, 317
Silverman, D., 238
Simpson, D., 260, 263
Sjoberg, G., 77
Sköldberg, K, 12
Smelser, N. J., 68, 70, 80
Smolinski, W. J., 149, 155,
      195–196, 220, 257–258, 261
Snow, C. P., 30
Society for Industrial and
      Organizational Psychology, 121
Sokolowski, R., 110
Somerville, M. A., 25
Somit, A., 91, 107
Spencer, J., 68, 80
Spooner, M., 46, 298, 299, 334
Squires, G., 23
Steffen, W., 90
Stember, M., 5, 215
Stoddard, E. R., 24
Stoker, G., 99
Stoll, C., 235
Stoller, P., 10, 47
Stone, J. R., 93, 98, 110
Struppa, D. C., 31
Sturgeon, S., 92, 93, 98
Sullivan, A., 275
Swedberg, R., 68, 70, 80
Swoboda, W. W., 34, 39
Szostak, R.:
  on concepts, 293
  on deductive theory selection, 198–199

on disciplinary method,
    200–201, 204–205, 237–239
on disciplinary perspective, 62, 81
on grand theory, 103
on integration, 302
on interdisciplinary study, 178
on mapping, 23–24, 187
on meaning, 25
on method, 104, 111, 113
on perspective, 54
on phenomena, 83–88
on relativism, 91
on research evaluation, 241
on scope, 144

Taffel, A., 94, 113
Tanenhaus, J., 91, 107
Taper, M. L., 64, 113
Tashakkori, A., 202
Taylor, S. J., 202
Teddlie, C. B., 202
Thomas, G., 121
Toppinen, A., 52
Trow, M., 42
Trowler, P. R., 56, 58

Vars, G. F., 295
Vernon, P. E., 298
Vernoy, J., 69
Vernoy, M., 69
Vess, D., 74, 299
Vickers, J., 9, 11, 39, 79, 235
Vico, G., 33

Walker, D., 334
Wallace, R. A., 57, 61

Watson, J. D.:
    analysis, 220, 225–226
    The Double Helix: A Personal
        Account of the Discovery of the
        Structure of DNA, 177
    evaluation, 229–230, 232–233
    experiments/models, 235
    extension, 287–288
    integrating insights, 304–306
    on interdisciplinary
        interpretation, 264
    interdisciplinary
        understandings, 313
    knowledge, 190–191
    methods, choosing, 206
    on theory, 254–255, 257
    theory-based insights,
        conflicting, 266–269
Weingart, P., 36–37
Welch, J., IV, 158
Wentworth, J., 44, 123, 132
Wheeler, L., 14
Whitaker, M. P., 91, 254, 256
White, L. M., 72–73, 76–77
Wiersma, W., 214
Williams, J. M., 187
Willnat, L., 91
Wolf, A., 57, 61
Wolfe, C., 144–145, 179,
    248, 251, 284
Wright, S. P., 67

Xio, H., 215

Zeki, S., 81
Zetterberg, H. L., 67

Subject Index _____

Abstract thinking, 45
Academic credibility, 177
Academic Search Complete, 328
Academy, 51–52
Acid rain, 218–219
Activity, 123
Adequacy:
   decision making for, 189–194
   description of, 189
   disciplinary, 39, 43–44, 143
   disciplinary methods, identification of,
      200–212
   for interdisciplinary work, 124–125
   in-text evidence of, 212–213
   literature search to develop, 177
   theories, identification of
      relevant, 194–200
Admission, Review, and Dismissal (ARD)
   meeting, 278–279
Aesthetics, 75
AGLS (Association for General and Liberal
   Studies), 328
AIS (Association for Integrative
   Studies), 37, 327
Altruism:
   grants and, 289–290
   integrative technique of
      extension, 287
Ambiguity, 42–43
Analysis:
   of problem from disciplinary
      perspectives, 225–228
   of problem from each disciplinary
      perspective, 217–224
   See also Cultural analysis; Insights,
      evaluation of
Answers, 277

Anthropogenic Forces Degrading Tropical
      Ecosystems in Latin America: A Costa
      Rican Case Study (Nagy):
   integration of insights, 306–307
   integrative technique of redefinition, 285
   interdisciplinary understanding, 314
Anthropology:
   assumptions of, 91
   description of, 67–68
   epistemology of, 96
   perspective of, 60
   research methods of, 107
Antidisciplinary view, 39
Applied professions, 4
Appropriation, 286, 317
ARD (Admission, Review, and Dismissal)
   meeting, 278–279
Art/Art history:
   assumptions of, 92
   cognitive discord in, 56–57
   description of, 73
   disciplinary perspective of, 55
   epistemology of, 97
   evaluation of strengths/weaknesses of, 231
   perspective of, 61
   research methods of, 109
Assessment, of integration, 132
Association for General and Liberal Studies
   (AGLS), 328
Association for Integrative Studies
   (AIS), 37, 327
Associations, interdisciplinary, 327–328
Assumptions:
   common ground, creation of, 279–280
   communication and, 273
   definition of, 89
   of disciplines in humanities, 90, 92–93

of disciplines in natural sciences, 89, 90
of disciplines in social sciences, 89–91
integration, basis of, 301
integrative technique of
       redefinition, 283–286
integrative technique of
       transformation, 290–292
interdisciplinary, 38–41
ontological, epistemological, value-laden,
       251–253
source of conflict between
       insights, 250

Bias:
   disciplinary, 145
   personal, 146–147
   reflection on, 240
"Bilingualism" metaphor, 24
Bioethics, 174
Biological anthropology, 67
Biology:
   assumptions of, 90
   epistemological assumptions in, 252
   epistemology of, 94
   focus of, 63
   integrative technique of
          extension, 287
   perspective of, 60
   relevance to human cloning, 174
   research methods used by,
          105, 210, 211, 212
Bloom's taxonomy, updated, 115–116
Body of research, 170
Books:
   literature search with, 182
   LOC classification system, 183
   LOC subject headings, 183–184
Boolean Search Strategy, 184, 331–332
Border disciplinarity, 152–153
Borrowing, 192–193
Boundaries:
   "boundary crossing" metaphor, 22–23
   crossing of disciplinary
          boundaries, 57
   disciplinary boundaries, gaps
          between, 30
   work of interdisciplinary studies, 5
Breadth:
   of knowledge from discipline, 190–193
   triangulation of depth, breadth,
          integration, 124–125
"Bridge building" metaphor, 23
Burden of comprehension, 192

Case study, 240
"Categories of Phenomena About the Human
       World" (Szostak)
   for literature search, 180, 182–183
   table of, 86–88
Checklist, evaluation of previous
       research, 240–241
Chemistry:
   assumptions of, 90
   epistemology of, 94
   focus of, 63–64
   perspective of, 60
   research methods of, 105
Choice. See Decision making
CISMI Carleton Interdisciplinary Science
       and Math Initiative, 329–330
Clarity, 147
Classification approach, 84, 86–88
Classification system, Library
       of Congress, 183
Classroom, 33
Cloning. See Human cloning
Close reading:
   for assumptions, 253
   for evidence, 235
   of insights, 181
   of texts, 97
   for theory expansion technique, 282
   for theory-based insights, 257
Cognitive abilities:
   in Bloom's taxonomy, 115–116
   decision making, 137–139
   for integration of insights, 296–299
Cognitive advancement:
   from integrated insights, 41
   from interdisciplinary studies, 12
Cognitive decentering:
   chart of, 41
   definition of, 40
Cognitive discord, 56–57
Cognitive fluidity, 84
Cognitive map, 192
Cognitive process:
   activities involved in
          integration, 120–122
   common ground and, 274–275
   required for common ground, 276–277
Cognitive psychology:
   assumption/insight on suicide
          terrorism, 254
   common ground findings of, 272–274
Cold War, 35–36
Collaboration, 44

Collective Rational Strategic
Choice Theory, 303
College, 51–52
Columbia River ecosystem:
adequacy in relevant disciplines for study
of, 190–191
disciplines that illuminate problem of, 171
See also Northwest Passage: The Great
Columbia River (Dietrich)
Columbia University, 35
Common ground:
challenges in creation of, 280–281
definition of, 271–272
extension technique, 286–289
importance for integrative
process, 275–280
as integration basis, 301
integrative techniques, value of, 292
intuition for creation of, 297
organization technique, 289–290
redefinition technique, 283–286
theory expansion technique, 281–283
theory of, 272–275
transformation technique, 290–292
See also Integration, of insights
Communication:
common ground theory, 272–274
skills of interdisciplinarian, 45
Communicative competence, 45
Complex problems:
cognitive decentering and, 40–41
disciplinary inadequacy, 39–40
disciplines unable to address, 30–31
interdisciplinarian traits and, 42–43
justification of interdisciplinary
approach, 152
Complexity, 152
Composing Race and Gender: The
Appropriation of Social Identity in
Fiction (Silver):
disciplinary perspectives on, 223–224
integration of insights, 309
integrative technique of
redefinition, 286
interdisciplinary understanding, 317–318
justification of interdisciplinary
approach, 157
statement of problem/question, 150–151
Comprehensive perspective, 127–128, 129
Computer searches, 181–184
Computer-assisted education, 235–236
Concept formation, 71
Concept/principle map, 163, 165

Concepts:
common ground and, 284
common ground, creation of, 279–280
definition of, 61, 250
disciplinary jargon, 145–146
disciplines and, 61–62
element of discipline, 4
embedded in theories, 253
integration, basis of, 301
integrative technique of redefinition,
283–286
integrative technique of transformation,
290–292
literature search to identify, 177
relationship to theory, 102
source of conflict between insights,
250–251
Conceptual framework, overarching, 126–127
Conceptual interdisciplinarity, 18
Conflict, 248
See also Insights, identification of
conflicts in
Content/textual analysis, 239
Contested terrain, 6
Context:
contextualizing problem, 177
for problem/question, 147–148
Continuous variables, 290
Costa Rica. See Anthropogenic Forces
Degrading Tropical Ecosystems in Latin
America: A Costa Rican Case Study
(Nagy)
Courses, for interdisciplinary studies, 324
Creativity:
creative breakthroughs, 30
creative imagination, 139–140
for integration of insights, 296, 298–299
skill of interdisciplinarian, 46
Creole, 24
Criminal profiling:
common ground on, 286
disciplinary perspectives on, 221–222
integration of insights, 307–308
interdisciplinary understanding, 119, 315
Critical humanities, 72
Critical interdisciplinarity, 18
Critical social theory, 69–70
CRM (customer relationship management), 288
Cultural analysis:
conflicting theory-based insights, 268–269
expert's definition of problem, skewed, 234
for humanities research, 208–209
integration of insights, 308–309

interdisciplinary understanding, 315–317
See also The Practice of Cultural Analysis:
Exposing Interdisciplinary
Interpretation (Bal)
Cultural anthropology:
definition of, focus of, 67–68
on suicide terrorism, 254
Current Index to Journals in Education
(journal), 328
Curriculum:
of discipline, 7
general education movement and, 35
of universities, 32
Customer relationship management
(CRM), 288
Customer service, 288
Customer Service: The Ultimate Return Policy
(Schoenfeld), 288

Data:
of expert, possibly skewed, 234–236
identification/analysis of, 241
Data management table:
example of, 182
for organization of information, 181
Databases:
interdisciplinary resources, 328–329
for literature search, 184
search strategies for, 331–332
Decentering, cognitive, 40–41
Decision making:
for adequacy in relevant disciplines,
189–194
choice of research methods, 210–212
interdisciplinary research process as,
137–139
Defining elements of disciplines:
assumptions, 89–93
epistemology, 93–101
method, 104–112
phenomena, 83–88
theory, 101–104
Depth:
of knowledge from discipline, 190–193
triangulation of depth, breadth,
integration, 124–125
Dialectical thinking, 45–46
Differences, 20
Disciplinarity, 51
Disciplinary, 5
Disciplinary adequacy:
of interdisciplinarian, 43–44
necessity of, 39

for research process, 143
See also Adequacy
Disciplinary bias, 145
Disciplinary boundary, 57, 128–129
Disciplinary categories:
description of, 52
list of, 53
Disciplinary decisions, 247
Disciplinary depth, 9–10
Disciplinary inadequacy, 39–40
Disciplinary jargon, 145–146
Disciplinary knowledge, 126
Disciplinary methods:
choice of, 210–212
criterion for choice of, 204–209
definition of, 200
of experts, 236–240
of humanities, 201
identification of, 200–212, 241
interdisciplinary position on, 201–202
of natural sciences, 200
number needed in research project,
209–210
qualitative methods, implications of,
203–204
quantitative *vs.* qualitative
debate, 202–203
of social sciences, 201
Disciplinary perspective:
analysis of problem from, 217–228
caveats concerning clarification
of, 59, 61–62
clarified definition of, 58–59
common ground and, 280
commonality of categories of, 77–78
definition of, 53–54
drawing on, 59
humanities, 71–77
in interdisciplinary studies
definition, 11, 12
knowledge structure, 51–52
misconceptions about "perspective"
term, 54–56
natural sciences, 63–67
natural sciences/humanities, overall
perspectives of, 60–61
overview of discussion of, 51
problems with concept of, 56–57
social sciences, 67–71
strengths/weaknesses of understanding,
228–232
theory and, 102–103
Disciplinary reductionism, 301

Disciplinary specialization:
   critique of, 28–31
   definition of, 28
   trend towards, 34
Disciplinary understanding, 21
Discipline:
   definition of, categories of, 3–5
   use of term, 52
Disciplines:
   boundary crossing, 22–23
   categories of, 52, 53
   conflicts between insights, sources of,
       250–255
   criticism of, 36
   formation of, 31
   as foundation for interdisciplinary studies,
       15–16, 38–39
   history of, 32–34
   integration and, 122
   interdisciplinarity and, 16–17
   interdisciplinary critique of, 28–31
   in literature search, 179
   origins of, 32
   receptivity to, 43
   role in interdisciplinary studies, 322–323
   structure of, 51–52
   studies *vs.*, 8, 9
   theory-based insights, conflict between,
       255–266
   training/attitudes and common ground,
       283–284
   See also Adequacy; Elements of disciplines
Disciplines, identification of relevant:
   mapping the problem, 163–168
   most relevant disciplines, 169–175
   potentially relevant disciplines, 160–163
Dissertations Abstracts database, 329
Diversity, 44
DNA structure. *See The Double Helix: A
   Personal Account of the Discovery of the
   Structure of DNA* (Watson)
*Double Exposures: The Subject of Cultural
   Analyses* (Bal), 308
*The Double Helix: A Personal Account of the
   Discovery of the Structure of DNA*
   (Watson):
   analysis of problem/insights, 225–226
   choice of disciplinary method, 206
   conflicting theory-based insights, 266–267
   disciplinary perspectives on
       DNA structure, 220
   evaluation of expert's understanding of
       problem, 229–230

   expert's definition of problem, skewed, 232
   historical background, 177
   integration of insights, 304–306
   integrative technique of extension, 287–288
   interdisciplinary understanding, 313–314

Earth science:
   assumptions of, 90
   disciplinary perspective of, 55
   epistemology of, 94
   focus of, 64
   perspective of, 60
   research methods of, 105
Ecology and Society (journal), 330
"Economic man," 233
Economics:
   assumptions of, 91
   description of, 68
   epistemology of, 96
   expert's definition of problem,
       skewed, 233
   integrative technique of extension, 287
   perspective of, 60
   research methods used by,
       107, 210, 211, 212
Education:
   computer-assisted education, 235–236
   general education movement, 35
Educational Resources Information
   Center (ERIC) database, 328
Efficiency, 250
Elements of disciplines:
   assumptions, 89–93
   epistemology, 93–101
   method, 104–112
   phenomena, 83–88
   theory, 101–104
Empiricism:
   definition of, 77
   epistemology and, 95
   scientific method and, 104, 106
Encyclopedia articles, 182
End product:
   in definition of integration, 296
   interdisciplinary understanding as, 310
Enlightenment, 32–33
Enterprise, 42
Environmental studies, 7, 290–291
Epistemological assumptions,
   252–253
Epistemological position:
   common ground theory and, 274
   definition of, 93

Epistemology:
    definition of, 75, 93
    epistemic norms of a discipline, 94
    epistemological approaches, 98–101
    epistemological position, 93
    expert's definition of problem, skewed, 234
    of humanities, 77, 95
    identification of, 241
    interdisciplinarity and, 16–17
    of natural sciences, 94–95
    of social sciences, 95, 96
ERIC (Educational Resources Information
        Center) database, 328
Etymology, 27–28
    See also Interdisciplinarity, origins of
Evaluation:
    of insights, 217
    of integration, 132
    See also Insights, evaluation of
Evidence:
    of expert may be skewed, 234–236
    identification/analysis of, 241
    sources of conflict between theory-based
        insights, 264, 266
Examination, 33
Existing literature, 178
Experiments:
    epistemological assumptions, 252
    strengths/weaknesses of, 237, 238
Expert interdisciplinarian, 44
Experts:
    data/evidence, possibly skewed, 234–236
    definition of problem, skewed, 232–234
    help with identification of disciplines, 162
    methods used by, 236–240
    strengths/weaknesses of understanding,
        228–232
    weaknesses of insights, 225
Exposure, 308, 316
Extension technique, 277, 286–289

Faith, 291–292
False consensus bias, 121
Federated Searching, 332
Feedback, 142–143
Feminism:
    description of, 75–76
    epistemological approach of, 99
Fiction. See Composing Race and Gender:
        The Appropriation of Social Identity in
        Fiction (Silver)
Fields, 19
Focus, of specialization, 28–29

Focus question, 151–157
    See also Problem definition/statement of
        focus question
Fool's Gold: A Critical Look at Computers in
        Childhood (Alliance for Childhood), 236
Foundation, disciplines as, 15–16, 38–39
Fresh Water Scarcity in Texas (Smolinski):
    conflicting theory-based insights, 261
    disciplinary perspectives on, 220–221
    justification of interdisciplinary
        approach, 155
    statement of problem/question, 149
    theories from disciplines on, 195, 196–197
    theory-based insights, 257–258
Fruit basket analogy, 120
Functionalism, 69

General Education in a Free Society (Harvard
        University), 35
General education movement, 35
Globalization, 40
Goal:
    of integration, 131
    knowledge requirements and, 193
Grading, 33
Graduate students, 202
Graffito. See The Practice of Cultural
        Analysis: Exposing Interdisciplinary
        Interpretation (Bal)
Grand theory:
    description of, 101
    importance to interdisciplinary work,
        102–104
    insights into problem, 174
Greeks, 31
Guidelines, for interdisciplinary research
        process, 141–142

Harvard University, 35, 274–275, 330
Heuristic process, 138–139
High-Tech Heretic: Why Computers Don't
        Belong in the Classroom and Other
        Reflections by a Computer Contrarian
        (Still), 235–236
Historical background, literature
        search for, 176–177
History:
    assumptions of, 92
    categorization of, 52
    description of, focus of, 73–74
    as discipline, 4
    epistemology of, 97
    evidence in, 235

evolution of, 5
perspective of, 61
research methods used by,
    109, 210, 211, 212
H-NET, 328–329
Holistic thinking, 46–47, 122
Human capital theory, 267–268
Human cloning:
depth/breadth of knowledge
    for study of, 191
disciplines with insights
    into, 170–171, 173
most relevant disciplines, identification of,
    174–175
potentially relevant disciplines,
    identification of, 161, 162
as time-sensitive problem, 213
Human world, phenomena about, 86–88
Humanism, 35
Humanities:
approach to understanding, 76–77
assumptions of, 90, 92–93
category of traditional disciplines, 4
choice of disciplinary method for study,
    206–209
conflicting theory-based insights, 262–264,
    268–269
disciplinary form of, 34
disciplinary methods used in, 201
disciplinary perspectives on problems,
    222–224
disciplines of, 53
epistemology of, 95
expert's definition of problem, skewed, 234
expert's understanding of problem,
    231–232
graffito, theories from disciplines on, 198
integration of insights, 308–309
integrative technique of extension, 288–289
integrative technique of redefinition, 286
integrative technique of transformation,
    291–292
interdisciplinary studies involving, 28
interdisciplinary understanding, 315–318
of interest to interdisciplinary students,
    71–76
justification of interdisciplinary approach,
    156–157
learning/thinking processes, 78
methods of, 108–110
overall perspectives of, 61
phenomena of, 85
postmodernism's influence on, 103

sources of conflict between theory-based
    insights, 264–266
statement of problem/question, 150–151
theories within same discipline, 196
theory-based insights, 258–259, 260
Humility, 44

Ideographic theory, 198
IDR (interdisciplinary research), 11
Imagination, creative, 139–140
Implicature, 286, 317
Inclusiveness, 179
Index, 184
Inferences, 66
Insights:
concepts and, 102
disciplinary method and, 204–205
disciplinary perspective vs., 54–56
of discipline on problem, 173–174
evaluation of, 217
integration into new whole, 117–120
integration of, 41
in interdisciplinarity, 13
interdisciplinarity origins and, 27
in interdisciplinary research process,
    141–142
from interdisciplinary studies, 12
in interdisciplinary studies definition, 11
justification of interdisciplinary approach,
    152–153
literature search, mistakes in, 179–180
theory and, 104
theory identification for disciplinary
    adequacy, 194–200
See also Common ground;
    Integration, of insights
Insights, evaluation of:
analysis of problem from disciplinary
    perspectives, 225–228
checklist to evaluate previous research,
    240–241
data/evidence, possibly skewed, 234–236
expert's definition of problem, skewed,
    232–234
methods used by experts, 236–240
strengths/weaknesses of expert's
    understanding, 228–232
weaknesses, identification of, 225
Insights, identification of conflicts in:
disciplinary/interdisciplinary
    decisions, 247
importance of, 248
location of insights, 249–250

sources of conflicts between insights,
    250–255
theory-based insights, 255–266
theory-based insights, addressing
    conflicting, 266–269
Instrumental interdisciplinarity, 17–18
Integrated result, 131
Integration:
    Bloom's taxonomy, updated, 115–116
    cognitive activities involved in, 120–122
    common ground, importance of, 275–276
    conflicts in insights and, 248
    definition of, 6, 116
    goal of, 131
    importance to interdisciplinarity, 123–124
    of insights, 41
    interdisciplinary integration,
        definition of, 122–123
    in interdisciplinary research
        process, 20–21, 141–142
    methods for assessing, 132
    "new whole," nature of, 117–120
    prerequisites for, 124–131
    product/purpose of, 323
    role/nature of, 323
    summary of, 132–133
    techniques, familiarity with, 130
    traits of term, 116–117
    work of knowledge integration, 19
    See also Common ground; Insights,
        identification of conflicts in
Integration, of insights:
    basis of, 301
    cognitive qualities, internal
        dispositions for, 296–299
    definition of integration, 295–296
    examples of, 302–310
    important to interdisciplinary research
        process, 299–300
    interdisciplinarian's work, 301
    process of, 300
    when integration occurs, 302
An Integrative Approach to the Elimination of
    the "Perfect Crime" (Delph):
    disciplinary perspectives on, 221–222
    integration of insights, 307–308
    integrative technique of redefinition,
        285–286
    interdisciplinary understanding, 119, 315
    justification of interdisciplinary
        approach, 156
    statement of problem/question, 149–150
Integrative knowledge, 130

Integrative Learning: Opportunities to
    Connect, 330
Integrative mind-set, 130–131
Integrative skills, 126–130
Integrative techniques:
    challenges in creation of common
        ground and, 281
    for common ground, 277–278
    extension technique, 286–289
    organization technique, 289–290
    redefinition technique, 283–286
    theory expansion technique, 281–283
    transformation technique, 290–292
    value of, 292
Intellectual vertigo, 218
"Inter," 5–6
Interdisciplinarians:
    common ground, responsibility, 277–278
    integration of insights, cognitive
        qualities/internal dispositions for,
        296–299
    integration of insights work of, 301
    literature search, challenges of, 177–178
    natural sciences, interest of, 63–67
    social sciences, interest of, 67–71
    traits, skills of, 41–47, 278
Interdisciplinarity:
    cognitive outcomes of, 323–325
    common ground theory and, 272–274
    competing impulses behind term, 16–17
    integration, importance of, 123–132
    line between disciplines and, 5
    problem as focus of, 6
    use of term today, 17–21
Interdisciplinarity, origins of:
    disciplines, formation of, 31–32
    disciplines, history of, 32–34
    etymology, research model of, 27–28
    insights and, 27
    interdisciplinary approach to learning,
        thinking, producing knowledge, 38–41
    interdisciplinary critique of disciplines,
        28–31
    interdisciplinary studies, emergence of,
        34–37
    traits, skills of interdisciplinarians, 41–47
Interdisciplinary common ground, 272
Interdisciplinary decisions, 247–248
    See also Decision making
Interdisciplinary integration:
    comprehensive definition of, 296
    definition of, 116, 122–123
    See also Integration; Integration, of insights

Interdisciplinary learning, 43–44
Interdisciplinary research (IDR), 11
Interdisciplinary research process:
  adequacy in relevant disciplines, 189–213
  analysis of problem, evaluation of
      insights, 217–241
  cautions concerning steps of, 142–143
  characteristics of, 137
  clear guidelines, benefit to students of,
      141–142
  common ground, 271–292
  creative imagination for, 139–140
  as decision-making process, 137–139
  identification of conflicts in insights,
      247–269
  identification of relevant disciplines/choice
      of most relevant, 160–175
  illustration of, 141
  integration of insights, 295–310
  interdisciplinary understanding, 310–318
  justification of interdisciplinary approach,
      151–157
  literature search, 175–185
  problem definition/statement of focus
      question, 144–151
  as "tall order," 140
Interdisciplinary resources, 327–334
Interdisciplinary studies:
  cognitive outcomes of, 323–325
  definition of, 11–12, 321–322
  disciplinary perspectives in, 52–62
  "discipline" part of term, 3–5
  disciplines, role of, 322–323
  emergence of, 34–37, 322
  integration, role of, 323
  "inter" part of term, 5–6
  interdisciplinarity, competing impulses
      behind, 16–17
  interdisciplinarity, use of term, 17–21
  knowledge formations, 10–11
  metaphors used to describe, 22–24
  premise of, 15–16
  "studies" part of term, 6–10
  what it is not, 13–15
Interdisciplinary Studies Project (Project
    Zero), Harvard Graduate School of
    Education, 274–275, 330
Interdisciplinary understanding:
  definition of, 11–12, 310
  description of, 21
  examples of, 313–318
  in interdisciplinary research process,
      21, 141–142

  of problem, 6
  as product of integration, 323
  testing, 311–313
  ways to express, 311
Interdiscipline, 52
Interdisciplines.org, 185, 330
Interfaces, of disciplines, 153–154
Internal dispositions, 296–299
Internet:
  online resources, 329–330
  scholarly knowledge, 184–185
Interpenetration, 128–129
Interpretivism:
  epistemological approach of, 93, 95, 99
  limitations of epistemology, 100
  methods of, 108, 111–112
Interview, 240
In-text evidence, 212–213
Introductory course, for interdisciplinary
    studies, 324
Intuition:
  for common ground, 278
  for integration of insights, 297
  use of term, 283–284
Issues in Integrative Studies (Association for
    Integrative Studies), 37, 185, 330
Iterative process, 139

Jargon, disciplinary, 145–146
  See also Terminology
Journal of Interdisciplinary History
    (journal), 331
Journals, interdisciplinary, 330–331
JSTOR (Journal Storage), 329
Justification of interdisciplinary approach:
  criteria for, 151
  examples of, 154–157
  insights produced by at least two
      disciplines, 152–153
  no single discipline has been adequate, 153
  problem is unmet societal need, 154
  problem/question is at interfaces of
      disciplines, 153–154
  problem/question is complex, 152

Keywords:
  of disciplines, 173
  search strategies, 331
Kin Altruism Theory, 304
Knot theory, 64
Knowledge:
  common ground in form of, 273
  disciplinary knowledge for integration, 126

division into disciplines, 31
Enlightenment, scientific revolution
    and, 32–33
humanities approach to understanding,
    76–77
integrative knowledge for integration, 130
interdisciplinarity and, 16–17
interdisciplinary approach to learning,
    thinking, producing
    knowledge, 38–41
from interdisciplinary studies, 21
interdisciplinary understanding, 310
"mapping" metaphor and, 23–24
other sources of, 184–185
outside disciplines, 59
pluralism development, 37
professionalization of, 33–34
required depth/breadth from
    discipline, 190–193
structure of, 51–52
unifying/integrating, 20
unity of, 35
work of integration of, 19
Knowledge domain, 4
Knowledge formations:
boundary crossing, 22–23
definition of, 10
types of, 10–11
Knowledge production:
change in, 21
interdisciplinary approach to, 38–41
pluralism in, 37

Laboratory, 33
Language. *See* Terminology
Law, 175
Leader member exchange
    (LMX) theory, 121
Learned thinking process, 276–277
Learning:
interdisciplinarity and, 324
interdisciplinary approach to, 38–41
love of, 42
Library catalogues, 178
Library of Congress (LOC):
classification system of, 183
subject headings, 183–184
Library Trends, 45 (2) (journal), 331
Library-based computer searches:
challenge of, 181
identification of sources, 182–183
indexes, database, other
    collections, 184

Library of Congress classification
    system, 183
Library of Congress subject headings,
    183–184
Literature:
evaluation of strengths/weaknesses
    of, 231
of interdisciplinary studies, 322, 324–325
Literature (English):
assumptions of, 92
description of, 74
epistemology of, 97
perspective of, 61
research methods of, 109–110
Literature search:
challenges, 177–178, 180–181
description of, 175–176
disciplines in, 179
library-based computer search techniques,
    181–184
mistakes commonly made, 179–180
other knowledge/knowledge
    formations, 185
purposes of, 176–177
scholarly knowledge, 184–185
suggestions for initial phase of research,
    178–179
theory identification and, 194
The Little Prince (de Saint-Exupéry), 28–29
LMX (leader member exchange)
    theory, 121
Locations, of insights, 249–250
Logic:
definition of, 75
in religion, mathematics, 291–292
Love of learning, 42

Mapping:
concept/principle map, 163, 165
research map, 163, 164
system map, 163–166, 167
theory map, 166, 168
"Mapping" metaphor, 23–24
Martyrdom Theory, 303
Mastery, of discipline, 189
Mathematics:
assumptions of, 90
epistemology of, 94
focus of, 64–65
perspective of, 60
research methods of, 105
*Mathematics and Religion: Processes of
    Faith and Reason* (Arms), 291–292

Metaphor:
    definition of, 22
    to describe interdisciplinary work, 22–24
    for interdisciplinary understanding, 311
    jigsaw puzzle, 117, 118, 119
    "moving toward integration," 131
    skill of interdisciplinarian, 45
    testing interdisciplinary understanding, 312
Metaphysics, 75
Methods:
    definition of, 104
    element of discipline, 4
    of experts may be skewed, 236–240
    of humanities, 108–110
    identification of, 200–212, 241
    for integration assessment, 132
    of natural sciences, 104–106
    of positivism, interpretivism,
        postmodernism, 111–112
    of social sciences, 106–108
    theory and, 103
Mind-set, integrative, 130–131
Mistakes, in literature search, 179–180
Mode of thinking, 19
Model:
    of DNA structure, 313
    of integration, 126
    for interdisciplinary understanding,
        311, 314
    testing interdisciplinary understanding, 312
Modernism:
    advantages/disadvantages of
        using, 207–208
    assumptions of, 90
    epistemological approach of, 95, 98
    limitations of epistemology, 100
Molecular biology, 5
Monodisciplinarity, 274–275
Monopsony Exploitation Theory, 261, 268
Morality, 117–118
Most relevant disciplines, 169–175
Mountains Beyond Mountains (Kidder), 317
Multidisciplinarity:
    definition of, 13
    interdisciplinarity *vs.*, 17
    as not integrative, 123
Multidisciplinary studies, 13–15
Music/Music education:
    assumptions of, 92
    description of, focus of, 74–75
    epistemology of, 97
    perspective of, 61
    research methods of, 110

Narratives:
    examples of interdisciplinary
        understandings, 313–314,
        315–316, 317–318
    for interdisciplinary understanding, 311
    testing interdisciplinary understanding, 312
Narrow interdisciplinarity, 274
Narrowing, 169–175
Narrow-range theories, 101, 174
Native studies, 11
Natural sciences:
    analysis of problem/insights, 225–226
    assumptions of, 89, 90
    category of traditional disciplines, 4
    choice of disciplinary method, 206
    conflicting theory-based insights, 261,
        266–267
    disciplinary methods used in, 200
    disciplinary perspectives on problems, 220
    disciplines of, 53
    epistemology of, 94–95
    evaluation of expert's understanding of
        problem, 229–230
    expert's definition of problem, skewed, 232
    humanities and, 77
    integration of insights, 304–307
    integrative technique of extension, 287–288
    integrative technique of redefinition, 285
    interdisciplinary understandings, 313–314
    of interest to interdisciplinary
        students, 63–65
    justification of interdisciplinary
        approach, 155
    learning/thinking processes, view of
        humanity, 78
    methods of, 104–106
    overall perspectives of, 60
    phenomena of, 85
    problem solving approach, 65–67
    statement of problem/question, 148–149
    theories from disciplines, 195–197
    theory-based insights example, 257–258
Natural thinking process, 276–277
New Directions: Science, Humanities, Policy
    (web site), 328
New whole:
    in interdisciplinary integration definition,
        122–123
    nature of, 117–120
Nomethic theory, 198
Nonlinear thinking:
    in integration process, 300
    skill of interdisciplinarian, 46

Nonscholarly knowledge:
  for further perspectives, 240–241
  for interdisciplinary research, 185
*Northwest Passage: The Great Columbia
    River* (Dietrich):
  as example of integrative work, 131
  justification of interdisciplinary
      approach, 155
  statement of problem/question, 148

Occupation sex discrimination. *See* "On the
    Need for Integrating Occupational Sex
    Discrimination Theory on the Basis of
    Causal Variables" (Fischer)
"On the Need for Integrating Occupational
    Sex Discrimination Theory on the Basis
    of Causal Variables" (Fischer):
  analysis of problem from disciplinary
      perspective, 226, 227
  choice of disciplinary method for study, 206
  conflicting theory-based insights,
      261–262, 267–268
  disciplinary perspectives on OSD, 221
  evaluation of expert's understanding of
      problem, 230–231
  expert's definition of problem, skewed,
      233–234
  justification of interdisciplinary approach,
      155–156
  statement of problem/question, 149
  theories from disciplines on, 197–198
  theories within same discipline on, 195
  theory-based insights, 258, 259
Online resources, 329–330
Ontological assumptions, 251–252
Oral histories, 185
Organization, of information in literature
    search, 181
Organization technique, 278, 289–290
*Organized Environmentalism: Towards a
    Shift in the Political and Social Roles and
    Tactics of Environmental Advocacy
    Groups* (Englehart), 290–291
Other sources of knowledge:
  knowledge outside the disciplines, 185
  literature search for, 175–176
  scholarly knowledge, 184–185
Overarching conceptual
    framework, 126–127
Overarching questions, 218–219
Overlap:
  of insights from disciplines, 193–194
  in perspectives, 172

Paradigm shift, 40
Paradox, 42–43
Participant observation (PO), 239
Periodical literature, 182
  See also Journals, interdisciplinary
Personal bias:
  disciplinary perspectives and, 224
  statement of problem free of, 146–147
Perspectival approach, 84
Perspective:
  analysis of problem from each disciplinary
      perspective, 217–224
  clarified definition of disciplinary
      perspective, 58–59
  of discipline on problem, 169,
      170–173, 179
  integration as comprehensive, 127–128
  misconceptions about term, 54–56
  See also Disciplinary perspective
Perspective taking, 120–121, 122
Phenomena:
  about human world, 86–88
  classified, 84
  defining element of disciplines, 83–84
  disciplines and their illustrative
      phenomena, 85
  exclusion of, 241
  methods of experts and, 237
  potentially relevant disciplines,
      identification of, 161
Philosophy:
  assumptions of, 92
  branches of, 75–76
  epistemology of, 98
  perspective of, 61
  relevance to human cloning, 175
  research methods of, 110
Physics:
  assumptions of, 90
  epistemology of, 94
  focus of, 65
  perspective of, 60
  research methods of, 105
Pidgin, 24
Plato's Academy, 31
PO (participant observation), 239
Point of origin, 132
Point of view, 277
Political science:
  assumption/insight on suicide
      terrorism, 254
  assumptions of, 91
  description of, 70

epistemology of, 96
perspective of, 60
research methods of, 107
Positivism:
   epistemological approach of, 93, 95, 98
   limitations of epistemology, 100
   methods of, 108, 111–112
Postmodernism:
   advantages/disadvantages
      of using, 207–208
   challenge of, 264
   epistemological approach of, 98–99
   epistemology of, 95
   influence on disciplines, 103
   influence on methodology, 106
   limitations of epistemology, 100
   methods of, 108, 111–112
Potentially relevant disciplines:
   definition of, 160
   identification of, 161–163
   narrowing to most relevant
      disciplines, 169–175
Power, 40
The Practice of Cultural Analysis: Exposing
      Interdisciplinary Interpretation (Bal):
   choice of disciplinary method for study,
      206–207
   conflicting theory-based insights of cultural
      analysis, 268–269
   disciplinary perspective, analysis of problem
      from, 226, 227, 228
   evaluation of expert's understanding of
      problem, 231–232
   expert's definition of problem, skewed, 234
   integration of insights, 308–309
   integrative technique of extension, 288–289
   interdisciplinary understanding, 315–317
   justification of interdisciplinary
      approach, 156
   sources of conflict between theory-based
      insights, 264–266
   statement of problem/question, 150
   theories from disciplines on, 198
Pragmatic interdisciplinarity, 17–18, 35
A Preface to Grants Economics: the Economy
      of Love and Fear (Boulding), 289–290
Prerequisites, 124–131
Problem definition/statement of focus
      question:
   defining scope of problem/question,
      144–145
   disciplinary bias, 145
   disciplinary jargon, 145–146

examples of, 148–151
guidelines for, 147–148
literature search for, 176
personal bias, 146–147
selection of researchable, 144
Problem description, 66
Problem representation, 66
Problem solving:
   natural sciences approach to, 65–67
   social sciences approach to, 71
Problem-focused research, 154
Problems:
   analysis from disciplinary perspectives,
      225–228
   cognitive decentering and, 40–41
   definition of problem, skewed, 225
   disciplines unable to address complex,
      30–31, 39–40
   expert's definition of problem, skewed,
      232–234
   insights into, evaluation of, 225–241
   interdisciplinarian traits and, 42–43
   interdisciplinarity for solving real-world, 38
   in interdisciplinary research process,
      141–142
   justification of interdisciplinary approach,
      151–157
   knowledge from disciplines and, 193
   mapping, 24, 163–168
   most relevant disciplines, identification
      of, 169–175
   potentially relevant disciplines,
      identification of, 160–163
   in research steps, 140
   situating/contextualizing, 177
   in transdisciplinary study, 15
Process:
   assessment of integration, 132
   interdisciplinary integration as, 123
   interdisciplinary research as, 138–139
   in interdisciplinary studies definition, 11, 12
   See also Interdisciplinary research process
Product/process, new:
   from integration, 323
   for interdisciplinary understanding, 311
   testing interdisciplinary understanding, 312
Professionalization, of knowledge, 33–34
Profiling. See Criminal profiling
Proposition formation, 71
Psychology:
   assumptions of, 91
   computer-assisted education and, 236
   description of, fields of, 68–69

epistemology of, 96
evaluation of strengths/weaknesses of,
    231–232
perspective of, 60
research methods of, 107
See also Cognitive psychology
"Purview," 54

Qualitative methods:
    misconceptions about, 203
    quantitative methods vs., 108, 111,
        202–203
    theoretical implications of using, 203–204
Qualitative Research Methods (Berg),
    202–203
Quantification of evidence, 77
Quantitative methods, 108, 111, 202–203
Quantity, 180
Questions:
    asked by disciplines, 4
    for interdisciplinary understanding, 311
    justification of interdisciplinary approach,
        151–157
    for most relevant disciplines, 169–175
    overarching questions, disciplinary
        perspective and, 218–219
    See also Problem definition/statement of
        focus question
Quotations, 257

Rationalism, 77
Rationality, 290
Reading, 178, 181
    See also Close reading
Reality, 40–41
Reason, 291–292
Receptivity, 43
Redefinition technique:
    for common ground, 275, 277
    concepts, importance of, 284
    description of, 283
    disciplinary training/attitudes
        and, 283–284
    examples of, 285–286
    for integration of insights, 309
    need for common vocabulary, 284
    student use of, 281
Reductionism, 106, 301
Reflection, 42, 240
Reflexivity:
    epistemological self-reflexivity, 95
    interdisciplinary research as reflexive, 139
    reflexive scholarship, 12

Relevant disciplines, adequacy in:
    decision making for, 189–194
    description of, 189
    disciplinary methods, identification of,
        200–212
    in-text evidence of, 212–213
    theories, identification of relevant, 194–200
    See also Disciplines, identification of
        relevant
Relevant information:
    collection of in literature search, 180–181
    natural sciences selection of, 66
Religious studies:
    assumptions of, 93
    description of, 76
    epistemology of, 98
    perspective of, 61
    relevance to human cloning, 175
    research methods of, 110
Research:
    design, 71
    disciplines with insights into problem,
        173–174
    map, 163, 164
    need for interdisciplinary, 325
Research methods. See Disciplinary methods
Research model, of interdisciplinarity, 28
Research process:
    awareness of, 130
    epistemology and, 95
    integration, importance of, 123–132
    integration of insights, 54–55
    interdisciplinary, 20–21
    See also Interdisciplinary research process
Resources, interdisciplinary, 327–334
Resources in Education (journal), 328
Results, 131
Role taking, 120–121

"Sacred" Terror Theory, 303
Samuel Taylor Coleridge: The Rime of the
    Ancient Mariner (Fry):
    conflicting theory-based
        insights, 262–264
    theories within same discipline, 196
    theory-based insights, 258–259, 260
Scholarly knowledge, 184–185
Sciences:
    integrative technique of redefinition,
        285–286
    integrative technique of transformation,
        291–292
    interdisciplinary studies involving, 28

specialization in, 34
See also Natural sciences; Social sciences
Scientific method:
   research methods of natural sciences, 105
   steps of, 104, 106
Scientific revolution, 33
Scope, 144–145
Search, 331–332
   See also Literature search
Self-Sanction Theory, 302–304
Seminar, 33
Skewed understanding, 225
Skills:
   definition of, 42
   of interdisciplinarian, 45–47, 278
Social identity. *See Composing Race and*
   Gender: The Appropriation of Social
   Identity in Fiction (Silver)
Social movement theory, 290–291
Social Science Reference Sources, 161
Social sciences:
   analysis of problem from each disciplinary
      perspective, 226, 227
   assumptions of, 89–91
   category of traditional disciplines, 4
   choice of disciplinary method for study, 206
   conflicting theory-based insights,
      261–262, 267–268
   disciplinary methods used in, 201
   disciplinary perspectives on problems,
      221–222
   disciplines of, 53
   epistemology of, 95, 96
   evaluation of expert's understanding of
      problem, 230–231
   expert's definition of problem, skewed,
      233–234
   humanities and, 72, 76–77
   integration of insights, 307–308
   integrative technique of extension, 288
   integrative technique of organization,
      289–290
   integrative technique of redefinition,
      285–286
   integrative technique of transformation,
      290–291
   interdisciplinary understanding, 315
   of interest to interdisciplinary students,
      67–70
   justification of interdisciplinary approach,
      155–156
   learning/thinking processes, view of
      humanity, 78

   methods of, 106–108
   ontological assumption in, 251–252
   overall perspectives of, 60–61
   phenomena of, 85
   postmodernism's influence on, 103
   problem solving approach, 71
   statement of problem/question, 149–150
   theories from disciplines on OSD, 195,
      197–198
   theory-based insights about OSD, 258, 259
   value assumptions, 252
Society, 154
Sociobiology, 15
Sociology:
   assumptions of, 91
   description of, fields of, 69–70
   disciplinary perspective of, 55, 56, 61
   epistemology of, 96
   integrative technique of extension, 287
   quantity of material produced by, 180
   research methods of, 108
Solution, of integration, 130
Sources:
   of conflicts between insights,
      248, 250–255
   identification of, 182–183
   information about, 181
   locations of insights, 249–250
Specialization:
   critique of, 28–31
   scientific revolution and, 33
   trend towards, 34
Statements, 257
Statistical analysis, 238
Strengths:
   of disciplinary methods, 238–240
   of expert's understanding of problem,
      228–232
"Studies":
   as integral part of interdisciplinary
      studies, 8
   meaning of, 6–7
   plural, reasons for, 8–10
   traditional disciplines not referred to as, 7
Subdiscipline, 52
Subject headings, 183–184
Suicide terrorism:
   assumptions/insights into, 253, 254
   concepts of, 250–251
   conflicting insights about, 248, 249
   integration of insights, 302–304
   interdisciplinary inquiry about, 153
   literature search on, 176

theories on, 253, 255
theory expansion technique, 281–283
theory-based insights into, 182, 256
Surveys, 237, 238
Sustainability: Science, Practice, and Policy (journal), 331
Symbolic interactionism, 69
Symbols, 67
Synthesis:
    definition of, 295–296
    in natural sciences problem solving, 66
    traits of, 116–117
    when it occurs, 302
    See also Integration
System, 152
System map:
    example of, 167
    function of, 163–166
Szostak's typology of selected theories, 198–200

Table:
    data management table, 181, 182
    for linking discipline with perspective, 170–173
Terminology:
    common ground and, 273, 279
    disciplinary jargon, 145–146
    integrative technique of extension, 288–289
    integrative technique of redefinition, 283–286
    need for common vocabulary, 284
Terrorism. *See* Suicide terrorism
Terrorist Psycho-logic Theory, 302
Testing, interdisciplinary understanding, 311–313
Texas. *See Fresh Water Scarcity in Texas* (Smolinski)
Theory:
    of common ground, 272–275
    common ground, creation of, 279–280
    concepts, relationship to theory, 102
    correlation with method, 108, 111
    definition of, 101
    disciplinary method and, 204–205
    of discipline on problem, 170, 174
    element of discipline, 4
    grand theories, 101
    identification of, 241
    identification of relevant, 194–200
    importance to interdisciplinary work, 102–104
    of integration, 126–128
    integration, basis of, 301

literature search to identify, 177
narrow-range theories, 101
source of conflict between insights, 250, 253–255
Theory expansion technique, 281–283
Theory map, 166, 168
A Theory of Justice (Rawls), 75
Theory-based insights:
    close reading of insights, 257
    description of, 255
    sources of conflict between insights produced by different disciplines, 264–266
    sources of conflict between insights produced by same discipline, 257–264
    into suicide terrorism problem, 256
Thesaurus, 184
Thinking:
    cognitive processes for common ground, 276–277
    creative, for common ground, 278
    holistic, 122
    integration of modes of, 19
    interdisciplinary approach to, 38–41
    nonlinear, 300
    skills of interdisciplinarian, 45–47
Time:
    disciplines as time-dependent, 5
    saved by literature search, 176
    use of current scholarship, 213
Topical databases, 184
Traditional interdisciplinarity, 35
Traits:
    definition of, 42
    of interdisciplinarians, 42–44
    of interdisciplinarians for common ground, 278
Transdisciplinary studies, 15
Transformation technique, 278, 290–292
Triangulation, 124–125, 209–210
Tropical ecosystems. *See Anthropogenic Forces Degrading Tropical Ecosystems in Latin America: A Costa Rican Case Study* (Nagy)
Truth, 252
Tunnel vision, 29

Undergraduate students, 202
Understanding:
    humanities approach to, 76–77
    integration, new whole from, 117–120

in interdisciplinary research process,
141–142
See also Interdisciplinary understanding
Unification, of knowledge, 20
University:
disciplinarity and, 34
disciplinary knowledge in, 51–52
origins of, 32
reforms, interdisciplinary
studies and, 36–37
Urban studies, 7

Value, 117–118
Value-laden assumptions, 252, 253
Variables, continuous, 290
Verification, 66–67
Vocabulary. *See* Terminology

Water. See *Fresh Water Scarcity in Texas*
(Smolinski); *Northwest Passage: The
Great Columbia River* (Dietrich)
Weaknesses:
of disciplinary methods, 238–240
of expert's understanding of
problem, 228–232
of insights, identification of, 225
Wealth, 306–307
Web of Knowledge, 329
Web sites:
interdisciplinary associations, 327–328
online interdisciplinary resources, 329–330
Wide interdisciplinarity, 118, 274
Women's studies, 11
WorldCat, 329
Writing, 33

About the Author _____

Allen F. Repko is Director of the Interdisciplinary Studies Program at the University of Texas at Arlington. He earned his PhD in History at the University of Missouri–Columbia. Dr. Repko's research and teaching interests include interdisciplinary history, theory, and practice as well as U.S. foreign policy. He currently consults on the design and implementation of interdisciplinary programs.